THE DEVIL WITHIN

The Devil Within

Possession & Exorcism in the Christian West

BRIAN P. LEVACK

YALE UNIVERSITY PRESS
NEW HAVEN AND LONDON

For information about this and other Yale University Press publications, please contact:
U.S. Office: sales.press@yale.edu www.yalebooks.com
Europe Office: sales@yaleup.co.uk www.yalebooks.co.uk

Set in Adobe Caslon Pro by IDSUK (DataConnection) Ltd
Printed in by TJ International Ltd, Padstow, Cornwall

Library of Congress Cataloging-in-Publication Data

Levack, Brian P.
   The Devil within : possession and exorcism in the Christian West / Brian Levack.
     pages cm
   ISBN 978-0-300-11472-0 (cl : alk. paper)
1. Exorcism—Europe—History. 2. Demoniac possession—Europe—History. I. Title.
   BV873.E8L48 2013
   133.4'26094—dc23

                                                                    2012042933

A catalogue record for this book is available from the British Library

10 9 8 7 6 5 4 3 2 1

Contents

Illustrations

Preface

M Y INTEREST IN THIS subject began in 1972 when my wife, Nancy, and I cared briefly for a four-month-old foster child whose teenage parents had severely beaten him. When this infant was committed to our care, he had suffered numerous broken bones, including a fractured skull, which had caused him to experience recurrent seizures. He also had cigarette burns on different parts of his body. When we asked how this infant could have been subjected to such extreme physical abuse, we learned that family members had come to the conclusion that he was possessed by the Devil and decided therefore to use physical force to expel the evil spirit. The child's mother also believed that her aunt, who often had violent seizures herself, had sent the Devil into this infant because her niece had laughed at her while experiencing these fits. I later discovered that our foster child's abuse was not that unusual. In the last fifty years there have been numerous incidents in which parents or relatives have used physical force to expel demons from children they believed were possessed.

At the time this infant came into our home I was developing a scholarly interest in the subject of witchcraft prosecutions in Europe during the early modern period. In studying witchcraft, I learned that witches in the sixteenth and seventeenth centuries were often accused of having caused demonic possession by commanding demons to enter the bodies of their victims and seize control of their physical movements and mental operations. Research on the apparent possession of a young woman in early seventeenth-century England and an investigation of a cluster of possessions in late seventeenth-century Scotland led me to undertake a much broader, European-wide study of this phenomenon. This book is the product of that sustained inquiry. Its main purpose is to 'make sense' of the pathological behaviour that demoniacs displayed in both Catholic and Protestant communities during these years.

For most people in early modern Europe, demonic possession made perfectly good sense. For them the afflictions suffered by demoniacs—the convulsions, contortions, muscular rigidity, swelling, vomiting of alien substances, contempt for sacred objects, and speaking in languages previously unknown to them—were the result of the Devil's entrance into the inner caverns of their bodies and the control he thereby acquired over their physical movements and mental operations. This belief that the Devil was responsible for the symptoms of possession was consonant with the dominant tradition in early modern Catholic and Protestant theology, which assigned him considerable power in the natural world. Demonic responsibility for possessions also made sense to the uneducated, who acquired at least a rudimentary knowledge of the demonic world from the clergy who preached and ministered to them.

This supernatural, demonic interpretation of the symptoms of the possessed, however, has not satisfied most modern scholars, either because they do not accept the possibility of demonic power in the world or, even if they do, because such an interpretation of the phenomenon is incapable of verification. They have therefore offered alternative explanations of 'what was really happening' when Christians in the early modern period acted in this unusual way. The two explanations that have gained the widest currency are that demoniacs were either faking the symptoms of their possession or that they were physically or mentally ill. These interpretations of possession cannot be readily dismissed, because some demoniacs actually did pretend that they were possessed, while others apparently suffered from severe psychological disorders. But neither interpretation provides a satisfactory explanation of the majority of possessions, in which the manifestation of the symptoms spread rapidly from one demoniac to another in convents, orphanages, and small villages. Pretending to be possessed required coaching and planning that was not possible when large numbers of demoniacs suddenly began to exhibit such pathological behaviour, and it is equally implausible to think that those demoniacs who began to exhibit the same symptoms were all afflicted by the same neurological or psychosomatic maladies.

A third, more plausible interpretation of demonic possession that applies to both individual and collective possessions holds that demoniacs were performers in religious dramas who were following scripts they learned from others. In cases of group possessions, the newly afflicted simply imitated those whom they observed. This theatrical interpretation of demonic possession is compatible with those based on fraud and disease, but it goes beyond them in its explanation of why most early modern demoniacs uttered blasphemies and curses, violated moral and social conventions, and showed contempt for sacred objects. Unlike the theory of disease, which interprets the experiences of demoniacs in terms of modern medical or psychiatric theory, the theatrical interpretation of possession takes seriously the religious beliefs of the possessed and their families. Without understanding these religious beliefs, the 'epidemic' of demonic possessions that occurred in early modern Europe does not make complete sense.

The argument that demoniacs were actors in religious dramas is not new, but I develop this theatrical interpretation of possession in two ways. Whereas most of those who have written about the performative aspects of possession have focused on voluntary possessions, especially those that were fraudulent, I argue that *all* demoniacs, including those whose possession occurred spontaneously or involuntarily, assumed dramatic roles. Consciously or not, demoniacs followed scripts that were encoded in their religious cultures. I also argue that these scripts were strikingly different for Catholics and Protestants. I want to show that all possessions are culturally specific—that they are rooted in the distinct religious cultures in which demoniacs and other members of their communities were immersed.

This book is concerned primarily with the early modern period of European history, which is broadly defined as the years between 1450 and 1800, but it also deals with earlier and later periods. My discussion of possession and exorcism in the time of biblical antiquity explores the different ways that Christians in the early modern period interpreted the accounts of Christ's exorcisms in the New Testament, while references to possessions and exorcisms in the Middle Ages and the works of medieval scholastic theologians provide a context for understanding the early modern phenomenon. In the later chapters I discuss possessions in the nineteenth and twentieth centuries. These possessions not only testify to the persistence of religious belief and practice in a 'secular' world but allow for comparisons between modern possessions and those that took place centuries earlier.

The surge in the number of possessions in early modern Europe had its origins in movements for religious reform that arose in the fifteenth, sixteenth, and seventeenth centuries. The most significant of these movements were the Protestant Reformation, which began in the early sixteenth century, and the Catholic Reformation, which had begun earlier but gathered new strength in response to the Protestant challenge. Both reformations urged the cultivation of personal piety, and the efforts by both Catholics and Protestants to achieve sanctity contributed to the late sixteenth-century increase in the number of possessions. The different ways in which Catholic and Protestant demoniacs acted and spoke when possessed and the different strategies that priests and ministers employed to dispossess them were deeply rooted in the religious cultures of their day. Studying demonic possession in this period offers us an opportunity to appreciate the variety of religious beliefs and experiences in the age of the Reformation and to compare those beliefs and experiences with those of both believers and sceptics in the modern world.

Acknowledgements

In researching and writing this book I have benefited from the advice and criticism of many of my colleagues. I am particularly indebted to Douglas Biow, Alison Frazier, Steve Friesen, Jo Ann Hackett, Julie Hardwick, Al Martinich, Martha Newman, and Michael White for reading drafts of individual chapters and making valuable suggestions for revision. My wife, Nancy Levack, who is an author and editor in her own right, listened patiently to many paragraphs that I read aloud, gave the entire manuscript a close reading, and provided the invaluable perspective of a non-specialist who shared my interest in the topic.

For help of various sorts I wish to thank Robert Abzug, Michelle Brock, Jorge Cañizares, Stuart Clark, Edwin Curley, Owen Davies, Rainer Decker, Sarah Ferber, Julian Goodare, Tamar Herzig, Derek Hirst, Rab Houston, Neil Kamil, Pierre Kapitaniak, Richard Kieckhefer, Ildikó Kristóf, Erik Midelfort, Bill Monter, Wayne Rebhorn, Jim Sharpe, Angela Smith, Jeff Smith, Gretchen Starr-Lebeau, Hans de Waardt, Gerhild Scholz Williams, and Charles Zika.

Over the past ten years I have read papers on the topic of demonic possession at the University of Edinburgh, Washington University, the University of Queensland, the University of Kentucky, the University of Oslo, the University of Melbourne, and the University of Adelaide, and also at meetings of the American Society for Legal History, the Faculty Seminar in British Studies at the University of Texas, the Western Conference on British Studies, and the Devil and Society conference in Toronto. These meetings gave me the opportunity to discuss my work at different stages of completion, and the comments and questions from the audiences helped me clarify many of my thoughts on the subject.

Finally I wish to thank Heather McCallum, my editor at Yale University Press in London, for her sustained interest in my work over the years, her encouragement to write this book, and her advice on how to make my work accessible both to scholars and to a more general, non-academic audience.

Austin, Texas
June 2012

CHAPTER I

Making Sense of Demonic Possession

During the sixteenth and seventeenth centuries the reading public in Europe was treated to a steady diet of stories describing the extraordinary behaviour of people who were said to have been possessed by demons. The unfortunate victims of these attacks, usually referred to as demoniacs, reportedly experienced violent convulsions, their limbs stiffened, and they demonstrated extraordinary physical strength. Their faces became grossly distorted, their eyes bulged, and their throats and stomachs swelled. They experienced temporary loss of hearing, sight, and speech, vomited huge quantities of pins, nails, and other materials, spoke in deep animal-sounding voices, suffered various eating disorders, and engaged in self-mutilation. They conversed in languages of which they had no previous knowledge, uttered blasphemies and profanities, violated conventional standards of morality, went into trances, foresaw the future, and disclosed secrets unknown to others. A few of them were reported to have levitated.

These accounts of demonic possession were not the only stories of the marvellous, the wondrous, and the preternatural that literate Europeans read about in the books, pamphlets, and broadsheets that proliferated in the first age of print. These same readers might also have read about a race of people in distant lands who had only one large foot; a child in Saxony born with bovine feet, four eyes, and the mouth and nose of a calf; the occurrence of no fewer than three eclipses of the Sun and two eclipses of the Moon in a single year; and a woman in England who gave birth to fifteen rabbits.[1] A six-volume anthology of such wonders, including a number of demonic possessions, was first published in 1560,[2] and forty years later the French Huguenot minister Simon Goulart published another anthology of such occurrences.[3] Some of the 'prodigies in nature' described in these collections, like the afflictions of the possessed, were assigned religious, prophetic, or even apocalyptic significance.[4] But whereas many of the signs and wonders described in these 'prodigy books' gradually lost their religious significance, or were reclassified as 'curiosities' that were studied from an empirical, scientific perspective, or dismissed as fictional, the afflictions of demoniacs remained a subject of considerable religious and medical interest and controversy well into the eighteenth century.[5]

One reason for the enduring popular and learned interest in demonic possession was that the symptoms displayed by demoniacs differed only in degree from those of some people who were not believed to be demonically possessed. To be sure, the manifestations of demonic possession appeared to be wondrous, but only a few of these, such as levitation, were universally regarded as lying outside the order of nature. The possibility that an unschooled person might speak in a foreign tongue, while highly unusual, was not impossible, and many early modern Europeans knew of people who went into trances and prophesied the future.

Possession narratives struck a responsive chord with a large segment of the literate population because of their immediacy, their human dimension, and their moral relevance. Readers of these accounts tended to take the reported experiences of people who lived in their own countries more seriously than the sighting of creatures in foreign lands or the descriptions of monsters in classical literature. Readers could, moreover, sympathize with the plight of demoniacs and may well have wondered whether a member of their own families might become the next victim of demonic fury. And while wonders in nature were often accorded prophetic significance, they were not likely to have had as great an impact on a reader's religious practice or moral conduct as an account of a demonic possession. Descriptions of demonically inflicted human suffering, whether intended to tempt the pious or punish the sinner, were instructive, admonitory, and frightening.[6]

It is impossible to determine with any degree of precision how many people in Europe were reputedly possessed by demons during the early modern period. Judicial records mention the names of demoniacs only when they accused witches of causing their afflictions or when they were prosecuted for fraud. Since demoniacs were considered to have been involuntary victims of demonic assault, they were not liable to criminal prosecution for what they did while under the Devil's influence. But references to possessions in the records of witchcraft prosecutions, published narratives of possessions and exorcisms, demonological treatises by theologians and inquisitors, and records of exorcisms performed at shrines and other locations support the claim that the number of possessions in the early modern period was exceptionally large and probably greater than at any time before or since.

The number of people reputedly possessed by demons in early modern Europe certainly reached into the thousands. Many of these possessions were collective or group phenomena in which the symptoms spread rapidly among people living in close-knit communities. In 1554 a group of eighty-two women in Rome, most of whom were Jews who had recently converted to Christianity, became possessed within a very brief period of time.[7] In 1593 more than one hundred and fifty adults and children were reportedly possessed in the Silesian town of Friedeberg, and another forty demoniacs were afflicted in the town of Spandau a few years later. The demonologist Henri Boguet claimed that people in Savoy experienced fits and convulsions on a daily basis in the closing years of the sixteenth century.[8] Demons allegedly possessed hundreds of nuns in some fifty different French, Italian, and Spanish convents, the most famous being that of the Ursuline nuns in the French city of Loudun between 1632 and 1638. Between 1627 and 1631 as many as eighty-five persons in the village of Mattaincourt in Lorraine experienced demonic seizures which resembled those that took place in convents.[9] An Italian inquisitor claimed that the entire population of the Italian village of Belmonte north of Rome became possessed in the 1650s, while more than one hundred men, women, and children were afflicted in the same way in the German diocese of Paderborn a few years later.[10] Even if some of these figures were exaggerated, the phenomenon approached, if it did not actually achieve, epidemic proportions.

The historical sources

Demonic possession is a methodological land mine for historians. The most basic challenge is determining the factual accuracy of contemporary accounts of specific possessions. There is of course no such thing as a completely objective report of a historical event, but the separation of fact from fiction is especially difficult when the report includes apparently unnatural or preternatural elements. How, for example, can we take as observed fact the possession narrative of the French demoniac Nicole Obry when it claims that a black beast, believed to be a demon in animal form, crept out of this woman's mouth when someone tried to administer her medicine? Or the report that a Franciscan monk at Querétaro, Mexico in the late seventeenth century pulled a large toad out of the mouth of the demoniac by the leg and threw it on her bed?[11] Should one be expected to believe that the head of the young Scottish demoniac Christian Shaw really pivoted 180 degrees or that the possessed woman Katherine Gualter vomited a live eel, eighteen inches long, followed by twenty-four pounds of various substances 'of all colours' twice a day for two weeks?[12] Did the nuns at Loudun really understand questions put to them in Turkish, Spanish, and Italian as well as in the language of a 'savage' Brazilian tribe? Reports of such occurrences lead one to question whether any details of these accounts can be trusted. Should they not be treated in the same way as the observation of St Jerome when he reported that the Roman pilgrim Paula, while visiting the tombs of prophets in the Holy Land, saw female demoniacs hanging upside down in mid-air without their skirts falling down over their heads?[13]

The veracity of such reports can be questioned on a number of possible grounds. In some cases authors of possession narratives may have deliberately misrepresented the actual course of events to boost sales, much in the manner of the less reputable tabloid newspapers today. Alternatively the authors could have exaggerated the severity of the demoniacs' afflictions or even invented some of the details of the case to heighten fear of the demonic, demonstrate the sanctity and power of the exorcist, or prove that only his Church had the power to cast out demons. The author of a possession narrative written in 1573 produced a second edition of the episode more than forty years later in which he incorporated a symptom of a completely different possession that had occurred in the intervening period.[14] During the Reformation era reports of possessions and exorcisms were often designed to win converts to either Catholicism or a particular Protestant denomination, making the veracity of all such accounts of possession fundamentally suspect.[15] The biblical reports of Christ's expulsion of unclean spirits from demoniacs during his public ministry provide an early example of such misrepresentation for confessional purposes. Although the historical Jesus probably did perform many exorcisms, the specific incidents reported in the Gospels should not be considered part of the historical record. The purpose of these stories was not to report what actually happened but to illustrate Christ's power and thus win converts to Christianity.

Even if the author of the narrative intended to present an accurate account of a possession, he might have unconsciously distorted what really happened. In many instances the author did not witness the actual possession but relied on the accounts given by others, which in turn might well have come to them second- or third-hand. Even if the author had been an eyewitness to the possession, his testimony was suspect. We know from criminal trials today that testimony by eyewitnesses can be just as unreliable as that given in a confession. In the case of possessions, observers shocked by the immoral behaviour of demoniacs or fascinated by their strength or disgusted by their regurgitations could easily have exaggerated the extent of their affliction or the level of their deviance. Clerical writers who were preoccupied with the presence of demonic spirits in the world could just as easily have exaggerated the physical or moral effects of demons on the behaviour of parishioners under their pastoral care.

When the demoniac was reported to have spoken in these possessions, there is good reason to think that the words of the possessed were those of the person who had written the account, not a transcript of what the demoniac had actually said.[16] The prayer that the English demoniac Mary Glover reportedly delivered during her possession in 1602, for example, was almost certainly written by John Swan, a Puritan minister who witnessed the efforts to end Mary's torments and wrote a pamphlet to record her spiritual struggles. It is highly unlikely that Mary ever said the prayer.[17] When a possessed twelve-year-old Silesian girl discussed theologically learned issues with Tobias Seiler, the author of this young girl's possession narrative, we can safely assume that Seiler, the educated pastor and school superintendent in the girl's parish, composed the entire discourse.[18]

The cultural assumptions that authors of narratives made regarding the Devil could easily lead them to exaggerate the physical symptoms of the demoniac.[19] When for example the author of a possession narrative reported that witnesses smelled a loathsome odour during a possession, such as the members of the congregation that had observed the convulsions of Mistress Kingesfielde in London in 1564, it is impossible to tell whether they actually smelled the offensive odour or whether they thought they did because they had been told that there were terrible smells associated with the Devil and Hell.[20]

Yet even if we accept the likelihood that all narratives of possession have been filtered through the lenses of observers who were predisposed to see and hear certain things, we cannot dismiss such reports as entirely fictional. Unlike confessions of witches, which could easily have been contaminated by the inducement of testimony under torture, accounts of demonic possession represented efforts to describe unusual human behaviour. Authors may have exaggerated the activities they had witnessed or read about, but they had little reason to invent the entire narrative. We have good reason to be sceptical of accounts of monsters sighted in the New World in the same way that we have good reason to be sceptical of the sightings of the Loch Ness monster today, but accounts of possessions that were witnessed by large numbers of people, sometimes in public venues, must be granted at least a measure of credibility, especially when observers who disagreed on the causes of the demoniacs' behaviour did not deny that they had witnessed it.

The symptoms of early modern possession

What led early modern Christians to claim that one or more demons had entered the body of a person, known as the demoniac or energumen, and temporarily gained control of that person's physical movements, mental faculties, and speech? These 'signs' of possession varied significantly: there was no single model of demonic possession in early modern Europe. Rather there was a large repertory of signs that could appear in different combinations. The number of symptoms varied from case to case, but it was very rare for a person who manifested only one or two of these signs to have been diagnosed as a demoniac.

The signs of possession can be divided into those that were physiological, indicating that the afflicted person had experienced an alteration of anatomy or bodily functions, and those that were verbal or behavioural, in that they involved changes in speech, personality, or moral conduct.[21]

Convulsions

The most commonly reported physiological symptoms of possession were recurrent bodily convulsions in which the person trembled, shook, shuddered, writhed, or had seizures. These fits were often accompanied by frothing or foaming at the mouth. The convulsions were sometimes so severe that the demoniacs thrashed against stationary objects. One report of the possession of a nun at Loudun in 1635 claimed that the demon Asmodeus, manifesting his supreme rage, shook the girl backwards and forwards a number of times, 'making her batter as an hammer with so great, great quickness that her teeth crashed, and her throat made a forced noise'.[22] The English demoniac Richard Dugdale had 'astonishing fits', each lasting three hours, which were so severe that they wrenched him out of his chair.[23]

Physical pain

Almost as common as convulsions were bodily pains that ranged from minor irritations, such as pinpricks or the feeling that ants were crawling under the skin, to those described as torments or torture. The demonologist Johann Weyer (1515–88) reported that in 1494 the nuns at Wertet had pieces of flesh torn from their bodies.[24] In 1571 the Venetian healer and demoniac Elena Crusichi, known as 'la Draga', claimed that the 'awful beast' that possessed her 'gives me so much pain that I feel like I am finished. He eats my guts and destroys my legs [and] my throat and he takes my memory, and he does not let me eat, and he wishes to kill me.'[25] Those who observed the possession of Margaret Murdoch in late seventeenth-century Scotland testified that her body showed signs of having been pinched and pricked and that her flesh was blistered and burnt as if it had been seared by a hot iron.[26] Self-mutilation and attempts at suicide, as in the case of Jeanne Féry at Mons in 1584 and Françoise Fontaine at Louviers in 1591, also belong in this category of physical harm to the demoniac.[27]

Rigidity of the limbs

A third type of commonly reported physiological symptom was the stiffening of the arms and legs in such a way that they could not be relaxed. The limbs of the twelve-year-old Silesian demoniac Magdalena Lieder were so firmly crossed for upwards to an hour that no man could pull them apart.[28] The Mexican demoniac Francisca Mejia's body reportedly turned 'so stiff that not even the strength of many robust men was sufficient to bend her frail arm but an inch.'[29] Two demoniacs in Utrecht in 1595 were observed lying on the ground, one of them 'as stiff as a piece of wood', for five hours. The stiffness of limbs was one of the physical symptoms demoniacs shared with hysterics, which helps to explain why Jean-Martin Charcot and his colleagues in nineteenth-century France equated the two conditions.

Muscular flexibility and contortions

The opposite of muscular rigidity was the body's ability to display exceptional muscular flexibility. In 1637 one of the possessed nuns at Loudun was able to extend her legs in a straight line with both of her thighs touching the ground.[30] A more common demonstration of this symptom was the arching of the demoniac's back, a feat that only a skilled gymnast or contortionist might be capable of performing today. In 1563 the body of eighteen-year-old Anne Mylner of Chester arched into a hoop at the same time that her stomach began to swell, and the efforts of a godly minister for two hours to return her back to its normal extension failed.[31] During the exorcisms of Ursuline nuns at Auxonne in 1662 some of the demoniacs could supposedly bend all the way backwards and lick the floor.[32] This arching of the back often came toward the end of an exorcism, as the Devil's resistance to expulsion reportedly increased in intensity.[33]

Preternatural strength

Many demoniacs displayed preternatural strength, by which is meant physical ability inconsistent with one's age or physical appearance. This was often demonstrated by an inability to restrain the demoniac. Some of the possessed, like a man exorcized by Christ, broke whatever chains or ropes had been used to bind them. At Augsburg in 1571 five people could not hold the demoniac Anna Bernhausen still.[34] A more active display of superhuman strength was the ability to lift heavy objects. One of the nuns possessed at Auxonne in 1658 was reported to have hoisted a heavy marble vase full of holy water with two of her delicate fingers.[35] A less frequently recorded demonstration of preternatural strength was the ability to turn one's head to face the rear or to have it 'twisted almost round', as was described in the case of the Goodwin children in Boston in 1688.[36]

Levitation

In still rarer instances the demoniac was reported to have levitated. During her exorcism in the church at Louviers in 1591, the body of the sixteen-year-old servant girl Françoise Fontaine reportedly rose higher in the air than the altar before being thrown to the ground.[37] A demon allegedly 'raised from the earth the body of the [Mother] Superior' at Loudun during her exorcism in the 1630s, and many of the other nuns in her convent were also reported to have floated in the air.[38] The sisters in the Ursuline convent at Auxonne were said to have done the same. Most reports of levitation came from Catholic convents, but two seventeenth-century Protestant demoniacs, Christian Shaw in Scotland and Margaret Rule in Massachusetts, were also reputedly lifted off the ground.[39]

The opposite of levitation was the gaining of excessive weight, which made it impossible to lift even one part of the demoniac's body. One of the possessed nuns at Loudun was said to have exhibited this rare symptom of demonic possession during her exorcism. To prove that she was in fact possessed, one of the exorcists invited the duchess of Aiguillon, who visited Loudun in 1637, to attempt to lift the head of the possessed nun. To her surprise, the duchess had no difficulty doing so, and after others had performed the same feat, she said sarcastically to one of the exorcists that this hardly qualified as a proof of possession.[40]

Swelling

Observation of the swelling of the throat, face, tongue, or stomach and the bulging of the eyes was far more frequently reported than claims of levitation for the apparent reason that swelling, unlike levitation, straddled the borderline between the natural and the unnatural. Agnes Brigges had 'a great swelling in her throat and upon her jaws',[41] while William Somers's tongue swelled 'to the size of a calf's tongue and his eyes as great as beast's eyes'.[42] All seven of the Lancashire demoniacs of 1597 'had their bodies swollen to a wonderful bigness', and the stomach of one of them, Margaret Byrom, a thirty-three-year-old kinswoman of Mistress Starkey, 'swelled as big as a woman with child'.[43] An inquisitor saw the stomach of the Mexican demoniac Juana de los Reyes grow to an unnaturally large size before returning to normal when touched with a relic.[44] Veronica Steiner's head, breast, and neck swelled so much that they all became deformed.[45] The Scottish demoniac Margaret Laird's throat swelled so much that attendants had to loosen her clothes.[46] The demonological interpretation of such swelling was that the Devil introduced a substance into the demoniac's body and moved it around internally. Those who doubted the validity of specific possessions could easily attribute such swelling to natural causes, including in some cases pregnancy. For this apparent reason swelling was rarely cited as evidence of a true possession.

Vomiting

A recurrent element in many narratives of possession was the vomiting or extrusion of alien objects. Pins and needles were the most common materials, but the list of ejected substances includes nails, glass, blood, pottery, feathers, coal, stones, coins, cinders, sand, dung, meat, cloth, thread, and hair. A girl from Beckington in England apparently held the record for the number of extruded pins (two hundred), while a fifteen-year-old girl from Louvain reputedly coughed up twenty-four pounds of liquid a day in 1571. Claims of such excessive amounts of regurgitated substances, including the four hundred chamber pots of blood supposedly vomited by a demoniac in Germany in the late seventeenth century, call into question the credibility of such contemporary testimonials and raise the difficult question of which elements of possession narratives can be accepted at face value.

Loss of bodily function

In contrast to displays of contortionism and preternatural strength, some demoniacs reportedly experienced a loss of bodily function. Most often this took the form of a temporary loss of sight, hearing, or speech. The Italian exorcist Zacharia Visconti considered the loss of one's voice one of the most frequent effects of possession.[47] A loss of feeling was less common, but that insensitivity reportedly occurred during a number of possessions. An English demoniac at Nottingham in 1597, for example, had needles thrust into his hands and legs to see if he was faking, but he was senseless and no blood flowed.[48] Mary Glover had no reaction when her flesh was burned, while a Scottish demoniac in 1755 reportedly delivered a baby without any pain during her possession.[49]

The most extreme loss of bodily function was a lapse into a cataleptic state, sometimes described as a trance. The English demonologist Richard Bernard reported the case of a demoniac from Warwickshire who sometimes 'fell into a deadly trance, therein continuing the space of a day, representing the shape and image of death, without all sense and motion, saving breathing and her pulse, neither was she moved with pinching, or the like.'[50] The demoniac Nicole Obry was able to alternate repeatedly between the active and passive modes of possession. After writhing, contorting her body and acquiring a rigidity of her limbs, she lapsed into alternating states of lethargy and senseless stupor. On more than one occasion she became temporarily deaf, blind, and speechless. After needles were put into her lifeless hands she revived, only to return to a catatonic state.[51]

Many demoniacs, including those who fell into a cataleptic state, lost their powers of memory. The most common manifestation of this amnesia was the inability of demoniacs to remember what they had said during their seizures. This loss of memory occurred only in so-called somnambulistic or trance possessions; in 'lucid' possessions the person retained consciousness throughout the experience and was aware of the demon within.

Fasting

A relatively uncommon loss of bodily function among demoniacs was the inability to eat or drink for long periods of time. In the early fifteenth century the reforming nun Colette of Corbie cured a demoniac whose body had become rigid and who could not eat or drink.[52] In 1669 the twenty-year-old English demoniac Jane Stretton abstained from all sustenance for nine months.[53] In the late seventeenth century the New England minister Cotton Mather (1663–1728) reported that one of the 'miseries' that demons inflicted on the demoniac Mercy Short was 'extreme fasting for many days together'.[54] More often than not, however, fasting was associated with good or divine possessions, such as that of the Maid of Schwindweiler in 1585, who reputedly did not eat or drink for seven years but whom God miraculously kept alive during the entire period.[55] In these cases the fast could be viewed as part of a divine ecstatic experience or a programme of asceticism that God had ordered.[56]

Nevertheless, the fasting of a person possessed by a good spirit might lead to a suspicion that the Devil was responsible for the inability to eat or drink. When the early fifteenth-century saint Lidwina of Schiedam stopped taking solid food and then refused to swallow, the suspicion arose that she was possessed by a demon.[57] A person who abstained from taking food could also be exposed as a fraudulent demoniac. This apparently happened when a young female demoniac from the German town of Moers, who 'hath not taken any food these sixteen years and is not yet neither hungry nor thirsty', was 'detected' as a fraud after being interviewed by Elizabeth the Winter Queen during her exile in the Netherlands.[58] Some modern historians have retrospectively diagnosed such instances of fasting as cases of anorexia nervosa.[59]

The widest variety of observable signs of possession, which most directly reflected the specific social and cultural environments the demoniacs inhabited, were verbal and behavioural. These differed from the physiological symptoms in that they involved changes in the speech, personality, or conduct of the demoniac.[60] There is scant evidence that demoniacs displayed this latter type of symptom in Christian Europe before the thirteenth century.[61]

Language

The most striking verbal symptom of possession was the ability to speak in languages previously unknown to the demoniac. To contemporary observers, this linguistic proficiency provided the most persuasive evidence that a demon, not the afflicted person, was the speaker.[62] In these demonstrations of linguistic facility, Latin was usually the language of choice, because it was the language of the Church and therefore the language that the Devil allegedly used to parody Christianity. For this reason Latin was sometimes referred to as the Devil's tongue.[63] But demoniacs sometimes spoke phrases in Greek and Hebrew, and in the Dutch Republic stories circulated in the early seventeenth century about 'a wench who spoke all languages'.[64] In the French-speaking cantons of Switzerland the main 'foreign' language in which demoniacs spoke was, not surprisingly, German, but one Swiss demoniac responded not only in German but also in five or six other languages.[65] The demoniacs in Paderborn in 1656 were reportedly familiar with all languages and could answer questions in Latin, Greek, and Hebrew.[66] Some of these utterances were remarkable for their content. An illiterate demoniac from Saxony spoke in both Greek and

Latin regarding a war that was about to be fought, while an illiterate woman in Italy quoted verses from Virgil's *Aeneid* in the original Latin.[67]

Less impressive than the ability to speak in these unfamiliar languages was the ability to understand questions put to them in those tongues. Nicole Obry was asked questions in Flemish, German, French, and Latin but answered only in French or Flemish. Two German demoniacs exorcized at Schlehdorf in 1667 answered questions only in German on the grounds that the demons occupying their bodies had been forbidden, presumably by Satan, to answer in Latin.[68] Marthe Brossier was asked questions in Greek and English but answered only in her native French dialect.[69] The failure of demoniacs actually to speak in these languages led to the suspicion that their acclaimed linguistic ability was specious. In Lancashire two young, unschooled female demoniacs, aged ten and twelve respectively, answered questions put to them in Latin 'as if they had soundly understood them', but they were unable to understand one word once they came out of their fits, nor did they ever speak in Latin.[70]

The acclaimed linguistic facility of demoniacs was consistent with the belief of theologians that demons, who were believed to be fallen angels, had the high intelligence with which God had endowed all angelic spirits. Theologians also believed that because demons were spirits without bodies such as those of humans, they themselves did not have the power of speech. Hence they could speak only through the demoniacs whose bodies they occupied. As one demoniac reportedly said, the Devil 'uses all my appendages and organs—my neck, tongue and lungs—in this way through me for speaking or wailing, so that while I do hear the words that he speaks in this way through me and from my organs, I am completely unable to resist.'[71]

The counterpart of demoniacal speech in 'good' spirit possessions is speaking in tongues. In modern Pentecostalism this verbal facility is considered to be a gift from the Holy Spirit at the time of baptism, a recurrence of the experience of the Apostles at the time of the first Pentecost. Speaking in tongues, however, should be distinguished from the linguistic facility of early modern demoniacs in that Pentecostal speech 'is incoherent, repetitive syllabification, having neither the form nor the structure of human speech.'[72] However sceptical contemporaries may have been of the authenticity of demoniacs' ability to speak in Latin, Greek, or Hebrew, they never claimed that their spoken words were mere babbling.

Voice

A further sign of possession was a noticeable change in the demoniac's voice, which was often described as deeper and gruffer than the normal voice of the afflicted person. Demoniacs often spoke from their bellies or from very deep in their throats. The English demoniac John Fox 'spoke with an audible voice within him, which seemed sometimes to sound out of his belly, sometimes out of his throat, and sometimes out of his mouth, his lips not moving.'[73] This 'belly speech' often bore a closer resemblance to the sound of an animal than the voice of a human being. In one English case the demoniac sounded like 'a great trotting horse'; in another she barked like a dog.[74] Two young demoniacs in the German town of Brakel in 1657 grunted like snuffling pigs.[75] Such animal speech was consistent with the belief that the Devil took the shape of various animals when he appeared to human beings.[76] Sometimes the possessing demons were themselves identified as animals, as when four of the five demons that inhabited the young French demoniac Loyse Maillat were identified as Wolf, Cat, Dog, and Griffon.[77]

In some cases the demoniac spoke in two voices, that of the Devil and the normal voice of the demoniac. The contrast between the deep, hoarse, masculine voice of the Devil and that of the demoniac was most striking when the possessed person was a young girl. In a number of instances, including that of the German demoniac Veronica Steiner, the demoniac prayed to God and praised his name when speaking in her natural voice but blasphemed, cursed, and railed against the established religion when speaking in that of the Devil.[78] In some cases the demoniac engaged in a dialogue with the Devil, alternating voices in the manner of a ventriloquist conversing with his puppet. Needless to say, all such possessions displaying two voices of the demoniac were lucid, in that the demoniac remained conscious throughout the experience.

Trance experiences and visions

Demoniacs sometimes described the visions they had while in a trance. The main characteristic of trances, which are deliberately induced in modern possessions, is that the possessed person loses consciousness during the experience. These visions, as well as the prophecies sometimes delivered in this unconscious state, were culturally specific, in that they reflected the religious culture in which they arose.

The trances of demoniacs are sometimes referred to as ecstasies or raptures, terms that imply an exaltation of the mind and emotions. The word ecstasy, however, is most commonly used to describe positive experiences, such as heightened spiritual awareness, falling in love, reaching a sexual climax, or acquiring poetic inspiration. When referring to possessions in the early modern period it usually denoted a divine rather than a demonic possession. Psychiatrists define trances and ecstasies as altered states of consciousness.

Clairvoyance

Another display of demoniacs' exceptional mental prowess was clairvoyance, the power to perceive matters beyond the range of the ordinary senses. The prophecies that demoniacs uttered in their trances belong in this category, as does their knowledge of the secrets of others and the location of hidden objects. Clairvoyance was closely related to the magical power of divination, the ability to discover knowledge unknown to others, a power that early modern Europeans also attributed to witches. The demoniacs at Paderborn could predict the future and tell what was happening at a distance. Anne Gunter told people who were brought before her how much money they had in their purses.[79] The twelve-year-old son of one Mr Crook in Lancashire in 1676 'could tell in his fits what was adoing in places far distant from him, whereof he could have no information by his senses, nor by any other ordinary means of conveyance'.[80]

Blasphemy and sacred objects

In keeping with the belief that the voice the audience heard was that of the Devil, demoniacs often uttered blasphemies, obscenities, and curses, and denied fundamental doctrines of Christianity. In Catholic countries they railed at priests, insulted the Virgin Mary, condemned the Church and the sacraments, and spat on crucifixes. In 1717 a nun in Mexico City trampled on the communion host after taking it out of her mouth, spat on an image of the Child Jesus, and furiously beat a crucifix.[81] Demoniacs displayed horror when presented with sacred objects, such as relics. Many of these attacks on Christianity came during exorcisms, as the exorcist conversed with the demon he believed was inhabiting the afflicted person's body. Blasphemy was far less common in Protestantism, but the late sixteenth-century English demoniac William Somers denied the existence of God.[82] Since Protestantism was a religion of the Word, Protestant demoniacs most commonly indicated rejection of their religious culture by indicating an inability to read the Bible or even listen to its being read.[83]

Immoral gestures and actions

The actions and gestures of the demoniac, just like their words, conveyed a rejection of Christian morality and piety. Child demoniacs disobeyed their parents, nuns made lewd sexual gestures, and some female demoniacs took off their clothes. During Mass in an Italian village demoniacs not only shrieked in animal voices and contorted their bodies but also pulled up their dresses.[84] At Loudun in 1632 the Ursuline nun Sister Clara 'fell into strange convulsions . . . exposing her person in the most indecent manner, without a blush and with foul and lascivious expressions and actions'. Other possessed nuns at Loudun 'made use of expressions so indecent to shame the most debauched of men, while their acts, both in exposing themselves and inviting lewd behaviour from those present, would have astonished the inmates of the lowest brothel in the country'.[85] Many demoniacs, both Protestant and Catholic, had difficulty praying or worshipping at divine service.

The definition of possession

The multiplicity of observable signs of demonic influence and control of demoniacs' bodies as well as their occasionally contradictory nature make it difficult to formulate a precise definition of demonic possession in early modern Europe. For the purposes of this study possessions had two essential features. The first was that contemporaries regarded the afflictions and behaviour of afflicted person as pathological or abnormal. The physiological symptoms, which included convulsions, contortions, paralysis, loss of vision, and levitation, were pathological in the sense that they deviated from established medical norms. In 1755 the English court physician Richard Meade wrote that 'in the whole catalogue of diseases, which afflict mankind, there is no other that seems so much to surpass the force of nature as this, in wretchedly tormenting the patient by fierce distractions of the mind and excessively strong tho' involuntary motions of the body.'[86] The English demoniac William Somers was reported to have foamed at the mouth in such an unnatural way that the foam did 'hang down from his mouth to his breast . . . in such abundance as is not able to be uttered by any human creature'.[87] These abnormal somatic symptoms of possession may be termed physiopathological.

A similar criterion of abnormality characterized the verbal and behavioural signs of possession, such as speaking in previously unknown foreign languages, clairvoyance, and the public violation of conventional standards of conduct. These symptoms can also be classified as pathological, in the sense that they deviated from established practices. Verbal and behavioural symptoms of possession, as opposed to those that are physiological, may be termed psychopathological.

The second feature of demonic possession, which is closely related to the first, is that family, friends, pastors, and medical doctors who observed the demoniac would conclude, after weighing the options, that the Devil was responsible for such abnormal behaviour. In other words, contemporaries concluded that the afflicted person was possessed by demons. This book will deal only with those persons who were defined as such by their contemporaries. Demonic possession is a social construct, based on a widely shared belief in the possibility that a maleficent spiritual being can cause the abnormal or pathological behaviour described above. When this book refers to demoniacs, it means those people who were identified as such by their contemporaries.[88]

The definition of possession used in this book excludes four groups of people whom contemporaries often referred to as being possessed. The first were those who displayed many of the same symptoms as demoniacs but whose afflictions were believed to have been caused by beneficent or superior spirits, a broad category that in Christianity included God and the angels. These possessions are usually referred to as good, positive, or divine, and they can be distinguished from demonic possessions by both their proclaimed source and the intentions of the possessed. In the late Middle Ages and early modern periods many aspirants to sanctity, especially women, fell into trances and raptures, had hallucinations and visions, fasted for long periods of time, and demonstrated clairvoyant and prophetic powers. They also demonstrated an ability to speak previously unknown languages. While some signs of divine possession, such as stigmata, were not usually manifested by demoniacs, and while the divinely possessed only occasionally exhibited feats of abnormal strength, the symptoms of the two types of possession were similar enough for authorities to develop techniques to determine whether the possessing agent was a good or demonic spirit. This art of discerning spirits, a term derived from St Paul, usually resulted in the inclusion of some possessed women in one category or the other. The boundary between the two, however, was so thin that some women once believed to be aspirants to sanctity, especially nuns in France, Spain, and Italy, were later numbered among the Devil's victims. This crossover group that eventually came to be viewed as possessed by demons are included in this study.

The second group of people sometimes identified as having been demonically possessed consisted of those whom the Devil assaulted externally. Demonologists often made a distinction between *obsession* and *possession* on the grounds that the former involved an external assault on the afflicted person's body rather than an internal occupation. The Latin word *obsessio* bears the connotation of a military siege. Possession, by contrast, connoted breaching the walls and actually invading the fortress.[89] In obsession the Devil can appear to victims, strike them, and harass them in various ways that affect their bodies and emotions, whereas in possession 'the demon takes possession of the faculties and organs of the person in such a way as to produce not only in her, but also by her, actions that that person could not bring about herself.'[90] Medieval theologians often contended that saints were not subject to possession, only obsession, since it was believed that God would not allow the Devil to inhabit their bodies. Thus demons tormented St Anthony mentally and physically while he was in the Egyptian desert, but they did not occupy his body. When demons reportedly slapped the saintly Tuscan nun Veronica Giuliani in the head while she tried to pray, knocked her off ladders, kept her awake at night, hissed like serpents, and gave off foul smells they were obsessing, not possessing her.[91] The French priest Jean-Marie Vianney, who was canonized in 1925, claimed to have been obsessed by the Devil for thirty-four years. In this book I have classified as demoniacs only those persons whose bodies were putatively invaded by demons; hence its title, *The Devil Within*

Despite this theoretical distinction between obsession and possession, the two categories have often been confused, possibly because *obsessio* was sometimes used to identify both external and internal attacks by the Devil. In the late sixteenth century, an English pamphlet reported how the Devil, taking the form of a small bear having neither head nor tail, lifted a Somerset woman out of her bed, rolled her like a hoop through three rooms and down a high set of stairs before her husband and his brother demanded that the demonic intruder depart in the name of God. Although this was clearly a case of obsession, the published narrative referred to the woman as having been 'possessed with the Devil'.[92] In similar fashion Father Surin, the exorcist at Loudun who was reportedly possessed by the demons he had expelled from the possessed nuns, has been interpreted as an instance of obsession rather than possession, mainly because Surin never allowed the Devil to control his mental faculties during the entire experience.[93]

The symptoms displayed by the bewitched girls at Salem, Massachusetts, in 1692, which have often been considered signs of demonic possession, suggest that the girls were merely obsessed. The girls' afflictions included fits, distempers, skin lesions, pinpricks, choking sensations, and loss of hearing, sight, and memory. They also made 'foolish, ridiculous speeches' and assumed odd postures, crept under chairs, and crawled into holes. Of these symptoms, only the vaguely described fits and distempers and the sudden loss of hearing, sight, and memory might indicate genuine possession. Some historians have nonetheless considered the afflictions of these young girls to be classic cases of demonic possession.[94] The problem with this classification is that the girls' symptoms did not include the most distinctive features of early modern possessions. They did not exhibit muscular rigidity or flexibility, vomit alien objects, or speak in languages that they had not previously learned. Nor did these alleged victims of witchcraft or any observers claim that evil spirits had actually invaded the bodies of the girls and taken control of their physical and mental functions. The only roles ascribed to the Devil were as the ultimate source of the girls' symptoms and producer of the spectres of the witches that the girls claimed they could see and that they were the source of the witches' powers. One can argue that the girls at Salem were obsessed, but the claim that they were possessed by the Devil does not agree with early modern European demonological theory.[95]

The third group of demoniacs I have excluded from this analysis are those who presented themselves to exorcists to be cured of minor medical ailments which they and their exorcists believed were caused by the Devil. Very few if any of the hundreds of demoniacs who sought the services of the Piedmontese exorcist Giovan Battista Chiesa in the late seventeenth century or the German priest Johann Joseph Gassner in the mid eighteenth century displayed the classic symptoms of possession discussed above. Chiesa and Gassner are relevant to the study of possession because of what their careers tell us about the theory and practice of exorcism, but the symptoms of possession displayed by their patients, which were often common illnesses such as fevers, headaches, and sore throats, resist classification as pathological. Occasionally Chiesa and Gassner would exorcize an epileptic or a paralytic but hardly ever someone who was demonstrating preternatural strength or the prowess of a contortionist. Nor did these demoniacs display the linguistic facility, clairvoyance, or repulsion of sacred objects that demonologists had identified as common symptoms of possession ever since the thirteenth century. I have not included the thousands of these demoniacs who underwent routine exorcisms in my estimate of the number of possessions in early modern Europe. Nor do I place in that category the hundreds of demoniacs who flocked to shrines and other holy places to be exorcized.[96] I do, however, discuss these mundane possessions in Chapter 10 as one form of possession that has occurred frequently in Europe since the early eighteenth century, when the number of classic and much more widely publicized possessions began to decline.[97]

The exclusion of mundane possessions and routine exorcisms raises the question of whether there was an 'epidemic' of possession in early modern Europe. There is little doubt that exorcism, considered as a form of spiritual physic, was commonplace in early modern Europe. In this sense possession was hardly a fringe phenomenon; it was part of the warp and woof of the religious life of the time.[98] But classic possessions, characterized by the pathological symptoms described above, were obviously not so plentiful. The term 'epidemic', a medical term referring to a communicable disease that spreads rapidly through a community, can only refer to large group possessions, in which the spread of symptoms gave the impression that the malady was contagious. Even in these cases, however, the term is misleading, since it implies that possession was a communicable disease. The late nineteenth-century writers who first used the word 'epidemic' to describe cases of possession believed that demoniacs were 'really' victims of the contagious 'disease' of hysteria.[99]

A fourth group of early modern Europeans whom I have excluded from consideration in this book are those who were described as possessed simply because they were sinners. Theologians and demonologists, most notably the sixteenth-century Genevan minister Pierre Viret, claimed that all human beings were possessed by devils, because sin, the Devil's speciality, was the natural and perdurable state of mankind. Luther anticipated Viret's view of possession when he claimed that all sinners were demon-possessed.[100] So too did the Lutheran minister Daniel Schaller, who said that possession involved the seizure of the souls and hearts of men. The sixteenth-century English physician and moralist Andrew Boorde included all sins in the category of possession.[101] All these writers, following St Paul, used the term 'demonic possession' to describe the condition of human society in the Last Days. Such 'ethical possessions' differed from the physiopathological and psychopathological experiences that are the essential elements of the phenomenon that is the subject of this book.

Interpretations of possession

How then did early modern Europeans and subsequent generations make sense of the individual and group possessions that contemporaries described in agonizing detail? How did they account for physical and social behaviour that deviated so dramatically from what was considered normal or conventional?

Demonic occupation

The dominant contemporary interpretation of these experiences was that the Devil, often identified by his biblical name of Satan, or one or more of his subordinate demons, invaded the body of the demoniac and seized control of that person's physical movements, senses, and mental faculties. Because demons were viewed as being incorporeal, they 'could go in and out of our bodies, as bees do in a hive'.[102] Once they had penetrated the human body, which was then viewed as being porous or permeable and hence vulnerable to supernatural attack, they roamed around its inner caverns, indiscriminately attacking organs and anatomical parts. When they attacked the brain, they gained control of the demoniac's memory, imagination, and reason.[103] According to the Italian exorcist Giovan Battista Zaretti, who exorcized the nuns of Santa Chiara in 1636, demons, once inside the body, ascended quickly to the demoniacs' heads, sending them into a deep sleep, and then started attacking their hearts, causing them excessive pain. When a surgeon gave the nuns purges and tried to bleed them, the demons were said to have blocked the canals of the their bodies to prevent anything from exiting. The demons then reportedly closed off the women's lower orifices so that blood would flow from their mouths.[104]

Belief in possession by demons was deeply ingrained in early modern European culture. Long-standing popular beliefs regarding the presence of evil spirits in the world and their frequent interactions with human beings provided the foundation for such claims, and they received endorsement from biblical scholars and scholastic theologians.[105] The accounts of Christ's expulsion of unclean spirits from demoniacs in the New Testament provided what was considered to be unimpeachable support for the reality of demonic possession, while medieval theologians gave a rational, philosophical explanation of how demons, who were believed to be incorporeal spirits, could achieve penetration and occupation of a human body.

From the earliest days of Christianity the belief existed that more than one demon could possess a person. The scriptural basis for this belief was the answer a demoniac gave when Christ asked him to identify himself and he replied that his name was Legion. The number of men in a Roman imperial legion was about six thousand, but demonologists felt free to speculate on the number that were active in any one possession. The eight-year-old demoniac Loyse Maillat in Burgundy was possessed by five demons, while Rollande du Vernois hosted two such spirits, one named Cat and the other given the unimaginative designation of Devil. Jeanne des Anges, the Mother Superior of the convent at Loudun, was reputedly possessed by seven demons, each one occupying a different part of her body and each one identified by name.[106] Other demons remained anonymous. According to the theologian and exorcist Sebastian Michaelis, 6,660 unnamed demons possessed Louise Capeau at Aix-en-Provence in 1609, a claim that the chief demon Beelzebub made while speaking in Capeau's voice. This estimate, obviously suggested by the exorcist, was probably based on the identification of one of the two beasts accompanying the dragon in the Book of Revelation as the number 666, rather than an erroneous knowledge of the number of Roman legionaries.[107] The German Jesuit Georg Scherer claimed in 1584 that the sixteen-year-old demoniac Anna Schlutterbäurin was possessed by 12,652 demons—the highest number ever recorded. This estimate was based on the contention that the Roman legion actually had 12,500 soldiers.[108] By this criterion the legion of demons possessing Anna included a few reserves available for service if the others faltered.

Medieval and early modern theologians contended that possession by a demon could take place in two ways. The most common was direct invasion by the Devil, who could act only with the permission of God. This requirement of divine permission represented a rejection of the belief of dualist heretics such as Cathars that the Devil was the coequal of God and was the creator of the material world, from entrapment in which Christ tried to free human beings. In the face of such claims it was imperative for theologians to reassert God's sovereignty by claiming that the Devil could not invade the body of a human being without God's permission.

The second method of possession, which was recognized only after the prosecution of witches had begun in the early fifteenth century, was that the Devil entered the body of the demoniac at the command of a witch. In such circumstances, the afflictions suffered by the demoniac were considered to be *maleficia*, the acts of magical harm inflicted by witches on their neighbours or enemies. The idea that witches, who were defined as people who could cause magical harm and who made pacts with the Devil, could command demons to do their bidding derived from traditions of learned or ritual magic, in which male magicians summoned up demons and commanded them to perform magical deeds. As accusations of witchcraft gradually devolved on to illiterate women who were viewed as sexual slaves of the Devil, demonologists tended to minimize the power witches exercised over demons. But the older belief that witches could command demons to perform magical acts on their behalf persisted in the belief that they could command them to possess another human being.

Christians of all denominations believed that the demons could be expelled from bodies they had invaded and occupied. This dispossession of demoniacs was usually referred to as exorcism. In the Catholic Church exorcism was an elaborate and often public ritual in which a priest or designated official tried to expel the demon by commanding the demon to depart, reciting various formulae, applying sacred objects to the body of the demoniac, and sometimes using physical force. Protestants objected to the Catholic ritual on the grounds that it did not have scriptural sanction, that it emphasized the human power of the exorcist rather than appealing to the deity, that it was essentially magical and superstitious, and that its purpose was to perform a miracle in an age when they had ceased. In order to dispossess a demoniac Protestants were supposed to use only the scripturally warranted methods of prayer and fasting, but some Protestants occasionally used methods otherwise reserved for Catholics.

The belief that demons actually entered the bodies of human beings, while perfectly understandable and plausible to many people in early modern Europe, has often met with expressions of scepticism, both among contemporaries and modern scholars. This scepticism has been of two varieties. The first, which prevailed mainly in the early modern period, did not reject the possibility that demons could possess human bodies. These possession sceptics simply denied demonic agency in specific cases of alleged possession. The second and more fundamental variety of scepticism was the denial of the very possibility of demonic intervention in the natural world and the Devil's involvement in human affairs. While this position is not incompatible with a belief in the existence of spirits, it has found its most determined proponents among rationalists who, like the ancient Jewish Sadducees, denied the existence of all spirits.

This reluctance of modern scholars to accept contemporary supernatural explanations of demonic possession is understandable. There is broad agreement, or at least there should be, that it is not the function of historians either to propose or to endorse supernatural explanations of past events. In the Middle Ages historians did this almost as a matter of course to illustrate the role of Providence in human affairs, but modern historians have for the most part abandoned explanations of historical events that cannot be supported by a critical examination of the sources.[109] A modern historian might *believe* that the Devil can possess human beings, but such a position can be based only on that historian's religious faith. Historians can and should, however, take seriously the beliefs of contemporaries that Satan was the cause of a demoniac's afflictions.[110] The problem with many modern scholarly treatments of possession is that in denying the reality of supernatural agency they also fail to take seriously the belief of contemporaries that Satan was responsible for the demoniacs' behaviour and that their beliefs had a great deal to do with the ways in which demoniacs acted.

The two most common sceptical, rational interpretations of possession are that demoniacs were faking the symptoms of their possession and that they were suffering from illnesses that had natural causes. These efforts to explain what really was happening when demoniacs displayed the signs of possession cannot be readily dismissed, since it is apparent that some demoniacs did in fact pretend to have been possessed, while others clearly had contracted some sort of disease or illness that produced symptoms similar to those displayed by demoniacs. Nor can these two sceptical interpretations of possession be dismissed as anachronistic, since contemporaries offered the same interpretations as modern historians.

Fraud

As the number of demoniacs increased in the sixteenth century, Catholic and Protestant authorities claimed that significant numbers of them were faking their possession. They conducted tests to determine whether possessions were authentic, often during exorcisms, and if the demoniacs failed those tests they became liable to prosecution in either the ecclesiastical or the temporal courts. Counterfeit demoniacs, as they were known in England, simulated possession for a variety of reasons. The most common were to attract attention, violate moral or social norms with impunity, receive alms from sympathetic neighbours, or accuse enemies of having caused their possession by means of witchcraft.

Authorities tried to detect fraudulent demoniacs for different reasons in Catholic and Protestant lands. Catholic efforts in this regard originated in the discernment of divine from demonic possessions, an initiative that began in the late Middle Ages to determine whether female aspirants to sanctity were possessed by good or evil spirits. This process of discernment inevitably became linked to the question of whether specific divine or demonic possessions were genuine or false, and that question of sincerity or deception became more important than determining the type of spiritual experience of the possessed.[111]

The main method of making this determination in Catholic possessions was to subject the possessed to a variety of tests. Investigations of feigned sanctity often differed from those used to detect counterfeit demoniacs. In the case of the divinely possessed, investigators often sought to determine whether the person had actually fasted for long periods of time. (One aspirant to sanctity was discovered to have secretly gone on eating binges between periods of fasting.) Another question was whether stigmata, which were far more common among the divinely possessed than demoniacs, were self-inflicted wounds. This proved to have been the case with the Portuguese nun Maria de la Visitación, who confessed to this deceit as well as to having falsely claimed that she had had visions.[112]

The administration of tests to detect fraud in demoniacs usually focused on their alleged feats of preternatural strength and their demonstration of linguistic skill, but occasionally the possessed were also tested for clairvoyance and levitation.[113] In December 1632 the archbishop of Bordeaux sent a group of Catholic physicians to investigate whether Mother Jeanne des Anges had exhibited any supernatural signs. In particular, he wanted

them to determine whether the assistants of the exorcists had fed information to Mother Jeanne so that she could demonstrate knowledge of events
in faraway places or could say eight or ten words, correct and well
constructed, in several different languages, or whether she, being bound
hand and foot on a mattress on the floor, could rise and float in the air for
a considerable time.[114]

In 1601 a French exorcism ended after more than five months when the
demoniac, a priest by the name of Gorbal, was questioned in Spanish,
Gaelic, and Breton. The demon did not understand any of these languages.[115]
In 1621 the French monk and professor of philosophy Claude Pithoys,
who later converted to Protestantism, published a treatise titled *La
Descouverture des faux possedez* (The Discovery of Fake Possessions) in
response to Catholic efforts to exorcize Elisabeth de Ranfaing, a young
widow from the town of Nancy in Lorraine. Pithoys's efforts to discredit
the possession included the argument that many of Ranfaing's symptoms
had natural causes or were the result of diabolical illusion, but he also
considered the possibility that the symptoms were deliberately simulated.
He revealed that an unscrupulous physician, after failing to seduce
Ranfaing, plied her with various medicines to produce convulsions. To test
the authenticity of the possession Pithoys recommended that the demoniac be addressed not in Latin but in Greek or Hebrew and that she be
given both consecrated and unconsecrated hosts to see if she responded to
both in the same hostile manner.[116]

In the sixteenth century Catholic authorities defined 'simulation of
sanctity' and 'simulation of diabolic possession' as crimes.[117] Criminalization
did not, however, lead to a torrent of prosecutions. Most of those that
resulted in investigations took place in the tribunals of the Spanish and
Roman inquisitions.[118] The secular courts in Catholic territories rarely
brought legal action against fraudulent demoniacs. One such case occurred
in Regensburg in the early fifteenth century, when municipal authorities
arrested and tortured a woman who preached that she was filled with the
spirit of God.[119] French secular courts also heard a few such cases. But the
regulation of spirituality was the traditional preserve of the ecclesiastical
courts, so even when fraudulent possession was defined as a serious crime
of deception, ecclesiastical authorities took the initiative in prosecuting it.

The exposure of counterfeit demoniacs in Protestant territories differed
from those in Catholicism in three respects. First, there was little if any
concern in Protestantism with good or 'divine' possession; Protestant
attention focused exclusively on the demonically possessed. Second,
Protestant authorities were willing to use the secular machinery of the
state as well as that of the Church to prosecute counterfeit demoniacs.

Third, Protestant authorities used the investigation and occasional prose-cution of fraudulent demoniacs for confessional purposes. They were intended in many instances to identify the falsely possessed as Catholics or their exorcists as being 'popishly affected'.

The confessional purpose of such exposures was evident in the work of Samuel Harsnett, who served as chaplain to Richard Bancroft, the bishop of London, in the early years of the seventeenth century. In 1603 Harsnett published a fierce anti-Catholic treatise, *A Declaration of Egregious Popish Impostures*, claiming that a cluster of exorcisms performed by the Jesuit William Weston in aristocratic households in Essex in the mid 1580s were fraudulent. Harsnett also intended to discredit three exorcisms conducted by the Puritan preacher John Darrell, against whom he had written an earlier treatise in 1599.[120] Harsnett claimed that Darrell's methods of dispossession were almost indistinguishable from Weston's and were equally fraudulent. In exposing these exorcisms as counterfeit, Harsnett made it clear that the possessions themselves were also 'pretended'—that the demoniacs as well as the exorcists were impostors. During the trial of Darrell, as a result of which the minister was deprived of his benefice, four of the demoniacs whom Darrell had exorcized confessed that they had faked their symptoms.[121]

The English belief that most cases of possession were fraudulent received confirmation from two prosecutions in the secular courts in which demoniacs confessed that they had faked their symptoms. The first case was that of Anne Gunter, the sister-in-law of the Regius professor of divinity at Oxford, whose fits and regurgitation of pins in the presence of the College fellows gained the attention of a number of prominent English academics and physicians, including William Harvey, in 1604. Anne had accused three women in her Berkshire village of causing her possession by witchcraft. After the women were acquitted, the attorney general, Sir Edward Coke, brought charges against Anne and her father, Brian Gunter, in the Court of Star Chamber for having conspired to indict the women. Star Chamber was the only court in the land that had jurisdiction over such an offence. The prosecution attracted the attention of both Harsnett, who kept Anne under house arrest and pressured her to confess her guilt, and King James I (r. 1603–25), who interviewed Anne on four separate occasions in an effort to detect the fraud. During the course of the trial Anne confessed that her father had induced the symptoms of posses-sion by burning brimstone to induce her fits and had forced her to swallow the pins that she had regurgitated.[122]

The second case, also tried in the Court of Star Chamber, involved the prosecution of Thomas and Elizabeth Saunders of West Ham, Essex, and their daughter in 1622 for having encouraged their granddaughter, Katheren Malpas, to pretend that she had been bewitched and possessed by an evil spirit. Under examination by William Coventry, the attorney general, Elizabeth admitted that she had devised the scheme so that her daughter and granddaughter might secure financial contributions from 'such persons as should come to see her in pity and commiseration'. This simulated possession also involved accusations of witchcraft, for Katherine had accused two women of causing her afflictions by means of maleficent magic. Instead of bringing charges against the women, however, the Essex assizes prosecuted Katherine for pretending to be bewitched and for then maliciously and falsely accusing one of the women of witchcraft. For this offence she was placed in the stocks and committed to a house of correction for eight months.[123]

By the late seventeenth century the belief that all early modern demoniacs faked their possession became widespread among English writers. In his sceptical witchcraft treatise, *The Displaying of Supposed Witchcraft* (1677), the English physician John Webster (1611–82) referred to all earlier instances of demonic possession in his country as 'diabolical counterfeiting'.[124] Some modern scholars, seeking a rational explanation of what was 'really happening' in early modern possession, have emphasized the fraudulent nature of the most highly publicized cases of demonic possession in England and France in the sixteenth century.[125] Fraud, however, cannot provide a comprehensive explanation for all early modern European possessions. To argue that all demoniacs were impostors requires that we classify all possessions as volitional, that is, that the demoniacs or the persons directing them deliberately staged the possession. The narratives of early modern possessions do not support such a premise. Many appear to have originated involuntarily, when the demoniac simply began to display abnormal, unnatural, or pathological symptoms. Those might very well have had medical or psychological causes, which were also unlikely to have been volitional. It is true that demoniacs or their family members might then have seized that opportunity to feign additional symptoms, but such an intervention does not mean that the entire possession was counterfeit. We are still left with the challenge of explaining the elements of the possession that were not apparently volitional.

Illness

The second interpretation advanced both by sceptical contemporaries and modern 'rational' scholars is that demoniacs were suffering from a physical or mental illness. This interpretation cannot be readily dismissed. The reported symptoms of demoniacs, even if they were greatly exaggerated for polemical purposes, make a prima facie case for the argument that these individuals had serious medical or psychological problems. Even some early modern writers who subscribed to a demonological interpretation of possession also accepted a medical interpretation, since they believed that the Devil was the ultimate cause of all disease—that the Devil, like God, worked through nature rather than against it.[126]

Until the late nineteenth century, the diseases that medical practitioners and demonologists considered the most likely causes of possession were the three classic psychosomatic maladies of epilepsy, melancholy, and hysteria. Hippocrates and other ancient Greek physicians had identified all three of these diseases as having both mental and physical symptoms: they originated in internal organs but had pathological effects on the functioning of both the body and the mind. Two of these diseases, epilepsy and melancholy, had particular appeal to those who thought the Devil was the cause of all disease, since both maladies had acquired a supernatural interpretation that coexisted with the natural interpretation. Ever since the time of Hippocrates epilepsy had been known as the sacred disease, and in the fourth century CE melancholy acquired the nickname of 'the Devil's bath'. Hysteria, however, failed to acquire a similar supernatural label or interpretation, so it became the preferred medical diagnosis of possession in the seventeenth and eighteenth centuries. By the late nineteenth century the medical interpretation of possession had become the exclusive preserve of secularists.

In the second half of the nineteenth century the French neurologist Jean-Martin Charcot, who epitomized this modern, secular approach to medicine, developed a comprehensive theory of hysteria that comprehended both epilepsy and melancholy, which he claimed was the 'real' explanation of what was happening when people were reportedly possessed by the Devil in the sixteenth and seventeenth centuries. Armed with this new theory of *hystéro-épilepsie*, Charcot and his colleagues began to diagnose specific early modern instances of possession retrospectively as examples of hysteria. As part of this campaign of historical revisionism, a group of his associates republished a number of early modern possession narratives, to which they attached explanations of what they thought was 'really' going on during possession. The identification of demonic possession with hysteria thus became the established historical explanation.

The protean concept of hysteria as defined by Charcot broke down into more specific aetiological categories in the twentieth century, but the process of reinterpreting what was once called demonic possession as some sort of neurological, emotional, or cognitive disorder has continued to the present day. In the past four decades researchers have suggested that demoniacs were afflicted by, among other things, bipolar disorder, catatonic schizophrenia, epilepsy, palsy, Tourette's syndrome, chorea (a nervous disorder marked by a spasmodic movement of the limbs), ergot poisoning, anorexia, and trance disorders. The most popular of these explanations is that demoniacs suffered from a dissociative identity disorder (DID), more commonly referred to as multiple personality disorder, which is one of many aetiological stepchildren of hysteria. Modern psychiatrists find DID a persuasive naturalist explanation of demonic possession because demoniacs usually alternated between two distinct personalities—those of the possessed person herself and the demon who apparently spoke through her.

The use of modern psychiatric theories to diagnose early modern cases of possession has two serious limitations. The first is that the theories fail to account for the many different signs of possession reported in contemporary narratives. Those in the early modern period who rejected the naturalist interpretations of possession were quick to point out this weakness. In defending the reality of the possession of seven persons in Lancashire in the mid 1590s, the Protestant minister George More noted that while a sceptic might be able to explain one specific sign of possession, he could not account for all or even most of the eighteen signs More had enumerated in this particular case.[127] The same critique applies today. For example, the argument that demoniacs were victims of Tourette's syndrome might serve as a plausible explanation of the compulsive, involuntary cursing, blasphemies, and twitching of demoniacs, but it says nothing about their feats of abnormal strength or those episodes in which the demoniac did not utter profanities. In a similar vein, the regurgitation of alien objects, when not deliberately faked, might be diagnosed as the medical disorder known as allotriophagy or pathological swallowing, but such vomiting of alien objects was always just one sign of an apparent possession.[128] Ergot poisoning might be used to explain the convulsions of demoniacs but does little to account for their violation of moral and cultural norms. Interpretation of possession as the effects of ergot poisoning is also unlikely to explain cases of possession among adults, whom it rarely affected, as well as those that originated in areas where the contamination of the grain supply was not reported.

The second limitation, closely related to the first, is that all such psychiatric diagnoses are ahistorical. They suffer from the assumption that pathological or abnormal behaviour in all societies and at all periods of time can be attributed to the same psychopathological syndromes or complexes. Taken to their extreme, such assumptions can lead to the argument, epitomized in the work of the German philosopher Traugott Oesterreich and to a lesser extent the psychologist Morton Klass, that all possessions, ancient or modern, regardless of the differences in the cultures in which they take place, are essentially the same.[129] Such diagnoses are apparent in efforts of modern psychiatrists as well as some anthropologists and historians to seek universal explanations of both historical and contemporary possessions.[130] Their studies are anachronistic in that they use models derived from the observation and treatment of people living in the modern era to explain the mentality and anxieties of people living in a very different historical period. More seriously, they fail to recognize the cultural specificity of illnesses, especially those that have a mental or psychic component.[131]

Despite its serious limitations, modern psychiatric theory, especially that which relates to anxiety disorders, can play a role in making sense of demonic possession. It can do so, however, only if it is used to explain a limited number of symptoms of the possession, in most cases those that were evident when the afflictions began. Psychiatric theory might, for example, explain how stress or anxiety can express itself psychosomatically, such as when demoniacs began to experience convulsions, demonstrate preternatural strength, or lose control of their senses. The other symptoms, however, especially those of a verbal or behavioural nature, can only be explained in terms of the religious culture in which the possession takes place.

Cultural performance

The two explanations of demonic possession that have held the greatest appeal for 'rational' minds—disease and fraud—do not by themselves provide a satisfactory explanation of what was really happening during early modern European possessions. Fraud may provide a persuasive explanation for a limited number but hardly for all of those that took place. Disease might render certain symptoms of possessions, especially those evident in their initial stages, intelligible, but neither physical nor mental illness can explain all the things the demoniac said or did. A more comprehensive understanding can be gained by viewing demoniacs as well as all those who participated in the effort to cure them as performers in religious dramas. Whether unconsciously or not, they were playing roles and following scripts that were encoded in their respective religious cultures.

The idea that demoniacs were actors is not new. Sceptical contemporaries, especially Protestants, frequently accused demoniacs of acting or pretending that they were possessed. Modern historians have also developed an analysis along such lines, and in this they have drawn inspiration to some extent from the work of cultural anthropologists.[132] This scholarship, however, has focused primarily if not exclusively on volitional possessions, in which the demoniacs were aware that they were following a script and performing before an audience. Modern scholars have been even more attentive to the theatrical dimensions of early modern exorcisms, especially those conducted publicly, and they have also fruitfully studied the representation of possessions and exorcisms in early modern dramas.

This book argues that all possessions, not just those that were feigned or otherwise volitional, were theatrical productions in which the demoniacs and also their families, neighbours, physicians, pastors, and exorcists played their assigned roles. All these participants in the drama of possession acted in the way that members of their religious communities expected them to act.

Those expectations, and therefore the scripts that demoniacs followed, were significantly different for Catholics and Protestants. There were many religious cultures in early modern Europe. Even before the Protestant Reformation, one can distinguish between the religious culture of the monastery and that of the laity. The cultivation of lay piety, especially after the Council of Trent in the mid sixteenth century, made it especially difficult to talk about a single Catholic culture in the early modern period. The Protestant Reformation gave birth to a wide variety of beliefs and ideals, most notably within Lutheranism and Calvinism, but also in the more radical religious sects. The new Protestant confessions led to different interpretations of the Mass, the means of obtaining salvation, the nature of efficacy of sacraments, the relationship between Scripture and Tradition, the definition of sanctity, the sovereignty of God, the intercession of the saints, and the enforcement of morality. These differences between various Catholic and Protestant cultures, especially between post-Tridentine Catholicism and Calvinism or Reformed Protestantism, help to explain why possessions and exorcisms took many different forms during the age of the Reformation.

Social conditions

Understanding demonic possession as a form of theatre helps us make better sense of the phenomenon than identifying it as fraud, which occurred only in a small minority of cases, or as the product of physical or mental illness, which fails to explain the profound differences between the experiences of Catholic and Protestant demoniacs. But none of these three non-supernatural explanations of possession, including the broadly applicable theory of cultural performance, explores the social circumstances that caused some demoniacs to pretend they were possessed, led others to experience profound religious anxiety, or yet others to follow the possession scripts encoded in their religious cultures. All possessions, in other words, were influenced by the position that the demoniacs held in their communities and their efforts to deal with, and sometimes change, that position. The study of these circumstances addresses not so much the question of *what* was happening when demoniacs acted the way they did, but *why*. This inquiry, which has been the main concern of modern social and political historians, represents yet another effort to make sense of demonic possessions in early modern Europe. The social circumstances in which possessions took place, however, do not provide a full explanation. They are most valuable in disclosing the variety of conditions in which possessions occurred and in setting the stage for the theatrical performances, in all their religious complexities, which were to follow.

Subsequent chapters will address these interpretations in detail, but it is first necessary to ask on what basis early modern Catholics and Protestants arrived at or confirmed their belief that demons were in fact responsible for the afflictions of the possessed. They did this either by appealing to the passages in the New Testament in which Christ expelled demons or to the works of medieval scholars who offered theological and philosophical explanations how demons could exercise power in the natural world. These inquiries are the subject of the next two chapters.

CHAPTER 2

Possession and Exorcism in Christian Antiquity

A STUDY OF DEMONIC possession in the early modern period must begin with the biblical accounts of the exorcisms performed by Christ. The main reason for this starting point is that both Protestants and Catholics appealed to these biblical texts to prove the reality of the phenomenon they were observing in their own day. Biblical possessions and exorcisms also provided scripts that demoniacs and exorcists followed in the religious theatre of possession. The account of Christ's exorcism of a boy with a 'dumb spirit' in Mark 9: 17 had such an emotional impact on the young Augustinian monk Martin Luther that he reportedly became possessed himself, falling into a fit, dropping to the ground, and exclaiming in an animal-like voice, 'It isn't me; It isn't me.'[1] His experience reveals how suggestive and emotive the biblical accounts of possession and exorcism could be fifteen hundred years after they were committed to writing.

A further reason for beginning this study with the Bible is that the demoniacs cured by Christ became the subject of a large body of philosophical, hermeneutical, and theological literature in the early modern period. This literature dealt with the authenticity of possessions, the validity of exorcisms, the existence of spirits, the relationship between the natural and the supernatural realms, the possibility of miracles in a post-Apostolic age, and the Second Coming of Christ. This literature disclosed large areas of agreement among all Christians on some issues, but it also revealed how divisive the contentious world of biblical scholarship became in the age of the Reformation. These intellectual divisions existed not only between Catholics and Protestants, who were the main antagonists, but also among Christians belonging to the same religious denominations. In many cases these controversies touched on fundamental doctrinal issues.

Possession and exorcism in the New Testament

One of the reasons why the phenomenon of possession has endured throughout the history of Christianity is that it has a firm foundation in the Bible. The New Testament recounts a number of incidents in which Christ and the Apostles expelled 'unclean spirits' or demons from the bodies of human beings. Since Christians have consistently believed the Bible to be the inspired Word of God, these passages have supported the Christian belief that demons have the ability to enter a human body and literally take possession of it; that is, assume control of its physical and mental functions. These passages have also supported the Christian belief that these invading demons can be expelled from their human hosts.

Although Scripture has inspired belief in possession, the brevity of the biblical accounts, the language in which they were written, and variations between the biblical writers in describing the same incident have sparked considerable debate regarding the nature of the demoniacs' afflictions and the effectiveness of their exorcisms. These controversies have contributed to or reflected divisions within Christianity throughout its history, especially between Protestants and Catholics at the time of the Reformation.

Although there were about fifty references in the New Testament to the performance of exorcism by Christ and his disciples, only five of Christ's exorcisms provided enough detail to inspire imitation. All five accounts appear in the synoptic Gospels, that is, the texts known as Matthew, Mark, and Luke. The accounts in these three Gospels differed in length, emphasis, and detail, but in their main points they agreed. Some modern scholars have used these texts in their quest to discover the historical Jesus, such as to support the claim that his profession was that of exorcist or healer.[2] The reason for briefly summarizing the episodes here is to see to what extent they served as models or inspiration for possessions and exorcisms in early modern Europe. These summaries are consistent with the biblical texts that were widely available to Christians in the sixteenth and seventeenth centuries: the Latin Vulgate used by Roman Catholics; the Bible translated into German by Martin Luther in 1534; the three English translations of 1538 (the Great Bible), 1559 (the Geneva Bible) and 1611 (the King James Version); and the Dutch Bible authorized by the States-General in 1637.[3]

The first of these five exorcisms, recounted in Mark 1: 21–8 and Luke 4: 31–7, was the expulsion of an unclean spirit or demon from a man in the synagogue at Capernaum in Galilee at the beginning of Christ's public ministry. The story says nothing about the man's symptoms before he entered the synagogue. It is unclear from the text whether the demoniac approached Jesus or Jesus sought him out. When Jesus confronted the man, the demon, speaking through the man, declared: 'What have you to do with us, Jesus of Nazareth? Have you come to destroy us? I know who you are, the Holy One of God.' In this way the unclean spirit acknowledged Christ's sanctity and his ability to destroy him. In response Jesus rebuked the demon, saying: 'Be muzzled and come out of him.'[4] The Greek word for muzzled meant silenced and physically constrained, so Christ's command was interpreted as a demonstration of the power of his spoken word over the demon. Only upon the spirit's departure does the text explain that the exorcism sent the man into convulsions and that he cried out in a loud voice. The account concludes by reporting the reaction of the crowd to this incident, which was amazement at Christ's power over demons and their obedience to his commands. The reference to more than one unclean spirit suggests that this was not the only such exorcism that amazed local crowds. Indeed, the same evening, after healing Simon's mother-in-law, Mark reported that Jesus was brought all the sick and those possessed by demons. He cured the sick and expelled many demons.[5]

The second and most problematic of the instances of possession in the Gospels was that of the Gadarene or Gerasene demoniac (Matthew says there were two such men), who came out of the tombs (possibly burial caves) where he resided to meet Jesus as he came ashore on the eastern shore of the Sea of Galilee. In this story, which appears in Matthew 8: 28–32; Luke 8: 26–39; and Mark 5: 1–20, the man had already displayed some of the symptoms later identified with demonic possession before he encountered Jesus. He had broken the chains with which he had been bound so that no one was able to subdue him, and 'continually night and day . . . he was crying out and bruising himself with stones'. Luke adds the significant detail that for a long time the man had worn no clothes. When Christ commanded the unclean spirit to come out of the man (or men) the demon, speaking through the man, pleaded with Jesus, whom he recognized as 'Son of the Most High God', not to torment him. When Jesus asked the demon to identify himself, the spirit replied: 'My name is Legion; for we are many.' The word legion in this context simply meant a large number, not the specific number of 6,000 men in a Roman legion.

This exorcism had a most unusual ending. When the exorcized demons begged Jesus not to send them out of the country but instead let them possess a herd of 2,000 pigs, Jesus granted this request, transferring the spirits from the demoniac's body into those of the animals.[6] This repossession, however, caused the pigs to rush down a steep bank into the sea, where they all drowned. The herdsmen who witnessed this spectacular event reacted differently from the crowd in the synagogue at Capernaum.

When they saw the demoniac sitting clothed and in his right mind, they were afraid and entreated Jesus to depart from their region.

The third demoniac whom Jesus exorcized was the daughter of a Syrophoenician woman in the region of Tyre. The incident is related in Mark 7: 25–30 and Matthew 15: 21–8. The woman's ethnicity was significant because she was the only one of the demoniacs in these five exorcism texts who was a Gentile. Despite Christ's efforts to remain unnoticed when he entered a town in the vicinity, the woman, whose daughter had an unclean spirit, upon hearing that Jesus was secluded in a house, found him and fell down at his feet, asking him to cast an unclean spirit out of her child. For reasons not divulged in the text, Jesus said to her, 'Let the children first be fed, for it is not good to take the bread of the children and throw it to the dogs.' At that point she not only recognized Jesus as 'Lord' but replied that the dogs under the table should eat the crumbs left by the children. Jesus said: 'For saying this go, the demon has gone out of your daughter.' When the woman returned home, she found her child lying in bed and the demon apparently gone.

The story of the demoniac often identified as the epileptic boy told early modern readers much more about the actual afflictions of this youth than those of the daughter of the Syrophoenician woman. The Gospels (Mark 9: 14–29, Matthew 17: 14–21 and Luke 9: 37–43) relate the story of a man who had asked Christ's disciples to cast a 'dumb spirit' out of his son, who would become rigid, foam at the mouth, grind his teeth, and be cast to the ground whenever the evil spirit seized him. The father reported that the son had been going into convulsions since childhood and that the spirit had been trying to destroy him by throwing him into fire and water. Jesus said that he could help the man if he would believe, and after he expressed his faith, Jesus commanded the 'dumb and deaf spirit' to depart and not re-enter the boy. When the disciples asked Christ why they had failed to cast out the spirit, Jesus replied, 'This kind can come forth by nothing but by prayer and fasting'.[7]

The fifth of Christ's possession cases served as the occasion of a controversy regarding Christ's ability to cast out demons.[8] The controversy arose late in the public ministry of Jesus, by which time his fame as an exorcist was widespread. After exorcizing a blind and mute demoniac to the amazement of a crowd of onlookers, either the Pharisees who wished to discredit him (according to Matthew), the scribes (according to Mark), or someone in the crowd (according to Luke) claimed that he had cast out demons by the power of Beelzebul, the prince of demons.[9] Mark added that Jesus was himself accused of being possessed by Beelzebul, reflecting the recurrent claim that he was mentally ill. ('He has Beelzebul.') In one of the most frequently cited passages of Scripture, Jesus argued that if Beelzebul drove out demons by his own power, his demonic kingdom would be destroyed, for 'if a kingdom is divided against itself, that kingdom cannot stand'.[10] According to Matthew, Jesus went on to explain that if he cast out demons by the spirit of God, 'then the kingdom of God has come upon you'. This last text provided a scriptural foundation for the connection between exorcism and the Apocalypse.[11]

The symptoms of biblical possessions

The biblical accounts of these five exorcisms say very little about the possessions that Jesus terminated. This should hardly surprise us. Like many other texts relating to Christ's public ministry, these stories were intended to demonstrate Christ's authority over demons, not the power of the demons over human beings. The biblical accounts, therefore, bear little or no resemblance to early modern narratives of possession, which were intended mainly to document the power of the Devil in human affairs and only secondarily to recount the success or failure of efforts to drive him out.

Since these biblical stories were concerned with Christ's exorcisms rather than the possessions themselves, the authors had no need to enumerate or describe in any detail the actual afflictions from which the demoniacs suffered. They only needed to show that the demoniacs suffered from a serious illness and that Christ demonstrated his sacred power by curing them. Hence the demoniac in the synagogue was reported to have simply convulsed and cried out, and when Jesus demanded the demon's expulsion, the unclean spirit reacted violently, tearing and convulsing the man whom he had possessed. Instead of blaspheming in the manner of an early modern demoniac, he affirmed the holiness of Jesus.

The story of the Gadarene demoniac (or demoniacs) describes the preternatural strength of the man who broke the chains and fetters that bound him, mentions that he was naked, and reports that he bruised himself with stones, but it says nothing about his falling into a trance, seeing visions, levitating, or violating moral norms. The account of the exchange between this demoniac and Jesus, which did not involve blasphemy or heresy but rather respect for Christ, once again was intended to demonstrate the power of Christ over the demons, both in driving them from the man's body and transferring them to the herd of swine. The passage also emphasized the way in which the exorcism spread the word of Christ's miraculous power.

The story of the epileptic boy refers to more symptoms of possession than all the other accounts of possessions combined, but the number of observable signs that it refers to still cannot begin to match the later descriptions of most early modern possessions. The boy, whose father brought him to Jesus to be cured, was described as possessed by a mute and deaf spirit which threw him to the ground, sent him into convulsions, made his body rigid, and caused him to foam at the mouth and grind his teeth. These symptoms are consistent with epilepsy, which was known as the falling sickness, and the identification of the boy as 'moonstruck' or 'lunatic' in Matthew 17: 15 has been rendered as 'epileptic' in modern editions of the Bible.[12]

Two other symptoms of the epileptic boy's afflictions suggested comparison with early modern cases. Like many early modern demoniacs, the boy was described as both deaf and mute.[13] The sixteenth-century exorcist Zacharia Visconti considered the loss of a demoniac's voice one of the most frequent effects of demonic possession in his day.[14] This might explain why the opening quotation of Valerio Polidori's *Thesaurus exorcismorum*, the anthology in which Visconti's treatise was included, is Matthew's account of this exorcism.[15] The second point of comparison is the boy's urge since his childhood to throw himself into fire and water. Many demoniacs in early modern Europe, especially Protestants plagued by their own sinfulness, considered suicide, and some of them succeeded.[16]

Mark and Matthew provided no indication as to why the Syrophoenician woman's daughter was considered to be possessed. Nor was there a verbal exchange between Christ and the demon. Jesus simply announced that the demon had departed once the mother had decided to feed children with the scraps of the table before throwing the crumbs to the dog. Mark apparently had little concern with either the causes of the possession or the means by which Christ performed the exorcism. His main purpose in telling the story was to illustrate the appeal of Jesus to the Gentiles in the region of Tyre, where he was preaching. Since Christ did not engage in any ritual of exorcism that was capable of subsequent imitation, the story had the potential to reinforce the Protestant approach to dispossession.

In the last of the five major biblical accounts of a possession and exorcism, the incident that sparked the celebrated Beelzebul controversy, the demoniac whose malady triggered the debate was described only as mute and blind. Once again there was little disclosure of the nature of his possession. The purpose of the text, related at considerable length, was to identify the true source of Christ's power as an exorcist and to respond to sceptics who might doubt it.

The demoniacs cured by Christ did not manifest the full range of symptoms in early modern European possessions. The only symptoms identified in the five exorcism stories were temporary loss of speech, hearing, or sight; convulsions that in one instance involved foaming at the

mouth and the grinding of teeth; the demonstration of preternatural
strength and anatomical rigidity; and violent self-abuse. To this might
be added clairvoyance in the recognition that Christ was the Son of
God, although that was not supposed to reflect the demon's preternatural
cognitive abilities. These symptoms were compatible with the afflictions
of early modern demoniacs, and they worked their way into many
sixteenth- and seventeenth-century possession narratives, but they were
not the distinguishing characteristics of early modern possessions.[17] The
texts do not even hint that the biblical demoniacs had entered trances or
had visions, hallucinated, spoke in foreign tongues, or acted immorally. All
of the maladies that biblical demoniacs suffered could be described as
neurological or physiological disorders, and only the Gadarene demoniac,
who was reported to have cried during his possession and recovered his
'right mind' after Christ exorcized him, displayed some of the signs of
mental illness. No wonder that some modern scholars have identified
all the maladies afflicting biblical demoniacs as illnesses and concluded
that the historical Jesus was essentially a healer. In Luke the distinction
between Christ's healing and his exorcisms is blurred, as when the Gospel
reports that Jesus 'cured' demoniacs.[18]

The argument that the biblical accounts provided scripts for early
modern demoniacs to follow also fails to recognize the complexity and
prolixity of those sixteenth- and seventeenth-century scripts. Demoniacs in
early modern Europe were doubtless familiar with the accounts of possession in the New Testament, and the narratives of their possessions pointed
out those similarities,[19] but since their symptoms were far more varied and
involved the Devil's assumption of power over the demoniac's mental as
well as physical functions, their performances drew on many more sources
than Scripture. It is hard to imagine that the cameo appearances of demoniacs in the Gospels served as models for the more spectacular cultural
performances of their early modern counterparts. Those performances
reflected a set of Christian beliefs regarding demons that developed
between the time of Christ and the age of the Reformation, mainly in the
thirteenth and fourteenth centuries.[20]

Exorcisms in the New Testament

New Testament possession texts said more about the expulsion of the
demons than about the symptoms of possession, but nevertheless did not
provide a template for future exorcisms. One reason for this is that Christ
did not need to request or rely upon the assistance of a deity to expel an evil
spirit. Because of his divine status, he was able to introduce a charismatic

form of exorcism that did not use any ceremonies or rituals.[21] The apparent absence of ritual, coupled with the absence of an invocation to a deity, made it relatively easy for Protestants to claim that Catholic exorcisms lacked scriptural warrant.

The only elements in Catholic exorcisms that appeared to have scriptural authority were the exorcist's addressing the demons directly and his demand that the Devil identify himself. Even that exchange, however, was controversial in Catholic theological circles, since some early modern demonologists, including the Spanish Jesuit Martín Del Rio, warned against interrogating the demon on the grounds that the Father of Lies was unreliable.[22] A further problem for Catholics who might have sought scriptural guidance in this respect was that Christ's commands to the demons, if given at all, were fairly simple. In the case of the epileptic boy and the Syrophoenician woman's daughter, he expelled the demon without even giving a verbal command.[23] Even if Christ had said more when he cast out unclean spirits, the authors of the Gospels were not particularly interested in how he drove out demons; only in the fact that he did so.[24]

For their part, Protestants could appeal to the biblical account of the epileptic boy to support their approach to dispossession. When the disciples asked Jesus why they had failed to expel the boy's unclean spirit, he replied that such expulsion could only be done by prayer and fasting. When Protestants tried to cure a demoniac, they insisted on using only those biblically sanctioned procedures.[25] In this way they expressed their belief that the dispossession was entirely in God's hands; they could only beseech the deity to expel the demon by his power. Prayer was the antithesis of magic, in that the former was contingent upon God's response whereas the latter exalted the power of the human practitioner. By insisting that only prayer and fasting could expel demons from their human hosts, Protestants supported their frequent claim that Catholic exorcisms were magical.

Protestants could also appeal to the New Testament to support their belief that faith in Christ was necessary to drive out demons. Faith was of course central to Protestantism, since Luther had argued that salvation could be attained through faith alone. Protestants claimed that the faith of the epileptic boy's father in Jesus was necessary for the boy to have been cured. They could also appeal to Mark 16: 14–18, in which the resurrected Christ told the Apostles as they were going into the world that those who believed in him would not only be saved but would be able to cast out demons in his name. Another text that appeared to support the Protestant emphasis on the importance of belief in exorcism was the account of the inability of seven itinerant Jewish exorcists, the sons of the high priest Sceva, to cast out demons in Christ's name, since they did not believe in Christ.[26]

The problem for Protestants who encountered a case of possession was that they could not do very much about the situation. Their reliance on Scripture as the only source of religious belief and conduct (the principle known as *sola scriptura*), allowed them to argue that the Catholic ritual of exorcism was magical and superstitious, but it handicapped them in their efforts to stop the violent convulsions and bodily torments of people in their communities. The problem was analogous to their own inability (theoretically) to do anything themselves to achieve their own salvation, which was dependent solely on God's freely granted grace. Catholics had the psychological advantage of thinking that they could actually *do* something to relieve the demoniac's symptoms, just as they were convinced that they could *do* something to merit their own salvation. The possibility that they might be able to drive out demons helps to explain why some Protestants employed traditional Catholic methods of exorcism to cure demoniacs in their midst. The prosecution of witches who were believed to have caused possessions represented another way in which Protestants could at least attempt to relieve the demoniac of her afflictions.

The cessation of miracles

Protestant appeals to Christian antiquity in order to discredit Catholic exorcisms were not restricted to claims that these magical and superstitious rituals lacked scriptural warrant. Protestants also claimed that miracles, a broad category of supernatural intervention in the natural world that included exorcisms, had not been possible since the end of the Apostolic Age or at the closing of Scripture shortly thereafter. This claim reflected the Protestant critique of Roman Catholicism, especially its reliance on saints, relics, and shrines, all of which were closely associated with the performance of miracles, as intermediaries between humans and God.[27] The doctrine was intended to discredit all modern Catholic exorcisms as counterfeit while not denying the authenticity of the possessions and exorcisms in the New Testament or the dispossessions performed by Protestants using the methods of prayer and fasting.[28]

The Protestant doctrine of the cessation of miracles had its roots in the writings of Luther and Calvin, but it achieved its most sustained and cogent expression in the work of sixteenth- and seventeenth-century English Protestant theologians.[29] The doctrine was grounded in the belief in the sovereignty of God: that is, the belief that he would not delegate any of his power to a human or supernatural creature. Specifically, it proclaimed that although God had performed miracles in biblical times to strengthen and confirm the people's faith in Christ and had given the power to his

Apostles to continue the work of converting pagans to Christianity, this authorization ended no later than the fourth century, when Rome converted to Christianity.[30] Bishop John Hooper of England wrote in 1550 that the miracles of the early Church had been so successful in proving the truth of Scripture that 'there is now no more need of new miracles'.[31]

The miracles that the Protestant doctrine intended to debunk included the full spectrum of divine power which Catholic saints had traditionally displayed to prove that they were holy and theirs was the true Church founded by Christ. The English Protestants who promoted the doctrine, however, were mainly concerned with exorcism. The two most effective critiques of the Catholic position appeared in John Deacon and John Walker's *Dialogicall Discourses* (1601), which these two divines wrote in response to the possession and dispossession of William Somers in 1597, and Richard Baddeley's *The Boy of Bilson* (1622), written after the twelve-year-old William Perry, whom the Jesuits had exorcized, had been exposed as a fraudulent demoniac.[32] Deacon and Walker cited Calvin in arguing that the true miracles effected by Christ and written down by the evangelists were fully sufficient to confirm true saving grace, while those who knew miracles were occurring were wicked and had 'such curious brains as (not contenting themselves with eternal salvation) do desire to leap beyond the limits and bounds of the kingdom of heaven'.[33] Baddeley prefaced his possession narrative with 'A Discourse concerning Popish Exorcising', in which he issued a point-by-point refutation of the Jesuits' claim 'that the use of miracles is a necessary, perpetual, and profitable character and note of the true Church of Christ'.[34]

Despite its utility in the Protestant war of words against Catholics regarding demonic possession, the Protestant assertion that miracles had ceased by the end of the Apostolic Age exposed itself to criticism on a number of fronts. First and most ironically, it lacked the scriptural support that Protestants demanded in other theological and liturgical controversies. Strained efforts to find textual support in the New Testament came to naught. The writings of the Church Fathers provided only marginally more support than Scripture.[35] In one of his sermons St Augustine had declared that 'miracles now cease', but in another text he admitted that miracles continued to be performed in his day.[36] Even the most sceptical Protestant might have had difficulty agreeing that all miracles performed during the early Middle Ages were fraudulent. The lack of consensus on when miracles had actually ceased made the doctrine appear even more speculative. Even if that time could be determined, a Catholic might have asked why Christ had allowed priests in the early years of Christianity the 'special privilege' of performing exorcisms in his name and then denied this privilege to those in subsequent generations. And did the denial of Christ's delegation of this power to Christians at a particular time question the power of God himself?

Regardless of its theological merit, the promotion of the doctrine of the cessation of miracles had little impact on the propaganda wars over exorcism that raged in the age of the Reformation. The most effective way for Protestants to debunk exorcisms, which could hold a large popular audience in awe, was to demonstrate that these latter-day miracles were fraudulent, not to proclaim that they were impossible. Only by demonstrating their counterfeit nature could Protestants hope to undermine Catholic claims. Hence the Huguenot response to the 'Miracle of Laon' in 1566 was to show that the demoniac, Nicole Obry, had faked her symptoms, while Samuel Harsnett, who believed firmly that miracles had ceased, devoted more time to exposing the impostures of Catholic (and radical Protestant) exorcists than in arguing the fine points of Augustinian scholarship regarding miracles.[37]

Even then, Protestants could not prevail in this propaganda war with the Catholics. Popular faith in the possibility of miracles, reinforced by the need of people to rid themselves of terrible afflictions, guaranteed that the Catholic practice of exorcism would survive Protestant criticism in the seventeenth century and secular assaults by *philosophes* in the eighteenth century. All that Catholics needed to do in response to Protestant criticisms was to seek more proof for the authenticity of miracles, especially those that involved the exorcism of evil spirits.[38] The Roman Catholic belief in miracles has continued to the present day, as is evident in the requirement that saints cannot be canonized until evidence is produced that they have been responsible for at least two miracles after death.

Protestants and the reality of biblical possession

The basic dilemma facing early modern Protestants in the controversy with Catholics over exorcism was that they could not deny the authenticity of the possessions and exorcisms recorded in the Bible. This dilemma explains why they formulated the chronologically based doctrine of the cessation of miracles. Only by arguing that miracles had ceased at some point in Christian antiquity could they attest to the historical validity of the Gospel exorcisms while proclaiming all later efforts, especially those by Catholics in the age of the Reformation, as fraudulent.

The only other way that sceptical Protestants could escape this scriptural dilemma was to reinterpret the scriptural possession stories in non-literal terms. These efforts, however, required a direct challenge to the literalist biblical scholarship of early modern Protestantism. They also challenged the belief of many Protestants that possession in the modern world was still possible.

During the seventeenth and eighteenth centuries a small band of Protestant scholars proposed three solutions to this dilemma. First, they argued that the demoniacs in the Bible were physically or mentally ill. The danger inherent in this interpretation was that it implied that the persons identified in the Bible as possessed by an unclean spirit had been described erroneously. This was in effect to deny the infallibility of the Word of God. The second line of argument, equally novel in Protestant theology, was that the demons identified as such in the New Testament should be viewed metaphorically rather than literally. The third argument was that the unclean spirits in the Bible were not Christian devils but demons of Hellenistic origin that had undergone a transformation when they became part of Jewish religious culture.

The first scholar to challenge Protestant scriptural orthodoxy in these terms was the celebrated English theologian and polymath Joseph Mede (1586–1639), a fellow of Christ Church, Cambridge. Mede's close association with the Calvinist theologian William Twisse and the Presbyterian reformer Stephen Marshall suggest that he too may have been a Calvinist, but in any event he was an ardent Protestant, whose posthumous book, *The Apostasy of Later Times* (1641), presented an uncompromising attack on the Roman Catholic Church. This millenarian tract, which bore the subtitle *The Gentiles' Theology of Demons*, made the bold assertion that the demoniacs Christ exorcized were madmen. This radical claim alone explains why Mede did not agree to publish the book in his lifetime.

The Apostasy of Later Times begins with an interpretation of John 10: 20, 'He hath a Devil, and is mad', and proceeds from there to identify different types of madmen with different types of demons. By proposing a natural, medical explanation of possession Mede made the Bible compatible with seventeenth-century natural philosophy, although the main purpose of the treatise was to show that the Christian concept of demons was derived from the beliefs of Gentiles, which had perverted Christianity in the form of Roman Catholicism.[39]

Ten years after the publication of Mede's book the philosopher Thomas Hobbes included a section on demons in Book 4 of *Leviathan* (1651), his groundbreaking treatise on politics. In an earlier chapter Hobbes, who was a Protestant and probably a Calvinist,[40] challenged the scholastic distinction between corporeal and incorporeal substances, the latter being in his view an oxymoron. For the materialist Hobbes there was no such thing as an incorporeal spirit. All spirits were substances and hence were corporeal, since they had dimensions and could be seen, even though they could not respond to touch. They were not flesh and bone, but they had thin subtle bodies, sometimes referred to as aerial bodies, in the same way that air was a substance. Such also were the 'spiritual bodies' that St Paul said would rise from the dead after the Second Coming. These bodies were not imaginary, such as phantasms produced by the imagination, but were 'subtle and invisible'. They were real and permanent creatures of God.[41]

How then did Hobbes deal with the biblical accounts of possession? How, he asked, could a corporeal spirit exist inside in 'a body of flesh and bone, full already of vital and animal spirits?' Acknowledging his debt to Mede, Hobbes asserted that the demoniacs in the Bible were not possessed by demons but were 'such as we call madmen or lunatics, or such as had the falling sickness, or that spoke anything which they, for want of under-standing, thought absurd'. If demoniacs were madmen, and the Devil was a metaphor for 'a disease, as frenzy, or lunacy', one might ask why Christ (who obviously knew their real identity) addressed them as demons. 'But if there be no immaterial spirit, nor any possession of men's bodies by any spirit corporeal, it may again be asked why our Saviour and his Apostles did not teach the people so; and in such clear words, as they might no more doubt thereof'. Why did Christ not address the fever or the lunacy? Hobbes's answer to this question was that Christ used 'the appellation of devils by which they were then commonly understood'.[42]

Hobbes's linguistic interpretation of the New Testament possession texts was even less likely than Mede's to change the Protestant literalist approach to biblical exegesis. However rational or plausible his commentary may appear to modern scholars, traditional Protestants were unwilling to change the way they interpreted biblical texts. The widespread view that Hobbes was an atheist—a claim rooted in his materialism and his mechanistic view of the natural world—gave Protestant writers another reason to ignore his biblical scholarship.[43] They made the same charge of atheism against the radical Dutch philosopher Baruch Spinoza, who while never specifically commenting on the exorcism texts, gained the reputation of 'a profane abuser of Scripture' who 'will have all those devils which Christ and his disciples cast out to be but diseases in men's bodies'.[44]

A charge of atheism such as was lodged against Hobbes and Spinoza would have been much more difficult to defend against the Dutch Calvinist minister Balthasar Bekker (1634–98), who in the early 1690s became the next prominent biblical scholar to argue for a metaphorical interpretation of the exorcism texts. Bekker advanced these ideas in *De betoverde weereld* (The Enchanted World), a long, discursive treatise originally published in two separate volumes in 1691 and 1693 respectively.[45] The book sold thousands of copies in the first few months of publication and was translated into German, French, and English.[46] Bekker was not as radical as Spinoza, in that he did not deny the existence of demons, nor did he deny the truth of Scripture. But he did employ some of the methods of Spinoza's biblical exegesis, and this led the Reformed minister Jacobus Koelman to accuse Bekker of advocating Spinozism.[47]

Like Mede and Hobbes, Bekker argued that the references in the New Testament to possession and exorcism should be taken figuratively to describe people who were insane or suffering from illnesses. The reason that the evangelists used these metaphors was to make Christ's exorcisms understood to 'the superstitious Jewish people'.[48] Bekker buttressed his interpretation with the scriptural text which stated that God had cast demons into Hell, where they were to stay until Judgement Day, giving them no physical power in this world.[49] He claimed that demonic possession was impossible because demons were pure spirit (a position different from that of Hobbes), and therefore could not have knowledge, which depended upon their having mental faculties and senses.[50] These arguments did not find support from the members of the Dutch Reformed Church. Having challenged the leading theologians of his age, Bekker was deprived of his benefice, and his book inspired the publication of 170 responses, most of which were hostile to his claims. One of the few Dutch clergymen who defended him, Eric Walton, was prosecuted for blasphemy and died in prison awaiting trial.[51]

The strength and durability of Protestant support for the reality of scriptural possessions and the effectiveness of exorcisms can be seen in the reaction of the English ecclesiastical establishment to the biblical commentary of Thomas Woolston on possession and exorcism in the early eighteenth century. Woolston was a mystical theologian whose radical views had already gained him a reputation for being mad even before he offered his interpretation of miracles in the New Testament. The main argument in his treatise on the subject, published in 1727, was that the 'miracles of Jesus, as recorded by the evangelists, were never wrought, but are only related as prophetical and parabolical narratives of what will be mysteriously and more wonderfully done by him'.[52] Appealing to the works of the Church Fathers, especially the third-century Christian writer Origen of Alexandria, he argued that the miracles of Christ's healings of bodily diseases, including the afflictions of demoniacs, must be interpreted allegorically.

Woolston took particular pleasure in debunking the great miracle of Christ's 'casting the devils out of the madman or madmen and permitting them to enter into the herd of swine'.[53] He found the circumstances of this supposedly factual incident perplexing, asking what the pigs were doing in a Jewish land, where one was forbidden to eat their flesh. If the answer was that local inhabitants were raising the swine to feed the nearby population of Gentiles, Woolston wondered why Jesus would have agreed to a request by demons to destroy the livelihood of the local inhabitants.[54]

For Woolston the story of this exorcism cried out for a metaphorical interpretation, which he supplied in his treatise. Drawing on the commentary of St Hilarion (291–371) and other Church Fathers, including Augustine, he argued that the possessed 'madman' represented mankind, and if there were two madmen, as Matthew says, they represented the Jew and the Gentile at the time of Christ's coming, 'who may be possessed with devils, in as much as they are under the rule of diabolical sins and subject to the worship of false deities'.[55] In this way Woolston reclassified the incident as an ethical possession in which Satan entered the sinner, as happened with Judas at the time he betrayed Christ. As discussed in Chapter 1, the sixteenth-century Calvinist writer Pierre Viret and Luther had identified resolute sinners as both lunatics and demon-possessed.[56] Woolston also interpreted the demoniac's breaking the chains that fettered him in a metaphorical sense, seeing his violence as hatred of the Church of Christ. In keeping with this interpretation he represented the herd of swine that the Devil entered as heretics or possibly 'Christians in general'. Woolston concluded his interpretation of this exorcism by claiming that if the exorcism had been recorded of Mohammed rather than Jesus, Christian divines would have used it to confute Mohammedanism and turned Mohammed himself into a witch, 'a sworn slave to the Devil'.

Woolston's revisionist interpretation of the biblical possession narratives, like Bekker's, was an effort to introduce a new methodology in scriptural studies. Most academic biblical scholars today would endorse the broad exegetical approach that he followed in this work. But there was little chance that many Protestants, even in an age of religious toleration, would display sympathy for either Woolston or his book. His *Discourse* engendered some sixty printed replies and led to Woolston's trial and conviction for blasphemy in 1729.[57] Unwilling to promise that he would stop publishing such incendiary and blasphemous works, he was imprisoned for one year and fined. He died in poverty in 1733.

Only four years after Woolston's death Arthur Ashley Sykes, an English latitudinarian divine, reopened this biblical controversy regarding possession by publishing an anonymous treatise, *An Enquiry into the Meaning of Demoniacks in the New Testament*. Sykes had no love for Woolston, claiming that the latter's intention had been to 'expose Christianity to contempt and ridicule', but Sykes nonetheless developed the very same points that Woolston, Mede, and Hobbes had made regarding demonic possession. He argued that the Jews had received their ideas of demons from the Greeks; that their demons were not the same as Christian devils; that the demoniacs whom Christ exorcized were either mentally or physically ill; and that the biblical exorcism texts should not be taken literally.

The most distinctive contribution that Sykes made to the possession controversy was to argue that the demons (*daimonion* in the Greek of the New Testament rather than the Latin *diaboli* or devils in later Christian redactions) were actually the souls of dead men.[58] In other words, they were ghosts. Sykes claimed that this idea originated with Hesiod and Homer, but as the English antiquarian Samuel Pegge indicated in his response to Sykes, the word *daimon* did not signify a departed soul either in the classics or in Scripture. Regarding the classics, Pegge claimed that the demons in Hesiod and Homer were a 'ministerial order of beings' distinct from the general population. In Hesiod they were a mythological race of mortal men who after their death lived on earth as pure spirits.[59] Nevertheless, the idea that demons were the souls of departed men did gradually develop in Greco-Roman culture by the time of Christ.[60] In dealing with Scripture Pegge was on much more solid ground. The Jewish belief that demons were the souls of the departed that had returned to inhabit the bodies of the living originated in Jewish mystical circles as part of the cabbalistic doctrine of the transmigration of souls in the twelfth century, and records of *dybbuk* possession in Jewish communities did not begin until the sixteenth century.[61] This belief did, however, surface among Christians from time to time, only to be dismissed by ecclesiastical authorities as false if not heretical.[62] It also appeared in the possessions of blacks in colonial Brazil, who claimed that 'the souls of deceased relatives come to speak through the mouths of the bewitched'.[63] The entities that possess people in non-Christian societies today include ancestors as well as deities and other spirits.[64]

Sykes went on to explain that since ancient Greeks and Jews at the time of Christ attributed medical disorders, especially the 'sacred' diseases of epilepsy and madness, to evil spirits, it became customary to say that individuals with such a disorder 'had a devil' or were possessed. For Sykes it was clear that the possessed boy in the Bible was an epileptic, while the man who broke his chains was a lunatic. More generally Sykes declared, 'I know not whether there is a single instance of a demoniac which may not fairly and justly be explained by epilepsy or madness.'[65] This sweeping statement would include the disciple Philip's exorcism of demons that were 'crying out in a loud voice', that is, raving in the manner of a madman.[66]

According to Sykes, the reason for New Testament writers' attributing the diseases and actions of the possessed to demonic spirits was in the final analysis linguistic: they were making use of the 'terms and language usual in their times' in describing the diseases that afflicted the people whom Christ exorcized. In so doing they felt no need to explain the actual causes of those diseases. Their only concern was to show that Christ miraculously cured them. In reading the Scriptures therefore 'we are not to regard the letter but the real and exact meaning of the sacred writers'.[67] This was a directive with which Woolston could well have agreed.

Like Woolston, Mede, and Hobbes, Sykes also failed to persuade his contemporaries. The publication of his treatise triggered more than thirty replies, and the metaphorical interpretation failed to gain real traction within Protestant clerical circles.[68] The argument that the biblical demoniacs were suffering from disease, especially lunacy, found a receptive audience among medical doctors, if the treatise by the royal physician Richard Mead can be viewed as representative.[69] But there was little hope that the Protestant clergy would accept this type of biblical linguistic revisionism. The Protestant theological establishment was still committed to a literal interpretation of Scripture. They felt a need to prove that possessions that took place in Protestant communities, as opposed to the fraudulent possessions by Roman Catholics, were authentic.

Eventually, however, the tide turned. The turning point appears to have occurred in the 1760s, when the metaphorical interpretation of Scripture began to win support within Protestant theological circles. The key figure in this shift in biblical scholarship in Germany was the Lutheran scholar Johann Salomo Semler, who entered this mine-filled controversy when the possession of Anna Elisabeth Lohmann, a twenty-one-year-old woman from Saxony, created a major stir in 1759. Lohmann's symptoms included paroxysms, rigidity of the limbs, facial contortions, temporary loss of speech, and insensibility. Insisting that this widely publicized possession was not authentic, mainly because Lohmann had not displayed the classic symptoms of language, clairvoyance, and preternatural strength, Semler came to doubt the authenticity of all possessions, including those reported in the New Testament.[70] In a Latin treatise published 1760, which drew on the writings of Mede, Bekker, and Sykes, Semler claimed that the demoniacs in the Bible were suffering from natural illnesses or were mad, that Greek and Jewish demons were nothing more than the non-mortal parts of men, that references to a spirit's possessing a demoniac in the Bible was simply a manner of speaking, and that the Apostles were full of the false opinions of the Jews of their day, including the apocalyptic expectation that Jesus would return again as an earthly ruler.[71]

Semler's ideas were hardly new, but they encountered a much more balanced reception than those of his early eighteenth-century English and Dutch predecessors. His treatise drew the expected number of responses, but many of them were positive. Even more surprising was the support he received from a number of Catholic biblical scholars who had adopted his metaphorical and contextual interpretation of Scripture.[72] A similar reception of the treatise by the English Dissenting minister Hugh Farmer, *An Essay on the Demoniacs of the New Testament* (1775), suggests that learned scepticism regarding the authenticity of demonic possession had taken hold within the clerical community. This scepticism, anchored in biblical scholarship, was far more influential in determining the response of elites to reports of possession than the views of medical doctors. By 1800 most Protestants, clerical and lay, had begun to doubt the authenticity of possessions reported in their communities or the press.

Jewish, Greek, and Christian demons

All these seventeenth- and eighteenth-century Protestant biblical commentators understood that the evil spirits referred to in the Bible reflected Greek beliefs in demons. They reached this conclusion mainly because the Greek work *daimon* or its variant *daimonion* was often used to identify an evil spirit in the New Testament, which was written in Koine, the Greek language that was used throughout the Middle East during the Hellenistic period (323–30 BCE) and continued to be used throughout the eastern part of the Roman Empire for the first two centuries after the death of Christ. The Koine word *daimonion* was also used in the Septuagint, the translation of the Hebrew Bible into Greek for the benefit of Jews who lived in Alexandria and other parts of the Hellenistic world and who had lost their facility in Hebrew. The Septuagint, whose translation had taken two centuries to complete, also influenced the writing of the New Testament, since it was the biblical text through which early Christians and the authors of the New Testament acquired their knowledge of the Hebrew Bible, which they called the Old Testament. The Septuagint was the original source of the claim by Christians that deities identified by Jews as false idols were in fact demons.[73]

Despite the importance of their discovery of Greek influences on the Jewish belief in demons, radical seventeenth- and eighteenth-century Protestant biblical commentators left many aspects of this process unexamined. Hobbes and Sykes, for example, attributed Jewish ideas of demons to the epic poetry of Hesiod and Homer, but failed to explain how beliefs regarding demons that originated in Greece in the eighth century BCE were transmitted to Jews in Palestine at the time of Christ. They did not assess the extent of Hellenistic influences on Jewish culture, which began in the third century BCE but became significant only in the first century CE.[74] They did not recognize that the original Greek word *daimon* could refer to either a good or bad spirit and that a Greek *daimon* actually had more in common with a Jewish or Christian angel than an evil spirit, in that it played an important role as a mediator between humanity and divinity.[75] Nor did they recognize that in Hellenistic culture *daimones*, rather than being incorporeal, as they became in the dominant Christian tradition, had some degree of materiality and occupied the natural sphere of sublunary air. Most important, they did not take into account the many different sources of the beliefs in evil spirits that prevailed in Palestine at the time of Christ.

So where did the belief in the evil spirits or demons that appear in the exorcism stories and elsewhere in the New Testament originate? The books of the Hebrew Bible, especially those written before the first century CE, say little about such spirits. As a monotheistic religion Judaism did not wish to establish a rival spiritual power to Yahweh. Most references in the Hebrew Bible are to the spirit of God, not to that of an evil rival. Evil spirits became more prominent in the post-exilic books of the Hebrew Bible, after Jews were exposed to the Persian dualistic religion of Zoroastrianism during the Babylonian captivity in the sixth century BCE But post-exilic Jewish evil spirits (which were identified by a variety of names in Hebrew) still lacked distinct personalities and had limited power.

Some scholars have identified a body of Hellenistic Jewish apocalyptic literature produced in the two centuries before Christ as the source of Jewish beliefs in evil spirits in first-century Palestine. These apocalyptical sources identified evil spirits with fallen angels and introduced the theme of a cosmic war between God and evil. The Book of Daniel, written in the second century BCE, identified the prophet's vision of four beasts as metaphors for four kingdoms and prophesied the destruction of the fourth, later identified in the early modern period as the Roman Catholic Church, and its replacement by a new kingdom of the 'saints of the most High'.[76] This Jewish apocalyptic literature had a direct influence on Revelation, the last book of the New Testament, which told the story of the war in Heaven and the transformation of fallen angels into demons. The only difficulty with regarding Jewish apocalyptic literature as a source for the Jewish belief in demons is that these works did not specifically identify the fallen angels with evil spirits, as the Christian tradition did.

The apocryphal books of the Hebrew Bible (i.e. those not included in the Jewish or Christian canons) make those connections explicit. The

Book of Enoch, written between the third and first centuries BCE, describes the origins of evil by telling the mythical tale of Semyaza, the leader of the fallen angels, who came to Earth, mated with women who gave birth to giants who caused widespread destruction on earth. Enoch calls these giants evil spirits.[77] The Book of Tobit, written in the second century BCE, not only makes the first reference in Jewish literature to the powerful demon Asmodeus, who resembled the Persian god of rage, but also suggests that this demon may have been exorcized. In a fit of jealousy Asmodeus, who was in love with a woman named Sarah, had killed her seven husbands. It is unclear whether the demon had actually possessed Sarah, but the book describes a ritual, directed by a healing angel called Raphael, that resulted in the subjugation of Asmodeus and forced him to flee. This account in Jewish literature may have prepared the ground for the prevalence of exorcism among Jews at the time of Christ and the success of Christ as an exorcist.

The third of the non-canonical books of the Hebrew Bible that contributed to the development of Jewish beliefs regarding demons was the Book of Jubilees, which was written in the second century BCE. This book describes how unclean spirits, under the command of a leader named Mastema, led astray the sons of Noah. The book includes Noah's prayer to God to restrain these 'malignant' spirits, who were 'created to destroy' and harm 'the sons of righteousness'. This text may have helped to prepare Christ's audiences for his exorcisms by showing that a holy man could control and direct the destiny of demons simply by praying to God, a theme that recurs in the story of the epileptic boy in the New Testament. The plea for God to prevent the return of evil spirits was echoed in the New Testament when Jesus commanded the mute and deaf spirit not only to come out of the epileptic boy but also 'never to enter him again'.[78]

The main Hellenistic contribution to the Jewish belief in demons came from the Jewish mystic, philosopher, and theologian Philo of Alexandria (20 BCE–40 CE). Philo, who was versed in the Scriptures as well as classical Greek philosophy and literature, achieved a synthesis of the two traditions. In his brief treatise, *On Giants*, Philo subscribed to the traditional Greek belief that demons could be good or evil, and in the tradition of Platonic philosophy he also identified these spirits with souls, which, being invisible, hovered in the air. Souls, demons, and angels were therefore entities that differed in name but were identical 'in reality'. They were part of the natural order, and some of these living, immortal creatures could descend into human bodies.[79] Philo then subscribed to the Jewish distinction between good and evil angels as well as good and evil souls, citing Psalm 78: 49, which reads that God in his wrath 'sent evil angels among them'.

In keeping with the Platonic tradition, the good angels entered philosophers and men committed to virtue, whereas the evil ones resided in
those committed to bodily pleasures. Philo was not describing demonic
possession as it was understood in the time of Christ, but *On Giants*
marked an important step towards the transformation of Greek *daimones*
into the Jewish demons or unclean spirits that Christ exorcized during the
public ministry.

The Jewish concept of demons in first-century Palestine, therefore, had
many different sources. References to fallen angels, unclean spirits, and
demons reflected the different literary traditions that influenced Jewish
writing at the time of Christ and in the first century of Christianity.[80] Only
some of these could be classified as Greek or even Hellenistic. Eighteenth-
century biblical scholars such as Sykes and Semler were correct in their
identification of a Greek contribution to Jewish thought regarding the
nature of demons at the time of Christ, but their equation of Jewish
demons with those of ancient Greece, or even those of the Hellenistic
culture of their day, neglected the various sources of Jewish ideas about
demons over the course of many centuries.

Satan and the Devil

Hellenistic culture played a limited role in the emergence of the belief
that the chief of demons in the New Testament was Satan, or, as he has
been known in Christianity, the Devil. Satan, a Hebrew word meaning
adversary, received first mention in the pre-exilic books of the Hebrew
Bible, where he appeared as an angelic spirit and messenger that was not
evil. At that time Satan was not a proper name. In the post-exilic books
of the Hebrew Bible, this angelic spirit became '*the* Satan', as in Job and
Zechariah, and in 1 Chronicles 21: 1 Satan became a proper name. But in
these books Satan had not yet become an evil creature. In Job he was a
member of God's council who accused human beings before God, and in
1 Chronicles, where he 'stood up against Israel', he still operated as the
instrument of an angry God. Satan was mentioned twenty-seven times in
the Hebrew Bible, but he could not be easily identified with the figure that
later became known as the Christian Devil.

In the New Testament, where Satan's proper name (which remained in
the original Hebrew) appears thirty-four times, he became the adversary
and tempter of Christ and the personification of evil. He also became the
Prince of Demons, and thus the equivalent of Beelzebul, whose name
refers to Baal, the chief rival cultic god to Yahweh in the Hebrew Bible.[81]
His later identification as 'the Devil' stemmed from the use of the word

diabolos, a Greek word meaning 'slanderer' or 'accuser', to refer to Satan in the New Testament.[82] *Diabolos* appears seventy-one times in the original Greek texts, and the word clearly referred to the 'adversary' Satan. The Greek word *diabolos* was Latinized in the fourth-century Vulgate as *diabolus*, which in turn was translated as *devil* in early English usage. In French *diabolus* became *diable*, in German *Teufel*, and in Dutch *duivel*. Bekker objected to the translation of *diabolos* as *duivel* rather than *demon* in the official Dutch translation of the Bible in 1637 on the grounds that it transformed the demon Satan into the singular Devil of medieval and early modern Christianity.[83] This translation led to the frequent Christian identification of all demons as devils, as in the King James Version of the Bible.[84] In 1737 the biblical scholar and natural philosopher William Whiston complained that 'the language of the moderns which speaks of devils in the plural number and supposes that the demoniacs were generally possessed by devils is wholly unsupported and unknown in the New Testament'.[85] Whiston was correct. The word Devil was meant to refer only to Satan and is therefore a proper name. Satan's subordinate spirits should have been referred to only as demons.[86]

Christian demons

Once Satan was established as the Devil, Christian writers devoted considerable thought to identifying his subordinates, a process that began in the early centuries of Christianity and continued through the Middle Ages and into the early modern period. The number of these demons grew rapidly as Christian writers demonized the pagan gods, whose worship they condemned.[87] Some of these demons were Greco-Roman gods such as Diana, whom Paul confronted at Ephesus. Others, including the powerful demons later called the princes of Hell, including Beelzebul, Asmodeus, Belial, and Belphegor, were the names of demons that appeared in the Hebrew Bible.[88] One of these princes, Leviathan, a sea monster which appeared six times in the Hebrew Bible, had been demonized by Jews in the first century CE. In Christian demonology Leviathan became the keeper of the gates of Hell and was represented in early modern art as the mouth of Hell. Lucifer, a Latin word meaning light-bearer, was constructed on the basis of a passage in Isaiah regarding a star that tried to be higher than others and fell to earth, thus becoming the name for Satan before the Fall. The princes of Hell were so powerful that Christian writers occasionally identified some of them as the equivalent of Satan.[89]

Exorcists in the early modern period acknowledged this demonological pluralism when they elicited the names of the spirits that invaded the bodies of demoniacs. While Protestants almost always referred to the spirit that possessed a person as Satan or the Devil,[90] Catholics, who were more likely than Protestants to believe in a graded hierarchy of demonic spirits, gave them a variety of names.[91] The most common name, besides Satan, was the demon Beelzebub, a prince of demons. In 1566 the French demoniac Nicole Obry claimed that her voice during her possession was really that of the demon Beelzebub,[92] who was also identified as the demon that possessed Marguerite Obry at Soissons in 1582, Marthe Brossier at Paris in 1598, and Jeanne des Anges at Loudun in 1632. Beelzebub had made his first appearance in the Hebrew Bible in 2 Kings 1: 3, which referred to him as the god of the city of Ekron. His name, which is translated into English as 'Lord of the Flies', was a play on the name of the Hebrew demon Beelzebul, which means 'the Lord is exalted'.[93] Beelzebub's status as a prince of demons derived entirely from his confusion with Beelzebul, by whose power Christ had been accused of driving out demons.

All seven of the demons that allegedly possessed Jeanne des Anges had biblical names, but many of the spirits that possessed the other nuns at Loudun had names such as Pollution, Elimy, Dansfin, Nephtaly, Agal, and Celse. The demons at Louviers in 1647 included not only Leviathan and Asmodeus but also Putiphar, Dagon, Ancitif, Arfaxat, Gonsang, Calconix, and Grongade.[94] One of the demons that vacated the body of the German demoniac Apolonia Geisslbrecht in 1582 gave his name as Schwamm, a German word meaning sponge or fungus.[95] When multiple demons were exorcized, the demoniacs sometimes made up names for them. Five of the English demoniacs whom the Jesuits exorcized in 1585 named their 'captain demons' Pippin, Maho, Philpot, Modu, and Soforce, while the names of others that ranked below the captains included Hillio, Hilco, Smolkin, and Hiaclito.[96] The demoniacs who accused witches of causing their possession at Berry in 1582/3 referred to more than eighty non-biblical possessing demons besides Satan.[97] In an exorcism of two English nuns in the Spanish Netherlands in 1651, the English priest Edmund Bedingfield identified by name three hundred demons, none of them having a biblical name.[98] Some demons had acquired their names in the late medieval period when ritual magicians had conjured them in the practice of their art.[99]

The assignment of names to the evil spirits that were believed to have invaded the bodies of Christians in the early modern period was just one indication of how Christian beliefs regarding the demonic realm had developed since the composition of the synoptic Gospels in the first century CE. The Bible had provided a limited amount of information about the identity, powers, and purposes of demons. It was left to Christian writers in the next fifteen hundred years to speculate on how the demonic world was organized, what functions these fallen angels performed, and why they possessed human beings. It was also left to theologians in the Middle Ages to develop a systematic body of knowledge regarding the metaphysical nature of these creatures and the powers they exercised in the natural world.

CHAPTER 3

Possession in Christian Demonology

THE WIDESPREAD BELIEF THAT demons could invade human bodies and seize control of their physical and mental faculties was an essential precondition of the surge in the number of possessions in early modern Europe. If theologians had not subscribed to this belief, ecclesiastical authorities would not have devoted as much attention as they did to demoniacs; preachers would not have given sermons on the subject; and large public exorcisms would not have taken place. Possessions would still have occurred in local communities, as they had throughout the history of Christianity, but a large wave of possessions, often described as an epidemic, would not have taken place.

These beliefs regarding demonic possession were never accepted blindly. Like many religious beliefs, they were often contested, and even those who proclaimed them most loudly often did so in response to those who doubted or denied them. The possibility of the Devil's invading and occupying a human body never became an article of Christian faith. It was not included in the Nicene Creed or even in the catechisms that proliferated in the age of print. Those who denied or even qualified the belief were occasionally accused of blasphemy or atheism, but no one was ever prosecuted for heresy on such grounds. In this respect the belief in possession was similar to the belief in witchcraft, which was also contested throughout the early modern period. Nevertheless, the belief in possession, which could invoke much clearer scriptural authority than witchcraft, became an important weapon in a major theological effort to prove the existence of spirits, a belief that had always been central to Christianity.

This chapter will address the question: on what grounds did demonological writers, clergymen, and educated laymen in the early modern period come to the conclusion that persons who displayed the various symptoms described in Chapter 1 were possessed by demons? On what grounds, moreover, did these believers in the reality of possession take issue with the growing number of sceptics who questioned or denied that belief? They could of course appeal to the authority of Scripture, which provided a basis for the belief in the possibility of possession, as it still does in some confessions today. Scripture, however, offered little guidance in determining why demoniacs behaved the way they did. As discussed in Chapter 2, the behaviour of demoniacs in the New Testament usually differed from that of their counterparts in the early modern period. Some Protestant writers, moreover, claimed that the scriptural accounts of possession should be interpreted metaphorically. Thus, when demonological writers in seventeenth-century Europe witnessed a young woman experiencing terrible bodily contortions, vomiting pins, and uttering blasphemies, they needed more than the scriptural examples of the demoniacs exorcized by Christ (none of whom displayed such symptoms) to determine that demons were responsible for her behaviour. They needed to find non-scriptural grounds to persuade both themselves and any potential sceptics that this young woman was in fact possessed by demons.

One possible tactic was to use theological arguments developed by scholastic theologians in the thirteenth century to show how demonic possession was metaphysically possible. Another approach was to relate possession to the widespread apocalyptic belief among Catholics as well as Protestants that the Antichrist had appeared and that the Devil, as prophesied in the Bible, was exceptionally active in the final days of human history. Yet another approach was to argue that the physiological symptoms displayed by demoniacs were so extreme that they could only have had a supernatural cause. This last approach not only supported a demonological diagnosis of a particular case of possession but also provided 'empirical' evidence to refute the claims of radical sceptics that evil spirits did not exist.

These arguments held sway in communities, especially those that were Catholic, through the eighteenth and into the early nineteenth century. Even though scepticism gained considerable strength in these years, it never completely dislodged the belief that demonic possession was possible. Consequently cases of possession continued to crop up throughout Europe during the age of the Enlightenment and in more recent times. As long as ecclesiastical authorities and writers were unwilling to follow Balthasar Bekker's lead and deny the Devil's ability to interact with human beings, cases of possession would arise and some clerics would insist that the Devil was their cause.

The nature of demonic power

Belief in the Devil never waned between the end of Christian antiquity and the thirteenth century. Satan was such an important figure in the New Testament, and his struggle with Christ was so titanic, that he could scarcely have been ignored. Satan had a prominent place in sermons and in the stories that monks circulated to inspire adherence to Christian morality. He was also a significant presence in art, literature, and folklore. But until the thirteenth century theologians generally did not make the Devil a subject of rational inquiry. This dearth of learned commentary, however, ended with the development of scholasticism, the dialectical method of inquiry taught in the cathedral schools and universities that transformed the study of theology, philosophy, and law. Inspired by the rediscovery of many texts of Aristotle and his Islamic commentators in the twelfth-century Renaissance, scholastics supplemented the two main sources of Christian doctrine, Scripture and Tradition (the latter being the teaching of the Church Fathers and Church councils), with a third source: reason. Scholasticism therefore represented an effort to reconcile faith and reason as far as possible, recognizing that certain doctrines were incapable of rational analysis. The most prominent of the scholastics, who synthesized the thought of his predecessors and placed theological concepts in a Aristotelian framework, was St Thomas Aquinas (1225–74), a Sicilian who lectured at the University of Paris. Demons and angels were not central concerns for Thomas, but in his massive *Summa theologica* he conducted a systematic investigation of the nature of spirits and of demonic power.

Aquinas claimed that angels, being purely intellectual creatures, were not in any way corporeal. Their immaterial constitution explains how they could exist in great numbers.[1] Since demons were believed to be fallen angels, they too were spiritual beings. Unless angels and demons were pure spirit, it would have been hard to imagine how hundreds or even thousands of demons could have occupied the body of a demoniac at the same time. Designating demons as immaterial spirits obviated the problem of explaining how even one of them could penetrate a human body, a feat that would be difficult if they were in any sense corporeal. Nevertheless, an alternative tradition in Christianity, rooted in Greco-Roman thought, held that demons, while immortal, were at least in some sense material. A number of early Christian writers, including Tertullian, Origen, and Lactantius, believed that the Devil was in fact corporeal, and the alternative, corporeal tradition acquired a place in Byzantine demonology.[2] Robert Burton referred to this body of demonological thought in *Anatomy of Melancholy*

(1621), and, as discussed in Chapter 2, Thomas Hobbes provided a philosophical foundation for it in 1651.[3] The dominant tradition in both
Catholic and Protestant thought, however, denied demonic materiality.
John Deacon and John Walker took pains to defend the spiritual nature of
demons in their *Dialogicall Discourses* (1603), and in 1615 the Puritan writer
Edward Nyndge attributed the Devil's 'nimbleness' in possessing human
beings to their spiritual nature, as they were not 'laden with any heavenly
matter as our bodies are'.[4] Renaissance demonologists, who emphasized the
ongoing interactions between spirits and the natural world, viewed demons
as spiritual beings that looked like bodies but were not.[5]

In addition to being able to invade a human body, Aquinas believed that
a demon had the power to control the movement of bodies from one place
to another. In this way a demon could, for example, cause the regurgitation
of alien substances in the human body and also assault the demoniac from
without. A demon also had the ability to create illusions and delude either
by confusing a person's vision or by taking images out of the memory and
impressing them on a person's imagination. This power greatly facilitated
a demon's ability to tempt human beings. Finally, this incorporeal demon
could take air and compress it into the shape of a corporeal creature. The
aerial body thus constructed was substantial, but the demon did not create
it from nothing (a power reserved to God alone); rather the demon
reshaped the air that God had already created. Whenever the Devil
appeared as a human being or an animal, as when he appeared as a man to
tempt a person, or as a beast at the witches' assemblies, it was by virtue of
his power either to create illusions or to form an aerial body.[6] The aerial
body, while substantial in itself, was not the Devil himself but the product
of the Devil's power over local motion. Such an aerial body could not,
therefore, invade a human body.[7]

By enumerating these powers of the Devil, Aquinas provided a theological foundation for the Christian belief in demonic possession. At the
same time he identified two limitations of the Devil's power that also
influenced the discourse on possession. The first was that everything the
Devil did must have the permission of God. Aquinas could claim no
originality in establishing this point; a long succession of Church Fathers
and theologians had insisted upon the same limitation. To claim otherwise
would have challenged the sovereignty of God and thus endorse, or at least
flirt with, the doctrine of dualist heretics such as Cathars, who conceived
of God and the Devil as rival and to some extent coequal powers. In mainstream Christianity the Devil has always been the creature of God. In the
sixteenth and seventeenth centuries Protestant theologians emphasized
this limitation of demonic power as much as, if not more than, Catholics.[8]

A problem lurked, however, in the claim that the Devil required the permission of God to exercise any of his powers. If God allowed the Devil to subject a person to demonic assault, the question could (and did) arise: why should God ever allow the Devil to inflict such excessive physical abuse, especially on a person of high moral calibre? For God to have permitted a possession that involved severe bodily harm (such as tearing flesh from the demoniac's body) could not reasonably be interpreted as punishment for sin if the demoniac was innocent, and it was also unreasonable to think that God would allow such Draconian means of temptation. According to medieval belief, God might work in mysterious ways, but allowing the Devil to subject a pious person to such physical abuse made the deity appear to be capricious if not tyrannical.

The second scholastic limitation on demonic power that influenced the discourse on possession was that the Devil could not force a person to sin. This was the way that Aquinas and others reaffirmed a central doctrine of medieval Christianity and early modern Catholicism—the freedom of the will. The Devil might tempt, which was one of his most important functions, but he could not deprive people of the responsibility to make moral choices and thus either gain salvation or suffer damnation. If the will was free, the question arose of what happened when the Devil possessed a human body, travelled through the body to the brain, and took possession of one's mental faculties. The way that most theologians in the scholastic tradition solved this problem was to argue that because the Devil seized control of the demoniac's mental faculties, he could thereby gain control of the will. The demoniac was freed from moral responsibility for his or her actions while under the Devil's influence in the same way that a child or a mentally ill person was not held morally responsible for his or her actions. The analogy with mental illness was particularly appropriate in cases of possession because many demoniacs were considered to be lunatics. The theory that demoniacs were not responsible for their behaviour, however, did not go unchallenged during the age of the Reformation, since Protestants claimed that the sinfulness of demoniacs was the proximate cause of their possession.[9]

Closely related to the question of free will was the issue of whether the Devil could possess, that is, inhabit and control, the soul during one's life. Most twelfth- and thirteenth-century theologians agreed that although demons might invade the body and cause physical or mental illness, only the Holy Spirit could possess the soul.[10] Demons could 'imprison' the soul and deny it access to the body, but they could not control it in the way that they could dictate the movements of the body. The most emphatic statement of this position came from the Franciscan friar St Bonaventure

(1215–74) in his commentary on *Four Books of Sentences*, Peter Lombard's foundational textbook of scholastic theology written in about 1150. Bonaventure explained that demonic possession was a mechanical operation that had little impact on the soul. In this theologian's view, God refused to give the Devil direct access to the person's soul.[11] The Devil could tempt the person to sin, which might lead him to lose his soul after death, but in this life he could only possess the body. Thomas endorsed Bonaventure's position on this question.[12]

The influence of Aquinas waned in the fifteenth century, as the nominalist philosophy originally promoted by the Franciscan friar William of Ockham (1288–1348) de-emphasized the role of reason in theology, claiming that only faith could give humans access to theological truths. But the theology of Aquinas continued to provide the most plausible, theologically grounded explanation of how the Devil could in fact possess a human being. Aquinas's demonology did not lead to an increase in possessions; nominalism actually played a greater role in that regard by positing an arbitrary God who by the dictates of his inscrutable will gave the Devil greater permission to wreak havoc in human society than Aquinas would admit. But Thomistic demonology helped exorcists and clerical authorities make sense of the new upsurge in possessions, and it served to counter any scepticism that either they or others might have entertained.

One illustration of how Thomistic philosophy served this theological purpose was the discussion of demonic possession in the notorious witchcraft manual, the *Malleus maleficarum*, written by the Dominican theologian and inquisitor Heinrich Kramer and first published in 1486. This widely circulated treatise set out to prove that witches existed, demonstrate the threat they represented to Christianity, and provide instructions to inquisitors and secular authorities on how they might successfully prosecute them. Much of the book consists of anecdotal accounts of witchcraft trials that Kramer himself had adjudicated, but its theological framework comes mainly from Aquinas, whom Kramer cited frequently.

Kramer dealt with the subject of demonic possession because witches were widely believed to have caused possessions by commanding the Devil to enter the bodies of their victims. This belief had encountered scepticism in the southern areas of Germany where Kramer had served as an inquisitor, and his express purpose was to clear up doubt that demons could, at the insistence of witches, 'take control of humans entirely'. He also used this publication to resolve doubt that such possessions could take place without the instrumentality of witches, even though this method of possession was not pertinent to his inquiry.[13]

To answer these questions Kramer relied on the theology of Aquinas, accounts of demonic possessions in church histories, and more recent witchcraft cases. Some of the possessions reported by clerical authorities harmed only the body, while others injured both body and mind. Some possessions involved internal and external temptation, while still others deprived the demoniac of the use of reason. The most relevant part of Kramer's answer, however, consisted of his reliance on the demonology of Aquinas to prove that the Devil could not possess the soul, 'because God alone glides into the mind, and also because the Devil is not the cause of guilt in the same way that the Holy Spirit is the cause of the grace that the Holy Spirit produces in the soul by His own working'.[14] The conclusion to be drawn from this was that the Devil could not be the cause of sin, 'which the Holy Spirit permits the soul itself to commit'.[15] In this way Kramer used scholastic demonology to show that possessions were not only possible but that they were to be interpreted in accordance with fundamental Roman Catholic doctrine.

The scholastic discourse on demonic power had a profound impact on other early modern writings about witchcraft and possession. In 1593 the Italian physician Andrea Cesalpino (1524–1603), who participated in an investigation by theologians, philosophers, and men of his own profession to decide whether the possession of a group of nuns was authentic, wrote an entire treatise on possession that included both the views of the scholastics and those of medical authorities. The section on the peripatetic philosophers was taken straight from Thomas Aquinas. The demonological views of the Dutch physician Jason Pratensis (1486–1558), who wrote the first textbook on neurology in 1549, derived ultimately from the same source.[16]

The scholastic view of demons as incorporeal beings that could penetrate a human body and also take on the appearance of physical bodies (by working on the imaginative faculty or by compressing air to form aerial bodies) served to confirm belief in possession among both the learned and the illiterate. It solved the philosophical problem of how one or more demons could gain access to a human body while confirming the belief that the Devil could appear to people in the shape of a human being and could be present at witches' assemblies in the form of a goat or a bull. Artistic representations of demons were not simply devices to make abstract theological ideas regarding immaterial spirits comprehensible. They were also representations of the aerial bodies or phantasms that scholastic theologians claimed the Devil was perfectly capable of forming.

In contrast to Catholics trained in the scholastic tradition, Calvinist clergy discouraged the popular belief that the Devil assumed aerial bodies and interacted with humans in that capacity. Calvinists thought much more of a Devil that threatened them spiritually and internally, tempting them to sin, rather than physically meeting with them and offering them power, sex, or money in exchange for their souls.[17] For this reason Calvinist sources only occasionally described the physical appearance of demons when they tempted a human being or when they presided at witch assemblies, which in any event were not referred to very often in Calvinist witchcraft trials. In similar fashion, Calvinist sources only occasionally describe the physical departure of a demon during an exorcism. The desired end of a Calvinist possession was the conquest of temptation, not the physical banishment of the demon. The demons that vacated the bodies of Calvinist demoniacs were usually not described as black birds or the grotesque creatures depicted in woodcuts and engravings of Catholic exorcisms. The possession narrative of the English Puritan Andrew Nyndge, for example, simply reported that the spirit disappeared out a window.[18] In a religious culture that emphasized the spiritual rather than the physical threat represented by the Devil, there was no need to describe him in physical terms. One consequence of this identification of the Devil as a spiritual tempter was that Protestants in the Reformed tradition had difficulty developing images of the supernatural entity that threatened them. The Bible provided little help in this regard, and the hostility of Reformed Protestantism to images gave Calvinists few visual images of the Devil to work with. Other Protestants, especially Lutherans, encountered no such difficulty in developing a concept of who the Devil was and what he looked like. Luther reported struggling with the Devil physically as well as spiritually.[19]

The increasing power of the Devil

Aquinas and those who appealed to his authority explained how it was possible for demons to possess a person, but their demonologies did not contribute to the growing sense in the fifteenth century that the Devil's power was increasing. Aquinas gave no indication that he was concerned with such a development. Indeed, until the fourteenth century scholastic theology kept the Devil under wraps. Satan was thought to be most powerful in the monasteries, where struggles of monks against the Devil sometimes achieved epic proportions, but even in those locations there was little fear that God would allow Satan to prevail. In lay culture the Devil was even less threatening, in many cases being depicted as a weak, if not comic figure.

The demonological enhancement of demonic power began in the fourteenth century, and was directly attributable to the work of theologians writing in the nominalist tradition, which replaced Thomism as the dominant theological tradition in the late Middle Ages. Nominalism challenged the rationalism of Aquinas by emphasizing the role of God's will in the governance of the world, placing limitations on human free will, and restoring the element of mystery in Christian doctrine. The nominalist view of divine power and will eroded or weakened the confidence of the older Thomistic tradition that the Devil's power in the world could be contained; an inscrutable, arbitrary God might give the Devil great latitude in the world for reasons unknown to humankind. This view of demonic power found powerful expression in the work of Jean Gerson (1363–1429), the brilliant theologian who became the chancellor of the University of Paris in 1395. Gerson took issue with many aspects of the scholasticism of Aquinas, including its confidence that God would always keep the Devil on a short leash.

The nominalist enhancement of demonic power and the erosion of confidence in the ability to resist him successfully coincided with the origin of witch-hunting in the early fifteenth century. It also coincided with a striking increase in the number of reported cases of possession. Not surprisingly, Gerson and the Dominican reformer Johannes Nider, who also wrote in the nominalist tradition, made major contributions to the demonological literature on both witchcraft and possession. Gerson was the central figure in the condemnation of all forms of magic, especially ritual magic, by the theology faculty of the University of Paris in 1398, and he was also a major contributor to the art of discerning spirits.[20] Nider was the first demonologist to develop the fantasy of the witches' sabbath in his treatise, *Formicarius* (The Ant Heap), written around 1437, and he argued that witches and demoniacs were involved in related activities.[21] Like Gerson, Nider helped to establish procedures to distinguish between genuine and false possession.[22]

As fear of the Devil's power increased, the threat that he represented began to change. He continued to be the cause of illness, physical harm, destruction and chaos, as he had been during the Middle Ages. But in the fifteenth and sixteenth centuries, as more of the laity became committed to a programme of cultivating personal piety, his role shifted more to that of tempter. Of course the Devil had always served that function; he had, after all, tempted Christ in the desert, and his temptations of early Christian saints, especially St Anthony, had become legendary during the Middle Ages. Religious writers in the sixteenth and seventeenth centuries such as Teresa of Avila warned that the Devil's temptations were especially powerful and persistent when a person was aspiring to sanctity.[23] In sixteenth-century Protestantism, which was preoccupied with sin and the difficulty of escaping its effects, temptation became the main function of the Devil.[24]

Possession and the Apocalypse

If medieval scholastic theologians provided an intellectual foundation for the belief in the reality and increasing frequency of demonic possession, later demonological writers gave greater plausibility to the recent increase in their number by claiming that they had eschatological significance. These early modern demonologists, many of whom were involved in exorcisms, often interpreted demonic possessions as signs that the world was about to end and that Judgement Day was at hand. By taking this approach, they could relate the experiences of demoniacs to a set of religious beliefs that commanded widespread support among Catholics as well as Protestants and among educated as well as illiterate members of society.

The belief that humanity was preparing for a titanic battle between good and evil, between Christ and the Devil, which would precede the Second Coming of Christ and the Last Judgement, was a major article of Christian faith. It was based primarily on the Book of Revelation, the final prophetic book of the New Testament, written by John of Patmos in the late first century CE.[25] Apocalyptic thought (the word *apocalypse* connotes the revelation of hidden knowledge) also drew on prophecies in the Hebrew Bible, which in turn had been influenced by Zoroastrianism, the dualistic religion of Persia with which Jews had come into contact during the Babylonian captivity. Apocalyptic thought was therefore a prominent feature of Judaism as well as Christianity. Jewish apocalyptic thought, which flourished in the two centuries before Christ, focused on the expectation that a Messiah would soon appear, a prophecy that Christians claimed Jesus had fulfilled.

The belief that the final battle between the forces of good and evil was about to occur gained credibility from other biblical references to the Last Days, the period preceding the end of the world.[26] During this brief period, so it was prophesied, the Antichrist would appear, sin would be prevalent, and the Devil's rage against God's creation would increase. In describing the war in Heaven and the expulsion of Lucifer and the other fallen angels Revelation 12: 12 warned: 'But woe to you O earth and sea, for the Devil has come down to you in great wrath, because he knows that his time is short.' Eschatology, the study of the Last Days, was concerned with what could be expected and what was actually transpiring in this final period of human history, when the Devil would unleash his full fury.

Apocalyptic and eschatological beliefs had been present throughout the history of Christianity, but they acquired urgency in the Reformation era, when confessional conflicts and social and economic turmoil portended the end of the world and when evangelistic preachers and parsons familiarized a broad segment of the population with the prophecies of Scripture. The Antichrist became a central motif in art and literature as well as the topic of countless sermons. The association of apocalyptic thought with *millenarianism*—the belief that Christ will come again and rule for one thousand years—has led to the assumption that eschatology was an eccentric body of thought, out of the mainstream of early modern Christianity—a belief that is still widespread today. But the belief in the Apocalypse, considered by itself without its millenarian variations, was a central element of Christian thought.[27]

Apocalyptic thought did not cause demonic possessions; rather it set them within a scriptural and historical framework that assigned the demoniacs and the exorcists a role in human history. It is not surprising that when demonologists observed the afflictions of demoniacs and the efforts to exorcize them, they gave them eschatological significance. Believing that humanity had entered the Last Days, in which the Devil was predicted to demonstrate unprecedented power, they readily interpreted the afflictions of demoniacs as evidence that the world would soon end. The pathological symptoms of demoniacs provided evidence of the Devil's raging fury, which Revelation predicted would be far more harmful and threatening than at any previous time.[28] The frenzies of the demoniacs actually mimicked the fury of the Devil in the Last Days. Thus exorcisms became battlegrounds for good and evil to re-enact the conflict that had taken place in biblical times and would be rehearsed once again at Armageddon. In the context of apocalyptic thought, possessions therefore made perfect sense to those who observed and wrote about them. If demonological writers entertained any doubts about the authenticity of possessions, the knowledge that this pattern of activity was part of a cosmic drama that would lead to the Second Coming of Christ could readily reassure them and provide a religious explanation for the greater frequency of possessions. Apocalyptic and eschatological beliefs helped many early modern Europeans make sense of the strange and inscrutable behaviour of demoniacs in their communities.

The Roman Catholic demonological writers most responsible for describing possessions in apocalyptic terms were the exorcists whose mission was to cast out demons. Their apocalyptic beliefs are apparent in the exorcist manuals of the late sixteenth and early seventeenth centuries. The most widely circulated was *Compendio dell'arte essorcistica*

(Compendium of the Exorcist's Art), compiled by the Franciscan friar from Bologna, Girolamo Menghi. First published in the vernacular in 1572, it went into seventeen editions, two of them in Latin, by 1609.[29] Although the *Compendium* contained seven exorcist rites, it was much more than a manual. It was essentially a demonological treatise, a theoretical and polemical work by a trained theologian. Its main purpose was to explain why it was so important to counter demonic power in the Last Days. Menghi explained that the frequency of possessions in his day fulfilled the prophecy in Revelation that the Devil had been allowed to ravage God's creation and torment human beings in the days immediately preceding the Second Coming. The exorcisms that he promoted were designed to assist in this final struggle against the forces of darkness before God's inevitable victory.[30]

Catholic apocalyptic interpretations of possession appeared in accounts of the spectacular exorcisms that took place in France during the wars of religion. The earliest was the exorcism of the demoniac Nicole Obry in the Cathedral of Notre Dame at Laon in 1566. Guillaume Postel's interpretation of her exorcism as an event in the history of the world and the account of her possession and exorcism by one of her exorcists, Jean Boulaese, were full of apocalyptic and millenarian references.[31] Boulaese considered this miraculous exorcism evidence of God's plan to convert the Jews (an important element of apocalyptic thought) and unite all men in the Last Age.[32] The exorcisms of the nuns that took place at Aix-en-Provence in 1611, when Father Louis Gaufridy was convicted and executed as a witch for causing their possession, and the exorcisms of three Brigidine nuns at Lille in 1613 were placed within the same apocalyptic interpretative framework.[33] In his narrative of the possessions at Louviers in 1643, the Capuchin monk Esprit de Bosroger opened his account by situating the nuns' exorcism in the struggle between good and evil that had begun in Lucifer's revolt.[34]

The Spanish cases of possession that were assigned apocalyptic and eschatological significance were less spectacular than those in France, but they were no less illustrative of efforts to interpret exorcisms in this way. In 1607 a demon occupying the body of Marcia Garcia, a middle-aged woman from Madrid, reportedly told the exorcists that Lucifer was expecting victory over the archangel Michael once the Antichrist appeared, a statement of demonic confidence that was unusual in possession narratives. It is worth noting that the identification of the Devil as Lucifer rather than Satan in this possession as well as in that of the nuns at Louviers is consistent with the apocalyptic interpretation of these possessions. The name of Lucifer, which means 'light bearer' in Latin, was derived from the reference in Isaiah to a star brighter than all the others that was cast down from Heaven to Earth because of its pride. Lucifer thus became the name of the Devil in much apocalyptic literature.

Catholic demonologists placed only a handful of demonic possessions within an apocalyptic framework. The cases they chose to interpret in this way, however, provided some of the clearest illustrations of the association between possession and the Last Days, since all involved exorcisms. For it was exorcisms, rather than the initial symptoms of possession, that revealed the most dramatic conflicts between good and evil, between Christ and the Devil. The symptoms of possession, moreover, usually became most severe during exorcism, often just before the demon left the afflicted person's body.

In German lands, where apocalyptic thought was more pervasive than in any other part of Europe, Lutheran ministers took the lead in describing possessions in an eschatological context.[35] Because Lutherans did not use the Roman Catholic rite of exorcism, they made these associations in sermons, letters, academic treatises, and possession narratives. The German reformer Philip Melanchthon (1497–1560) urged those who used proper Protestant methods to expel demons to 'speak openly to the whole church about the coming judgment by the Son of God.'[36] In a possession narrative written in 1605 Tobias Seiler, pastor and school superintendent at Löwenberg in Silesia, described the possession of the twelve-year-old daughter of Georg Lieder in apocalyptic terms. The opening page of this possession tract included a quotation from Revelation 8: 13 predicting 'Woe, woe, woe to those who dwell on the earth' and a second one from John 12: 31, announcing that 'Now is the judgment of this world; now shall the ruler of this world be cast out.'[37] In 1594 a panel of Lutheran theologians and pastors charged with explaining mass possessions at Friedeberg and Spandau concluded that the only reason the possessions took place at this time was that the Second Coming of Christ was imminent.[38] In the same year Andreas Celichius, the Lutheran superintendent in Mecklenburg, having observed some thirty possessions, claimed that the only way to understand the horrible spectacles he observed was to recognize that the world was in the Last Days.[39]

Like many other apocalyptic writers, Seiler claimed that possession was only one sign of the Last Days: social disorder, prodigies in nature, unprecedented immorality, and the prevalence of sin all pointed in the same direction. But as Stuart Clark has argued, possession and its treatment provided the most vivid illustration of the end of the world, since it presented in stark terms the contrast between good and evil. This probably explains why Daniel Schaller, the Lutheran pastor of Stendal in

Brandenburg, in providing a series of proofs that the world was coming to an end, focused on demonic possession as the best current example of what the Bible prophesied. Schaller argued that 'the great swarm and number of demoniacs' in his time (the late sixteenth century) was so great that it heralded the Second Coming of Christ 'to break the hold of that hellish monster who has made his place in men's bodies and destroy entirely the work of devils with the Last Judgement.'[40] In 1605 the Protestant preacher Heinrich Riess claimed that the increasingly large number of exorcisms was a sign of the Last Days.[41]

The unrivalled Lutheran penchant for presenting possession in apocalyptic and eschatological terms stemmed from the biblicism that characterized Lutheranism from its inception. The Lutheran doctrine of *sola scriptura* and the Lutheran devaluation of Tradition and scholastic reasoning as sources of religious truth led to a reliance on Scripture that was unmatched in Roman Catholicism. This Lutheran focus on Scripture, coupled with use of the Bible as a guide to contemporary action, led Lutheran ministers and writers to see connections between the possessions described in the New Testament and those in their own day. Schaller, for example, claimed that just as the existence of a great number of demoniacs at the time of Christ portended his 'first bodily coming', a similar surge in possession in the late sixteenth century portended his return, as Revelation prophesied. Of course Schaller had no idea how many demoniacs there were at the time of Christ. Nor have we. Schaller assumed the number was high simply because of the attention the evangelists gave to exorcisms performed by Christ and the Apostles. Schaller had a much better sense of 'the swarm' of demoniacs in his own day, but even in that context the evidence remained anecdotal. The important consideration, however, is not the number of demoniacs in either period but the fact that Lutherans linked apocalyptic expectations, which flourished in both periods, with the Christian war against Satan and the promise of Christ to establish a new kingdom.[42]

Evidence of the connection between the increase in the number of possessions and apocalyptic thought was far less evident in Calvinism, not because biblicism was weaker in Calvinism, which it was not, but because the number of Calvinist possessions was so small. We have evidence of no more than one hundred possessions in Calvinist communities—a stark contrast to the thousands in Catholic areas and the hundreds in Lutheran and Anglican communities. Most Calvinist possessions, moreover, took place in the late seventeenth century, when possession was becoming less common throughout Europe.[43] The authors of possession narratives, preachers, and demonologists, however, made full use of these relatively infrequent cases by attributing their occurrence to the belief that the world was in its Last Days. One of the earliest Calvinist possessions that was interpreted in apocalyptic terms was that of the thirteen-year-old Puritan boy Thomas Darling in 1596. The editor of the account of Darling's possession, John Denison, used the bewitchment of Darling as proof that the prophecy in Revelation, 'The Devil, says he, has great wrath, knowing that he has but a short time', was coming to pass.[44] The group possession of children under twelve years old in an orphanage at Hoorn in Holland in 1674, an event reminiscent of the famous group possession at Amsterdam in 1566, took place in an atmosphere of revived apocalyptic expectations which pervaded the Calvinist world at the time.[45] Cotton Mather placed the Salem witch-hunt of 1692, which the Boston clergy believed involved both witchcraft and possession, in an apocalyptic framework when he used Revelation 12: 12 as the text of his sermon, 'Wonders of the Invisible World', which he delivered in August of that year. The sermon documented the heightened activity of the Devil during the Last Days.[46]

Eschatology cannot explain the entire phenomenon of demonic possession in early modern Europe. There is no evidence, for example, of apocalyptic or millenarian preaching or narratives with apocalyptic themes in the majority of possessions for which we have at least a literary record. Although apocalyptic and eschatological consciousness was a major feature of early modern Catholic as well as Protestant thought, it was more pervasive in Protestantism, whereas most possessions occurred in Catholic lands.[47] Nevertheless eschatology, when it was invoked in cases of possession, helped contemporaries make sense of an otherwise bewildering phenomenon.

Possession and the sceptical challenge

The belief in possession, however plausible, frequently encountered sceptical challenges. The most uncompromising of these came from a group of early modern philosophers and writers who denied the very existence of spirits, a position that threatened to undermine the belief in an array of demonic activities in the world, including witchcraft and possession. The most forceful statement of this position found expression in the late seventeenth century, and to refute it defenders of traditional Christian doctrine needed to do more than cite Scripture or appeal to scholastic theology. To meet the demands of the new science, especially the deductive, experimental approach of natural philosophers in the Royal Society in England, they needed to supply empirical evidence to supplement the proofs offered by Scripture and scholastic demonology.

Appealing to instances of demonic possession to prove the existence of demons was hardly new in the seventeenth century. In the thirteenth century Aquinas had dismissed the claims of some Aristotelian philosophers that demons did not exist by claiming that demoniacs performed deeds that could not be explained by natural causes. In particular, he argued that anyone who spoke a language that he himself could not understand was obviously possessed by a demon. In the fifteenth century the scholastic philosopher Jean Vineti developed a more systematic and sustained argument for the existence of demons. In a treatise condemning necromancers who summoned up demons, Vineti argued that the activities of exorcists and necromancers, both of whom had direct contact with demons, proved their existence. Possession provided the crucial proof because it had the unimpeachable authority of Scripture.[48]

Reliance on possession and exorcism as the main proof of demonic reality persisted through the sixteenth and seventeenth centuries. Demonologists like Heinrich Kramer echoed the traditional arguments of Aquinas, while German preachers used specific cases of possession to resolve the doubts of sceptics. Scholastic and scriptural arguments, however, were less persuasive in the seventeenth century, when many physicians argued that possession could have natural causes and Protestant biblical scholars contended that Scripture was not to be interpreted literally. The defenders of orthodoxy needed to provide more compelling empirical proof than had Aquinas, Vineti or Kramer to support their belief in the reality of possession and therefore the existence of spirits.

The most sustained contributions to this debate came from England, Scotland, and New England. The English discourse on the existence of spirits can be traced back to the late sixteenth century, when the radical Protestant layman Reginald Scot published a sceptical work on witchcraft that called into question the very existence of demons. Whether he declared that they did not exist, as at least one scholar has argued, or whether he simply denied that they had no role in the natural world, cannot be ascertained.[49] But that uncertainty does not obscure the radicalism of Scot's position or the claim of orthodox Christians that Scot had denied the existence not only of witches and demons but of God himself.

In 1597 King James VI of Scotland, one of the few demonologists to respond to Scot's scepticism regarding witchcraft, labelled him and those who agreed with him as Sadducees because of their apparent intellectual kinship with the members of a Jewish sect active in Judaea from about 200 BCE until 70 CE which denied the existence of spirits and the immortality of the soul.[50] In the 1650s and 1660s Meric Casaubon, the son of the famous humanist scholar Isaac Casaubon, attacked the new breed of

Sadducees in a treatise confuting the claims of an apparently growing group of thinkers who denied the existence of 'spirits, witches and the supernatural operations'.[51] The controversy over the claims of this so-called neo-Sadducism intensified in the 1680s with the publication of *Saducismus triumphatus* (Sadducism Triumphant) by the English cleric Joseph Glanvill, who was a member of the Royal Society, and *Satan's Invisible World Discovered* by George Sinclair, a Scottish natural philosopher from the University of Glasgow.[52] Both works, in an effort to provide empirical evidence for the existence of spirits, related stories about witchcraft, apparitions, poltergeists, and other preternatural phenomena to counter the claims of the seventeenth-century Sadducees. These stories were designed to prove the existence of God, for if one did not believe in spirits, the belief in God would likewise vanish. As Henry More, one of Glanvill's allies, put it: 'No spirit, no God.'[53] In this way the debate over the existence of spirits became part of the heated controversy over atheism in the late seventeenth and early eighteenth centuries.

The battle between the Sadducees and their opponents entered a new phase in 1691 when the English Presbyterian minister Richard Baxter published *The Certainty of the Worlds of Spirits* Baxter's entrance into the debate was significant for the purposes of this discussion because he used many more instances of demonic possession than either Glanvill or Sinclair to prove the existence of spirits. Glanvill and Sinclair had emphasized poltergeists, ghost stories, and especially reports of witchcraft. Baxter, however, turned the reader's attention to possession, including the account given by the earl of Lauderdale in 1659 of the possession of Margaret Lumsden in the town of Duns in Berwickshire in the late 1620s. He also mentioned the example of Mary Hill, an eighteen-year-old girl from Beckington who reputedly vomited up no fewer than two hundred pins and whose tongue swelled out of her mouth; a woman believed to be hysterical until she vomited long crooked nails, brass needles, and lumps of hair and meat; a girl from Louvain who vomited twenty-four pounds of liquid a day, followed by the dung of geese and doves, hair, coal and stones; and the demoniac who in one year reportedly vomited enough blood to fill four hundred chamber pots. Baxter also referred to Cotton Mather's recently published apocalyptic book, *Memorable Providences Relating to Witchcrafts and Possessions* (1689), which presented an account of the possession of the Goodwin children in Boston. One of the children, Baxter reported, had been 'visited with strange fits'. Their tongues were reported to have 'drawn down their throats' or 'pulled out upon their chins to a prodigious length'. 'Sometimes they would be deaf, sometimes dumb, and sometimes blind, and often all this at once.'[54] Mather interpreted these and other possessions as signs that the rule of Satan was in its final days and the Second Coming was imminent, a theme that, as we have seen, was an important intellectual prop to the belief in demonic possession. Like Baxter, Mather intended the publication of his account of the possession of the Goodwin children to refute the claims of atheists and 'the old heresy of the Sadducees, denying the being of angels either good or evil'.[55]

From a polemical point of view the attention given by Baxter to possession was a deft move. Just like Vineti in the fifteenth century, Baxter understood that demonic possession provided much more certain proof of the existence of spirits than witchcraft, because in observing possessions one could presumably hear the Devil speak and witness the bodily movements he controlled. Baxter's book also gave the debate over the existence of spirits a denominational character. During the 1690s, as the controversy intensified, the anti-Sadducees—those who accepted the reality of possessions and witchcraft—tended increasingly to be English Dissenters (the heirs of the seventeenth-century Puritans), New England Puritans, and Scottish Presbyterians.

In the 1690s a cluster of new possession narratives appeared in print that anti-Sadducees used to bolster their position. First there was the witch-hunt at Salem, Massachusetts, in 1692, which many contemporaries interpreted erroneously as a case of mass demonic possession. A narrative of the Salem trials by Deodat Lawson appeared in that year, followed by Cotton Mather's *Wonders of the Invisible World*.[56] Then there was the case of the 'Surey demoniac', Richard Dugdale, a teenage gardener from Lancashire who began to experience fits in 1688 and who testified to the reality of his own possession in 1689. Dugdale's affliction became the subject of a major controversy that peaked in 1689 with the publication of his possession narrative at the urging of 'believers of Satan's activating men's bodies by possession, witchcrafts, etc .... as a very likely expedient for rooting out atheism, debauchery, Sadducism, and Devilishness'.[57] This narrative, written by the Nonconformist minister Thomas Jolly, elicited a rejoinder from Zachary Taylor, who took the traditional Anglican position that the whole thing was a hoax.[58]

The crucial task in all these examples of demonic possession was to show that the symptoms were reported to be extraordinary or outside the normal course of nature. Fully aware of the sceptical claim that possessions were caused by natural illnesses, the anti-Sadducees needed to produce examples of symptoms so extreme that their supernatural origin could not be doubted. They had to meet the standard of the *Rituale Romanum* of 1614, which would allow exorcism only in cases of possession that were clearly of supernatural origin. The *Rituale* insisted that the exorcist 'must be thoroughly acquainted with those signs by which he can distinguish the possessed person from those who suffer from a physical illness'.[59] The problem with this standard is that those eager to classify the cases as demonic could easily exaggerate the severity of the symptoms. As we have seen, possession narratives exhibited rhetorical devices that make it difficult to accept them at face value.

All late seventeenth-century Calvinist possession narratives classified the symptoms of the demoniacs as impossible to diagnose medically. The statement that one of the possessed Goodwin children at Boston in 1688 was seized with strange fits 'beyond those that attend an epilepsy or cata-lepsy' shows how the authors of these narratives made the case for super-natural causation.[60] Another tactic was to explain that the parents of the demoniacs first consulted a physician to determine the cause of the child's afflictions, concluding that the Devil was at work only after the doctors could find no natural explanation. In this way the anti-Sadducees showed that they were conversant with current medical science, such as it was. Consultation with a physician before determining that the afflicted person was possessed became standard operating procedure in late seventeenth-century possession episodes.

The possession of Christian Shaw, the eleven-year-old daughter of the laird of Barragan in western Scotland in 1697, became a centrepiece in this effort to use episodes of demonic possession to bolster the anti-Sadducean position. Like most other cases of possession in Scotland (and there were relatively few) this one led to the trial and execution of seven witches for having caused the young girl's afflictions. No sooner had these witches been executed at Paisley, in 1697, than a number of pamphlets describing the case began to appear, including an anonymous account, *A True Narrative of the Sufferings and Relief of a Young Girle*, published in Edinburgh in 1698. This work has been attributed to Francis Grant, later Lord Cullen, the lawyer who prosecuted the Paisley witches, with the assistance of John MacGilchrist, a Glasgow solicitor who was Christian's uncle.[61] The polemical purpose of *A True Narrative* was clearly indicated in the preface, which used Shaw's possession to affirm the existence of God. Its purpose was also revealed by the title of the London edition of this work, *Saducismus debellatus* (Sadducism Conquered).[62]

Another anonymous pamphlet, *Witch-Craft Proven*, published at Glasgow in 1697, served the same polemical purpose at the *True Narrative*. This highly credulous work, erroneously attributed to John Bell, made no specific reference to the Paisley trials, but the place and date of publication and its professed purpose to prove the existence of spirits, leaves no doubt regarding its inspiration.[63] The author starts by painting a grim picture of a world in which spirits do not exist: 'For if there be no spirits then ... there is no eternal death, life, nor resurrection to be to be expected, nor any local place of punishment for the damned to be tormented in ... nor any heavenly joy and solace to be expected by the truly godly after this life.'[64] He then cites the presence of witches in all ages as evidence for the existence of wicked spirits, and those 'who are in covenant and league with them'.[65]

Seven years later an account of the possession of Patrick Morton, a teenage blacksmith from the Scottish burgh of Pittenweem in Fife, illustrated the lasting influence of the *True Narrative* and its theological message. This pamphlet not only compared Morton's symptoms to those of Christian Shaw but put the episode to the same polemical use, 'for proving the existence of good and evil spirits'. Claiming even more empirical evidence to support his cause, the author used this opportunity to claim that there were thousands of witnesses to the influence of evil spirits in both hemispheres.[66] Such claims appealed to those who needed empirical evidence for their belief in the reality of possession, but it did not thin the ranks of the Sadducees, who grew in number in the early eighteenth century. The only segment of educated opinion that was reluctant to embrace it was that of the clergy.

Scepticism and its limits

Throughout the fifteenth, sixteenth and seventeenth centuries those who defended the authenticity of contemporary demonic possessions resisted the arguments of the sceptics. True, some possessions may have been counterfeit and others may have been caused by natural illnesses, but others appeared to be genuine. The testimony of Scripture, the logic of scholastic philosophy, the widespread Christian belief that human society was in the Last Days, and the persuasive force of narratives of possession made it difficult for clerics to abandon their belief in the possibility of possession. To do so was to question the infallibility of the Word of God, dispute the logic of the scholastics, deny the overwhelming observable evidence that the world was in its Last Days, and convince themselves that it was not the Devil forcing innocent people to enter into bodily contortions and to utter blasphemies. To adopt the position of the sceptics would mean rejecting everything they had been taught since childhood about the Devil and the threat he represented.

The difficulty that early modern authorities had in abandoning their belief in possession can be demonstrated by looking at the writings of the Protestant physician and demonologist Johann Weyer. Also known by his Dutch name of Wier, Weyer is most well known for his sceptical views regarding witchcraft, but like most demonologists he also wrote about the closely related phenomenon of demonic possession. Although he attributed many possessions to melancholy or fraud, he argued that others were genuine. The only possibility that he unequivocally rejected was that witches were responsible for such possessions. In *De praestigiis daemonum* (1563) Weyer argued that a group of possessed nuns at the convent at Wertet, who were believed to have been possessed at the command of witches, were actually possessed directly by the Devil. After describing how these nuns 'had their legs, arms and faces wrenched totally backward' and climbed trees like cats, he concluded: 'It cannot be doubted that in fact Satan had possessed these maidens.'[67] By taking the position that some possessions were caused by demons and others by natural factors, Weyer did little to promote a naturalist interpretation. At best he confused the issue, illustrating the difficulty of distinguishing between demonic and medical explanations of the demoniac's afflictions.

It is clear from this one passage that Weyer was more sceptical regarding witchcraft than possession. One reason for their differential treatment was that Weyer, an evangelical Protestant, never denied the existence of a powerful Devil who could intervene in the processes of nature. In his view the Devil was responsible for deluding the women who were accused of witchcraft, and the women were morally accountable for their lack of faith. Once demonic power in the world was conceded, genuine possession by the Devil had to remain an option. A second reason for Weyer's greater scepticism was that while possession found support in numerous passages of the New Testament, the biblical passages cited to support the belief in witchcraft were highly controversial. Displaying his knowledge of biblical scholarship, Weyer explained that the Hebrew word *chasaph*, which was translated as 'witch' in 'Thou shalt not suffer a witch to live' (Exodus 22: 18) referred to a diviner or poisoner, not a person who had made a pact with the Devil.

The reluctance or inability of the sceptical Weyer to abandon his belief in the Devil's ability to invade the body of a human being goes a long way towards explaining why belief in the possibility of possession persisted among educated people far longer than the belief in witchcraft. As long as educated people continued to believe in the existence of a Devil that God allowed to intervene in the natural world, they could not reject entirely the belief in demonic possession. They might argue, as many Protestants did throughout the seventeenth and eighteenth centuries, that demonic possession was a rare or exceptional development, thereby demonstrating a sceptical frame of mind that became widespread in the last decades of the seventeenth century, but they still could not abandon the belief that the Devil could invade the body of a human being and take control of it.

One might think that the development of science in the seventeenth century, especially the emergence of the mechanical philosophy, which contended that the entire natural world (including human bodies) operated in a regular fashion in accordance with immutable laws established by God, would have undermined this belief. But the mechanical philosophy readily accommodated demonic as well as divine intervention in the world by claiming that both God and the Devil operated through the processes of nature rather than outside them. This helps to explain why seventeenth-century natural philosophers (as scientists were then called), including those learned in medical science, did not promote atheism (allaying the fears that the mechanical philosophy would lead in that direction) and did not undermine the belief in demonic possession any more than they undermined the belief in witchcraft. Throughout the seventeenth century demonology maintained a scientific standing that prevented members of the Royal Society in England, including Robert Boyle and Isaac Newton, from challenging the belief in possession as unscientific or irrational. For them the mechanical philosophy could not explain occult forces. As late as 1737 William Whiston, who succeeded Isaac Newton in the Lucasian chair of mathematics at Cambridge and whose scientific beliefs coexisted comfortably with his view of a mechanistic universe, could not deny the possibility of demonic assaults on the human body any more than he could deny Newton's theory of gravity, since the mechanical philosophy could explain neither of these apparently occult forces in nature.[68]

If the belief in demonic possession were to be successfully challenged in early modern Europe, the case against it had to come from clerical rather than scientific circles, from theologians and biblical scholars, not philosophers or scientists. It is no surprise that the mechanical philosophy found little support in these quarters.[69] Nor was there much of a chance that clergy would subscribe to the claim of the pantheist philosopher Baruch Spinoza, who claimed in 1661 that devils were fictions that men posited 'in order to find causes of hate, envy, anger and such passions'.[70]

The clergyman who made the strongest case in this regard was the Dutch Calvinist minister and biblical scholar Balthasar Bekker. Although Bekker was a Cartesian—an advocate of the ideas of the French philosopher and scientist René Descartes—his argument against the reality of both possession and witchcraft proceeded more from his biblical scholarship than from his subscription to Cartesian principles regarding the separation of mind and body and the operation of a mechanical universe.[71] In *De betoverde weereld*, Bekker presented a detailed exegesis of the Bible to prove that the Devil was incapable of intervening in the natural world.[72] 'The empire of the Devil,' he contended, 'is but a chimera and he has neither such a power nor such an administration as is ordinarily ascribed to him.'[73] Bekker did not doubt that the Devil existed, but he believed that God had confined him to Hell after the war in Heaven described in Revelation, and from that position the Devil was incapable of doing any of the things that scholastic philosophers claimed he could. To argue otherwise would have been to deny the sovereignty of God.

Since the Devil was chained up in Hell, he could not make pacts with human beings, as it was widely believed witches did, or give them the power to practise magic. Most important for our purposes, it meant that the Devil could not invade and occupy a human body. The fact that Bekker situated the Devil in Hell, which he believed to be located at the centre of the Earth, by itself prevented him from influencing the course of nature or human events. To seize that opportunity the Devil needed to be situated in the air, the realm that most Christian theologians believed he occupied, where he could more easily interact with human society.

Bekker's volumes were translated into French, German, and English, and they reached a broad audience, but his demonology, which was more radical than that of Reginald Scot, nonetheless failed to carry the day.[74] A large number of pamphlets attacked him for violating Calvinist theological orthodoxy.[75] The leaders of the Reformed Church, incensed that Bekker had challenged the most revered Calvinist theologians of the age, expelled him from his ministry for his faulty exegesis of the Bible. His treatment at the hands of the theological establishment presaged the similar ostracism that awaited the two English theologians, Woolston and Sykes, who dared to challenge the literal interpretation of Scripture, as discussed in Chapter 2. Clerical scepticism regarding the possibility of possession developed very slowly and was retarded by the persistent belief in the power of the Devil.

The limited impact of scepticism regarding possession can best be witnessed in Catholic territories, where a large majority of European possessions took place. As discussed in Chapter 1, the Catholic Church had always demonstrated a certain degree of scepticism about the authenticity of specific possessions. In the fourteenth century clerical authorities had developed a series of tests to determine the authenticity of apparent possessions, and techniques to discern fraudulent cases. The Spanish and Roman inquisitions had even prosecuted demoniacs who were shown to have faked their symptoms. Protestant criticism that most Catholic possessions were either fraudulent or caused by natural disease had made their task even more urgent. Catholic scepticism became even deeper with the publication of a new *Rituale Romanum*, which contained an authorized rite for exorcizing demoniacs and condemned the unofficial and semi-official rituals found in the anthologies of Girolamo Menghi and his associates. This manual, published during the pontificate of Paul V and reflecting the spirit of Catholic reform, made the tests for possession even more demanding and declared that every apparent possession was to be assumed to be the result of natural causes unless supernatural origin was not in doubt.

By the end of the seventeenth century, the scepticism that the *Rituale* displayed towards the reality of many cases of demonic possession contributed to the reduction in the number of reported cases in Catholic territories. Collective possessions, which were mainly a Catholic phenomenon, were far less common after 1660. But possessions did not come to an end in Catholic Europe. They persisted mainly because there continued to be a widespread demand for exorcism among the general population and because the Vatican was unable to overcome the willingness of local clergymen to appease that popular demand. One reason Catholic authorities were reluctant to take action was that they did not deny the possibility that genuine possessions could occur. Although the Vatican placed many of the exorcist manuals written in the sixteenth century and early seventeenth century on the Index of Prohibited Books and published new editions of the *Rituale Romanum*, that manual still prescribed a ritual for genuine cases of possession. The Vatican could not reasonably expect its clergy to appreciate the fact that the official Catholic rite of exorcism in the *Rituale Romanum* was intended to be used only in rare instances.

The clerical treatment of demoniacs in Mexico in 1691 reveals how demonic possessions could take place in the face of growing papal and inquisitorial scepticism. In 1691 an outbreak of possessions occurred among converts in the Franciscan mission of Querétaro in this Spanish colony. The demoniacs, possibly in reaction to the rigorous asceticism promoted by the evangelical branch of the Franciscans who staffed the mission, had fallen into paroxysms, vomited needles, thrown themselves violently to the ground, and uttered blasphemies. When the possessions, which spread rapidly throughout the mission, came to the attention of the Inquisition in Mexico, the inquisitors displayed the same scepticism that had become common among Catholics as well as Protestants in Europe by this time. In their view the reports of the possession strained credulity, and the claims made by the demoniacs that Lucifer was obediently doing God's work challenged the traditional view of the Devil as God's antagonist. It also pushed the orthodox belief that the Devil required God's permission to enter a person's body to an illogical extreme, according to which God would become the ultimate source of the demoniac's physical and mental torments.[76] The Holy Office wanted to deny the authenticity of these possessions not because they believed that possessions were impossible or because they thought the symptoms had natural causes but because the Franciscan interpretation of the possessions as ultimately God's work challenged the traditional concepts of both divine and demonic power. The problem they faced, however, was that the Franciscan belief in a capricious, tyrannical God had a firm foundation in the Augustinian and nominalist theology that flourished in both Catholic and Protestant quarters during the Reformation.[77]

Faced with this theological quandary, the inquisitors dismissed these particular possessions as the product of the demoniacs' fantasies and hallucinations. In so doing they contributed to the gradual relocation of the belief in the reality of possession to the uneducated people who were its main victims. This was the same strategy that sceptical officials adopted when dealing with charges of witchcraft. In this way the inquisitors could discredit the particular accusation without denying the belief in demonic activity that had originally given credence to both phenomena. In dealing with witchcraft accusations the strategy brought an end to prosecutions while allowing the clerical belief to persist well into the eighteenth century. We know that witchcraft prosecutions ended long before most educated people, especially members of the clergy, stopped believing in the reality of witchcraft. It was much more difficult, however, for ecclesiastical authorities to prevent exorcisms when local clerics encouraged them. Judicial authorities could take action against illegal witchcraft prosecutions, but they could do little to put an end to possessions. This explains why, when other incidents of possession occurred in France and Spain in the late eighteenth century, the Church could not prevent them. They could publish new editions of the *Rituale Romanum*, as they did in record numbers between 1751 and 1770, and try to discredit unauthorized exorcisms, but their efforts were limited by their inability to deny that some of the possessions might be authentic. Even the Spanish Benedictine Benito Feijoo (1676–1764), who claimed that 96 per cent of all demoniacs either faked or imagined their possessions, would not deny that the remaining 4 per cent were genuinely possessed. Among members of the clergy a rational and enlightened view of possessions ultimately ran up against a scriptural and theological roadblock that prevented the abandonment of the belief.

As the body of limited clerical scepticism grew during the late seventeenth and early eighteenth centuries, the belief in possession increasingly became the preserve of the less educated members of society and the clerics and exorcists who still catered to it. Until clerical establishments abandoned the belief, however, incidents of possession would continue to take place and secure clerical approval, as they still do in some religious communities today.

CHAPTER 4

Expelling the Demon

THE EXPULSION OF DEMONS from human bodies, often referred to as exorcism, was an essential component of the possession experience. Although its purpose was to heal demoniacs, the procedure more often than not aggravated their symptoms, allegedly agitating the demons within and causing the demoniacs greater suffering. The demons were said to have tormented their victims more severely as they vacated their bodies than at any time during their occupation. During exorcism the voices of the demons speaking through their victims became louder and more fearful than ever before. When the demons departed they were often described as ugly creatures, such as black birds, crows' heads, frogs, or hedgehogs. The demon's physical assault upon the body of the demoniac increased in intensity during exorcism. One Dutch priest claimed in 1650 that the Devil could tear a person into a thousand pieces during an exorcism.[1] Exorcists compounded this alleged demonic violence by taking forceful physical action against the possessed person on the presumption that they were struggling with the demon, not its human host.

This book is concerned only with the expulsion of demons from human beings who displayed the physical and psychological symptoms discussed in Chapter 1. The Catholic Church labelled such dispossessions 'major exorcisms', as opposed to the 'simple exorcisms' which until 1969 preceded the baptism of infants.[2] In Christian antiquity, the use of exorcism before baptism had symbolically represented the removal of original sin from the 'spiritually possessed' person and had nothing to do with expulsion of a demon that could take control of a person's physical movements and mental faculties. This book also excludes the exorcism of evil spirits from animals, crops, and inanimate objects, including buildings and the land itself.[3] Early sixteenth-century Spanish exorcists were known to have exorcized clouds, tempests, and hail as well as pests such as locusts and aphids.[4] Spanish priests in the New World even performed exorcisms of 'nature' on the grounds that this broadly defined entity, which included the physical landscape, was reputedly infested with demons.[5] Such symbolic rites of purification were categorically distinct from exorcisms that were intended to expel spirits from the bodies of human beings. The exorcism of ghosts or spectres, which Erasmus satirized as superstitious in his *Colloquies* (1518), also falls outside the boundaries of this study.[6]

Medieval and early modern writers often used the words exorcism and conjuration interchangeably, in that both involved the commanding of an evil spirit by invoking the name of God. The similar connotations of the two terms lent support to the Protestant argument that the Catholic liturgical rite of exorcism was a magical ritual.[7] The main distinction between the two practices is that they had different ends: an exorcist commanded evil spirits so that he could drive them out of a human body and thereby free the demoniac from an unwanted occupation, whereas the conjuror or necromancer commanded demons so that he could use their power for his own benefit or that of others.[8] This distinction between exorcism and conjuration was the basis of the different demonological and judicial treatment of exorcists and ritual magicians in medieval and early modern Europe.[9]

Because exorcism and conjuration bore similar connotations, Protestants were reluctant to use the word exorcism to describe their efforts to expel demons from their human hosts. Protestants denied that Christ had actually performed exorcisms during his public ministry, since he did not need to appeal to a higher power. Nor did Christ need to address the invasive demons at all; he could cast them out by a mere act of will, as in the episode involving the daughter of the Syrophoenician woman. In discussing the biblical possession narratives as well as their own efforts to expel demons from the possessed, many Protestants used the generic word *dispossession* in place of the etymologically loaded word, exorcism. In recent times they have adopted the even more neutral term of *deliverance*, which Catholics have also used in some instances.

Exorcism or dispossession was 'a form of healing used when demons or evil spirits were thought to have entered a person and to be responsible for sickness'.[10] The close association between exorcism and healing can be seen in the New Testament, in which Christ not only expelled unclean spirits from demoniacs but also cured scores of people of various diseases. The frequency of his cures and the references to his powers of healing in the same context as his expulsion of demons has led to the argument that the two processes were identical. Mark, however, suggests that healing and exorcism, while similar in many respects, were nonetheless distinct when he reported that Jesus 'healed many who were sick with various diseases, and cast out many demons'.[11] Exorcism was a form of healing; but not all healing, such as that of people with physical deformities, involved exorcism.

The purposes of exorcism

The curing of the demoniac has always been the proximate, ostensible, and proclaimed purpose of exorcism. The ritual of dispossession, however, was also intended to influence those who witnessed it. Although the Vatican recommended in 1614 that all exorcisms be conducted privately to avoid scandal, exorcisms rarely took place in complete privacy. Even when performed at shrines, as they often were in Catholic German territories, they probably attracted at least a few observers.[12] Publicity explains why exorcism always had a theatrical dimension. Theatre requires an audience, and even exorcisms performed before a small group of people, such as those restricted to family members, took on the character of dramatic productions. When performed before large crowds, the public function of exorcism became its primary motivation.

Conversion

The exorcisms performed by Christ clearly had a public and a theatrical dimension. They were intended, at least in the eyes of the evangelists who wrote about them many years after the death of Christ, to prove that Jesus was the Son of God and that he did not cast out demons by means of demonic power. According to the Gospels, the crowds that witnessed these dispossessions were astonished by the immediate transformation of the demoniacs after Christ had exorcized them. The evangelists claimed that the possessing spirits themselves, speaking through the demoniacs, acknowledged Christ's divine status.

During the early centuries of Christianity exorcism became an instrument for converting pagans to the new religion. Instead of demonstrating directly the miraculous power of God, which was the purpose of the possession narratives in the New Testament, early Christian exorcisms served the purpose of proving that only Christians were capable of expelling demons in God's name. In the third century Tertullian and Cyprian both claimed that there was no better proof of Christianity, since each exorcism represented a victory over a pagan deity, which was identified as a demon. The exorcisms also revealed the intercessory power of the saints who performed them. The mere presence of an exorcist saint was reported to have sent demoniacs into convulsions. When St Martin of Tours came into a church, according to his fifth-century Life, 'the demoniacs who were there howled and trembled as criminals do when the judge arrives'.[13]

Instruction

After 1200, by which time Europe had been effectively Christianized, the public function of exorcism began to change. No longer necessary to demonize pagan gods and win converts to Christianity, except as part of missionary work in foreign lands,[14] exorcism served the purpose of confirming and disseminating demonological ideas. This new function, which coincided with the development of scholastic demonology, reflected a significant change in the signs of possession. Before 1200 most demoniacs displayed mainly physical symptoms, such as convulsions, contortions, and preternatural strength, but at this point demoniacs also began speaking in foreign languages and even prophesying. As exorcisms began to last longer, exorcists spent more time extracting information from the possessed regarding demons and their alleged powers. This information confirmed and sometimes amplified ideas they already had regarding the demonic underworld.

The growth of large public exorcisms and the publication of possession narratives in the early modern period gave exorcists the opportunity to communicate the demonological knowledge obtained during exorcisms to a broader audience. Exorcists usually had some grounding in demonology. Even if they had not studied theology at a university, they could have learned basic demonological ideas from the exorcist manuals that were widely available in the late sixteenth century. Exorcists deployed the knowledge of the Devil that they had acquired from these and other sources in their dialogues with the demons. In this way the people who attended these public rituals or who later read about them in possession narratives could acquire or increase their knowledge of the demonic world. If they had any doubts regarding the existence of demons, which some of them may have had, witnessing or reading about exorcisms could resolve those doubts. Preaching at the time of exorcisms might also have persuaded them that the Last Days were at hand.

In a treatise on demoniacs written in 1599 at the time of the exorcism of Marthe Brossier, the French polemicist Pierre de Bérulle gave a new twist to the idea that exorcism served a pedagogical function. The main purpose of Bérulle's treatise was to prove that possessions and exorcisms had increased since the establishment of Christianity and that the Church, rather than the state, had exclusive authority over the performance of these rites. Bérulle also claimed, however, that possessions and exorcisms served instructional purposes. God allowed the Devil to possess human beings and gave power to the Church to expel them so that atheists could see with their own eyes how the Devil could be tamed in God's name.[15] In this way Bérulle anticipated the arguments of late seventeenth-century anti-Sadducees that possessions provided empirical evidence for the existence of all spirits, including God himself.

Protestant dispossessions served somewhat different pedagogical functions from Catholic exorcisms. Protestants generally were not interested in forcing the possessing demons to identify themselves. Most English possessions, for example, referred to Satan or the Devil as the occupying demon and did not inquire further into the nature of his power. They exhibited little concern about the minor demons that were subordinate to him. For Protestants the main threat that the Devil represented was spiritual rather than physical. They were much more concerned with the Devil's ability to tempt than to cause physical harm. The primary goal of Protestant dispossessions, which consisted entirely of prayer and fasting, was to help the demoniac overcome the Devil's temptation and avoid eternal damnation. Relief of the demoniac's suffering was a secondary objective.

Confessional propaganda

The main function that Catholic exorcisms served during the Reformation era was to prove that Catholics, unlike Protestants, were able to cast out demons. Protestants claimed that Catholic exorcisms were magical and superstitious as well as ineffective. The English minister Henry Holland stated that exorcisms were 'all in vain'.[16] The Catholic response to this criticism was to demonstrate in a public, theatrical way that only the Catholic Church could cast out demons. As the one true Church established by Christ, it alone could perform miracles, the most spectacular being exorcism. Exorcism also served as a means to verify the truth of Catholic doctrine, especially the real, substantial presence of the body of Christ in the Eucharist. In the exorcism of the German demoniac Apolonia Geisslbrecht in 1582, the demon finally admitted after extensive interrogation and pressure, that the Eucharist was the real body of Christ.[17]

Catholics made the most effective use of exorcisms as anti-Protestant propaganda in France, southern Germany the Netherlands, and England. In each of these areas, however, Catholics found themselves in different competitive relationships with their Protestant adversaries.

France

The most theatrical and publicized of these exorcisms took place in France, where the conflict between the dominant Roman Catholic Church and a large Huguenot minority had led to violent warfare in the late sixteenth century. Although Catholics had an overall numerical advantage, Huguenots had strength in certain towns and provinces, and many of the exorcisms took place in or near those areas. The exorcism of Françoise Fontaine at Louviers in 1591, for example, took place immediately after the Huguenots had regained military control of the city. The Franciscan theologian Jean Benedicti conducted a number of exorcisms in the confessionally divided city of Lyon.[18] In the late sixteenth century, moreover, the conservative and fanatical Catholic League staged exorcisms not only to demonstrate the truth of Catholicism but also to persuade the large Catholic majority and the moderate Catholic leadership not to tolerate the new Protestant heresy of Calvinism.[19] After the Edict of Nantes in 1598, which gave the Huguenots toleration and control of enclaves in which they formed a majority, the exorcisms were intended to convert these Huguenots to Catholicism by discrediting their spiritual credentials.

In this anti-Huguenot propaganda the Catholics had a distinct advantage, in that all they needed to do was demonstrate the effectiveness of their ritual. Huguenots and Protestant foreign commentators might claim that the possessions were counterfeit or the product of natural causes, but it was difficult to compete with apparent Catholic success in driving out demons. On one occasion both Huguenots and Catholics tried their hand at dispossessing the same demoniac, but the Protestant methods of prayer and fasting, which were less theatrical than those of Catholics, could not be as easily manipulated or exploited in the manner of Catholic exorcisms.

Four of these French Catholic exorcisms in particular demonstrate the confessional appeal and effectiveness of such psychodramas. The first was the dispossession of Nicole Obry, a sixteen-year-old laywoman from Vervins in the diocese of Laon in Picardy in 1566. The exorcism took place in the Cathedral of Notre-Dame-de-Liesse at Laon. Picardy was a major theatre in the early years of the French wars of religion. Although Catholics had a majority in the province, the Huguenots had considerable influence there and represented a real threat to Catholic dominance. When reports stated that Obry had displayed many of the physical signs of possession, Catholic authorities sensed an opportunity to acquire ecclesiastical capital from her distress. The exorcism was conducted by the bishop of the diocese and was accompanied by long processions before large crowds. The ceremony was designed to show the effectiveness of the Catholic sacrament of the Eucharist, which Protestants considered to be magical and idolatrous. Its purpose was to demonstrate that as the body of Christ it had the ability to drive out demons. When the Eucharistic host was first brought to Obry, it aggravated the symptoms of her possession. This indication of the demon's reaction to the Catholic sacrament was effective anti-Protestant propaganda, especially when the demon, Beelzebub, identified Huguenots as his servants. When the Eucharist eventually succeeded in relieving Obry of her afflictions, it provided further proof that Catholicism was the one true faith. The Catholics claimed that the successful exorcism was a miracle—*Le miracle de Laon*—as a further refutation of the Protestant claim that miracles had ceased at the end of the Apostolic Age. A large number of narratives on this possession and exorcism continued to serve the purposes of Catholic propaganda after the event. The main Protestant responses to this onslaught of Catholic propaganda was to prove that the possessions and exorcisms were fraudulent.[20]

The Miracle of Laon had a profound impact on subsequent possessions and exorcisms in France. The published accounts of the episode provided scripts not only for other demoniacs to follow but also for the three most famous exorcisms that Catholic authorities performed in France between 1582 and 1634: the exorcism of four lay demoniacs of varying ages at Soissons in 1582, the exorcism of the young laywoman Marthe Brossier in Paris in 1598; and the mass exorcism of the Ursuline nuns at Loudun in 1634.[21] These exorcisms all served the purposes of Catholic propaganda against the Huguenots, and they all used the Eucharist as a method of expelling the demon. One of the possessed boys at Soissons was relieved of his symptoms when the Eucharistic host was forced into his mouth, just as in the exorcism of Nicole Obry. The demon Beelzebub that possessed Nicole Obry appeared in all three of these later exorcisms. All three were performed publicly before crowds estimated in the thousands. In all of them militant Catholics organized processions and preached sermons against Protestantism.[22] Narratives and treatises describing these exorcisms, many of them modelled on the accounts of the Miracle of Laon, became integral components of a massive Catholic propaganda campaign.[23]

Southern Germany

German Catholic exorcisms were not as spectacular or as common as those in France, but they served similar confessional purposes.[24] Southern Germany was the main battleground of the Counter-Reformation in central Europe. As in France, these exorcisms took place in religiously divided areas. Lyndal Roper has argued that in Augsburg, a religiously divided territory with a Protestant majority of the population but a Catholic government, the Counter-Reformation proceeded mainly by means of exorcism. Between 1560 and 1580 there was an 'exorcism mania' in Augsburg.[25] The priests who took the lead in the staging of public exorcisms were the Jesuits, the leaders of the Counter-Reformation in Germany.

The most famous exorcism in Germany in the sixteenth and seventeenth centuries was that of Anna Bernhausen, a maid-in-waiting to a member of the wealthy Fugger family, in 1570. The exorcism was performed at the Bavarian shrine at Altötting by Peter Canisius, who became known as the 'Second Apostle of Germany' (Boniface was the first) in recognition of his missionary work throughout the region. This exorcism owes its fame or (from a Protestant perspective) notoriety to the wide circulation of a narrative by Martin Eisengrein, a convert from Lutheranism who was both professor of theology at the Jesuit college at Ingolstadt and provost of the collegiate church at Altötting.[26] As a result of the publication of this pamphlet, Anna Bernhausen's possession and exorcism became the subject of a heated theological controversy between Catholics and Lutherans.

What distinguished Bernhausen's exorcism from those that took place in France was that it occurred at a shrine rather than in the city, where exorcism mania had already reached a fever pitch. The reason for this change of venue was that the Catholic government of the city had banned public exorcisms because of the scandal they had caused. The relocation to Altötting did not reduce the number of exorcisms in southern Germany. To the contrary, the episode revived the reputation of Altötting as a place of pilgrimage, and hundreds of demoniacs visited the shrine to be exorcized over the course of the next hundred years.[27] But the performance of exorcisms at this shrine and many others throughout Catholic Germany did mean that large crowds, such as those that had assembled at Laon and Soissons, could not witness them.

A relatively small number of Germans also witnessed the exorcism in 1582 of Apolonia Geisslbrecht, a thirty-year-old woman in the small town of Spalt, in the diocese of Eichstätt, about forty kilometres south of Nuremberg.[28] Apolonia's possession had begun when she called upon the Devil for help as she quarrelled continually with her abusive, drunken husband. At that point a tall man, promising her a variety of pleasures, allegedly appeared to her, and Apolonia gave this attractive, seductive man her hand. This was hardly the first time that a person's guilt for having some sort of commerce with the Devil triggered a possession. When her afflictions began, Apolonia was brought to the local church, where

Wolfgang Agricola, the dean of Spalt, performed all the tests to prove that Apolonia's possession was authentic. Then, as the woman's symptoms became more acute, he went to her house with three other priests, two theology students, and a group of neighbours. There he used the Eucharist and the priest's vestments to exorcize her in her bedroom. He placed the small cloth on which the Eucharistic host rested and then the host itself on Apolonia's head, thereby recalling the way in which the Eucharist had been used in the exorcism of Nicole Obry and the Soissons demoniacs. This method of exorcism, designed to prove the truth of the Catholic doctrine of the Eucharist and more generally the Roman Catholic faith, had an immediate effect, according to the possession narrative written by Sixtus Agricola with the assistance of Georg Witmerus. According to this narrative, after a long struggle the demon admitted that the Eucharist was the true body of Christ. The pamphlet compared the 'miracle' of the successful exorcism to the raising of Lazarus from the dead.[29]

Although only a few Catholics and probably no Protestants witnessed the deliverance of Apolonia Geisslbrecht, Agricola's possession narrative served the same polemical purpose as Martin Eisengrein's account of the exorcism of Anna Bernhausen. Dedicated to the bishop of Eichstätt, the pamphlet became a weapon in the efforts to bring Protestants in southern Germany back into the Catholic fold. Agricola claimed that he wrote the pamphlet to prove the authenticity of the possession and the effectiveness of the exorcism against the claims of the sceptics, by which he could only have meant the Lutherans. He suggested that the Lutherans themselves recognized the importance of the exorcism in this confessional conflict because during Apolonia's possession a Lutheran preaching friar, the son of a neighbour, came to Spalt and offered to exorcize Apolonia. Agricola wanted to entice the preacher to take part in the Catholic ceremony, but upon hearing of this requirement, the young man left the village.[30] Agricola's pamphlet, like Eisengrein's, was published in Ingolstadt, where the first Jesuit college in Germany had been established in 1549 in an effort to promote the Counter-Reformation in the region.[31]

Georg Scherer's sermon on the possession and exorcism of Anna Schlutterbäurin in 1583, which was also published at Ingolstadt, served a similar anti-Lutheran purpose. Anna lived in the religiously divided town of Mank, and when Emperor Rudolf II (r. 1576–1612) heard of her torments, he pressured Anna's Protestant lord to send her to Vienna to be exorcized. Responsibility for the entire possession was pinned on the Lutherans. The girl's seventy-year-old grandmother, who admitted taking the girl to Lutheran services, was tried and executed as a witch for having caused Anna's possession by demons in the shape of flies that she kept in bottles. During the exorcism the demons that spoke through Anna vilified Catholic ecclesiastics while praising Lutherans and Turks. Scherer claimed that Lutherans were incapable of casting out demons and boasted that Catholic prayer and holy water were responsible for the girl's deliverance.[32]

The Netherlands

In the religiously divided Dutch Republic, which came into existence as a result of the revolt against Spain in the late sixteenth century, Catholics occasionally used exorcism as a propaganda tool in their confessional battles with the Dutch Reformed Church. Protestantism became the official religion of the new state, which acquired the right to seize Catholic church property and introduce a programme of Protestant reform, but large concentrations of Catholics in many areas and the religious diversity of the population (which also included Lutherans, Mennonites, and Jews) as well as divisions among the Calvinists led to a de facto policy of religious toleration that had few parallels in seventeenth-century Europe.[33] But although Dutch Catholics could practise their religion without fearing political reprisals, they could not perform exorcisms in public. They needed to stage them in the privacy of their churches or in the countryside, where they were more likely to avoid detection.[34] This situation, coupled with the success of Protestants in responding to Catholic claims, prevented Dutch Catholics from fully exploiting their exorcisms to gain converts from Protestantism.

One example of the difficulty Dutch Catholics had in using exorcisms as effective propaganda became apparent in the casting out of the Devil from the body of a young cloth-maker, David Wardavoir, in the predominantly Protestant city of Utrecht. Wardavoir's apparently successful exorcism by unidentified Catholic priests had been a major source of Catholic boasting throughout the Dutch Republic in the early 1590s. In order to counter this propaganda, an anonymous Protestant pamphlet, published in 1595, gave a rival account of Wardavoir's deliverance in typical Calvinist fashion, claiming that he had fought off Satanic attacks only by means of prayer and his faith in Jesus Christ. The pamphlet sought to discredit Catholic exorcism as magical, endorsed the strict Protestant insistence on using only prayer and fasting to cast out demons, and reiterated that the Devil could be defeated only through God's Word. The pamphlet also articulated the Calvinist theme that his Wardavoir's faith had helped him resist the temptation to worship the Devil, that is, to become a witch.[35] We do not know what effect the publication had on public opinion, but it probably helped to neutralize the impact of Catholic propaganda regarding the incident. It did not result in a noticeable increase in the size of the Catholic population of the city.

In 1650 an exorcism conducted by a Catholic priest in Uden, an autonomous Catholic enclave in the Dutch Republic, also failed to realize its potential as Counter-Reformation propaganda. The incident involved a verbal exchange between the exorcist, Joannes Houbraken, the Catholic parish priest of a neighbouring village, and Cornelis Prouninck, the Protestant bailiff whose job was to inventory the church property that the Protestant Dutch Republic was preparing to confiscate. When the bailiff attended a Mass at which Father Houbraken was to exorcize sixteen demoniacs, the two men became involved in a dispute over the Catholic doctrine of transubstantiation and the miraculous nature of exorcism. At one point the demoniacs, led by Houbraken, threatened to send their demons into Prouninck and tear him into a thousand pieces. The bailiff, fearing he might be murdered, came close to pulling his gun, but the demoniacs backed off and Prouninck left the church. The Catholic community used the incident and the exorcisms that followed to prove that they belonged to the one true Church, but the incident more than anything revealed the limitations of the Counter-Reformation in this religiously diverse and administratively decentralized state.[36]

England

After Queen Elizabeth restored Protestantism as the official state religion in 1559, English Roman Catholics faced even more serious obstacles than their coreligionists in the Netherlands to use exorcism as an instrument of religious propaganda. By the term of a statute passed in 1585, Catholic priests were banned from the country, and discovery could result in a trial and execution for treason.[37] These dangers did not deter Jesuit missionaries from serving the Catholics in the country and from trying to convert Protestants to the Catholic faith. Exorcism became one of the main methods of bringing about these conversions. The theological rationale was the same as Catholics used in France: that there can only be one true Church, that the principal mark of that true Church is the ability to perform miracles, and that the greatest of these miracles is the casting out of devils. The exorcisms began in the mid 1580s when the Jesuit priest William Weston spearheaded a campaign to exorcize large numbers of demoniacs, which they estimated to be more than five hundred.[38]

Since the established Church of England wielded far more political and legal power than the Dutch Reformed Church, the government was much more effective in responding to the activities of the exorcists. Within a year all the priests who performed the exorcisms, including Weston himself, had been arrested and imprisoned. Many years later, when exorcisms once again became a major concern of the clerical establishment, Samuel Harsnett, the chaplain and assistant to Richard Bancroft, bishop of London, published *A Declaration of Egregious Popish Impostures* (1603), which reported the findings of a legal investigation of the exorcisms the priests had conducted at Denham, Essex in 1585 and 1586.[39] Four of the demoniacs who testified at the trial of Weston and his colleagues were Protestants who had converted to Catholicism during their exorcism. The other two, Annie Smith and Richard Mainey, both eighteen years old, were already Catholics at the time of their deliverance. During their exorcisms Mainey and two of the converts, Sarah and her sister Friswood, reportedly had visions confirming the Catholic belief in the Real Presence of Christ in the Eucharist. They also demonstrated the power of relics of recent Catholic martyrs.[40] The book, however, did not stop Catholic priests from continuing their efforts to win converts by casting out demons. In the first half of the seventeenth century English Catholic missionary priests performed more than sixty exorcisms, far more than the recorded number of Protestant possessions during the same period. Many of these exorcisms took place in Lancashire, a religiously divided county that had a disproportionately large Catholic population. There is no record of the number of conversions the campaign netted.[41]

The exorcism of Thomas Ashton, a weaver in the parish of Wigan in Lancashire, by four Catholic priests in 1696, provides an example of how Catholics tried to use exorcisms to gain converts as their numbers dwindled in the late seventeenth century. The only account of the exorcism comes from Zachary Taylor, the sceptical and virulently anti-Catholic Anglican minister of the parish. Since Taylor was not present at the exorcism, he had to rely on the report by the curate and reader of the parish who witnessed the event, which took place before a reportedly large crowd of Catholics and Protestants at the house of Thomas Pennington in Orrel. The most distinctive feature of this exorcism was Ashton's statements of Catholic doctrine on such matters as the existence of Purgatory, the Real Presence of Christ in the Eucharist, the effectiveness of praying before images, and the belief that outside the Catholic Church there was no salvation. These statements were prompted by questions from the lead Catholic exorcist, one Father Brooks.

Because of their intelligence and knowledge of the supernatural realm, demoniacs in the Middle Ages were occasionally allowed to preach. The recognition that Christ was 'the Holy One of God' by the demoniac in the synagogue at Capernaum provided a biblical precedent for accepting the truth of demoniacs' pronouncements. But the belief that the Devil was the Father of Lies, coupled with the blasphemies uttered by demoniacs, led most Catholic exorcists to elicit endorsements of Protestantism from demoniacs during the age of the Reformation. The statements of Catholic theological orthodoxy by Thomas Ashton therefore gave Taylor the opportunity to identify the Devil as 'a good Roman Catholic'.[42]

Protestant exorcisms

Protestants were certainly eager to refute Catholic claims of success in driving out demons, but they almost always did so defensively, to counter the impact of Catholic propaganda. Very rarely did Protestants take the offensive in this conflict and use their skill in expelling demons to prove that they, rather than the Catholics, were the true Church founded by Christ. Both their theology and their ecclesiology made it difficult for them to do so, since they believed that the departure of demons from their human hosts depended completely upon divine grace, and Protestants had no distinctive means of exorcism besides prayer and fasting to drive out demons. In the propaganda war with the Catholics over demonic possession, therefore, Protestants always found themselves at a competitive disadvantage against the powerful theatrical exorcisms of Counter-Reformation Catholicism. Without holy water to sprinkle, candles to light, adjurations to recite, and sacraments to administer, the ministers were ecclesiastically and psychologically impotent. This disadvantage became readily apparent in 1566 when French Huguenots attempted to exorcize Nicole Obry, an effort that came to naught.[43] The unnamed Lutheran preacher never even got a chance to exorcize Apolonia Geisslbrecht at Spalt.

The most sustained effort to outdo the Catholic exorcists came from the Dutch Reformed minister Johannes Bergerus, a man of scandalous repute who after arriving in Utrecht in 1599 began a career as an exorcist. His efforts to cast out demons were intended to challenge the Catholics' corner of the exorcist market, but his tactics angered mainstream Calvinists more than Catholics. Members of the Dutch Reformed Church in the city objected to his work mainly because he used superstitious remedies that smacked of magic, such as a wolf's eye and heart, pulverized teeth from a human corpse, and witches' excrement, to heal his clients. In this way Bergerus undercut the efforts of the Dutch Reformed Church to depict Catholic exorcists as magicians. Yet his theatrical exorcisms did encourage his large body of followers to hope that his exorcisms would prove that they, rather then the Catholics, belonged to the true Church of Christ. In this hope they were disappointed, since most of his exorcisms apparently failed.

The dispossessions conducted by the English Puritan minister John Darrell in the 1590s represented another Protestant attempt to beat the Catholics at their own game. Like Bergerus, Darrell did not use Catholic methods of exorcism, such as relics, holy water, or invocation of the saints in his efforts to drive out demons. In fact, he stuck very closely to the prescribed Protestant methods of prayer and fasting, which he skilfully transformed into major theatrical productions. According to the Puritan minister George More, Darrell's goal in exorcizing demoniacs in Cleworth, Lancashire was to show that the Church of England was the one true Church established by Christ.[44]

Nevertheless Darrell, just like Bergerus in Utrecht, gave greater offence to English Protestants than to his Catholic rivals. Appealing to the Calvinist doctrine of the cessation of miracles, Bishop Bancroft and Samuel Harsnett argued that Darrell's exorcisms, despite using only the prescribed scriptural methods of dispossession, were nonetheless popish, because they represented efforts to perform miracles in the post-Apostolic age.[45] There is considerable irony in Harsnett's appeal to Calvinist theology in this context, for by this time he had already challenged some of the essential tenets of Calvinist theology.[46] In any event, the controversy was more about ecclesiastical politics than theology. Bancroft and Harsnett wanted to suppress Darrell and other Puritan exorcists because their rituals were a form of Puritan propaganda that threatened the authority of the bishops. Harsnett and Bancroft also believed, not without cause, that Puritan exorcisms were designed to prove that the true Church established by Christ was embodied in the Puritan congregations, not the Church of England.[47]

The exorcists

Just as the functions of exorcism changed over time, so too did the qualifications for performing the rite. In the early centuries of Christianity the practice of exorcism was open to all Christians, clerical or lay, regardless of social status or gender. The words of Christ in Mark 16: 17 enjoining all who believed in him to cast out demons provided a clear scriptural warrant for this policy.[48] Priests, however, gradually assumed the primary responsibility for healing both the sick and the possessed. In the third century the Church established the minor clerical order of exorcist as one of the steps leading to ordination, thereby reinforcing a preference for the clergy to perform the rite. Nevertheless, some lay Christians continued to heal demoniacs.

In late antiquity the belief that casting out demons was a mark of sanctity reinforced the belief that saintly men were the most successful exorcists.[49] The Lives of the saints in the early Church are replete with accounts of their exorcisms. St Martin of Tours (316–97), for example, exorcized a man whose symptoms included compulsive biting by thrusting his arm into the man's throat, thereby forcing the demon to exit through his anus. St Hilarion (291–371), who reputedly exorcized two hundred demoniacs at the same time, drove an entire legion of demons from a man who had displayed preternatural strength by stomping on the man's feet, claiming 'Writhe! Writhe! Thou mob of demons!' Upon this command many demons reportedly departed through the man's mouth, making a ruckus in many voices as they left.[50] The belief that saints were the most effective exorcists explains why demoniacs in late antiquity often went to the shrines of deceased saints to be healed. This practice continued throughout the Middle Ages and into the early modern period, although not as frequently as in the early years of Christianity.[51]

When possessions experienced a revival of popularity in the thirteenth century, saintly men continued to perform exorcisms. The exorcisms of St Francis of Assisi, St Dominic, and St Bonaventure became legendary.[52] St Anthony of Padua (1195–1231) once ordered the departure of a demon that had forced a young man to eat his own excrement. As the demon left the man's body, it physically assaulted Anthony, one of the few instances of violent confrontations between a demoniac and an exorcist during this period. The tradition of exorcisms by men who later were canonized continued into the early modern period: St Ignatius Loyola, St John of the Cross, and St Peter Canisius all acquired fame as exorcists.[53] As the demand for exorcisms increased, however, many came to be performed by priests who were never likely to qualify for canonization. In his sixth discourse on magic Martín Del Rio explains that while a proven remedy for possession would be to seek the help of 'those saintly men who, by general agreement have the power to work miracles ... this remedy is scarcely used these days because there are hardly any such men in existence, especially in this part of Europe'.[54]

The prominence of saints as exorcists in late antiquity and the Middle Ages explains why medieval theologians argued that the effectiveness of exorcisms depended at least to some extent on the moral state of the exorcist. In this respect exorcisms were different from the sacraments, which were effective by virtue of the act itself, regardless of the moral state of the person who performed it. For this reason Catholic writers insisted that an exorcist be a person of high virtue.[55] At the same time, however, they admitted that the ability to cast out demons provided no *guarantee* of the holiness of the exorcist.[56]

Protestants would have agreed with the Jesuit Georg Scherer's statement that the ability to cast out demons (like any other bestowal of grace) was a freely granted gift from God, but they rejected the Catholic restriction of exorcism to the clergy. In keeping with their insistence that Christianity must emulate the practice of the early Church, Protestants claimed that any Christian, lay or clerical, could perform an exorcism, since the resurrected Christ had said that all those who believed in him would be able to cast out demons in his name.[57] In 1600 the English Puritan minister George More, who worked with John Darrell to dispossess seven demoniacs in Lancashire, wrote that such deliverance was 'no extraordinary gift, peculiar to any one man, but common to all the faithful, as well as to another, and that the mean and simple people may have as great privilege and power to cast out Satan by their faith and fasting and fervent prayer as either he, or I, or the best and chieftest preacher'.[58] More attributed the power to expel demons to the ordinance of Christ, not to 'powers inherent in any individual, in spite of papist claims to the contrary'.[59]

Despite the clear preference of the Catholic Church for having the clergy perform exorcisms, laymen continued to conduct the ritual, especially as the frequency of possessions increased in the late Middle Ages. In *Malleus maleficarum* (1486) Heinrich Kramer indicated both the concern of the Church with this practice and the difficulty of remedying the situation. Appealing to the authority of Thomas Aquinas, Kramer argued that although it was desirable for an ordained priest, preferably a monk, to perform the rite, it was not unlawful for other devout persons, even women, to cast out demons from those who had been bewitched.[60] There had in fact been a number of female exorcists in the Middle Ages, and at least two such women were active in sixteenth-century Venice.[61] Other Catholic writers, such as the Spanish demonologist Pedro Ciruelo, were less accommodating to lay exorcisms. In his treatise on superstitious practices, Ciruelo insisted that only ordained priests be allowed to perform public exorcisms.[62]

In the late sixteenth century, when the number of demonic possessions reached new heights and when exorcism manuals became widely available in print, the number of exorcists increased dramatically. Many of the new practitioners were lay healers who believed that demons were the cause of the illnesses they were hired to cure. In Germany wandering practitioners known as *Teufelsbanner* developed profitable businesses by charging fees for their services.[63] Others who met the popular demand for exorcisms were parish priests who had no training in the art and did not have permission from their ecclesiastical superiors to practise. Alarmed by this situation, Jesuits in Bavaria and Augsburg took the lead in a campaign to bring an end to unauthorized exorcisms. They cracked down on unlicensed practitioners, ordered some demoniacs to be sent to

locations where ecclesiastical authorities permitted exorcisms, and occasionally encouraged the prosecution of offenders for witchcraft.[64] In Italy
Girolamo Menghi, who in his first two exorcist manuals had accepted the
legitimacy of lay exorcism, insisted in his last book, *Fustis daemonum*
(1596), that only ordained priests should be entrusted with this task.[65] One
argument in favour of this restriction was that only priests could administer the Holy Eucharist, which had become increasingly important in
Catholic exorcisms. Priests were also needed to bless sacred objects, and
only they could wear the vestments that were often used in exorcisms.
The official Catholic liturgical manual, *Rituale Romanum*, restricted the
practice of exorcism to 'a priest or any lawfully appointed officer of the
Church'.[66] The 1952 edition of the manual specified that the exorcist must
be a priest who has the particular and explicit permission of his bishop.[67]

Despite these official and semi-official efforts to restrict the practice of
Catholic exorcisms to the ordained clergy, laymen and unlicensed priests
continued to practise exorcisms. In the Netherlands most exorcisms in the
seventeenth century continued to be performed by laymen or priests
without ecclesiastical permission.[68] These unauthorized exorcisms explain
why some Catholic dioceses decided to elaborate or even expand upon the
Vatican's policy in their jurisdictions. The archdiocese of Malines in the
Netherlands, for example, did so in its *Pastorale rituale romano accommo-
datum* in 1649,[69] and in 1669 the Polish bishop Casimir Czartoriski
ordered that no one, under pain of excommunication, could perform the
office of exorcist without a written licence from him.[70] Throughout the
seventeenth century Jesuits, who took the lead in the campaign to exorcize
the growing number of demoniacs throughout Europe, struggled to
enforce the newly proclaimed clerical monopoly of the ritual.

The Vatican's requirement met its most high-profile test in Spain
regarding the claim that King Philip IV of Spain (r. 1621–65) had the
power to cure demoniacs. This claim, advanced by the Spanish political
theorist Juan Eusebio Nieremberg in 1643 and by Francisco de Blasco y
Lanuza in 1652, was based on the traditional belief that kings possessed
thaumaturgic powers. Nevertheless the argument that Spanish kings could
cast out demons ignited a controversy, leading to a three-day public forum
in 1654 to determine whether the Habsburg monarchs had the miraculous
power to cast out demons.[71] Unlike the power to cure scrofula, long
claimed by French and English kings, the power to cast out demons was
clearly miraculous, and therefore the debate centred on the question
whether this gift was 'a miraculous favour from heaven'.[72]

No report of the proceedings of this forum is extant, and the issue
remained controversial. Less than a year later, the philosopher and physician

Gaspar Caldera de Heredia argued that although it was possible for a monarch to have this power, it required clear proof, which was difficult to adduce. Caldera's argument, which reflected a long tradition of Spanish scepticism regarding possession and exorcism, tended to support the policy of the Vatican that denied laymen—in this case a divinely appointed lay king—the power to drive out demons.

Ten years before the publication of the *Rituale Romanum* the Church of England had issued a new set of canons that included a prohibition of all unlicensed exorcisms.[73] Canon 72 represented a direct response to the efforts of John Darrell and other Puritans to use exorcisms, and especially communal fasting and praying, to strength the Puritan cause.[74] The professed concerns of Samuel Harsnett, Bishop Richard Bancroft of London, and other members of the English ecclesiastical establishment were not completely contrived. In their eyes Puritans, despite their protestations that they were working for reform within the Church, represented an ecclesiastical threat to the unity of the Church of England. Puritanism, they feared, could lead the group to separate from the Church, as the so-called Brownists (followers of the separatist Robert Brown) had done in the 1590s. The establishment of separate congregations of Puritans, freed from the control of the episcopal hierarchy, validated the fears of the ecclesiastical establishment in the early seventeenth century.

A variety of motives drove exorcists to practise their art during this period of expansion. The attention they received from the broader community certainly played a part; they were, after all, co-stars of the demoniacs themselves in the sacred dramas they were now orchestrating. There is little evidence to support the claim that some exorcists were impostors, a charge that Harsnett, John Deacon, and John Walker made against John Darrell and Richard Baddeley made against the Jesuits who exorcized William Perry, the Boy of Bilson. Giovanni Levi has argued that Giovan Battista Chiesa, the son of a magistrate in Piedmont, assumed the role of exorcist and healer as part of an effort to maintain the same level of respect that his father had enjoyed as an official who mediated disputes among the people in the local community. A desire for profit probably drove others to capitalize on the promise of casting out demons. Edmond Hartley, a cunning man whom John Dee called in to dispossess the children of Nicholas Starkey in 1595, not only extracted a fee of forty shillings a year from Starkey but demanded a house and property as compensation.[75]

In some cases exorcists used their power and prestige to satisfy their sexual appetites. The most blatant of these cases was reputedly that of the Brazilian exorcist, Friar Luís de Nazaré, who acquired a reputation for copulating with young girls and then using the material from their pudenda to make medicinal remedies. In one late seventeenth-century case, having heard in confession that a young girl was pretending to be possessed in order to get her parents to allow her to marry a young boatman, Friar Luís volunteered to exorcize the young woman, took her to a remote country home, 'had carnal copulation with her', took alms for his services, and then joined the couple in wedlock.[76] The young Catholic priests who exorcized the English demoniac Sarah Williams at Denham in 1586 ran their hands 'along all parts of her body' and placed relics on the 'most secret part of her body', claiming that the Devil rested there. When the Devil eventually vacated Sarah's body, he exited through her 'nameless part, the Devil's portgate'.[77]

The search for ulterior motives, however, should not deny the genuine religious concern of exorcists to heal those whom Satan had apparently harmed and wage war against the Devil at a time when he was thought to be especially active. To ignore this religious motivation is to engage in the same type of reductionism that has hampered the study of possession itself. The religious objectives of Father Jean-Joseph Surin, the chief exorcist at Loudun, cannot be explained simply in terms of his desire for publicity or sexual voyeurism. Surin made a deliberate, religiously inspired effort to turn the Loudun episode of possession-cum-witchcraft into Mother Jeanne des Anges's spiritual journey.[78]

Closely related to these religious motivations for exorcizing demoniacs was the belief that the ritual would provide an antidote to, or relief from, witchcraft. Because the symptoms of possession were often considered to be the result of witches' maleficent magic, exorcism became one of the means by which priests tried to identify witches, facilitate their prosecution, and reverse the effects of their spells. During the exorcism of the nuns at Santa Chiara in northern Italy in 1636, the exorcists interrogated the demoniacs to discover who had caused their bewitchment.[79] In some cases the occupying demons, speaking through the demoniacs, said they would not vacate the bodies of the possessed until all the witches who had caused the possession had been tried and executed.[80] The exorcist appropriately refused to negotiate with the Devil, but this verbal exchange between the two parties formed part of an effort to drive out demons and identify witches at the same time.

The efforts of higher authorities, especially those of the Vatican, to control exorcisms paralleled the efforts of higher ecclesiastical and secular authorities to control the excesses of witch-hunting, with which possession was often linked. The challenge was greater in dealing with exorcists, since possessions, unlike witchcraft prosecutions, could not be monitored effectively. But the Vatican could try to enforce its rules on the qualifications of exorcists, ban the publication of unauthorized exorcism manuals, and occasionally take judicial or administrative action against those who operated without official warrant. Chiesa's career in Piedmont, for example, ended abruptly when ecclesiastical authorities arrested him and tried him for failing to follow the approved ritual of exorcism and for receiving payment for his services. Suspecting fraud, they had also investigated whether any of his cures were effective.

Methods of dispossession

What then were the procedures used to cast out demons in the early modern period? It is important to recognize that exorcism underwent a series of changes over the course of centuries. Richard Kieckhefer has noted that before the fifteenth century the techniques of exorcism were 'in large measure improvised'.[81] In the late fifteenth century Heinrich Kramer tried to give some uniformity to both the form and the content of the ritual, but it continued to change during the sixteenth century.

Adjuration

One constant feature of Catholic exorcisms, which can be traced back to the origin of the ritual in the period of biblical antiquity, was putting the Devil on oath. Indeed, the meaning of the Greek word *exorkizein* was equivalent to the Latin word *adjuro*, meaning to put someone on oath or demand that someone swear. The way that most exorcisms began was for the exorcist to command the demon in the name of God to speak truthfully. Jesus of course did not need to follow this procedure when he cast out demons. He might have actually done so in the manner of other Jewish exorcists, but since the evangelists were claiming that he was the Son of God, they did not report his use of any verbal formulae. The early Christian practice of putting the demon on oath was most likely to have been adopted from contemporary Roman judicial practice, in which the defendant was commanded to answer (i.e. swear to) the truth. This preliminary step prepared the way for an interrogation of the demon, which provided the rhetorical framework for most Catholic exorcisms.

Many Protestants objected to putting the demon on oath, both because there was no way to guarantee that he would tell the truth when sworn and because the practice of commanding the Devil for whatever reason, even to tell the truth, resembled the conjuring of the Devil in ritual magic.[82] There was a fine line between adjuring the Devil and conjuring him; until the fifteenth century the words *adjuro* and *conjuro* were used interchangeably.[83]

Conjuring, however, acquired the further connotation of summoning up a spirit as well as commanding him, and this became one of the main reasons why Protestants classified exorcism as magic. In *The Damned Art of Witchcraft* (1608) the English theologian William Perkins condemned the use of adjuration in exorcisms, insisting that 'for an ordinary man now to command the Devil in such sort is mere presumption and a practice of sorcery'.[84] The Calvinist reformer Peter Martyr reminded his audience that while they should not forsake demoniacs, 'yet we must not by adjurations command them to go forth'.[85] The equation of exorcism with magic was not simply a Protestant rhetorical strategy. Kieckhefer has shown that in the late Middle Ages exorcists and necromancers shared the belief that the power of the sacred could not only command but also constrain evil spirits.[86] Of course the exorcist and the necromancer conjured demons for ostensibly different purposes: the former to drive out the evil spirits and the latter to use demonic power to gain power or wealth or influence. Nonetheless, the Protestant association of the two practices carried persuasive force.[87]

These objections did not, however, prevent some Protestants from adjuring the Devil in the traditional fashion, making sure that they did so in the name of God rather than the exorcist himself. (Christ had given his disciples the power to exorcize in the name of Jesus, so there was no question among either Catholics or Protestants regarding the ultimate source of the expulsion.) In one notable Protestant dispossession, Edward Nyndge, who held an MA in divinity from Cambridge, actually used the word 'conjure' in his effort to get the Devil to vacate the body of his afflicted brother, Alexander. Amidst much praying for his brother's deliverance, Edward addressed the demon by saying: 'Thou foul fiend, I conjure thee, in the name of Jesus our Saviour, the son of Almighty God, that thou speak unto us.'[88]

The only Calvinist cleric who tried to establish regular procedures for conducting exorcisms was Jáanos Samarjai, a Hungarian minister who published a set of regulations for both Calvinists and Lutherans in 1636. Although Samarjai took pains to distinguish the Protestant from the Catholic ritual, he nonetheless prescribed words of exorcism and identified the psalms and prayers to be recited during the ceremony. His liturgy, even if was inspired by Scripture in the Protestant fashion, showed a Calvinist accommodation of traditional Catholic practice.[89]

Interrogation

Once the demon had been adjured and commanded to speak, the main task of the exorcist was to discover his identity. This task, which in judicial practice today is secured by asking the defendant simply to state his or her name, was far more challenging in the case of demonic possession, since it was the name of the demon, not that of its human host, that the exorcist wished to obtain. Although theologians had given demons many different names, exorcism offered the only means to obtain confirmation of those names from the demons themselves, who as spirits without the corporeal equipment to utter words themselves, could speak only through the human beings whose bodies they occupied.

Identifying the demon(s) was just the first step in the interrogation that lay at the centre of the exorcism. As the symptoms of possession became more complex in the late Middle Ages, especially when they began to include speaking in foreign tongues and blaspheming, the interrogation became more complex. This was especially the case in the early modern period, when exorcism served the purpose of Catholic propaganda. One consequence of this development was that exorcisms, which in Christian antiquity were relatively brief, would often continue for days or weeks.[90] During this process the exorcist would make every effort to suggest to the demoniac the information he endeavoured to secure from the demon. There was a deep suspicion, especially among sceptics, that demoniacs spoke in languages of which they had no previous knowledge simply by repeating phrases that the exorcists first articulated. It is no coincidence that Latin was the main language of Catholic exorcism. The same sceptics also claimed that the exorcists suggested to the demoniac the names of the demons occupying their bodies.

When exorcists for whatever reason could not extract the information they desired from the demoniacs, they often sought to obtain it by reading the gestures and bodily movements of the afflicted person, interpreting these as signs of the Devil's nature, power, and even his identity. The belief that the Devil could not speak but conveyed information on his nature and power through signs, such as diseases and natural disasters, led exorcists to read the body of the demoniac as a text. This was much more common in Catholicism than in Protestantism, which was much less concerned with the physical symptoms of possession.[91] Michel de Certeau has argued that the demonological knowledge of exorcists thereby enabled them to turn the silence of these afflicted persons into language.[92]

Although interrogation of the demon remained the central feature of Catholic exorcisms during the early modern period, a number of demonologists argued against its use on the grounds that the information extracted from the Father of Lies, as John 8: 44 had referred to the Devil, could not be trusted. Jean Bodin, Nicolas Rémy, and Martín Del Rio all cautioned against the practice, and the churches of both Protestant

England and Catholic Spain specifically condemned it. Despite these discouragements, the practice of interrogating demoniacs continued, and it remained a main feature of the rituals included in late sixteenth-century exorcism manuals.[93] Even demonologists recognized its value in certain circumstances, warning only against interrogation of the demon out of 'curiosity'.[94]

One of the main reasons for the persistence of interrogation was the need to obtain information on the identity of witches, who were often considered to have caused possessions. Only in the late seventeenth century did demonologists and judges come to the conclusion, especially in the wake of the Salem witch-hunt of 1692, that demoniacs could not be trusted to reveal the names of the witches who afflicted them because neither the testimony of the Devil nor his appearance as a spectre could be trusted.[95] This realization played an important role in ending witchcraft prosecutions, and it also explains the reduction in the number of cases of possession in the late seventeenth century.

Physical force

A reluctance to interrogate the Devil might help to account for the increasing use of physical force against demoniacs in early modern exorcisms. Torturing the demon, like interrogating him, had its origin in Roman judicial practice. Interrogation and torture have always been closely related. In Roman law, if a suspect of low social status was recalcitrant, he could be put to the question, that is, tortured, in order to extract the truth. In late antiquity exorcists sometimes used physical force against demoniacs on the assumption that they were torturing the demon rather than the demoniac whose body he controlled.[96] This procedure gradually died out in the Middle Ages, as both Church and state forbade the use of judicial torture.[97] When, however, torture was reintroduced in both secular and ecclesiastical courts in the thirteenth century, the harsh if not violent treatment of demoniacs once again gained favour. The practice was justified by the flawed theory that a person (or in this case the demon occupying the human body) will always tell the truth under duress and by the belief that the scourging of the body could save a person's soul. Contemporary opinion was divided on the legitimacy of this harsh technique. The Spanish Jesuit theologian Thomas Sanchez argued that it was superstitious to use it directly to expel the demon from the body of the possessed but legitimate if it was intended to wound the pride of the demon and persuade him to vacate the human body voluntarily.[98]

Early modern demoniacs were never subjected to the instruments of judicial torture, but exorcists did occasionally resort to physical violence in an effort to expel the possessing demon. In most cases this involved beating the demoniac, while in others it led to a physical struggle with the possessed. In an exorcism witnessed by Michel de Montaigne in Rome in 1581, the priest railed at the demoniac, 'dealing the poor wretch heavy blows with his fist, and spitting in his face'.[99] During the exorcism of Madeleine Demandols in 1611, spectators were invited to tread on the demoniac.[100] At Louviers in 1643 Bishop Péricard beat one of the possessed nuns to make Leviathan, the demon that had allegedly possessed her, enter a hole to find a charm that witches had allegedly used to cause her possession.[101] The English playwright Thomas Killigrew, who observed the exorcisms at Loudun, saw a priest step on the breast of one of the nuns, strike her as she lay on her back with her heels under her buttocks, and then 'set his foot upon her throat, commanding the devil to explain why he lay in that strange posture.'[102] In some modern exorcisms, especially those in charismatic religious communities, exorcism has resulted in the death of the demoniac.[103] This harsh physical treatment of demoniacs has been justified as retaliation for the tortures and 'torments' that the Devil inflicted on the possessed, such as throwing them to the ground, piercing their bodies, and threatening to tear them to pieces.[104] Claims that the demon sometimes assaulted the exorcist provided further justification for such physical retaliation.[105]

The use of violence to cast out demons was predicated on the assumption that body and soul, matter and spirit, were intimately connected and that disciplining or punishing the body could have a beneficial effect on the soul. This assumption, which was stronger in Catholicism than in Protestantism, explains the practice of prescribing physical penance for sins, the infliction of corporal punishment for moral crimes, and the practice of self-flagellation. Using this belief to justify violence against demoniacs, however, pushed the theory to its limits, since the exorcist assaulted a human body not to benefit the demoniac's soul but to expel an incorporeal spirit that was believed to have taken control of the person's body.

Considered as a lens through which one can study changing gender relations in early modern Europe, the use of physical force by male exorcists against female demoniacs conforms to a broader early modern pattern in which men beat their wives with impunity and communities removed troublesome women from their midst by prosecuting them or lynching them for witchcraft. However much such violence might have been justified on the grounds that the exorcist was really fighting the Devil, it remained an act of violence against a person who almost never had the physical strength of the exorcist himself. In the history of medicine the use of violence in exorcisms, the purpose of which was to heal the demoniac patient, fits into a pattern of subjecting the ill, especially the mentally ill, to harsh if not brutal treatment. One example of this abusive treatment is that demoniacs, like those diagnosed as mentally ill, were often tied down during their convulsions or fits. Such treatment of mental patients was once justified as using the body to cure the mind, which is a modern, secular variant on the traditional belief that disciplining the body benefits the soul.[106]

Sacred objects

The most distinctive feature of public Catholic exorcisms in France and Germany during the period of the Counter-Reformation was their use of consecrated communion hosts and other sacred or blessed objects to prove that only the Catholic Church had the power to perform the miracle of casting out demons. The use of the host was also intended to prove that Christ was really present in the Eucharist, as Catholics claimed. At the same time these exorcisms were intended to expose the inability of Protestants to achieve the same miraculous results.

The Eucharist became central to Catholic exorcisms only when Protestants challenged the Catholic doctrine of transubstantiation. If, as Catholics believed, the consecrated host was really and substantially the body and blood of Christ, it was a potent method of casting out demons. The Eucharist was often exhibited in a monstrance at the site of the exorcism, as the local priest did at Belmonte during a mass possession in the early seventeenth century.[107] More often it was administered to the demoniac, usually before the ceremony began after she had made her confession, which was another sacrament of the Catholic Church. Despite official Vatican disapproval of this method of exorcism, on the grounds that exorcists should not use the Divine Presence to conjure evil spirits, exorcists continued to use the Eucharist in exorcisms throughout the seventeenth century.[108] The priest appointed to exorcize Jeanne Féry in 1584 pressed the host firmly on her body.[109]

The display and administration of the Eucharist may have been central to many of the public exorcisms of the period, but it was far more common to place sacred objects on the body of the demoniac. One practice was to tie the naked demoniac to a holy candle the length of Christ's body or the trunk of the cross as the priest made a verbal declaration of exorcism.[110] Sprinkling the demoniac with holy water was another common method, although Aquinas had claimed this practice was only effective against external obsession, not possession. In many instances exorcists used holy water in conjunction with other types of water to test the authenticity of the possession. In the exorcism of Apolonia Geisslbrecht in 1582, the exorcists used holy water, baptismal water, and ordinary water in the ceremony not only to cure but also to test the demoniac. The substitution of unblessed for consecrated wine also served as a test to determine the reality of the possession.

Other traditional procedures included the demoniac's holding a blessed candle and the placement of crucifixes, images of the saints, or relics on the body of the afflicted person.[111] The exorcism of one sixteenth-century German demoniac involved the use of a piece of what was claimed to be the true cross as well as a crucifix blessed by the pope.[112] In the exorcism of Marthe Brossier the exorcists put relics of the true cross in the demoniac's mouth.[113] The vestments that priests used in saying the Mass were also believed to be conduits of sacred healing power. The priest's chasuble, the outer garment, might be laid on the body of a demoniac, whereas his stole was usually wrapped around the possessed person's neck. When an English Catholic exorcist 'turned his stole twice or thrice' around a demoniac's neck, the possessed boy asked him 'if he meant to hang him'.[114] One late medieval manuscript required that the demoniac actually be dressed in the chasuble and stole, while another required that the possessed be laid in front of an altar after Mass, inside a chalk diagram, with three stoles binding him.[115]

Protestants denied the inherent sacred quality of all these physical objects, just as they rejected the Catholic belief in the real presence of Christ in the Eucharist. Protestants regarded the use of holy water and other blessed objects as superstitious, condemned the cult of the saints, and viewed the clerical garments of the Catholic priesthood as symbolic of a sacerdotal power that priests did not have. The Swiss theologian Heinrich Bullinger had many of these procedures in mind when he condemned the methods of Catholic exorcists as 'ridiculous and absurd'. 'Why,' asked Bullinger, 'must one stand the possessed person in a bath of cold water, throttle him with the chasuble or mass-vestments, and use many other follies?'[116]

Other follies to which Bullinger referred included exorcisms by means of physical objects blessed by priests. The use of some of these materials, including herbs, salt, wine, rose-sugar, stones, and parchment, had originated in popular healing rituals. The pieces of parchment were often inscribed and then used as charms or amulets to be placed on the demoniac's body. By blessing these physical objects exorcists transformed natural or folk remedies into quasi-religious instruments of healing. It is difficult to distinguish between those methods that were part of, or at least resembled closely, an orthodox ecclesiastical tradition and those that were superstitious if not irreverent.[117] The use of holy water and blessed salt, which had been used in exorcisms as early as the ninth century,[118] fell into the former category, but amulets and purely natural remedies belonged in the latter category and were condemned by the Vatican in 1614. Jesuit priests in England in the late sixteenth century concocted potions of various ingredients that they then administered to demoniacs while they were bound to a chair. This drink made them giddy and led many of them to believe that they were in fact possessed.[119] Girolamo Menghi originally defended the practice of using medicinal herbs during exorcisms, but the Roman Inquisition censured him for doing so, and he reversed his position in the early seventeenth century.[120]

The only material object that Protestants were permitted to use in their rites of dispossession was the Bible itself, not because it was a physical object but because it contained the Word of God. In the effort to cast out the demon that was afflicting the Puritan demoniac Alexander Nyndge, a bible, open to the text of Luke 8: 26, in which Christ cast out an unclean spirit, was laid upon Alexander's body. This procedure bore an uncomfortable resemblance to the Catholic practice of laying relics, communion hosts, or priests' vestments on the demoniac. Protestants may have justified the use of the Bible in this way as an indication of their belief that only the power of Jesus, as expressed in the words of the synoptic Gospels, could cure demoniacs. But treating the Bible as a physical object was open to the criticism that it was just as superstitious as the Catholic practice of investing sacerdotal power in sacred objects. By being placed on the body of Alexander Nynge, the Bible became a quasi-magical object.[121]

Verbal remedies

Catholics, like Protestants, used prayer as a means of dispossession, but the prayers used in Catholic exorcisms were often not based on Scripture, and they included invocations to the saints that were anathema to Protestants. Particularly offensive in Protestant eyes was the invocation of the Virgin Mary, whose cult Protestants were determined to eliminate. Some exorcisms repeated the prayer 'Hail Mary' many times, and the Jesuit priest Peter Canisius, who wrote a massive scholarly tome on the cult of the Virgin Mary, began an exorcism at Altötting by invoking Mary's assistance.[122] Protestants argued that invocation of the saints violated the sovereignty of God, in whose name only dispossessions could be performed. It was indicative of Catholic practice that the Bavarian painter Christoph

Haizmann was exorcized at the shrine of the Blessed Virgin at Zell. In the Catholic areas of the Dutch Republic the invocation of the Virgin Mary was often added to the prescribed exorcism ritual.[123] One of the exorcisms in Menghi's *Flagellum daemonum* mentions the Virgin Mary three times in the first paragraph of the ritual, while the revelation of the names of the demons possessing Elizabeth de Ranfaing during her exorcism in 1619 was attributed to the power of the Virgin Mary.[124] Getting the demon to say the name of the Blessed Virgin remains a part of Catholic exorcisms today.[125] Other invocations that never received official approval were those that used names of God drawn from various Jewish or Greek sources.

Many of these invocations were included in the exorcist manuals published in the late sixteenth and early seventeenth centuries. Most were published in Italy, where exorcisms were performed more frequently than in any other part of Europe. The most prominent of these manuals were compiled by Girolamo Menghi. In 1572 Menghi published *Compendio dell'arte essorcistica*, a demonological treatise that promoted exorcism as the main means of countering the effects of witchcraft. He wrote this book in the vernacular so that it could reach a broad audience of parish priests within Italy. Menghi subsequently published three more manuals, *Flagellum daemonum* [The Scourge of Demons] (1576), *Fustis daemonum* [The Cudgel of Demons] (1584) and *Fuga daemonum* [The Banishment of Demons] (1596) in Latin so that they might reach a larger European audience.[126] The first two of these Latin manuals were republished, together with four others by Italian authors, in the *Thesaurus exorcismorum*, a massive tome of more than 1,200 pages, compiled by Menghi and Valerio Polidori and first published in 1608.[127] Two of the other four manuals included in this anthology were written by Polidori, while Zacharia Visconti's *Complementum artis exorcisticae* (Venice, 1600) and Petro Antonio Stampa's *Fuga Satanae* (Venice, 1605) rounded out the collection.

Most of the exorcisms in the *Thesaurus* consist of verbal formulae that the exorcist could use to cast out demons. In these formulae Protestants found further evidence that the exorcist was acting in the manner of a ritual magician. Of course Protestants also used words in their efforts to cast out demons. One German Protestant noted perceptively in 1592 that the main difference between Catholic and Protestant exorcisms was that in Protestantism the spoken words were not thought to have any intrinsic occult power.[128] Protestantism was of course a religion of the Word, but that was the Word of God in Scripture.

The first serious effort to eliminate superstitious and magical exorcisms in early modern Europe was made by Heinrich Kramer, the author of the *Malleus maleficarum*. Claiming that many methods of exorcism were illegal as well as ineffective, Kramer proposed specific requirements to meet the test of legality. In particular he insisted that the words used in exorcisms should not include any express or tacit invocation of the Devil and that blessings used in the ceremony contain no unknown names.[129] Kramer's emphasis on what was lawful (the natural concern of an inquisitor), coupled with the difficulty or unwillingness of ecclesiastical authorities to discipline offenders, did little to end or even reduce the incidence of the practices he condemned. Many of the methods of exorcism he deplored found their way into the manuals that were published in the late sixteenth and early seventeenth centuries, when the emphasis on using verbal formulae against the demon became popular.[130] Despite papal disfavour, the semi-official exorcisms publicized by Menghi and reprinted in various seventeenth-century anthologies retained their popularity, leading the Vatican to place them on the Index of Prohibited Books in the eighteenth century.[131] In Brazil two exorcist manuals by the friar Candido Brognolo also retained their popularity after they had been banned.[132]

Protestant exorcists sometimes mimicked Catholic practice, even though they denied such imitation. They occasionally adjured the Devil, asking him to identify himself and say who sent him, as was the custom in Catholic rituals. When Martin Luther, who was highly critical of the Catholic rite, tried unsuccessfully to exorcize a young girl from Meissen in the sacristy of the Wittenberg parish church, he nonetheless followed the Catholic practice of putting the Devil on oath.[133] In 1574 the two Protestant ministers who presided over the dispossession of Mildred Norrington in Westwell, Kent went further than Luther when they 'commanded Satan in the name of the eternal God and his son Jesus Christ, to speak with such a voice as they might understand, and to declare from whence he came'. After a long series of exchanges the demon replied that his name was Satan and that Alice Norrington, Mildred's mother, with whom he had been for twenty years, had sent him into her bastard daughter. He also disclosed that Alice had kept him in two bottles under the wall of her house.[134]

In dispossessing John Fox at Nottingham in the early seventeenth century, the Puritan minister Richard Rothwell also engaged in a dialogue with the demon. A later commentator on this episode observed that such dialogues were common among Catholic exorcists but rare among Protestants.[135] Another such instance occurred in the late seventeenth century, when English Dissenting ministers interrogated Satan in their effort to dispossess Richard Dugdale in Lancashire.[136]

When Protestant exorcists adopted the Catholic practice of commanding a demon to depart in the name of God, they rendered themselves vulnerable to the charge by more orthodox Protestants that they, like Roman Catholics, were commanding the demon in the manner of a necromancer.[137] When the Protestant alchemist and ritual magician John Dee tried unsuccessfully to exorcize Ann Frank, a nurse in his household, he gave credence to this identification of exorcism and magic. Dee 'anointed (in the name of Jesus) . . . her breast with the holy oil' to drive out the demons.[138] It is not surprising that Dee, who had been ordained a Catholic priest at the age of twenty-six before converting to Protestantism, used holy oil, a sacramental, in the manner of a Catholic exorcist. In his private diary Dee admitted that he learned the procedure from reading Menghi's exorcist manual, *Flagellum daemonum*.

The effectiveness of exorcisms

In the propaganda war between Catholics and Protestants over demonic possession, Catholics had a distinct advantage, in that they gained a reputation as being far more successful than Protestants in their efforts to exorcize demons. Testimony by demoniacs that Catholic exorcists had cured them provided the main evidence for Catholic success. Further evidence comes from the fact that people suffering from medical conditions, having heard of other dispossessions, actively sought out Catholic exorcists in the hope of a cure. Indeed, the belief that the seventeenth-century exorcist Giovanni Battista Chiesa actually healed demoniacs provides a plausible explanation for his fame throughout Piedmont. This confidence also explains why some Protestants, including a man in Calvinist Geneva in 1578, enlisted the services of Catholic exorcists.[139] Protestants sometimes freely admitted their failure to drive out demons and conceded that Catholic exorcists were better at their job than they were.[140] To be sure, Catholics also experienced failures, or at least protracted difficulties, in their efforts to cast out demons. In 1554 a French exorcist could not expel the demons that had possessed eighty-two women in Rome, and in 1666 Anna Mayer needed to be exorcized 120 times at Altötting before the seven demons vacated her body.[141] But there is little doubt that the success rate for Catholics was much higher than for Protestants.[142] Catholics were conscious of this competitive advantage and boasted about their success. Referring to Martin Luther's failed exorcism more than fifty years after the fact, the French Jesuit Louis Richeome boasted that neither Luther 'nor any heretic has never been able to do such exploits as our exorcists do against devils'.[143]

One explanation for the apparent success of Catholics in casting out demons is that they were able to inspire confidence that their rituals actually worked. The elaborate rituals of Catholicism assured demoniacs that something was being done to relieve their afflictions, and this assurance made it more likely that the possessed would find some sort of relief. By contrast, the Protestant biblically sanctioned methods of prayer and fasting were too laborious and contingent on divine intervention to inspire confidence that demoniacs would find quick relief of their suffering.[144]

A second reason for the greater effectiveness of Catholic exorcisms was that the Catholic ritual constantly reinforced the belief that the Devil was responsible for demoniacs' misfortunes. This reinforcement, which was absent from Protestant dispossessions after the original diagnosis, could at least have relieved the anxieties of those who were afflicted. In his study of Chiesa, Giovanni Levi has argued that exorcism was essential in societies that needed to explain illness and misfortune. Convincing people that demons were the source of such misfortune could bring immediate relief to the afflicted.[145] Of course the expectation that Chiesa would in fact cure his clients could also have been a self-fulfilling prophecy. Those who travelled to meet him and paid for his services wanted to believe that they were cured, and some of them apparently were.

The Hanoverian physician Johann Georg Zimmermann, who denied the reality of possession, attributed Johann Joseph Gassner's success to his charismatic authority. Zimmermann was 'well persuaded that Gassner cured the nerve-sick by means of his extraordinary mastery over the imagination and nerves of ordinary people'.[146] To claim that he was a practitioner of psychological healing is a fair assessment of his skill. Gassner was undoubtedly aware that his techniques influenced his clients' state of mind. It is not surprising therefore that the historian of psychiatry Henri Ellenberger views Gassner as an exemplar of the primitive form of healing from which modern dynamic psychotherapy emerged.[147]

The only Protestants who registered a significant degree of success in driving out demons belonged to the more enthusiastic sects, such as the English Puritans, the English Dissenters after the Restoration and the Methodists in the eighteenth century.[148] The dramatic exorcisms conducted by John Darrell in the 1590s, which the clerical establishment claimed were popish, provide a good example of how Protestants could also heal the illness of demonic possession. The main difference between men like Darrell and Catholic exorcists in this regard is that Protestant ministers set out to cure the soul rather than the body. Protestants always emphasized the spiritual as opposed to the physical symptoms of possession. Possession for Protestants was more a struggle against demonic temptation and an effort to win the soul of the demoniac than an attempt to bring relief from the physical torments that the Devil inflicted. Protestant dispossession was therefore an effort to help the demoniac overcome temptation and prepare for the reception of God's grace. The healing was spiritual both in the methods employed and the desired end. As 'physicians of the soul' Protestant exorcists tried to win over troubled minds, to relieve the religious melancholy that Robert Burton described. They sought to turn the mind of the afflicted person to sin and thus prepare the demoniac for a true conversion and rebirth in Christ.[149]

The effectiveness of Catholic exorcisms helps to explain the increase in demand for them, and that demand created a psychological disposition in the demoniac that was conducive to a cure. This demand also explains why there were so many Catholic possessions; there is little evidence of a corresponding Protestant demand. This Catholic demand, like possession itself, has a long history. Many of the demoniacs in late antiquity came to the shrines of the saints to be exorcized because they believed they were possessed. The same was true of demoniacs in the Middle Ages. The wave of possessions in Belmonte in the late sixteenth century was fuelled in large part by the demand of the inhabitants to be exorcized. In 1861 ninety-three possessed French women in Morzine who believed that they had been possessed by means of witchcraft pleaded for a collective exorcism.[150] This demand continues today and is the main reason why the Catholic Church has felt obliged to train a new generation of exorcists.

CHAPTER 5

Demonic Possession and Illness

Tʜᴇ ᴄʟᴀɪᴍ ᴛʜᴀᴛ ᴅᴇᴍᴏɴɪᴀᴄs were 'really' suffering from a medical condition that had 'natural' causes—from an organic disease or a mental illness—has been the most consistent secular, rationalist analysis of demonic possession since the period of Christian antiquity.[1] This interpretation of demonic possession has served the purposes of sceptics from the Middle Ages to the nineteenth century, and it has continued to serve the purposes of psychiatrists in the past one hundred and fifty years. It has also appealed to biblical scholars who have refused to accept a literalist interpretation of the exorcism narratives in the New Testament.

This chapter will argue that while some demoniacs were probably suffering from various illnesses or mental disorders, only some cases of possession, and none of those that were experienced in large groups, can be explained in this way. This chapter will argue further that in those cases where a medical diagnosis seems appropriate or plausible, the illness with which the possession was identified cannot account for *all* the symptoms that the demoniac displayed, especially those that reflected the religious cultures in which the demoniacs were immersed. In these cases the medical diagnosis usually can explain only the initial manifestation of the person's possession.

The contention that all possessions had natural, medical causes did not gain widespread support until the nineteenth century. The only European thinkers who subscribed to, or even flirted with, such a radical view before the advent of positivism in the late nineteenth century were Reginald Scot, Thomas Hobbes, Baruch Spinoza, and Balthasar Bekker. Most of the other 'sceptics', including the English clerics John Deacon and Samuel Harsnett, the 'enlightened' Spanish monk Benito Feijóo, and the German biblical scholar Johann Salomo Semler, carefully avoided making such a categorical statement, while the otherwise sceptical demonologist Johann Weyer attributed some possessions to direct demonic invasion. One reason for the reluctance of writers to make such a categorical denial of demonic power was the belief that the Devil worked *through* nature; that he was in fact the ultimate cause of all illness.[2] This belief made it possible for commentators to argue that the symptoms of possession had both natural and supernatural causes, especially when they identified the disorder as madness.[3]

The persistence of the belief in the demonic origin of all diseases is illustrated in the career of Giovan Battista Chiesa, who exorcized hundreds of patients in Piedmont in the late seventeenth century. In contrast to the claims of many Italian physicians of his day, who in the tradition of Hippocrates sought to identify the natural causes of the illnesses they treated, Chiesa claimed that all illnesses had a demonic or supernatural origin. Demonic causation was most readily apparent when physicians could not identify a natural cause of an illness or disease; that referrals of demoniacs to Chiesa helped to preserve their own medical reputations for diagnostic reliability. But when the natural cause of a disease was known, such as when a tumour developed in the place where a man had been hit by a musket volley, Chiesa claimed that the ultimate cause of the illness was the decision by the Devil, working through natural causes, to visit this misfortune on this particular person. This assignment of ultimate responsibility to the Devil (and never to a witch) not only justified the exorcism but also confirmed the prevailing popular belief that all illness had demonic origins. And since most of the people in Piedmont suffered from some sort of illness or disease, Chiesa could confidently state that 'Out of ten thousand of us, nine thousand are possessed by the Devil.'[4]

In the nineteenth century Chiesa's way of thinking about the relationship between the natural and the supernatural realms gave way to a rationalist, positivist conviction that supernatural forces had not influenced the course of human history. This secular outlook, while defensible as a historiographical assumption, has had two deleterious effects on the study of demonic possession in centuries past. First, it has prevented scholars from appreciating the role played by demoniacs' religious beliefs and anxieties in causing their afflictions. Second, it has led scholars to interpret the experiences of early modern demoniacs in terms of psychiatric models formulated in more recent times. The premise for such interpretations is that such models have universal applicability, a premise that both cultural historians and cultural anthropologists reject. All illnesses, including what was then called demonic possession, are socially constructed and can be understood only if they are studied in the cultural context in which they took place.

Medical explanations of possession

From the time of Christ until the eighteenth century a dominant tradition within Christianity attributed all illnesses to demons, and the passages in the New Testament describing Christ's exorcisms were widely understood in those terms. When medieval and early modern Christian writers claimed that demoniacs were suffering from diseases caused by the Devil, they usually attributed their torments to one of three diseases known to physicians in ancient, medieval, and early modern times: epilepsy, melancholy, and hysteria. The first two of these maladies were believed to have had a supernatural dimension and could therefore be considered as having a demonic or supernatural origin. Hysteria, on the other hand, steadily resisted such supernatural interpretation and therefore became the preferred explanation of possession in modern times.

Epilepsy

The medical diagnosis of demoniacs as epileptics held the greatest appeal to biblical scholars and physicians who wished to accommodate their medical knowledge with their religious beliefs. Ever since the sixteenth century the boy exorcized by Christ in Mark 9: 14–29 has been identified as an epileptic. Like others suffering from the illness, the boy could not speak, foamed at the mouth, ground his teeth, fell to the ground, lost consciousness, and tried to commit suicide. Matthew probably also had epilepsy in mind when he used *seleniazetai*, the Greek word for 'moonstruck', to describe the boy's condition, since it was believed that the Moon was a source of epilepsy. The literal translation of Matthew's description of the boy's illness is that he was a lunatic, which is the way in which the Vulgate and the King James Version of the Bible translated the word. In the early modern period lunacy as well as epilepsy was considered an alternative diagnosis of demonic possession.

Although many early modern physicians diagnosed epilepsy as a natural disease, others believed that it was caused by the Devil. In ancient Greece epilepsy became known as 'the sacred disease', because it was believed that the gods caused it. In his treatise on epilepsy, *On the Sacred Disease*, the Greek physician Hippocrates (*c.* 460–*c.* 370 BCE) challenged this supernatural diagnosis, attributing its popular name to magicians and others who were ignorant of its true causes.[5] The word epilepsy could also be taken to indicate demonic origin, since it was derived from the Greek word for seizure, and being seized in Greek meant being taken by a *daimon*.[6] Some early modern Europeans argued that *all* demonic possessions were cases of epilepsy. In 1602 Jean Taxil, a physician from Arles, who never wavered in his belief that the Devil was the cause of possession, wrote that it was almost impossible to find a case of a demoniac who was not an epileptic; the cause of the epileptics' violent convulsions was the Devil's fury.[7]

Besides experiencing recurrent convulsions, epileptics became speechless, lost consciousness, and fell to the ground. They foamed at the mouth and clenched their teeth. Their tongues often protruded, and their bodies became contorted. They reacted violently, kicking in all directions, sometimes harming themselves, and they occasionally tried to commit suicide.

The problem with a diagnosis of epilepsy as demonic possession in early modern Europe was that it could not explain the full repertory of symptoms of possession, especially those that were verbal and behavioural. Speaking in languages unknown to the demoniac, showing contempt for sacred objects, and prophesying could not easily be attributed to a disease that involved a loss of consciousness. This was the main reason why the French physician Michel Marescot dismissed epilepsy as a possible explanation of the possession of Marthe Brossier, who never fell to the ground during her possession and who retained her senses throughout the entire experience.[8] It also explains why early modern physicians who proposed natural explanations for the phenomenon, such as Jean Riolan (1538–1606) and Edward Jorden (1569–1632), preferred to attribute possession to either melancholy or hysteria, both of which covered a wider range of symptoms and did not result in a loss of consciousness.[9]

The failure of epilepsy to provide a plausible explanation for the behavioural symptoms of possession became evident in a case discussed by the highly respected French physician Jean Fernel (1485–1558). In his treatise on the causes of diseases Fernel explained that the afflictions of an unidentified nobleman's son that were first thought to be the result of the natural disease of epilepsy were actually caused by the Devil's possession of the young man. Fernel offered this revised diagnosis when the boy started speaking in Latin and Greek, reacted in horror on seeing that his father was wearing a medal of St Michael, and was offended at the reading of Scripture.[10] Fernel's demonic diagnosis persuaded the English physician John Cotta that the Devil could in fact possess a human being.[11] But the main implication of Fernel's analysis was that demonic possession could not be equated with epilepsy or any other neurological disease, since epilepsy, as understood at the time, did not affect the person's cognitive abilities.

This failure to account for other symptoms besides convulsions, contortions, foaming at the mouth, and falling to the ground explains why the diagnosis of the possession of Thomas Darling, a thirteen-year-old boy from Burton upon Trent, as a case of epilepsy did not win widespread support. Darling, who was exorcized by the Puritan minister John Darrell in 1596, experienced a succession of fits consistent with those of epileptics, but epilepsy could not provide a plausible explanation for Darling's vomiting or his visions of a green angel and a green cat. Nor could epilepsy explain Darling's ecstasies, which were comparable to those of many French women who aspired to sanctity. Indeed, Darling's insistence that he had the spirit of God in him raised serious questions about whether he was undergoing a good or a demonic possession.[12] Melancholy offered a much more persuasive interpretation of Darling's religious experience.

Melancholy

In the thirteenth century, when demoniacs began to exhibit verbal and behavioural symptoms, such as speaking in unknown languages, uttering curses and blasphemies, reacting to sacred objects with horror, having visions, and foreseeing the future, the claim that demoniacs suffered from melancholy became an alternative to that of epilepsy. By the late sixteenth century, when possession reached epidemic proportions, melancholy had become the diagnosis of choice among physicians in cases of possession.[13] In fact melancholy, which was reported to be widespread if not epidemic in early modern Europe, was considered the 'fountain of almost all other diseases' affecting society.[14] It was also viewed as more than a disease. At the time of the Renaissance, theologians, writers, and natural philosophers adopted this body of medical knowledge and diagnosis to explain a wide variety of life experiences. In this way melancholy became 'one of the fundamental axes of Renaissance culture'.[15] Although melancholy acquired a reputation as 'the English malady', it was by no means restricted to England.[16]

As defined by physicians in the sixteenth and seventeenth centuries, melancholy was a somatic disorder that affected the imagination and the emotions, giving rise to anxiety, depression, fear, sorrow, sadness, and chronic fatigue. It often struck those who had experienced the loss of a loved one. It was also believed to be a source of ecstasy, visions, hallucinations, and delusions, and therefore was often identified as a cause of madness or delirium. Although some writers identified a form of melancholy as a source of genius and literary inspiration, physicians who wrote about the condition emphasized its negative physiological and psychological effects.[17] It makes sense therefore that it should have become the preferred early modern medical explanation of demonic possession. To be sure, epilepsy was never ruled out as a cause, especially when the victim experienced seizures, lost consciousness, and fell to the ground. But melancholy provided a more plausible explanation of the verbal and behavioural symptoms of possession that attracted the greatest attention in the early modern period. One indication of its prominence in the medical discourse of the day is that in 1614 the papacy took pains to distinguish genuine demoniacs from 'those who suffer from melancholia or any other illness'.[18] This distinction was based on the belief that the two interpretations of possession were incompatible. The strategy of the papacy in dealing with possession, like that of the Spanish physician Andrés Velásquez, was to look for natural explanations of illness and, when not finding them, attribute them to the Devil's supernatural powers.[19]

The French physician Michel Marescot's analysis of the case of Marthe Brossier in 1598 illustrates the appeal of melancholy as the preferred medical diagnosis of demonic possession. Marescot dismissed both epilepsy and hysteria as explanations of Brossier's condition, the former because the young woman did not lose consciousness and the latter because she never experienced shortness of breath, the condition caused by choking that led to hysteria's being called 'the suffocation of the mother' in English.[20] But Marescot did believe that Marthe was delusional and hence melancholic, as she had imagined that she was possessed by the Devil. This melancholy was compatible with Marescot's main interpretation that Brossier was a fraud, since 'melancholic persons are both deluded and cunning'.[21] Jean Riolan made a similar diagnosis of possession in 1610, as did the anonymous French doctor who was asked to provide a medical analysis of the possessions at Louviers in 1647.[22] The sceptical English demonologist Reginald Scot, a contemporary of Marescot, also recognized that melancholy could 'move imaginations' and thus cause delusions.[23] Scot claimed that 'the melancholic humour (as the best physicians affirm)' was the source of the 'strange, impossible, and incredible confessions' made by witches.[24]

Ever since ancient times physicians, following Hippocrates and Galen, had believed that melancholy was caused by an imbalance of black bile, one of the four humours in the human body that determined personality. (The others were blood, phlegm, and choler or yellow bile.)[25] Thus the illness was believed to originate in the spleen. This natural explanation of melancholy, however, competed with a supernatural interpretation in which the Devil was considered its ultimate cause. This latter, demonic interpretation, which was employed mainly in the early modern period to explain the effect of the malady on the imagination, explains why it was often called 'the Devil's bath', a term first used by St Jerome in the fourth century. Since the disease was considered a source of despair, it was readily seen as a fitting instrument of the Devil.[26] It was also seen as a preparative to possession, in that the Devil used it to create emotional unease in the demoniacs he attacked either externally or internally.[27] The Italian exorcist Zacharia Visconti claimed that the Devil, by influencing one's humours, could blur one's senses, make one mute and deaf and generally make one sick with melancholy.[28] The Jesuit biblical commentator Cornelius à Lapide explained that 'The Devil utilizes bodily dispositions toward illness, notably melancholy, as no other bodily substance is as suited to the Devil's designs as is melancholy.'[29]

As with epilepsy, interpretations of melancholy as both natural and demonic were not necessarily incompatible. In his treatise on witchcraft, the Italian inquisitor Francesco Maria Guazzo asked rhetorically 'Is it not possible for sickness to spring from natural causes, and at the same time possible for demons to be the instigation of such sicknesses?'[30] According to Guazzo, Satan induced melancholy by first disturbing the black bile in the body and then dispersing the black humour that resulted from this agitation into the brain and from there throughout the inner cells of the body. In *Anatomy of Melancholy* the English author Robert Burton, who argued ambivalently that the general causes of melancholy 'are either supernatural or natural', cited a number of Renaissance medical and religious authorities, including the Swiss theologian Ludwig Lavater, who made the same argument as Guazzo. Burton, who cites Lavater frequently, claimed that the Devil mingled himself with the humour emanating from black bile whenever it was found 'in extremity', especially in those persons 'who are most subject to diabolical temptations and illusions'.[31]

Some physicians, such as the neo-Aristotelian natural philosopher Pietro Pomponazzi (1462–1525), studied melancholy from a strictly naturalist position in the tradition of Hippocrates and Galen. In his treatise on natural effects, Pomponazzi claimed that the occult qualities of nature, not the Devil, caused harm and disease. Having already caused a major scandal in 1516 by denying the immortality of the soul, Pomponazzi went further in this work, which was written in 1520 but not published until 1556, by denying the reality of miracles and the existence of demons.[32] A number of Spanish physicians and many of the doctors trained in German universities in the sixteenth and seventeenth centuries took a similar naturalist position.[33] Because of this naturalism, late medieval and early modern physicians ran the risk of being called atheists. The old saying 'Where there are three physicians, there are two atheists' originated in late medieval Europe.[34]

The majority of physicians in the sixteenth and seventeenth centuries, however, expressed greater ambivalence regarding the nature of melancholy and the causes of possession.[35] In 1558 the Spanish physician Pedro de Mercado published a dialogue between a physician, a theologian, and a melancholic in which the naturalist and the demonic interpretations of melancholy were given equal billing.[36] The seventeenth-century English physician Richard Napier diagnosed most of his patients who claimed to be possessed by the Devil as melancholics, but he concluded that eighteen of them were actually possessed by demons.[37]

The writings of the Dutch physician Levinus Lemnius (1505–68) shows how reluctant even physicians trained in the Hippocratic and Galenic naturalist tradition were to abandon a demonic interpretation of melancholy and possession. Like Pomponazzi, Lemnius attributed demonic possession to 'melancholy, frenzy, madness, epilepsy, and horrible diseases that in the case of young women and widows clearly result from uterine disturbances'. These disturbances caused 'dark and dense' vapours, which gave the appearance that these people were diabolically possessed. Although he insisted that 'the humours, not bad angels cause diseases', Lemnius admitted that demons could nonetheless aggravate the symptoms of disease, by positioning themselves close to the patient's body and inter-mingling with the person's food, humours, and breath, thereby intensifying their symptoms.[38] Another Dutch physician trained in the same tradition as Lemnius, Jason Pratensis, offered a similar demonological interpretation of disease.[39]

In his demonological treatise, *De praestigiis daemonum* (1563), the Lutheran physician Johann Weyer also thought that the Devil, who could move body parts around and impress mental images on the imagination, could cause melancholy by mixing himself with the melancholic humour, i.e. that which was affected by an imbalance of black bile, which he found an 'extremely apt and convenient vehicle for the execution of his impos-tures'. This, according to Weyer, was an enterprise in which Satan took great delight.[40] The Devil was thus the ultimate cause of the melancholic's insanity. This view of melancholy as the product of demonic manipulation helps to explain how Weyer could attribute many possessions to natural diseases, especially melancholy, while at the same time arguing that a very powerful Devil could possess human beings of his own accord.

Weyer's position found support from the Spanish physician Francisco Vallés (1524–92), who was responsible for introducing a Christianized version of Galenic humoral theory in Spain. Vallés argued in *De sacra philosophia* that the Devil penetrated the body from the outside in order to excite the melancholic humour.[41] Even in the late seventeenth century, by which time most medical theorists of melancholy had denied its demonic source, the natural philosopher Joseph Glanvill, in his efforts to counteract the scepticism of a new breed of Sadducees, revived the belief that possession was caused by the Devil's manipulation of the melancholic humour.[42]

One reason why melancholy could readily accommodate a demonic interpretation, especially in the context of possession, was that one form of the malady was religious melancholy, a term coined by Robert Burton to describe the profound anxiety or even despair that often accompanied the quest for salvation.[43] It is clear that many demoniacs, especially those in Catholic convents or in Protestant households, began to manifest the symptoms of possession when grappling in one way or another with spiritual or moral concerns. Since melancholy was viewed primarily as a mental or emotional condition, it offered both a medical and a demono-logical explanation of what was happening when demoniacs displayed their pathological symptoms, especially when those symptoms indicated mental stress or illness.

Religious melancholy was particularly persuasive in analysing the relatively infrequent possessions of Calvinists, who were more preoccupied with fears of eternal damnation than Catholics, Lutherans, or Anglicans and were more likely to have despaired of attaining salvation. Some Calvinist demoniacs, like Robert Brigges in 1584 and Joan Drake in 1647, were convinced that they had committed an unpardonable sin against the Holy Ghost and soon after displayed some of the symptoms of posses-sion. Other demoniacs, such as Christian Shaw, became possessed while undergoing conversion experiences in which they acknowledged their sinfulness in preparation for the possible reception of God's freely granted grace. Many of these demoniacs contemplated suicide while trying to determine whether they were saved or damned. Giving pastoral care to such troubled souls was a major challenge for Calvinist ministers, who tried to convince them that only God knew whether they were predestined to eternal damnation or happiness.[44]

Catholic and Lutheran demoniacs also appeared to have been victims of religious melancholy. Catholics were unlikely to have despaired of their chances for salvation in the manner of Calvinists, but they nonethe-less harboured deep religious anxieties. Moshe Sluhovsky has argued that the possession of many French female demoniacs originated in their difficulty in dealing with religious transgressions, especially those of a sexual nature.[45] Jean Delumeau has provided examples of how the lived experiences of Catholics, no less than those of Protestants, illustrated the pervasiveness of religious anxiety during the period that the theologian Paul Tillich has referred to as the age of anxiety.[46]

Protestant possessions tended to be more concerned with soteriology, whereas Catholic possessions were more commonly caused by reactions to the rigours of the new spiritual discipline imposed by the Catholic Reformation. But depressive anxiety was rife in all religious denominations in the sixteenth and seventeenth centuries, and it is not unreasonable to consider it a significant contributor to the wave of demonic possessions in these emotionally fragile decades. It is no coincidence that the age of the demoniac was also the age of melancholy and that both coincided with the age of the Reformation.[47]

However appealing the interpretation of possession as an expression of melancholy might be, it proved of limited value to contemporaries, and of little or no value to modern scholars. In defending the reality of possessions Jean Bodin argued that melancholy could never have taught Greek, Hebrew, and Latin to demoniacs who spoke those languages but had never learned them.[48] In the wake of the possessions at Loudun the French physician and poet Hippolyte-Jules Pilet de la Ménardière wrote that neither melancholy nor any medical diagnosis of possession could be so broad as to comprehend the full range of symptoms exhibited by the Ursuline nuns.[49] Appealing to Aristotle's *Physics*, he rejected the argument that their symptoms could come from the black humour or any natural cause.[50] Ménardière had his own demonological axe to grind, but he was correct in his argument that the symptoms of possession were so varied that no one medical diagnosis could account for all of them. The German physician Johann Lange had made essentially the same argument in trying to explain the behaviour of forty-five demoniacs in Rome in 1554. Lange had argued that medicine could help to explain some of the somatic symptoms of possession, but that only the expulsion of demons could result in a complete cure.[51]

In particular, melancholy offered a relatively weak account of the physiological signs of possession, especially the convulsions, seizures, and contortions that other physicians had attributed to epilepsy. To be sure, some medieval medical writers had included sudden movement as one manifestation of melancholy, but most of the reported symptoms of melancholy were mental and emotional. Angus Gowland has explained that melancholy 'had direct reference in early modern Europe to forms of behaviour and experience that were emotional'.[52] It is no accident, moreover, that a large majority of the disorders that physicians attributed to melancholy in the sixteenth century were diagnosed as cases of insanity.

The diagnosis of demonic possession as melancholy continued through the seventeenth century, but it gradually gave way to a diagnosis of hysteria. The transition can be seen in the work of the English physician and religious writer Sir Thomas Browne. In his widely cited *Religio medici* (1642), Browne declared that 'the Devil doth really possess some men, the spirit of melancholy others, the spirit of delusion others'.[53] At a witchcraft trial in 1662, however, Browne argued that the demoniacs who accused witches of having caused their possession might well have been afflicted with hysteria rather than melancholy. Nevertheless, melancholy remained on the medical menu of possible causes of possession. As late as 1697 doctors called in to examine the young Scottish demoniac Christian Shaw diagnosed her condition as hypochondriac melancholy.[54]

The medical diagnosis of demoniacs as melancholics continued into the modern period, only to the extent that it was gradually assimilated to, and subsumed under, the broader neurological disease of hysteria. Melancholy lost aetiological significance and was reclassified as the modern disorder of depression.[55] In 1952 the papacy deleted melancholy from the list of natural illnesses that it had distinguished from true demonic possession in the seventeenth century.[56] The main reason for melancholy's failure to provide a persuasive explanation of what was 'really happening' in cases of possession was the difficulty physicians had in explaining how the imbalance of black bile caused the seizures, convulsions, and other physiological symptoms of possession.[57] In the final analysis, melancholy offered a plausible explanation of possession only when it was believed to be the Devil's bath.

Hysteria

The inability of melancholy to explain the full repertory of symptoms displayed by demoniacs helps to explain why physicians began to identify hysteria as the natural disease from which demoniacs suffered. A diagnosis of hysteria had the advantage of accommodating both the physiological and the behavioural symptoms of demonic possession. The history of the disease reveals its remarkable ability over the centuries to explain a wide range of symptoms. In the early modern period it offered a natural explanation of the seizures, fits, and contortions associated with epilepsy—a malady with which hysteria was often identified—as well as the anxieties and mental disorders that were symptomatic of melancholy. Its chameleon-like ability to mimic the symptoms of any other disease has led to the criticism that it is 'a diagnostic waste bin, a heterogeneous congeries of complaints cobbled together linguistically, mostly a testimony to medical myth-making, incomprehension and ignorance'.[58]

In light of this diagnostic flexibility, it is surprising that hysteria was not taken seriously as an explanation of demonic possession until the early seventeenth century.[59] Hysteria had just as long a pedigree as melancholy, both of the illnesses having been identified and studied in ancient Greece. Like melancholy it was believed to have originated in the body, specifically in the uterus, the Greek word for which is *hystera*. The main source of its symptoms, which appeared mainly in unmarried women, was the upward movement of the cold uterus in the body in search of heat in the warmer organs. For married women sexual intercourse provided the heat that made it unnecessary for the uterus to ascend in this way. This medical theory explains why physicians often recommended marriage as the cure for hysteria. When married women contracted this disease the most common treatment was to introduce pleasant odours into the vagina, sometimes by having the husband anoint his penis.

The occasion of the introduction of hysteria into the medical discourse of demonic possession was the affliction of Mary Glover, a fourteen-year-old daughter of a London shopkeeper, in 1602. Shortly after being threatened by Elizabeth Jackson, an older woman with whom Glover had previously quarrelled, Mary began to experience violent seizures three or four times a day. She had such great difficulty in eating that she had to be force-fed. She then developed paralysis of her hand, arm, and eventually her entire left side. As her condition worsened she displayed writhing, tics, spasms, and contortions of her face and body, and her head turned back-wards. Her stomach and throat swelled. She experienced temporary periods of blindness and an inability to speak. In other words, she displayed many of the symptoms of demonic possession.

Glover's parents, who were members of a London Puritan congregation and were familiar with the spate of recent possessions in England, suspected that their daughter was one of these unfortunate victims of a demonic assault, and their interpretation most probably explains why Mary accused Elizabeth Jackson of causing her afflictions by witchcraft. This was a common response to demonic possession, especially in Protestant communities, where it was believed that prosecuting the witch would relieve the demoniac. In any event, Mary's identification of Jackson as the cause of her affliction led to Jackson's trial for witchcraft, and during the trial Mary's confrontation with Jackson resulted in a rehearsal of many of her symptoms, including frightening verbal outbursts.

At the trial, in which the court dismissed many claims that the possession was counterfeit (mainly because Glover endured the burning of her flesh without pain), Edmund Jorden, a prominent and respected physician, testified that Mary was not possessed by the Devil but was suffering from the natural disease of hysteria. This disease was known as the suffocation of the mother because one of its symptoms was a choking of the throat that produced shortness of breath. The traditional explana-tion for hysteria was that when the uterus ascended within the body, it emitted bad vapours that affected the heart and the brain. The judge in the case, Sir Edmund Anderson, dismissed Jorden's argument, but Jorden responded with the publication of *A Brief Discourse of a Disease Called the Suffocation of the Mother*, in which he declared that 'divers strange actions and passions of the body of man' that are usually attributed to the Devil have 'true and natural causes' that accompany this particular disease.[60]

Like the earlier theories that demoniacs were epileptics or melancholics, Jorden's interpretation of possession as hysteria was deeply flawed. However appropriate it might have been in the case of Mary Glover, it could not easily be applied to male demoniacs, such as those cured by Christ, and it was an unlikely explanation of the possession of children younger than Glover or of women who were much older.[61] Even Glover herself had not reached the age of menarche at the time of her possession. When Jorden was called in to examine another young demoniac, Anne Gunter, five years after Glover's case was resolved, he was unable to propose a similar diagnosis and attributed her symptoms to fraud. He reached this conclusion after he had found pins and pieces of glass in Anne's stools, which led him to conclude that she had deliberately swallowed them.[62]

The inability of hysteria to explain the regurgitation of alien objects, which was often a distinguishing feature of possession, also hampered its utility as an explanation of the phenomenon.[63] In 1691 the English Presbyterian Richard Baxter referred to a case first reported by the sixteenth-century Italian physician Antonio Benivieni (c. 1443–1502) in which a woman was believed to be hysterical until she vomited long crooked nails, brass pins, wax and hair mixed in a ball, and a lump of food larger than anyone could swallow. At that point his diagnosis changed to possession by an evil spirit.[64] The only plausible natural medical diagnosis of this case would have been allotriophagy or pathological swallowing, which was not proposed at the time.[65] It is even possible that Jorden himself was not fully persuaded of his own diagnosis in the case of Mary Glover, since he entertained the possibility that the young girl was faking her symptoms. He may also have been aware of the weaknesses of his argument and that the only reason he presented it in the first place was to support his friend and ally Bishop Richard Bancroft and his chaplain, Samuel Harsnett, who at the time were trying to discredit Puritan efforts at dispossession.[66]

The flaws in Jorden's analysis might explain why it gained little support, even among his sceptical English contemporaries, who relied increasingly on the view that possessions were counterfeit rather than the product of natural disease. His book did not go into a second printing, nor did other physicians follow his lead in their efforts to interpret English or continental European possessions. The book also failed to resolve the ambivalence of those medical authorities who thought that possessions could be explained by either natural or demonic causes or by some mixture of the two. Testifying in a witchcraft trial in 1664, Sir Thomas Browne admitted that the fits of some women might have been caused by hysteria (reflecting the diagnostic shift from melancholy to hysteria) but that the subtlety of the Devil played a crucial role in heightening the symptoms:[67] In 1677 the Nonconformist minister Richard Gilpin, who had received a medical degree from Leiden and had written his dissertation on hysteria, published *Demonologia sacra, or, a Treatise of Satan's Temptations*, the main purpose of which was to illustrate how the Devil worked through nature. This included his role in causing hysteria, which Gilpin asserted could not be studied from a strictly naturalistic point of view. In 1693 Cotton Mather, after considering various naturalistic interpretations of the possession of Margaret Rule, including hysteria, came to the conclusion that only the power of the Devil could explain all the symptoms displayed by demoniacs.[68]

It would be anachronistic to exaggerate the significance or modernity of Jorden's treatise. Not only did it fail to change the medical discourse on possession, but it failed to advance the diagnosis and treatment of the people who allegedly suffered from the malady. Although Jorden deserves credit for adding verbal and behavioural signs, such as 'the croaking of frogs, hissing of snakes, crowing of cocks ... laughing, singing, weeping crying, etc.', to the primarily somatic symptoms of the disease, his reliance on the traditional uterine interpretation of the origin of hysteria made his contribution far less significant in the history of medicine than some historians have claimed.[69]

Nevertheless, Jorden did propose in an imperfect and tentative way the medical explanation of possession that *eventually* commanded widespread support as the most plausible explanation of what was 'really happening' when a person manifested the signs of demonic possession. That triumphant moment did not come, however, until the late nineteenth century. Before it did, the medical understanding of hysteria underwent a number of fundamental changes that allowed it to embrace many more symptoms than Jorden had recognized. The first, which took place during the seventeenth century, was the recognition of a male version of the disease, hypochondria, which was believed to originate in the spleen. Hypochondria, which had once been considered a form of melancholy (since both originated in the spleen), became the twin brother of hysteria, and both disorders underwent transformation into neurological and mental maladies together.

The second development was the redefinition of hysteria as a neurological disorder rather than either a uterine disease or one of the spleen.

The English physician Thomas Willis (1621–75) was the first doctor to make this claim, arguing that the pathologies that produced hysteria and similar disorders were firmly rooted in the 'brain and the nervous stock' rather than in the uterus. This interpretation met opposition from those who thought hysteria might originate in the stomach or gut, but by the late eighteenth century a medical consensus that hysteria was an organic disease of the nervous system had emerged. The interpretation of hysteria as a neurological disorder meant that men were just as capable as women of contracting the disease, even if it had always been diagnosed more commonly among women.

This neurological interpretation made it possible for doctors to assimilate both epilepsy and melancholy to the contemporary definition of hysteria. The process of assimilation began with Willis and was complete by the late nineteenth century. The similarity between epilepsy and hysteria was so close that the two terms were sometimes used together or interchangeably. The incorporation of melancholy, with its primarily mental or emotional symptoms, into this expansive category of hysteria took more time. In the late seventeenth century Thomas Sydenham (1624–89) argued that emotional factors or what he referred to as 'distur-bances of the mind' caused the physiological symptoms of hysteria,[70] and in the early eighteenth century the physician Sir Richard Blackmore (1654–1729) wrote that hysteria could not easily be distinguished from 'melancholy, lunacy and frenzy'.[71] Nevertheless, it still took time for hysteria, which had always been considered a somatic, i.e. a bodily or organic illness that expressed itself through emotional distress, to be viewed as a psychological disorder that expressed itself somatically.[72] Responsibility for this new perspective rests mainly with Sigmund Freud (1856–1939), who developed the idea that hysteria was a form of psychoneurosis, a psychic or mental disorder manifested in bodily symp-toms.[73] Freud's emphasis on the psychological causes of hysteria, especially the traumas that nineteenth-century French neurologists posited as their proximate cause, signalled a major shift in psychiatry away from somatic explanations that included lesions in the central nervous system.[74]

The person most responsible for bringing all the symptoms of possession under the same hysterical umbrella was Jean-Martin Charcot (1825–93). Convinced that hysteria and epilepsy were manifestations of the same disease, which he called hystero-epilepsy, Charcot gradually assimilated to hysteria a wide variety of maladies, including various forms of sclerosis, which he studied in his clinic at the Salpêtrière hospital in Paris in the late nineteenth century. By the time he had finished his research, he had proposed that the illness he called 'grand hysteria' had four distinct phases.

The first was the epileptic phase in which the patient suffered fits. The second was the period of contortions in which the patient engaged in dramatic physical displays, often accompanied by intermittent shrieking. Some of these contortions were seemingly impossible, especially the ability to bend backwards with only the back of the head and the heels touching the ground. The third stage, which occurred mainly in female patients, was the entrance into erotic ecstasy. The final or terminal stage included the experience of delusions or hallucinations.[75]

The ability of hysteria to embrace or in a certain sense mimic other diseases explains why it endured as the most persuasive explanation of 'what was really happening' when a person was supposedly possessed by the Devil. Charcot made the categorical claim that demoniacs were actually hysterics, and he retrospectively diagnosed a select group of early modern demoniacs, most notably Sister Jeanne des Anges, the Ursuline mother superior at Loudun, in this way.[76] In 1885 Charcot's colleague and co-author Paul Richer published a massive study of historical possessions, including some that had occurred only a few years previously, using the analytical framework Charcot had developed.[77] In 1886 the neurologist Désiré-Magliore Bourneville, also one of Charcot's colleagues, claimed that Jeanne Féry, the French Dominican nun who had been possessed at Mons in 1584 and 1585, suffered the most severe form of hysteria, which included convulsive attacks, hallucinations, a refusal to eat, insensitivity to pain or anaesthesia, prolonged ecstasies, visceral sensations and a *dédoublement* or splitting of her personality.[78] Bourneville's book was one of nine volumes in a series he edited under the title *Bibliothèque diabolique* in which early modern possession narratives were reprinted with the purpose of showing that the demoniacs were really suffering from hysteria.[79]

Historians soon joined medical practitioners in the rush to diagnose demoniacs retrospectively as hysterics. In 1886 the Russian-born historian Alexandre Tuetey published a study of witchcraft prosecutions in the independent Huguenot principality of Montbéliard, arguing that the unfortunate women who were believed to have been possessed in that territory were really *hystéro-épileptiques*.[80] In 1892 the neurologist and historian Paul Ladame, a disciple of Charcot, analysed the demoniacs in Geneva in the early seventeenth century using the same diagnostic categories.[81] A few years later the German psychiatrist Otto Snell, inspired mainly by the work of Charcot, claimed that the symptoms of hysteria, including indecent gestures and difficulty in swallowing as well as convulsions and insensitivity to pain, were the same as those described in cases of possession.[82] Henry Charles Lea, the twentieth-century rationalist historian of the Spanish Inquisition and witchcraft, made Snell's interpretation of possession the centrepiece of his interpretation of what was 'really happening' when a demoniac displayed the symptoms of possession.[83] Even in the second half of the twentieth century, by which time hysteria had been purged from the lexicography of the medical profession and had morphed into other maladies, including a wide variety of dissociative disorders, some historians continued to identify hysteria as the condition from which demoniacs suffered.[84]

A retrospective medical diagnosis of demonic possession as hysteria suffered from a different flaw from that of Jorden's treatise. Charcot's description of hysteria was so protean, embracing many diseases that are today identified today as distinct, that the term lost any specific aetiological meaning. The word is after all a cultural construct, just like possession itself, and as such it has been applied to a wide variety of psychoneurotic disorders, especially those classified as dissociative, which involve a loss of identity, and those classified as the product of a conversion syndrome, such as amnesia, paralysis, blindness, and deafness.[85] It is possible, nonetheless, that the diagnosis of an early modern demoniac as suffering from a specific malady once identified as hysteria can have some interpretative value. It can serve this purpose, however, only if it is used to explain a limited number of symptoms of the possession, preferably those evident when the afflictions began. In studying possession in Haiti in the twentieth century, the anthropologist Alfred Métraux concluded that the symptoms of only the 'opening phase' of a possession were psycho-pathological, in that they conformed exactly in their main features 'to the stock clinical conception of hysteria'.[86]

Multiple personality disorder

One psychiatric theory that has been used to explain both past and present possessions is dissociative identity disorder (DID), or what is often referred to as multiple personality disorder.[87] DID is an aetiological stepchild of hysteria—one of the many characteristics of that illness that gradually acquired autonomous diagnostic status. (Other stepchildren are post-traumatic stress disorder and traumas caused by sexual abuse.) The main manifestation of DID is the patient's difficulty maintaining his or her own personal identity, a process sometimes referred to as identity fragmentation. Now, there is little dispute that early modern European demoniacs manifested a weak sense of personal identity. During possession many apparently suffered temporary loss of their own personal identity as the Devil, so it was believed, gained control over not only their bodies but also their mental faculties and their personalities. In some cases the demoniacs' human personalities coexisted with the demons that possessed them, leading to verbal exchanges between the possessed person and the demon that occupied the body. These situations occurred when demoniacs did not lose consciousness during possession and could recount when it had taken place. In these lucid (as opposed to somnambulistic) possessions the demoniac often spoke in two different voices.[88]

The diagnosis of early modern demoniacs as victims of DID, however, does not provide a comprehensive explanation of the afflicted person's behaviour. As well as leaving many of the symptoms of the possession unaccounted for, it fails to take into account the influence of the religious culture that the multiple personalities reflected. In this respect it exposes the weakness of all such retrospective psychiatric analyses. Modern categories of psychiatry are often inappropriate for the purposes of historical analysis because they tend to remove 'the subject at least partially from the immediate context to a timeless context of universal applicability'.[89] In cases of possession they fail to take into account the religious contexts in which the episodes occurred.

The case of Jeanne Féry reveals the difficulty of retrospectively diagnosing a demoniac as suffering from dissociative identity disorder. In 1996 three psychologists claimed that Féry's possession, which was recorded in a long autobiographical account as well as in a narrative written by her exorcists, was 'perhaps the earliest historical case in which DID can be diagnosed retrospectively with confidence'.[90] According to this diagnosis, the demons that possessed Féry were the alternate personalities with whom she identified. They included Belial, who was attended by subordinate demons representing the seven deadly sins, and Cornau (Horns), Garga (Throat), and Sanguinaire (Blood). Another alter ego was Mary Magdalene, who acted as Féry's helper in dealing with her possession.

Now, it is apparent that during her possession Féry lost a clear sense of her own personal identity. Whether this reflected a more fundamental weakness in the concept of the individual self in early modern European culture cannot be determined.[91] But the substitution of these demonic personalities for her own were not the only symptoms of Féry's possession. They also included violent seizures, numerous attempts at suicide, self-mutilation, episodes of prolonged sobbing and intense physical pain, sleep disturbance, temporary blindness, eating disorders, facial contortions, the discovery of lost objects, and loss of knowledge and skills. The three psychologists claimed that the clinical picture of Féry's symptoms was 'quite familiar to contemporary clinicians working with dissociative disorders'. But to accommodate all these symptoms under the umbrella of DID would require that one use a medical paradigm as broad as hysteria itself, the illness that has splintered into DID and many other psychoneurotic disorders. To label this complex, diverse set of symptoms as a form of dissociative identity disorder is to characterize the entire experience on the basis of only one set of symptoms.

This is not to deny that Féry was experiencing a profound psychological crisis or that modern psychiatric theory might help to illuminate its causes. It is possible that conflicting desires led this troubled soul to detach what was unacceptable to her and create a separate identity to embody those desires. In other words she may have experienced a particular form of DID. But the only way to make sense of the entire possession, with all its symptoms, is to view it as a cultural performance that follows a script that was encoded in early modern Catholic culture. Whether or not Féry was faking the symptoms of her possession, as some contemporaries suspected and which she may have admitted in 1620, does not really matter. Either consciously or unconsciously Féry acted in the way demoniacs were expected to act and said the things that demoniacs knew as a result of their religious education. These included the names of the demons that were tormenting her and the knowledge that Belial had always been depicted as being accompanied by seven subordinates. The reference to Mary Magdalene as a helper does not make sense unless we understand the role this alternative personality played in traditional Catholic culture. To identify Mary Magdalene as an 'internal self-helper' in terms of DID only restates the question of why Féry introduced Mary into her discourse. The reason is most probably that Mary Magdalene had herself been possessed by seven demons, which Christ expelled from her body.[92] Even the odd fact that Féry believed she had made a pact with the Devil, which did not agree with early modern demonological theory, can only be explained in terms of late sixteenth-century popular demonology, in which people were often told about witches who made such contracts with the Prince of Darkness and then tried to break them. Dissociative identity disorder cannot even begin to explain Féry's belief that she made a pact with the Devil.

Freudian theory

The possession of the Bavarian painter Christoph Haizmann in 1677 offers further evidence of the limitations of a psychiatric diagnosis of possession and the plausibility of an interpretation based on cultural performance. In August of that year Haizmann began to experience 'certain unnatural convulsions' in the church at Pottenbrunn, near where he was painting. When these convulsions recurred with increasing severity he was taken to a local ecclesiastical official, to whom he confessed that he had made a pact with the Devil nine years earlier in a fit of depression (viewed then as melancholy) following the death of his father. His immediate fear was that the Devil was about to lay claim to his body and soul.

In an effort to break the pact Haizmann begged to be taken to the shrine of the Blessed Virgin at Zell in Styria, the destination of many pilgrimages. There he was exorcized for three days and nights, after which he returned to Pottenbrunn and from there went to Vienna, where his sister was living. In October his convulsions began to recur, this time together with temporary paralysis of his leg. He also had eight visions of the Devil, who appeared to him in various forms, including one in which the Devil had female breasts. Haizmann attributed the recurrence of his afflictions to a second pact, signed in ink, which he claimed he had made with the Devil. Using his professional skills, he made nine paintings of the Devil as he had appeared to him. These paintings are included in his autobiographical manuscript.[93]

Haizmann's case was similar to Féry's only in his belief that he had made a pact with the Devil. Because they were Catholics, moreover, both demoniacs hoped that they could break these contracts; Protestants would have been far less likely to be given that option. The most striking difference between Haizmann's experience and Féry's, however, is that the painter did not give any signs of having an identity crisis or any other dissociative disorder. The Devil never spoke through him, nor did Haizmann assume the identity of the Devil. Aside from his convulsions and partial paralysis, Haizmann did not display any of the usual symptoms of possession. A contemporary might easily have concluded that this young painter was a repentant witch rather than a demoniac. It is entirely possible that the priests who treated him got their demonological categories confused. Such conflation of these two demonic types did occasionally occur in the early modern period, as shall be discussed in Chapter 8. Nevertheless Haizmann was identified as a demoniac and thus was submitted to the ordeal of Catholic exorcism.

Haizmann's autobiographical account and paintings made him an attractive subject for retrospective psychiatric analysis by Sigmund Freud in his paper, 'A Seventeenth-Century Demonological Neurosis', published in 1923.[94] Long before he wrote this analysis, however, Freud, who had studied with Charcot in the 1880s and had later come to the conclusion that sexual trauma was the root cause of all cases of hysteria, had developed a much broader theory of the human mind according to which frustrated sex drives lay at the root of all psychoneuroses, including hysteria.[95] For obvious reasons Freud did not consider this 'case history of a neurotic' an example of hysteria. The word appears only once, in the introduction to his forty-page paper, in which he refers to Charcot's study of early modern art.[96] Nor did Freud express interest in any other cases of possession as examples of hysteria or multiple personality disorder. The only reason he focused on this one was because it provided a case study for his over-arching libidinal theory of the mind.[97] Freud argued that Haizmann had contracted a paranoid psychotic illness rooted in an Oedipal complex, in which the Devil acted as the painter's father-substitute. The inverted or negative dimension of the complex was the boy's passive homosexual attachment to his father, which he resisted because of the father's implied threat of castration.[98] His submission to exorcism represented a flight to his mother, the Church, to avoid the threatened castration by his father.

Freud's interpretation of Haizmann's possession as a case of 'paranoia', a term later subsumed within the broader concept of schizophrenia, was no more satisfactory in explaining what 'really' happened in Haizmann's possession than was Bourneville's identification of Féry's possession as a case of hysteria. The problem did not lie in Freud's effort to provide a psychological explanation of Haizmann's distress. An interpretation focusing on Haizmann's acute spiritual anxiety might provide a plausible explanation of the convulsions with which his possession began. Rather the problem with Freud's analysis was that it was ahistorical. He used a theoretical model that he claimed had universal applicability to explain a specific historical event, and he failed to take into account the historical context in which the possession occurred.[99] The form and content of that experience, which involved making pacts with the Devil and describing his physical appearance in a series of paintings, cannot be explained without reference to the religious culture in which Haizmann was immersed. Only a person who had heard sermons about demonic temptation and seen images of the Devil in human or animal form or with multiple female breasts (which were plentiful in seventeenth-century Catholicism) could have constructed a narrative as evocative of early modern Catholic culture while at the same time confusing or conflating so many of the demonic themes of seventeenth-century literature.[100]

Religious anxiety

Efforts by medical doctors and psychiatrists to link possession with illness therefore cannot be equated with, or attributed to, a single illness or disease. The symptoms of possession are too varied to support a comprehensive medical model. Even when the illness is described in broad terms, for example as melancholy, hysteria, multiple personality disorder, or an altered state of consciousness (a term that is more descriptive than diagnostic)[101] the diagnosis cannot comprehend the wide variety of behaviour that demoniacs have exhibited in the past, especially those symptoms that are culturally specific, such as the ability to speak in languages previously unknown to the demoniac or the revulsion of the demoniac from objects considered sacred in the demoniac's religion. As discussed earlier, epilepsy, melancholy and hysteria all denoted different types of condition, even if they shared some common features. Each emphasized particular symptoms of the possession and redefined them in medical terms. The entire phenomenon defied reduction in medical terms.

Nevertheless, the *similarity* between at least some of the physiological symptoms displayed by demoniacs and those displayed by hysterics suggests that we are dealing with closely related phenomena.[102] Even if the authors of possession narratives exaggerated the symptoms of the possessed, and even if a number of demoniacs faked their possession, it is difficult to deny that those who were identified as demoniacs experienced profound psychological traumas that expressed themselves somatically.

One psychological interpretation that can account for some of the physiological symptoms of early modern possessions while not removing the demoniacs from their proper historical context is that they suffered from anxiety neuroses rooted in their religious experiences. The sources of such anxiety, which varied greatly from one religious denomination to the next, will be discussed in detail in the next chapter. For Jeanne Féry and Christoph Haizmann it was both regret and the terror that they had made pacts with the Devil. For many young Catholic laywomen and nuns it was terror, because they had violated the strict code of sexual morality that was being proclaimed as part of the reforms instituted after the Council of Trent. For Nicole Obry it was the sense of failure she felt because her family had not made the pilgrimages her deceased grandfather had requested in a vision. For aspirants to Catholic sainthood it was the fear that they had failed to adhere to the strict religious discipline prescribed as a means to attain mystical union with the divine. For many Calvinists it was the profound and desperate anxiety that they were not been numbered among the elect and thus were consigned to eternal damnation.

Religious anxieties of this sort could readily have expressed themselves in the physiological symptoms of possession, especially convulsions, eating disorders, swelling of the stomach, and the sensation of being pricked with pins. These were almost always the initial symptoms of possession, and the ones that demoniacs accused witches of having caused. Sometimes the demoniacs were described at first as having contracted a sickness that had no natural explanations. The more extreme symptoms, such as the displays of preternatural strength, levitation, contortionism, and ecstasies became part of the possession experience only when the experience was well under way and sometimes not until the demoniacs underwent exorcism. These more sensational elements of possession, moreover, entered into the picture when the demoniacs, either consciously or not, began to act the way demoniacs were expected to act—in other words, when they became cultural performers.[103]

Illness and group possessions

The rapid spread of the symptoms of possession from one demoniac to another in convents, villages, orphanages, and other close-knit communities presents the clearest challenge to the sufficiency of a physiological or even a psychoneurotic interpretation of demonic possession. These cases, taken together, account for the great majority of early modern European 'classic' possessions. Some involved the members of a single family or household. The possessions that occurred in more than fifty Catholic convents often affected between ten and twenty demoniacs, while the mass possessions, which affected more than one hundred people took place in villages and towns. We have evidence of more than one hundred and fifty such group possessions during the early modern period.[104] When Samuel Garnier, Henri Boulet and other disciples of Charcot used the medical term 'epidemic' to describe the prevalence of demonic possession in the early modern period, they were referring to these collective phenomena.[105]

It stands to reason that the spread of the symptoms of demonic possession from one person to another cannot be attributed to physiological or neurological factors. Epilepsy, for example, cannot spread rapidly within a community in the manner of a communicable disease.[106] Nor can hysteria, no matter how it has been understood. Charcot's explanation that the observation of other hysterics might have produced traumas that he considered essential to the origin of his patients' maladies stretched the definition of trauma beyond recognition. Charcot and modern psychiatrists have also claimed that hysterics have inherited a predisposition to the disease.[107] It is highly unlikely, however, that all the demoniacs in communities where the symptoms spread rapidly had inherited the same predisposition.[108] It is even more unlikely, for example, that villagers in Mattaincourt, Paderborn, and Belmonte all developed multiple personality disorders or experienced altered states of consciousness within the same month. One might plausibly refer to collective stress, caused by shared fears and concerns of people in the same close-knit community, but an analysis based on this type of collective anxiety, sometimes referred to as mass psychogenic illness, takes us out of the realm of medical, psychiatric diagnosis and into that of collective mentality and emotion.

Understanding group possessions thus requires that we abandon a search for medical causes, including those of a psychiatric nature, and explore the dynamics of group behaviour and the development of what the clinical psychologist Adam Crabtree calls the group-mind.[109] The reasons for the 'contagion' of these possessions might still lie in the psychology of the possessed, but the question becomes not how a psychosomatic disorder recurred in numerous instances but why individuals acted or performed in the manner of their siblings, colleagues, or neighbours. The same question can be asked of other 'psychic epidemics' in the past, such as the dancing manias of the late medieval and early modern periods, the collective religious singing and dancing of the French Huguenots known as Camisards in the early eighteenth century, and the behaviour of partici-pants in religious revivals of eighteenth- and nineteenth-century America. The convulsions, trances, visions, and prophecies of these groups, especially the Camisards, closely resembled the symptoms of possession.[110] The medical historian George Rosen and the cultural historian Clarke Garrett have both argued that such phenomena can only be understood in their cultural and social contexts and that those contexts are profoundly religious.[111]

Two common features of all such epidemics of religious group behaviour are shared belief and imitation. The epidemics took place in settings where all the members of the group had similar or identical religious beliefs, aspirations, and anxieties, and they spread by means of a process of imitation. In such environments it was relatively easy for one member of that community, while observing the behaviour and speech of others, to come to the conclusion that she was also possessed and either consciously or subconsciously imitate the performance of other members of her community.

Such imitation does not necessarily mean that the demoniacs whom they aped were faking possession, although we cannot categorically rule out that possibility. It does suggest, however, that these demoniacs, like children (and many demoniacs were children or adolescents), were highly suggestible. One example of such demoniacal imitation occurred in the village of Belmonte, Italy in 1596, where a woman's shrieking during Mass led others to follow her example, 'filling the church with the cries of various animals'. The friar who was saying the Mass reported that he saw bodies 'contorted into all possible positions' and women pulling up their dresses. The shrieking, which the friar said resembled Hell, did not cease until the Mass ended.[112]

Another instance of group possession of this sort occurred in late nineteenth-century Russia, where demoniacs known as *klikushi* or shriekers, when put in the presence of sacred objects, barked like dogs, uttered blasphemies, experienced seizures and shrieked the names of those they claimed were responsible for causing their maladies. Such barking, howling, and blaspheming, as well as the shrieking, are of course easy to imitate, and they can be contagious in the same way as group singing and dancing. In her study of these Russian demoniacs Christine Worobec cites the instance of Vasilisa Alekseeva, who began to manifest the symptoms of possession only after observing a group of shriekers in a Russian monastery.[113]

One reason why many demoniacs were so suggestible and thus readily imitated others in their communities is that they had come to believe that they too were actually possessed. Early modern medical authorities accepted this possibility. The Swiss physician Paracelsus (1493–1541) argued that one could actually become possessed by believing that one was.[114] In his treatise on the possessions at Loudun, the Scottish physician Marc Duncan, assuming for purposes of argument that the nuns were not faking, speculated that because of 'madness and error of the imagination', the women believed themselves to be possessed without being so.[115] Duncan argued that the nuns' constant vigils, fasts, and meditations upon Hell and the Devil's temptations, as well as their listening to sermons on the presence of the Devil in their convent, might have led them to believe that they were possessed or bewitched. Duncan also argued that the nuns' confessors might have concluded that their penitents were possessed and then persuaded them they were thus afflicted. He explained that the nuns' beliefs could easily spread to others in the convent, by the force of their imagination.[116] Duncan's reference to the nuns' imagination reflected the influence of Pomponazzi, who had argued that the imagination was especially powerful among people who lived in confined quarters.[117]

The widespread early modern belief that demoniacs were melancholics provided further support for the argument that these troubled souls imagined or came to believe that they were possessed. The sixteenth-century medical theory of melancholy held that the production of an imbalance of black bile in the spleen activated the imagination. The demonological theory of melancholy, which held that the Devil manipulated the melancholic humour, also emphasized the Devil's effect on the imagination. Religious melancholy, which minimized or ignored the medical theory, placed even greater emphasis on the supposed effect of melancholy on the imagination. Melancholy itself was not viewed as contagious, but the belief in self-possession that it allegedly fostered could quickly spread in a close-knit community of highly suggestible people who had similar religious anxieties. The cultivation of collective imagination, therefore, offers a plausible explanation for how possessions could spread rapidly among French nuns, Dutch orphans, and children in pious Protestant households.

Neither the medical theory of melancholy nor its demonological alternative continued to have influence in the eighteenth century, but the idea that demoniacs imagined they were possessed lived on into the period of the Enlightenment. In the early eighteenth century the sceptical Spanish monk Benito Feijóo claimed that those demoniacs who were not either genuinely possessed or impostors 'imagined' that they were possessed by demons.[118] In the following century Russian shriekers, who acted out a highly ritualized drama that had been a part of Russian Orthodox culture since the late Middle Ages, participated in this performance only after they came to believe that they were possessed.

Demoniacs who were conscious of their own pathological behaviour (i.e. those experiencing lucid as opposed to somnambulistic possessions) often believed that they were possessed. In Utrecht groups of demoniacs insisted that they were possessed when sceptical authorities challenged the validity of their possessions.[119] In the Aragonese village of Tosos in 1812 the demoniacs and their families argued with secular and ecclesiastical authorities, claiming that they were actually possessed.[120] The psychiatrist Samuel Pfeifer has shown that even in modern Western societies the belief that demons can cause one's own mental disorders remains strong among those afflicted with behavioural disorders. A large number of the Protestant outpatients in his clinic in Switzerland believed that evil spirits were the cause of their psychological problems.[121] In other words, they believed that they were demonically possessed.

All these group possessions, just like those that were experienced individually, had a theatrical dimension, in that the participants acted out scripts that were encoded in their religious cultures. One of the appeals of all rituals, religious or secular, is their theatrical nature. Demonic possessions, no less than religious processions, singing hymns, or the Catholic Mass, were religious rituals, and they do not make complete sense unless we can appreciate their theatrical nature. To that theatrical dimension of demonic possession we now turn.

CHAPTER 6

The Performance of the Possessed

T HE MOST FRUITFUL WAY for modern scholars to make sense of demonic possession is to see it as a theatrical performance that reflected the religious cultures of the demoniac, the community, and the exorcist. Others have of course seen possession in very different ways. To those who believed in the existence of the Devil and his ability to intervene in the natural world, the violent seizures, contortions, swellings, and blasphemies were clearly the work of the Devil, and if they had any doubts about the Devil's ability to make human beings act in this way, they could have been reassured by demonologists and the preachers that it was all part of God's plan for humanity. Physicians and psychiatrists, from Jean Riolan to Sigmund Freud, have also had no difficulty in making sense of demonic possession. For them it was a manifestation of a disease or illness that had natural causes, which they described in the medical idiom of their day. Many Protestants in the early modern period, and some modern historians, have made sense of early modern possessions by claiming that demoniacs faked the symptoms of their possessions.

These different interpretations have proved to be unsatisfactory for the purposes of historical analysis. The supernatural interpretation, while perfectly consistent on its own terms, has no place in historical analysis, since it cannot be supported by a critical examination of the sources. The medical interpretation, while useful in explaining some of the symptoms of demonic possession, fails to account for many others, especially those that reflect the specific religious beliefs of the demoniacs. The interpretation based on fraud, while undoubtedly accurate in some instances, cannot be applied to involuntary possessions, and it discounts the religious beliefs and practices of demoniacs even more than the argument that they were suffering from natural illnesses. The proposition that thousands of demoniacs faked their possessions for a variety of reasons presupposes an implausible consistency of motivation and behaviour, especially among the uneducated, who saw little advantage in faking their possessions and often lacked the skill to make a convincing simulation.

The theory that demoniacs, their neighbours, and the clergy who attended to them were engaged in theatrical performances rooted in their specific religious cultures overcomes the limitations of the medical and counterfeit interpretations while still relying on those theories in some cases. It provides an explanation that can apply to all possessions, Protestant as well as Catholic, while respecting their cultural specificity. It recognizes that some demoniacs were suffering from medical or psychological disorders and that others were clearly faking possession. But its main contention is that all demoniacs, whether ill or not, whether duplicitous or not, were following theatrical scripts that were encoded in their religious cultures. In other words, demoniacs acted in ways they were either taught to act or were expected to act. Their religious cultures did not *determine* what they said and did while under the Devil's influence; rather they offered them a set of beliefs and practices that they articulated and acted out, often at the prompting of others.

The perception that demoniacs were fairly accomplished actors is not new; it dates from the early modern period itself. This characterization of demoniacs, however, has always been used to describe *voluntary* demoniacs—those who were faking possession and hence deliberately performing for an audience. These demoniacs were able to respond to social cues, displaying their symptoms only when an audience was available to witness them or when they were brought into the presence of the witch who had accused them. The argument presented here is that *all* demoniacs, including the vast majority who were *not* faking their possessions, were nonetheless playing roles in sacred dramas. Involuntary demoniacs usually assumed those roles gradually. Their original symptoms, which were almost always physiological, were in most cases the product of some sort of religiously induced anxiety. Their assumption of the role of the demoniac took place as members of the community—usually ministers, physicians, and family members—interpreted their behaviour as the effect of demonic possession. Efforts by exorcists, who were following their own scripts, not only played their prescribed roles in this drama, but enhanced the performance of the possessed by adding more lines to their scripts and aggravating their symptoms. The family members, neighbours, and clergy who witnessed possessions also had their own parts to play in these religious dramas, assuming the role of a chorus that would join the demoniac on stage. The entire performance thus became the product of the interaction of the demoniac, the exorcist, and the audience.[1] The scripts could therefore be adapted to specific circumstances. Possessions were always scripted, but they could accommodate a certain amount of ad-libbing.

The argument that all possessions and exorcisms were cultural perform-ances applies both to the thousands of possessions in the early modern period and to those that took place in the early history of Christianity. Exorcisms performed in those years were dramas that were instrumental in spreading the new faith. The inspiration and model for these theatrical productions were the exorcisms performed by Christ, which the authors of the synoptic Gospels had dramatized to illustrate his power over demons. In this way the biblical accounts of Christ's exorcisms became the original possession scripts. As Michael White has argued, the Gospels themselves were dramas that were originally read aloud. Thus the early accounts of Christ's life, including his exorcisms, were shaped by the conditions of their performance, including the religious concerns of the audience and the narrators.[2] So the possessions and exorcisms as represented in the Gospels reflected the culture of the early Church.

Possessions in late antiquity, which were intended to promote the Christian religion, were also quintessentially theatrical. Performed in cathedrals, churches, or the shrines of saints, where they could be observed by others, possessions were transformed into what Peter Brown has referred to as psychodramas.[3] The renewed attention to possessions in the thirteenth century, when the symptoms of demoniacs began to reflect the influence of the evangelical revival of that century, was at least partially the result of the recovery of the Gospels as drama. Barbara Newman has argued that the 'new demoniacs' of that century, who were predominantly female, played a role in the re-enactment of sacred history that mendicant friars were promoting in their preaching.[4] The flood of possessions in the late twentieth and early twenty-first centuries also lend themselves to a theatrical interpretation, as will be discussed in Chapter 10. In each of these periods the scripts followed by both demoniacs and exorcists changed, thus reflecting the changing religious cultures in which they took place. In the early modern period, Catholic and Protestant cultures resulted in radically different scripts for both the possessed and their exorcists.

Possession and exorcism as theatre

Historians and literary scholars have pointed out the remarkable similari-ties between early modern possessions and exorcisms on the one hand and theatrical performances on the other. The comparisons suggest themselves most readily in situations where exorcisms were witnessed by large groups of people and when the exorcists could orchestrate the production; in other words, when the demonic performance had a director and a large audience. In his analysis of the possessions of the Ursuline nuns at Loudun, Michel de Certeau argued that the holding of the exorcisms in large public spaces before thousands of onlookers, the ability of the nuns to begin and end their convulsions when cued, and their playing the roles of the demons which were believed to be occupying their bodies made the ritual resemble a theatrical production.[5] Henri Weber has labelled all these public French exorcisms 'baroque spectacles'.[6] Early modern exorcisms had many of the ingredients of modern dramas, including sex and violence, and they were performed before large audiences, sometimes numbering in the thousands. When the number of onlookers reached 10,000, as at Laon in 1566, and 25,000, as at Loudun in 1634, the exorcisms moved outside in what became, in effect, open-air theatres. At Laon the crowds were so large that authorities had to build a higher and larger platform to accommodate the throng of onlookers.[7] Other spectators lined the streets to watch the daily procession of the demoniac from her temporary residence to the cathedral. At Soissons a new stage built for the same purposes measured twenty-four feet long and seven or eight feet high.[8]

Catholic exorcisms were especially suitable for theatrical interpretation, because the exorcist could follow one of many scripts that were published in the manuals of the day, such as the massive *Thesaurus exorcismorum* of 1608. Even more important, they were theatrical because they involved cultural interactions between the performers and the audience.[9] The purpose of the exorcisms (besides healing the demoniac) was to demonstrate that the Catholic Church was the one true Church. The exorcists, appropriately dressed in clerical 'costume' and carrying the props of their religion, such as the monstrance holding a consecrated host, an aspergillum for sprinkling holy water, or a burner for incense, were performing a religious ritual. The body of the demoniac was in many ways the central prop in the drama: Michel Foucault has described it as a theatrical stage on which the exorcism was performed.[10] Like all dramatic productions and rituals, these exorcisms could be repeated until they no longer attracted attention.

Protestant dispossessions were rarely performed before crowds as large as those at Catholic events. The Puritan minister John Darrell claimed that the prayers of one hundred and fifty people were responsible for the dispossession of William Somers in 1597.[11] The crowd that gathered in a barn in Altham, Lancashire, to witness the dispossession of Richard Dugdale in 1689 was so great that a hayloft collapsed under the weight of those who squeezed in to get the best view.[12] An even larger assembly of about a thousand people assembled to witness the examination of the demoniac Anna Mayer by the Lutheran governor of Stuttgart in 1695, but the officials who investigated this possession decided in the end that Mayer, who was a Catholic, was afflicted by a natural disease and sent her back to her native town of Rottenburg.[13] Although Protestants, when they did decide to conduct an exorcism, could not match the extravagance of the Catholic ritual of exorcism, which they considered to be superstitious and magical, they could nonetheless use their own procedures for dispossessing demoniacs by means of prayer and fasting to theatrical effect. Darrell, an accomplished showman, turned sessions of Protestant prayer and fasting into dramatic healing rituals.[14] The efforts of the New England minister Samuel Willard to dispossess Elizabeth Knapp in 1672 provided a 'gripping spectacle' for the crowds that witnessed his public performances.[15] These dispossessions often attracted onlookers as well as participants, and like many French Catholic exorcisms, they were intended as a form of religious propaganda.[16] No wonder that Samuel Harsnett, their most serious critic, claimed that such Protestant rituals were no less popish than the Catholic exorcisms undertaken by English Jesuits in the 1580s.

Since possessions had all the elements of good theatre, including a receptive audience, it is not surprising that they provided dramatic material for the playwrights of the age, who apparently recognized the theatricality of possessions and exorcisms more readily than have modern scholars. Their exploitation of this material for dramatic purposes made the knowledge of possessions available to those who might not have witnessed a possession at first hand or read about one in pamphlets. Thus a reciprocal relationship was established between possession and exorcism on the one hand and dramas that exploited such themes on the other. The incidents of possession that were widely known through the publication of possession narratives informed the plays, and those plays in turn informed the popular perception of possession and exorcism. It is even possible that these dramas provided scripts for those who became demoniacally possessed. The report that the body of the English demoniac Alexander Nyndge was 'wondrously transformed as it was before, much like the picture of a Devil in a play, with a horrible roaring voice, sounding Hell-bound' suggests that attendance at one of the plays might have inspired Alexander's performance or his brother's description of it.[17]

In his analysis of this reciprocal relationship between possession and the theatre, Stephen Greenblatt points out the paradox that English exorcists, despite their participation in these sacred dramas, did not want their rituals and performances to be considered theatrical because the theatre was the

realm of the fictional, and these writers desperately needed their audiences
to accept the possessions as real. The dramatic representation of possessions as fictional explains why the sceptical English clergyman Samuel
Harsnett supported such representations in the early seventeenth century.[18]
Indeed, the most compelling depictions of possession in early modern
literature come from Ben Jonson, who in *Volpone* (1606) and *The Devil is
an Ass* (1616) mocked the belief in possessions.[19] In both of these plays the
symptoms of possession were presented as clearly fraudulent. In *Volpone*,
the fake demoniac Voltore, who is coached by Volpone, acts out the symptoms of possession, including the vomiting of crooked pins, in a highly
histrionic manner. The character Fitzdottrel in *The Devil is an Ass* pretends
to be possessed to invalidate a legal document that had resulted in the loss
of his estate. He completely convinces the judge, Sir Paul Eitherside, that
he is truly possessed. The demon Pug (who had persuaded Satan to send
him to Earth at the beginning of the play) tells Fitzdottrel that his coach,
the swindler Meercraft, will 'teach you such tricks to make your belly swell,
and your eyes turn, to foam, to stare, to gnash your teeth together and to
beat yourself, laugh loud and feign six voices'.[20] Meercraft tells him how to
use soap to produce the appearance of foam in the mouth, just as Darrell
had done with the demoniacs Thomas Darling, the Lancashire Seven, and
William Somers.[21]

Shakespeare, who was influenced by Harsnett's scepticism, presents the
possession of Edgar, disguised as Poor Tom, in *King Lear* (1605) as clearly
fictional. He mocks Tom's diet, claiming that in the fury of his possession
caused by the Devil he eats cow-dung for salad, swallows a rat and a dog,
and 'drinks the green mantle of the standing pool'.[22] In this context
Shakespeare also mocks the belief in the Devil himself, referring to Satan
as the 'foul fiend' and the Prince of Darkness. Greenblatt explains that in
King Lear, 'demonic possession is responsibly marked out for the audience
as a theatrical fraud, designed to gull the unsuspecting'.[23] *Twelfth Night*,
written four years before *Lear*, does not display the same degree of scepticism and mockery, but the introduction of Sir Topas, a Calvinist minister
modelled on John Darrell, to cure Malvolio's 'possession' can hardly be
taken as an endorsement of the reality of possession or the effectiveness of
exorcism, especially since Shakespeare represents Malvolio's possession as
love madness.[24]

Not all theatrical representations of possession and exorcism in early
modern dramatic productions were intended to suggest that these experiences and practices in real life were fraudulent. To be sure, many English
dramas clearly stated or implied as much, as did the anonymous Lutheran
play of 1675, *Der visierliche Exorcist*, which lampooned the tactics of a

Catholic exorcist 'who drives out the fleshly spirits that torment maidens by using fraud and games to beat them out'.[25] But in kingdoms where a more credulous view of possession prevailed, plays reinforced belief in demonic power and the heroic efforts of priests to break that power. This was most evident in Spain, where the theatrical representation of possession and exorcism presumed their authenticity. In her comparative study of exorcism in English and Spanish literature, Hilaire Kallendorf points out that the exorcism scene in the Spanish comedy, *El pleyto que tuvo el diablo con el cura de Madrilejos* (The Lawsuit that the Devil had with a Priest of Madrilejos) is void of sarcasm or scepticism about exorcism and conveys unqualified support for the Catholic Church and its rituals.[26]

Modern playwrights and film directors have continued to exploit the theatrical potential of possession and exorcism, although they have not exhibited the same degree of scepticism as their early modern predecessors, perhaps because the authenticity of possessions is no longer a pressing theological issue. The possession of the Ursuline nuns at Loudun inspired two major motion pictures: *Mother Joan of the Angels* (1961) by the Polish director Jerzy Kawalerowicz and the extravagant if not sensational movie *The Devils*, directed by Ken Russell in 1971. A modern case of possession and exorcism in Washington, DC in 1949, the subject of William Peter Blatty's novel *The Exorcist* (1971), was made into a motion picture in 1973 and produced in a new version in 2000. A book by Matt Baglio, *The Rite*, which chronicles the training of an American priest as an exorcist in Rome, was released as a motion picture in 2011, although not to critical acclaim. Demons, demoniacs, and exorcists have had enduring appeal to playwrights and to theatre audiences.

Staging possessions

Anthropologists who have emphasized the theatrical nature of possessions in African and Caribbean cultures have focused on voluntary possessions— those in which the individual deliberately tries to make contact with the supernatural world. In his classic study of ritual possession in Haiti, Alfred Métraux argues that 'every possession has a theatrical aspect', but he limits that analysis to those who deliberately set out to become possessed. Métraux distinguishes these religious actors from the 'hysterics' who thought of themselves as victims of the Devil and whose experience was morbid and frightening.[27] Since Métraux considers demonic possessions involuntary and sees no reason why a person would want to invite evil spirits into their bodies, he does not explore the theatricality of demonic possessions.[28]

The most theatrical possessions in early modern Europe were those in which the apparent victims of demonic assault simulated their possessions. They did so because the appearance of possession offered them some benefit or advantage, such as the temporary freedom to violate moral or legal norms with impunity, the acquisition of fame, or financial gain. Since they needed to convince others that they were possessed, they learned how to feign convulsions, utter blasphemies and curses, swallow and regurgitate pins and other materials, speak from the belly through the art of ventriloquism, and pretend that they were hallucinating.[29] Contemporaries familiar with the theatre were more likely to detect the histrionics of fraudulent demoniacs than those who were not. François Hédelin, the only French cleric who concluded that the nuns at Loudun were deliberately faking their possessions, was himself a playwright and wrote a book on dramatic theory that established standards for dramatic techniques and presentation. One reason Hédelin visited Loudun was to gather information on crowd behaviour for a project that would redefine the audience for dramatic spectacle.[30]

The theatrical performances of Marthe Brossier, the twenty-five-year-old demoniac from Romorantin, acquired greater notoriety than those of any other early modern European demoniac. There is little doubt that Brossier's possession, which began in 1598 and continued intermittently through the following year, was fraudulent. At the very beginning of her career as a self-proclaimed demoniac, ecclesiastical authorities forbade priests in her diocese to exorcize her 'fictitious spirit', and she failed every test to prove the authenticity of her demonic experience. She went into convulsions when told that ordinary water was blessed but failed to respond appropriately when holy water was used in its place. She also went into convulsions when the opening lines of Virgil's *Aeneid* were read to her, thinking that they were excerpts from the bishop's exorcism manual. A panel of theologians and doctors who examined Brossier in Paris discovered that she did not understand Latin or Greek and that there was little evidence she had contracted a disease. Capuchin monks and theologians who subsequently challenged these findings produced no credible evidence to the contrary.[31]

Marthe Brossier was not as accomplished an actress as other fraudulent demoniacs, but she was by far the most widely travelled. After her failure to win support in her own diocese of Orléans, she travelled with her father to Paris, where she hoped to exploit anti-Huguenot sentiment in the wake of the promulgation of the Edict of Nantes, which had given freedom of worship to the Huguenots in 1598. After Marthe had been exposed as a counterfeit demoniac, King Henri IV ordered her and her father to return to Romorantin, where the local judge had instructions to keep her from travelling to other locations. In December 1599, however, the prior of the Capuchin monastery abducted her, and she was taken to Tarascon and Avignon to give further anti-Huguenot performances. From there she went to Rome to see Pope Clement VIII. She remained in Italy at least until 1604, when she was reported as having experienced convulsions in Milan. Marthe Brossier thus gave a new dimension to the theatre of the possessed by turning her possession into a travelling road show, not unlike those of itinerant troupes in early modern Europe or the national tours of Broadway shows in modern America.

The fraudulent possession of Anne Gunter in 1604 did not acquire the same international exposure or notoriety as that of Marthe Brossier, nor did it involve a public exorcism, but it was nonetheless a theatrical performance before a smaller, academic audience. Like that of Brossier, it also involved the participation of the demoniac's father, who wrote the plot and served as stage manager. When the sixteen-year-old Anne took sick in 1604, experiencing convulsive fits of undetermined origin, her father, Brian Gunter, recognized the opportunity to settle disputes he had with some of his neighbours in the village of North Moreton, Berkshire, not far from Oxford. He therefore deliberately induced many more symptoms of possession in his daughter, putting her head in the smoke of burning brimstone, administering intoxicating drinks to her, forcing her to swallow salad oil to make her vomit, beating her, and thrusting pins into her while she was asleep. In need of an appropriate setting for her performances, he sent her off to Exeter College, where her brother-in-law, Thomas Holland, the Regius professor of divinity, was principal.[32] There, before gatherings of up to forty fellows, students, and dons, Anne performed her various tricks on cue whenever an audience had assembled. As might be expected, many of these observers noted inconsistencies in her actions or discovered that she could not pass various tests they devised to prove the authenticity of her fits. Dr John Harding, the Hebrew reader for the University of Oxford and president of Magdalen College, observed that although Anne claimed to be able to read while blind, she could not continue her reading once the lights went out.[33] The second son of the Scottish earl of Murray, a student at Exeter, discovered the different means she used to untie her shoes and garters and move them along the floor.[34] When tried before the Court of Star Chamber for conspiring to indict her father's enemies for witchcraft, Anne confessed her tricks and explained her father's role in her fraudulent possession.

This book argues that all possessions—not just those that were pretended—should be understood as cultural performances that had meaning for the demoniacs, the ministers, and the audience.[35] In these possessions the demoniacs did not necessarily know they were acting; they simply assumed a role that was available to them in their religious culture. For this reason the quality of their acting skills was uneven. One group of such demoniacs who were apparently aware that they were performing comprised those whose possessions straddled the poorly defined boundary between the demoniac and the saint. Like the counterfeit demoniacs with whom they were sometimes erroneously identified, they were particularly good at following scripts, responding to cues, and interacting with their audiences. Nicole Obry in France, Thomas Darling in England, and Benedetta Carlini in Italy all fall into this category. Even though they were not pretending to be possessed, all three have won high marks for their acting ability.

The possession of Nicole Obry apparently originated in her guilt over her family's failure to make a pilgrimage that her grandfather's ghost had requested in a vision. Dismissing the possibility that her grandfather's soul had actually entered her body, the clergy who examined Nicole first thought that her grandfather's good angel had possessed her, but on second thought they decided that it was Beelzebub. They persuaded the young woman that this was the true cause of her afflictions, and after that she played the role of a demoniac brilliantly, despite the fact that she had no theatrical training or experience. The reason for her successful performance was most probably that her exorcists directed the entire show, feeding her all of Beelzebub's theological pro-Huguenot comments and cooperating with her successful cure by means of the Eucharist. Like many other French demoniacs, Nicole was suspected of fraud, but she lacked any apparent motivation for this type of deliberate dissimulation.

The possession of the thirteen-year-old Thomas Darling, of Burton upon Trent, whom John Darrell dispossessed in 1596, resembles that of Nicole Obry in some respects. When Darling, who was arguably more pious than Obry, displayed some of the common symptoms of possession, such as vomiting and falling into convulsions, the Puritan ministers who observed him concluded that he was possessed by the Devil. Suspicion of having caused his possession soon fell on Alice Gooderidge, an old woman with three warts on her face who, on a chance encounter with the boy in the woods (after he had farted in her presence), told him he was going to Hell. The narrative of Darling's possession, written mainly by Jesse Bee, a relative of Darling by marriage, and edited by the Puritan John Denison, was intended to establish the connection between witchcraft and possession, much in the same way that the published account of

1 Christ expels an unclean spirit. The eighteenth-century Dutch artist Gerard Hoet depicts Christ healing the demoniac in the synagogue at Capernaum at the beginning of his public ministry. The engraving was included in a Dutch Bible to illustrate the exorcism text of Mark 1: 23.

2 Christ exorcising a demoniac. This thirteenth-century manuscript illustration depicts the demon as a man with wings who is addressing Christ. The image was intended to represent the exorcism at Capernaum, in which the demon asked Christ, 'What have you to do with us, Jesus of Nazareth?'

3 St Eligius performing an exorcism. St Eligius (c. 590–659) was the bishop of Noyon. Painted in the fifteenth century by an anonymous artist, Eligius is shown praying, while two men are restraining the demoniac. The departing demon, depicted here as exceptionally large, has horns and bat wings.

4 St Catherine of Siena exorcizes a possessed woman. This seventeenth-century French engraving depicts St Catherine of Siena (1347–80) performing an exorcism of a female demoniac. Most exorcisms were performed by men, but Catherine's holiness qualified her for this role.

5 Exorcism of a young German woman in the fourteenth century. A sixteenth-century panel painting of an exorcism that took place in 1370 at the shrine of the Virgin Mary at Zell in Styria shows the exorcist has wrapped his stole around the woman's neck. The demoniac had been so tortured by the demons that she had killed her parents and infant, shown on the floor to the left. The numerous exorcised demons are leaving through the window.

6 The exorcism of Nicole Obry at the Cathedral of Laon in 1566. In the foreground Obry is being carried in a procession to the cathedral, while in the centre a crowd gathers below an improvised stage to witness different scenes of the exorcism. Near the top the exorcized demons are departing.

7 Administration of the Blessed Sacrament to Nicole Obry in 1566. French exorcists used the Eucharist in exorcisms as part of a propaganda campaign against the Huguenots to prove that Christ was really present in the Eucharist and that the Catholic Church was the one true Church established by Christ. Catholics considered both the Eucharist and exorcism to be miracles.

8 Execution of Urbain Grandier at Loudun in 1634. Grandier was one of three French priests convicted of causing the possession of nuns by means of witchcraft in the first half of the seventeenth century. The exorcism of the nuns takes place in the background.

9 St Ignatius of Loyola healing the possessed. This large painting by Peter Paul Rubens, originally placed above the altar in the Jesuit church at Antwerp in 1618, depicts St Ignatius, the founder of the Jesuit order, with one hand on the altar and the other raised to God. The people below him include a male and a female demoniac in the midst of their convulsions.

10 The exorcism of Madeleine Bavent in 1643. The first nun to be exorcised at Louviers, Bavent was subsequently accused of witchcraft, apostasy, sacrilege, and of having 'lewdly prostituted her body' to demons and warlocks at the witches' sabbath.

11 An Italian exorcism in the seventeenth century. This engraving by Jacques Callot depicts an unidentified woman during her exorcism. The woman's back is arched, her limbs are extended, and her head is twisted to her left. A picture of the Virgin Mary, whose help was often solicited in Catholic exorcisms, is in the background. The inscription explains that the demoniac's deliverance was attributed to this painting. The framing of the print in a proscenium arch gives the scene a dramatic character.

12 Christoph Haizmann's two paintings of the Devil. The Bavarian demoniac Christoph Haizmann, a painter working in Austria, made nine paintings to illustrate his encounters with the Devil. In the first painting, the Devil has four breasts and talons. In the second the Devil, holding the apple of temptation and smoking a pipe, exhibits human features, including multiple breasts, as well as the features of a goat.

13 The symptoms of hysteria I. Jean-François Badoureau depicts Louise Lateau, a patient in Jean-Martin Chacot's clinic, experiencing a hysterical attack in the late nineteenth century. The drawing shows the inflexibility of the woman's crossed legs and her extruded tongue. Charcot, who made the original sketch for the engraving, claimed that the symptoms of possession were the same as those of hysteria and that demoniacs in the early modern period were really suffering from hysteria.

14 The symptoms of hysteria II. Hysterics were observed arching their backs in the second stage of a hysterical attack, as depicted in this sketch of a patient in Charcot's clinic. Many demoniacs were reported to have demonstrated similar agility. The exercise was difficult but not impossible to perform.

A
TRVE AND
FEAREFVLL VEX-
ATION OF ONE
ALEXANDER NYNDGE:

BEING MOST HORRIBLY TORMEN-
ted with the Deuill, from the 20. day of *Ianuary*,
to the 23. of *Iuly*. At Lyering ſwell in
Suffocke: with his *Prayer after his
Deliuerance*.

WRITTEN BY HIS OWNE BROTHE.
EDVVARD NYNDGE Maſter of Arts, with the
Names of the Witneſſes that were
at his Vexation.

¶ Imprinted at London for *W. B.* and are to bee ſold by
EDVVARD WRIGHT at *Chriſt-Church gate*.
1 6 1 6.

15 Title page of *A True and Fearefull Vexation of One Alexander Nyndge* (London, 1615). The inclusion of images of actors on the title page of this possession narrative was probably intended to illustrate the connection between the Devil and the theatre. Alexander's brother Edward, who wrote the narrative, says that Alexander during his possession resembled the 'picture of a Devil in a play'. Puritans objected to the theatre because male actors playing female roles, as depicted on this page, violated the biblical prohibition of transvestitism and because plays were considered to be the work of the Devil.

16 William Hogarth, *Credulity, Superstition, and Fanaticism*. The English artist William Hogarth has, here, satirized religious enthusiasm and the beliefs it inspired. Hogarth linked witchcraft, indicated by the witch on a broomstick held by a Methodist minister, and demonic possession, indicated by William Perry, the Boy of Bilson, vomiting pins beneath the lectern. The woman in the foreground delivering rabbits is Mary Tofts, who was believed to have delivered fourteen rabbits in 1726. By including her in this engraving, of 1762 Hogarth linked popular belief in 'prodigies' with the 'irrational' belief in possession and witchcraft.

the possession of the five children of Robert Throckmorton in 1589 had linked the two beliefs and practices. For this reason the narrative of Darling's possession said that he had actually vomited devils upon becoming possessed. It also reported that when the Gospel of St John was read to him, the boy went into 'a marvelously sore fit' once he came upon the ninth verse of the first chapter.[36]

What made Darling's possession different from those of most other demoniacs was that he insisted throughout the whole process that he was possessed by the spirit of God, not the Devil. The script he followed indicated much greater faith in Jesus Christ than the professed belief of most other Puritan demoniacs that they were going to Hell. When sent into one of his many fits, Darling said to Satan: 'Do you say that I will worship you? I will worship the Lord of Hosts only', and after reacting violently to a verse from John, he demanded cheerfully: 'Read on in God's name.' During the entire experience he spoke with two voices, one being his and the other that of a demon. Towards the end of his possession he commanded Satan with these words: 'Away Satan away! You are a liar and the father of lies.' These were hardly the words of a conventional Protestant demoniac. Like all Protestant demoniacs he was involved in a struggle with Satan, but unlike almost all of them, he played a role of an aspiring Puritan saint rather than a miserable sinner who was resigned to a sentence of eternal damnation.[37]

Like Nicole Obry, Thomas Darling was accused of being a counterfeit demoniac, and during John Darrell's trial before the Court of High Commission a few years later he was persuaded or coerced to admit as much. But shortly after he testified in that proceeding, he withdrew his confession. He had no ostensible reason to fake his possession, and his claim that he was possessed by the spirit of God appeared to carry conviction. Nevertheless, this young boy was a voluntary demoniac, in that he deliberately scripted his possession, incorporating elements that reflected both divine and demonic inspiration. His possession may not have been a 'little dramatic masterpiece', as D.P. Walker has claimed, but he composed an original script that drew upon various sources with which he was familiar from his religious education. The description of Hell that he gave in the voice of Beelzebub, for example, incorporated details he probably learned from the sermons he had heard about the demonic underworld.[38]

A third example of a possession that straddled the boundary between a divine and a demonic experience and also involved the display of theatrical talent was that of Benedetta Carlini, the abbess of the Theatine Convent of the Mother of God in the small Tuscan town of Pescia. Benedetta cultivated a reputation as a mystic who had become the bride of Christ. In the course of this mystical process she had displayed many of the signs of divine possession, including ecstasies, visions, stigmata, and vomiting. During an ecclesiastical investigation of the authenticity of her mystical possessions in 1619, another nun in the convent, Bartolomea, testified that she and Benedetta had engaged in a variety of sexual practices. In responding to these charges Benedetta insisted that it was not she, but a beautiful male angel named Splendiletto who had sometimes occupied her body and performed the immodest acts with Bartolomea. When Benedetta spoke as Splendiletto, her voice apparently changed, but, like Thomas Darling, she could speak in her natural voice as well. It is understandable why the suspicion arose during this investigation that a demon rather than a good angel had possessed her.[39]

In any case, Benedetta's representation of herself as possessed by a spirit served her purposes, since it insulated her from possible punishment. She displayed considerable skill as an actress, which she may have developed by performing in dramas, sometimes taking male parts, in the convent. She therefore knew how to dress and talk like a man. She was also familiar with the way possessed people acted, and that knowledge helped make her performance more credible. She knew, for example, that as a credible demoniac she should not admit remembering any sexual encounters with Bartolomea. It is tempting to conclude that she had feigned her possessions, first to gain fame as a mystic and then to avoid punishment as a sex offender. Judith Brown has suggested, however, that by putting so much effort into representing herself as a woman possessed, Benedetta may have become part of the audience—that she may have convinced herself that she had an alternative identity.[40]

The common element in all these 'authentic' possessions was that the demoniacs, once they had experienced the initial symptoms of possession for any number of possible psychological or medical reasons, and once the ecclesiastical authorities in their community or diocese determined that they were possessed, acted the way that demoniacs in their religious culture were expected to act. Expressed in the language of the theory of role enactment, they assumed the role of a performer of a socially or culturally defined activity that involved either prescribed patterns of subjective experience or overt behaviour.[41] In this way they all became performers in the sacred drama of possession.

The possessions of the five daughters of Robert Throckmorton and seven of the maidservants in the Throckmorton household in Warboys, Huntingdonshire between 1589 and 1593 provide an example of how Protestant demoniacs could participate in the theatre of possession without being aware that they were acting or following a script. It does not appear that the Throckmorton children, who began to experience convulsions and fits in 1589, were deliberately simulating possession. Nor does it appear, at least on the basis of the one published account of the case, that their parents were coaching them. On the contrary, instead of taking the initiative in arranging this production, the parents belatedly endorsed what their children said and did. Nor did the local parson, Dr Dorington, play a role similar to that of the Puritan exorcist John Darrell in the following seven years. Nevertheless there are many indications that the children were engaged in a theatrical performance that even convinced one of the three women accused of bewitching them, Alice Samuel, that she had bewitched the children and caused their possession.[42]

After the diagnosis of their afflictions as a case of demonic possession, the five Throckmorton children assumed the culturally prescribed role that was available to them. The long published account of their possession and the prosecution of three witches who were held responsible for their afflictions show that these demoniacs were following scripts encoded in their Protestant religious culture. The sources of these scripts were the narratives of other English possessions and witchcraft prosecutions, the sermons they heard, and some of the religious literature produced by godly ministers of their day. The children's scripts therefore bore a distinctly Protestant stamp. They resisted participation in religious exercises, were unable to pray, reacted violently when Dr Dorington began praying after a meal at their house, could not read the Bible, would not keep holy the Sabbath, and enjoyed the Puritan vice of playing cards while under the Devil's influence. The demons that inhabited their bodies were the demonic familiars of Mother Samuel, a seventy-six-year-old woman who was accused of causing the girls' possession by means of witchcraft. Such familiars were unique to English witchcraft and had been prominent in the widely publicized trials of the Chelmsford witches in 1589, the year in which the possession of the Throckmorton daughters had begun.[43] The possession of the Throckmorton girls was the first such case in England that was linked to witchcraft, an association that became routine through most of the seventeenth century.

The possessions of Ursuline nuns at Auxonne between 1653 and 1658 provide another example of how demoniacs could participate in theatrical performances without realizing that they were doing so. Like the group possessions at Aix-en-Provence, Loudun, and Louviers, the possession at Auxonne originated in the nuns' sexual anxieties or guilt, but unlike those earlier group possessions, the proceedings at Auxonne did not focus on charges that priest confessors had sexual relations with them.

Instead they involved allegations of lesbian activity of the nuns with Barbe Buvée, the Mother Superior of the convent. Thus they did not follow the scripts of these other group possessions, and the only script they might have used, that of Benedetta Carlini in Italy twenty years earlier, would not have been available to them, as the Roman Inquisition's investigations of that episode had not yet been published. It is likely that the original symptoms that the nuns displayed were involuntary, probably resulting from their guilt for whatever sexual activities they had engaged in or the sexual fantasies they had entertained. In this connection it is interesting to note that only one of the many physicians called in to examine the nuns argued that they were acting fraudulently, and even he admitted that a few of them might have been genuinely ill. The report of another doctor in 1662 concluded that the nuns never displayed any legitimate or convincing sign of true possession, but he did not suggest that they were faking the symptoms of their possession. The only possible reason for doing so might have been the fear of prosecution for their immodest behaviour, but the investigation of Buvée for lesbianism did not commence until long after the nuns became possessed and had undergone exorcism. It is reasonable to speculate that their possessions were not deliberately staged.[44]

Yet these nuns did engage in theatrical performances. After displaying their initial symptoms, they acted more and more like other demoniacs, revealing hidden secrets, displaying preternatural strength, and worshipping the Blessed Sacrament with their bodies contorted in an arc. Responsibility for their having acted in this way probably lies with the exorcists, who were far more familiar with the conventional symptoms of possession than the nuns themselves and perhaps fed lines to them during their exorcism. The nuns were not very good actresses, but they performed when prompted. Unlike Nicole Obry, Thomas Darling, and Benedetta Carlini, however, they did not give any indication that they were deliberately putting on a show. Unlike those three demoniacs, the Auxonne nuns did not compose their own scripts by cobbling together various fragments of contemporary belief about possession. In some cases they may simply have been imitating the behaviour of their fellow nuns. The only deliberate step they might have taken was accusing Barbe Buvée of having sexually molested them. Everything else they said or did after their initial convulsions was part of the theatre of possession.

The performances of the nuns at Auxonne can be compared to those of hysterics whom Charcot and his colleagues examined and treated at Salpêtrière in the second half of the nineteenth century. Like early modern demoniacs, the hysterical patients of Charcot were engaged in theatrical performances, especially when they were hypnotized. The patients performed before large audiences; they responded to the 'stage directions' of medical personnel at the clinic; and they learned how to imitate other patients. Charcot concluded on the basis of his observation of these women that hysterics had an innate sense of drama and a talent for dissimulation. The women at Salpêtrière were often treated like actresses and posed for photographers. One of the hysterics, identified only as Blanche, was so talented that she was often compared to the great nineteenth-century actress Sarah Bernhardt, who actually observed one of Blanche's demonstrations at Salpêtrière. Blanche became a character in a play written by André de Lorde and Alfred Biset, *Une leçon à la Salpêtrière*, in 1908.[45]

Some of Charcot's hysterical patients were subject to accusations that they had deliberately deceived both their audiences and the doctors who were staging their performances. Some of these accusations of fraud were probably true. Some hysterics faked the symptoms of their illness for fear that if they did not perform as expected, they would have to leave the clinic. For the purposes of this comparison with seventeenth-century nuns we can say that these women became 'voluntary' hysterics. But fraud can no more easily explain the performance of all hysterics than the performances of all early modern demoniacs. Most demoniacs and hysterics acted the way they did while not fully conscious of what they were doing, a condition that rules out fraud. Certainly those who were hypnotized did not act voluntarily, except to the extent that they might have allowed themselves to be hypnotized.

Learning the scripts

How did demoniacs and those who participated in these cultural dramas learn their scripts? The most common method was by reading accounts of other possessions. The Bible was the source for many possessions, especially for Protestants. Because the scripts in the biblical accounts were brief and undeveloped, however, early modern demoniacs usually preferred to follow the scripts in more recent possession narratives. Marthe Brossier owned a copy of the possession narrative of Nicole Obry, which had been published thirty years earlier.[46] The nuns at Loudun had read Sebastian Michaelis's *Histoire admirable de la possession et conversion d'une pénitente* (1613), which was written to justify the prosecution of Louis Gaufridy in 1611. Michaelis's book became a foundational text for French demoniacs.[47] Anne Gunter had read the account of the possession of the Throckmorton children in 1589, thereby learning how to imitate their fits.[48] William

Somers had read the same account. In the trial of John Darrell in 1597 for his role in the exorcism of William Somers, the prosecution introduced published accounts of Darrell's exorcism of Thomas Darling, whom the preacher had dispossessed the year before.[49] In 1666 the German demoniac Anna Mayer was familiar with the possession of Anna Bernhausen in 1570, including the names of the demons that had possessed her.[50] The published accounts of the demonic possessions of Elizabeth Knapp in 1672 and of the Goodwin children in 1688, which were widely distributed throughout New England in the 1680s, helped to shape the performances of the afflicted girls at Salem in 1692 and 1693.[51] One reason for the relatively high proportion of literate demoniacs within both Protestant and Catholic communities was that they were able to read narratives of other possessions.[52]

Demoniacs, however, did not need to be literate to acquire knowledge of other possessions. Clergymen could just as easily communicate that knowledge to them orally. They could give sermons based on the exorcism texts in the New Testament, and they could also tell them about more recent possessions with which they were familiar. In 1585 Catholic priests in England related stories of possessions that they had either read about or witnessed at first hand to seven prisoners, leading the girls to believe that they themselves were possessed.[53] In 1704 a teenage boy from the Scottish shire of Fife began to display the signs of possession after his pastor read him the narrative of Christian Shaw's possession in the West Country seven years earlier.[54]

Whereas demoniacs learned their scripts from various sources, including narratives of other possessions, Catholic exorcists could also use the numerous scripts in published exorcists' manuals, which included a variety of verbal formulae for adjuring and expelling the demon. After 1614 they could follow the exorcism ritual in the official *Rituale Romanum* as well, although the unofficial manuals remained very popular. Exorcists not only followed these published scripts but also shaped the scripts of the demoniacs they were healing by feeding them lines in response to their commands or by confronting them with relics or crucifixes which might also provoke them to respond in word and action.

Protestant exorcists had their own scripts, which they usually learned from published narratives of recent Protestant possessions. Protestant exorcists were restricted to using the biblically sanctioned methods of prayer and fasting to drive out demons, although a few employed Catholic methods as well. The participation of the family and neighbours of the demoniacs in these prayers, in which the minister simply led the congregation, reflected the Protestant belief in the priesthood of all believers.

Sermons on biblical exorcism texts often supplemented the prayers for deliverance, as happened in the case of Mary Glover. For Protestant ministers who orchestrated these procedures, the scripts were available in the published sermons preached at earlier Protestant dispossessions.

Coaching

A drama coach was often involved in counterfeit possessions. John Darrell taught William Somers how to effect the illusion that a lump in his stomach travelled through his body by moving his fist under his bed sheets. In 1604, Brian Gunter coached his daughter Anne to vomit alien objects and go into fits, and in 1620 an old man taught William Perry, the Boy of Bilson, how to groan and moan, turn his neck and head both ways towards his back, 'gape hideously' with his mouth, grate his teeth, and 'put crooked pins, rags and such like baggage' in his mouth to make it appear that he vomited them.[55] After being exposed for not responding physically when the first verse of the Gospel of John was read in Greek and for making his urine blue by mixing it with ink, Perry confessed to his chicanery. In West Ham, Essex, Elizabeth Saunders, a yeoman's wife, testified before the Court of Star Chamber how she taught the demoniac Katheren Malpas to pretend that she was in a trance so that people would 'come to see her in pity and commiseration' and give her money.[56] In Scotland Mr Patrick Cowper, the minister in the fishing burgh of Pittenweem, coached the teenage demoniac Patrick Morton at every stage of his possession by reading him the narrative of Christian Shaw's possession and by helping him identify the witches whom he accused of having caused his possession.[57]

French priests were also suspected of coaching demoniacs, although none of the possessed ever confessed to fraud, as had William Somers, Anne Gunter, and William Perry. In December 1632 the sceptical archbishop of Bordeaux sent a group of Catholic physicians to investigate whether Sister Jeanne des Anges had exhibited any supernatural signs. In particular he wanted them to determine whether the assistants of the exorcists had fed information to her so that she could divine occurrences in faraway places, or could say eight or ten words, correct and well constructed, in several different languages, or whether she, being bound hand and foot on a mattress on the floor, could rise and float in the air for a considerable period of time.[58] In another French possession in the following century, the Jesuits claimed that the Franciscan brothers of Toulon coached the demoniac Marie-Catherine Cadière to exhibit the symptoms of possession.[59]

Contact with other demoniacs

In more close-knit environments demoniacs learned possession scripts from their neighbours. In the possession epidemics that took place in the Lorraine village of Mattaincourt in 1633, in a number of German towns, including Paderborn and Mecklenburg,[60] in four orphanages in the Dutch Republic as well as one in Rome in 1554, and in a number of French, Italian, and Spanish convents the symptoms of possession spread from one or two demoniacs to the entire community. It is likely that all the demoniacs in these communities found it therapeutic or otherwise advantageous, deliberately or not, to engage in the same cultural performance as the other members of the community. Dissemination of information about psychosomatic disorders can contribute to the development of the very same disorders among the audience. Ethan Waters has argued that the export of knowledge of American mental health problems, such as post-traumatic stress disorder, anorexia, and depression, has actually contributed to the spread of these maladies throughout the globe.[61] If the spread of psychiatric information can have this effect, then surely the observation of other demoniacs or the discussion of demonic possession in the wake of a possession could have led others to act accordingly.

Catholic and Protestant scripts

One of the most striking features of early modern possessions is that the scripts followed by Catholics and Protestants differed significantly, sometimes profoundly. The reason for this is that Protestants and Catholics had different beliefs, sometimes reflected in different liturgical practices, that affected how they described and interpreted possessions and how they thought those possessions should be ended. Catholics and Protestants had different views regarding the sacraments, the sources of religious truth, the Blessed Virgin Mary, the gravity of sexual offences, and the attainment of salvation.

Sacraments and sacramentals

Roman Catholicism was a sacramental culture. At its core was the belief that the sacred, which is by definition something hidden and mysterious, can be manifested through material objects and rituals. In this way Catholics invested the secular or the profane with sacred status.[62] Thus the seven sacraments, most of which were administered using materials, were believed to bestow grace on their recipients and were therefore instrumental in, if not essential for, salvation. Protestants, on the other hand believed that the sacraments were only a sign of God's freely granted grace, not conduits through which that grace flowed. Protestants moreover, reduced the number of sacraments from seven to two: baptism and the Eucharist. These were the only sacraments that had a scriptural foundation. Protestants characteristically considered the entire Catholic sacramental system superstitious and magical.

The most controversial differences between Catholics and Protestants regarding the sacraments were their beliefs regarding the Eucharist or the sacrament of the altar, more commonly known to Protestants as the Lord's Supper. This was for all Christians the central ritual in Christianity, but Protestants and Catholics held very different views regarding what actually took place during it. Catholics, following the exposition of Thomas Aquinas, claimed that when the priest consecrated the bread and wine during the Mass the two substances were miraculously transformed into the body and blood of Christ, although their accidents or appearances remained those of bread and wine. This doctrine of transubstantiation became the acid test of Catholic allegiance; so much so that Protestants in England were required to take an oath rejecting it in the seventeenth century.[63] Its importance explains why the consecration of the bread and wine was the central feature of the Catholic Mass and why Catholics engaged in practices in which they adored the consecrated host when it was displayed publicly. It actually *was* the body of Jesus Christ.

Among Protestants there was a range of doctrinal views regarding the Eucharist. The most conservative position, held by Lutherans, was that Christ was really present in communion but that the substances of the bread and wine and those of Christ's body and blood coexisted; hence the Lutheran doctrine was known as consubstantiation. Protestants in the Reformed tradition, however, adopted the argument of the Swiss reformer Ulrich Zwingli that Christ was not really present in the sacrament and that the ceremony was only a remembrance of Christ's sacrifice on the cross. English Protestant views included both Zwinglian and Lutheran elements, but Protestants of all stripes rejected the doctrine of transubstantiation. Calvinists actually rejected the Catholic ceremony as idolatrous. In 1635 a French Huguenot general, after sacking a Catholic town in the Netherlands, indicated his contempt for Catholic communion hosts by feeding them to his horses.[64]

The Catholic position regarding the Eucharist became central to the ritual of exorcism, which the Catholic clergy used to prove that by successfully casting out demons theirs was the one true Church founded by Christ. Beginning with the exorcism of Nicole Obry in 1566, the Eucharist became the main prop in these theatrical productions.[65] The exorcist would carry the host in a monstrance in a procession to the site of the exorcism and present it to the demoniac to elicit a hostile reaction. The communion host would then be used to expel the demon. At Laon the host was held up before Obry's face, aggravating all the symptoms of her possession. No wonder that Protestants made every effort to expose such exorcisms and possessions as fraudulent.

Catholics also emphasized the use of sacramentals—practices and material objects that did not bestow grace in the manner of sacraments but which nonetheless promoted the piety of those who employed them. Unlike the sacraments, sacramentals were not held to have been instituted by Christ. Among the most commonly used were holy water, relics, and holy oils, all of which Catholics used in exorcisms. The rite of exorcism was itself a sacramental. Protestants considered all sacramentals to be superstitious and magical, and they buttressed their claim by arguing that they had no scriptural warrant.

Scripture and Tradition

Protestants and Catholics disagreed fundamentally on the sources of religious truth. Catholics have always claimed that religious truth is embodied in both Scripture, the revealed word of God, and Tradition, which comprises the teachings of the Church Fathers and the councils of the Church. By contrast Protestants have always insisted on the doctrine of *sola scriptura*—that the Bible alone is the only source of both religious truth and proper religious and moral behaviour.

The biblicism of Protestantism had a profound effect on the content and form of possessions. It can most readily be seen in the way that demoniacs reacted to sacred objects during possession. Catholic demoniacs often demonstrated a horror of material objects that were held as sacred in Catholicism, such as relics, crucifixes, and other objects that had been blessed or consecrated. Protestants, however, considered such material objects magical and sources of false worship; what was sacred in Protestantism was the Word of God. Protestant demoniacs, therefore, reacted negatively to the presence or the reading of bibles; not so much to the physical books themselves, but to the Word they embodied. When the Starkey children in Lancashire went into convulsions 'some of them gave to scoffing and blasphemy, calling the holy Bible being brought up *bible babble bible babble*'.[66] In 1664 John Barrow, of Southwark, reported that if anyone in the presence of his possessed son James would take up a bible and 'mention the word of God or Christ in his hearing, he would roar and cry, making a hideous noise'.[67] The eldest of the Puritan Goodwin children in Boston in 1688 experienced 'dismal agonies' when anyone read an English bible in the room, even though she 'saw and heard nothing of it'. Her reaction was the same when someone tried to read either the Greek New Testament or the Hebrew Bible 'secretly or silently'.[68]

The Goodwin girl also reacted with 'hideous convulsions' to books that promoted Protestant beliefs, such as Protestant catechisms, even though she, a pious young woman, had 'once learned them with all the love that could be'. According to Cotton Mather, 'it would kill her to look into any book that (in my opinion) might have been profitable and edifying for her to be reading'. Nor could she read a book which proved that witches existed. On the other hand she could easily read 'popish' books and the English Book of Common Prayer, which New England Puritans also considered popish. The Devil, allegedly speaking through this young woman, claimed that the Prayer Book was her Bible.[69]

Protestant biblicism had a fundamental effect on the means by which clerical authorities endeavoured to expel evil spirits from the bodies of demoniacs. The Catholic ritual had developed over a long period of time and had incorporated many of the beliefs that had grown up around it. Catholic exorcism was a dynamic process that gradually became more elaborate than its original biblical model. Protestants insisted that the only approved methods of dispossession were the prayer and fasting used in the exorcism of the epileptic boy in the New Testament. Though some Protestants, most notably Lutherans, incorporated some elements of the Catholic ritual into their ceremonies, the contrast between the two procedures was the most striking difference between Catholic and Protestant possessions.

The Virgin Mary

The profound differences between Protestant and Catholic views of the Virgin Mary had a direct effect on the scripts of both demoniacs and exorcists. Because of the high place that Mary as the mother of Christ was believed to have in Heaven, where she was queen, she became the centre of many cults during the Middle Ages. As with the honouring of other saints, these devotional practices gave the impression that people actually worshipped Mary and thought of her as in some way divine. Protestants, committed to defending the sovereignty of God, to whom all worship was due (a position that medieval Catholic theologians had also insisted on in their struggle against dualist heretics) condemned Marian devotions and argued that Mary, as the mother of God, shared none of the divinity of her son.

Catholics continued to promote devotion to Mary, adding an important dimension to her 'worship' by promoting the saying of the rosary after the Catholic victory over the Turks at Lepanto in 1571. The intercessory power of the power of the Blessed Virgin Mary was considered to be so great that the recitation of the prayer 'Hail Mary' became a frequent part of the exorcism ritual, as it still is today. This explains why Christoph Haizmann was taken to the shrine of the Blessed Virgin at Zell to be exorcized. Appealing to the mother of God to intercede on behalf of demoniacs took its place alongside the use of the Eucharist in the effort to prove that Roman Catholicism was alone capable of driving out demons.[70]

Sin and salvation

One of the most profound differences between Protestantism and Catholicism concerned soteriology—the body of thought regarding the process of obtaining personal salvation. At the risk of oversimplifying a complex problem, Catholicism held that salvation was attainable for all and that although God granted initial or 'prevenient' grace gratuitously, the human will remained free either to accept it or reject it. Thus one could actually cooperate with God in the attainment of salvation, mainly by means of the sacraments, which provided further infusions of grace, and the performance of charitable works. This set of beliefs was a source of comfort to troubled souls, who felt that salvation was always within reach, even at the hour of death.

Protestants did not subscribe to a single set of beliefs regarding salvation, but all Protestant confessions accepted, at least in theory, the doctrine of predestination, the belief that before the world began God determined who would be saved. Protestants rejected the Catholic doctrine that the will was free in matters relating to salvation, and therefore they could not, like Catholics, play an active role in their quest for salvation. This belief caused widespread despair and occasional thoughts of suicide among Protestants, many of whom searched desperately for signs that God had predestined them to salvation and given them his freely granted grace. Calvinists developed the most radical formulation of this doctrine of predestination, claiming that the number of the elect was very small and that most men and women were damned to eternal perdition.

The doctrine of predestination was so difficult to accommodate that Protestants both within and outside the Calvinist camp struggled to modify it, to make it possible for a much larger group of Protestants to believe that they were or could be saved. Within Calvinism the followers of the Dutch theologian Jacobus Arminius challenged the harshest feature of the doctrine by claiming that the large majority of Christians were not predestined to Hell, arguing that God simply had foreknowledge of who would in fact be saved. This Arminianism, which denied that sin was part of God's creation, made deep inroads into English Protestantism in the seventeenth century, influencing not only the conservative followers of Archbishop William Laud but also many of the radical sects during the English Revolution of the 1640s, and it later came to characterize the main branch of eighteenth-century Methodism. Another development within English Protestantism that modified the harshest features of predestinarian doctrine was the formulation of Covenant Theology, which made it possible for Christians to believe they would be saved by performing the duties laid down in God's biblical covenants with humankind.

These modifications of the doctrine of predestination, reinforced by the pastoral reassurances that God's will in such matters could not be known, eased the burden of that doctrine, but they did not reduce the preoccupation of Protestantism with sin, which remained the main concern of Protestant demoniacs and the main source of the religious anxiety that was the proximate cause of their possessions.

The possession of the English Puritan Alexander Nyndge in late sixteenth-century England serves as an example of how Calvinist preoccupation with sin could dominate a possession narrative. In January 1573 Nyndge displayed a range of behaviours that convinced his brother Edward, the author of the narrative, that Alexander was possessed by the Devil. His chest and body swelled, his eyes bulged, he suffered convulsions, he bashed his head against the ground and the bedroom furniture, he demonstrated prodigious strength, he foamed at the mouth and became horribly disfigured. Edward's demonic diagnosis appeared to be confirmed when Alexander spoke in a base, hollow-sounding voice, which Edward identified as the voice of the demon that was tormenting him. As the narrative unfolds, the reader is told that the cause of the possession is Alexander's sinfulness and that the Devil has come not just to possess Alexander's body but his soul as well, a position which contradicted the traditional Catholic belief that the Devil could only possess the body.[71] The prayer that John Swan wrote for Mary Glover during her possession in 1602 said the same thing.[72] Later in the century the English Congregationalist minister Nathaniel Holmes, confirmed the Protestant position by saying that the Devil possessed the wicked, body and soul.[73]

The Calvinist belief in the Devil's ability to possess the soul was consistent with the Calvinist belief in a spiritual devil whose main activity was temptation. It also reflected the tendency of Calvinists such as Pierre Viret to think of possession as a spiritual or ethical rather than a physical operation. Among Catholics the Jesuit priest and exorcist Jean-Joseph Surin approximated the Protestant position on this question when he reinterpreted the possessions of the nuns at Loudun in mystical terms, claiming that the Devil was no longer confined to the body, as the scholastics had claimed, but was now also in the soul.[74]

Another example of a Protestant demoniac whose possession was marked by a deep sense of personal damnation was the English Puritan law student Robert Brigges. After attending a theological lecture in London on the topic of the unforgivable sin, which Mark 3: 28–30 identified as blaspheming against the Holy Spirit,[75] Brigges became convinced that he himself was an irredeemable sinner, hated by God and doomed to eternal damnation. In the following weeks and months he became more and more convinced that he was not numbered among the elect, and this conviction of irreversible damnation led him to make several attempts at suicide. When a physician in London diagnosed him as melancholic he became even more desperate. On Easter Sunday 1574 he swallowed a potion that he had taken without difficulty many times before, but this time he vomited his medicine and fell senseless for two hours. The following morning he lost his sight, and after that he gradually lost his hearing and feeling as well. With his faculty of speech still intact, he started reciting the Ten Commandments as a further indication of his obsession with his sins. Brigges's symptoms and speech began to attract the usual crowd of bystanders, who observed his emotional swings as he experienced demonic temptations to greed, murder, blasphemy, idolatry, heresy, and atheism. His struggles, which resulted from the internal spiritual anxiety that was endemic in Calvinism, were possible only in a religious culture that placed an inordinate emphasis on human sinfulness.[76]

Calvinist possessions could afflict both the pious and resolute sinners, but all Calvinist demoniacs had to deal with the overwhelming temptation to sin. This was true for the pious Goodwin children, who were possessed in Boston in 1688, as well as the Dutch boy who was sent to Tocutt (later renamed Branford) in Connecticut to reverse a long pattern of sinfulness. Despite his early career of lying and cheating and pretending that he was demonically afflicted, the boy (who was noted for his acting ability in his early life) had not yet succumbed to the ultimate temptation to conclude a pact with the Devil and thus become a witch. There was hope for even this obdurate sinner that he might resist temptation and be saved. In narrating this incident, Cotton Mather claimed that the boy's spiritual history illustrated 'the venom of sin, the wrath of God against sin, the malice of the Devil *and yet his limited power*'.[77]

The reminder that the Devil's power, however formidable, was limited inspired Protestant exorcisms, the main purpose of which was to help the demoniac resist Satan's temptations. For Protestant ministers who became involved in exorcisms the primary goal was to ask God to help the possessed person conquer sin. Relief from the physical symptoms of possession was a secondary concern and would occur only when the person was delivered from the effects of sin. This concern with the conquest of sin in Protestant exorcisms explains why the authors of possession narratives celebrated the spiritual victories of those who were delivered. These accounts of demoniacs overcoming temptation were intended to give hope to their readers that sin could be conquered and that they too might be saved, even if the doctrine of predestination told them their chances were slim. The English reformer John Parkhurst, bishop of Norwich, reported to the Swiss reformer Heinrich Bullinger in Zurich that two teenage demoniacs in the city in 1574 had happily resisted the temptation of the terrible adversary, ending with the departure of the adversary.[78] An anonymous Dutch Calvinist pamphlet of 1595 claimed that the demoniac David Wardavoir had triumphed over Satan through his faith in Jesus Christ.[79]

Giving the credit for the deliverance to God rather than to the demoniac was a consistent theme in Protestant possession narratives. Bishop Parkhurst ended his report of the dispossession of the two Norwich youths with the exclamation: 'To God be the praise!' When the evil spirit vacated the body of Thomas Darling in 1596, 'he fell flat on the ground, giving God thanks for his deliverance' and 'went presently into the town that it might appear what Jesus had done for him to the praise of his glory'.[80] When Mary Glover survived her spiritual ordeal, she thanked God for giving her the grace to break the will of Satan. Upon being exorcized by the Lutheran minister Johann Blumhardt in the nineteenth century, the demoniac Katharina Dittus proclaimed: 'Jesus is Victor.'[81] Such an attribution was unlikely to have been made in a Catholic exorcism. The proclaimed victor in a successful Catholic exorcism would have been either the demoniac, such as the woman exorcized by Jean Benedicti at Lyon in 1611, or the exorcist.[82]

Catholics did not place the same emphasis as Protestants on the pervasiveness of sin and the difficulty of resisting it. Nor did Catholic demoniacs usually reach the same state of spiritual despair. There were of course exceptions to this general pattern. Both the seventeenth-century Spanish priest Alonso Hidalgo and the French Jesuit Jean-Joseph Surin, who exorcized the nuns at Loudun, became convinced they were irrevocably damned, and in this mental state they began to display the symptoms of demonic possession. Both of these priests contemplated suicide.[83] But few

Catholics reached this state of desperation. The main reason is that Catholics had more weapons than Protestants to counter such a psychological state. Catholics had access to the sacrament of penance, through which their sins could be forgiven. Catholics also had ready access to the rite of exorcism, which meant that those who were demonically possessed could more easily be relieved of their suffering. Both Hidalgo and Surin, moreover, overcame their despair by convincing themselves that their possessions were signs of divine favour, a belief that illustrates the fine line that separated demonic and divine possession.[84]

Sexual morality

One of the most striking differences between Catholic and Protestant possession narratives was the much greater attention given to the sexual dimension of possessions in Roman Catholicism. Whereas Catholic demoniacs often entertained sexual fantasies, made sexually suggestive gestures, and accused the witches who caused their possession of enticing them sexually, Protestants rarely described sexuality as a central aspect of the possession experience. This is somewhat surprising, since both Catholic and Protestant authorities enforced strict standards of personal morality in the age of the Reformation, and they both punished sexual offences with greater severity than was customary in the pre-Reformation period. If anything, Protestant authorities were stricter than their Catholic counterparts in their condemnation of sexual crimes, which they prosecuted in both local ecclesiastical and secular courts.[85] One would expect therefore that sexual themes would be prominent features of Protestant possessions, especially since Protestant possessions were preoccupied with demonic temptation and sin.

The reason for this difference is that whereas Catholics were inordinately concerned with sexual offences, Protestants considered them just one category of sin that was no more serious than another. Late medieval and early modern Catholic literature on penance, especially the published manuals that gave guidance to priests hearing confessions, paid more attention to sexual sins than any others; they did not treat the seven deadly sins (one of them being lust) or any other enumerated sins equally. Moreover, within the general category of sexual sins Catholic constructed a hierarchy of such offences, ranging from fornication to bestiality, with rape of another man's wife only in the middle of the list, marginally less serious than the rape of a nun.[86] Protestants did not construct any such hierarchy of sexual transgressions, nor did they distinguish between mortal and venial sins, as did Catholics. All sins were equally abhorrent. The only sins that were more serious than others were the unforgivable sins of blasphemy and witchcraft, the latter involving blasphemy as well as apostasy. But sexual sins, especially the most common offences of adultery and fornication, were no more nor less serious than other moral failings that reflected an absence of discipline. When an unidentified English demoniac from Nottingham, almost certainly William Somers, was 'showed' a variety of sins, presumably in a vision, it included 'the filthy and horrible sins of whoredom both of the woman and the man', but it also included, without distinction, burglary, 'thieving and robbing by the high-ways with cruel murders', dancing, 'quarrelling and brawling with fighting and swearing', and the 'vain pastimes and unlawful games of dicing and carding'. It also included 'the deadly sin of drunkenness and the sin of gluttony set down by his eating so much that he fell off spewing and vomiting after it'.[87] This was a classic litany of the vices that Protestants were most determined to root out. The fact that Somers later confessed that he had faked his possession at the behest of John Darrell, the Puritan minister who came to Nottingham to dispossess him, does not reduce the importance of the script itself, which reflected Calvinist culture and may have been suggested by Somers's Puritan stepfather, John Cowper, who in response to the first report of William's possession confessed to one hundred and fifty sins of his own.[88]

The narrative that the Nonconformist minister Thomas Jolly wrote regarding the possession of Richard Dugdale, at Surey in Lancashire in 1688–9, reflected the same distinctive Calvinist view of the sinfulness of the demoniacs as Darrell's account of William Somers's possession. It is quite possible that Dugdale, like Somers, faked his possession, as the sceptical Anglican minister Zachary Taylor claimed. What is most revealing, however, is the way in which Jolly and a group of Dissenting ministers who testified regarding Dugdale's possession described the young man's experience. They claimed that his possession began when he was drunk and that the Devil tempted him by promising to make him a better dancer. During his possession, according to Jolly and his Nonconformist associates, Dugdale also started playing cards, dicing, and bowling, activities which, like dancing and drunkenness, were Calvinist vices. Noticeably absent in this Calvinist possession narrative was any reference to illicit sexuality.[89]

The second reason for the relative prominence of sexuality in Roman Catholic possessions is that reformers were especially concerned with the sexual offences of the celibate clergy, which had been a main source of anti-clerical sentiment, especially in France in Germany, in the fifteenth and sixteenth centuries. To be sure, they were also concerned with the

sexual conduct of the laity, especially after the implementation of the
reforms of the Council of Trent in the second half of the sixteenth century.
But a substantial majority of Catholic demoniacs, at least in France, Spain,
and Italy, were nuns who had taken vows of celibacy, and they often
accused priests, who had also taken such vows, of causing their possession
by witchcraft.

The most vivid example of the centrality of sexuality in narratives of
Catholic possessions (which of course must be treated sceptically as records
of historical fact) was the possession of Madeleine Bavent, a nun who had
entered the convent of the Franciscan Tertiaries at Louviers in 1620. Sister
Madeleine originally confessed that she entered the convent after having
been seduced by a Franciscan monk, who was reported to have had sexual
relations with three other girls as well. She later claimed, however, that she
had no memory of this sexual encounter and that her confession was based
on suggestions made by her accusers in 1643.[90] During her novitiate
at Louviers, the chaplain, Father Pierre David, who was interested in the
antinomian doctrines of the Adamites and Quietists, allegedly encouraged
her to strip naked and dance before him and even to receive Holy
Communion in that state. Father David's successor was Father Mathurin
Picard, whose sexual advances Bavent resisted but who, none the less,
according to Bavent's later testimony, forced her to have intercourse with
him on one occasion. Whether Bavent's claim that an incubus demon,
'exhibiting a huge penis, just like a man's', raped her in her cell was intended
to disguise another sexual assault by Picard or was a product of her imagination is unclear. It does provide further evidence, however, of the centrality
of sexuality in many Catholic possession scripts.[91]

The predominantly sexual script followed by Bavent and the nuns at
Louviers, which was similar to those in the possessions at Aix-en-Provence,
Loudun, and later at Auxonne and Toulon, found no counterparts within
Protestantism. The only case of possession in England that had a sexual
element was that of the seven children of Nicholas Starkey in Cleworth,
Lancashire in 1595. In that episode, however, the female demoniacs did
not exhibit any sexual fantasies in the manner of the French nuns at
Loudun. The sexual element arose only when Edmond Hartley, a cunning
man brought in to exorcize the children, kissed the young demoniacs and
thereby aroused suspicion that he was the witch who had been responsible
for their afflictions.[92] The sexual element was also absent in most New
England possessions as well as those in Geneva and the Dutch Republic.

Further evidence of the modest or non-existent place of sexuality in
Protestant demonology comes from the trials of witches in Protestant
countries. Central to Protestant witch-beliefs was the pact with the Devil,

which reflects the preoccupation of Protestant demonology with the Devil's role as tempter. Even in this context, however, sexual temptation was relatively infrequent, and it never assumed the major role it played in Catholic demonologies, such as the *Malleus maleficarum*.[93] In England, for example, witches were not accused of sexual commerce with demons until the witch-hunt conducted by Matthew Hopkins and John Stearne in 1645–7. The most explicit sexual charge against an English witch, claiming that the Devil had carnal knowledge of her body and 'suckt her in her breast and in her secret parts', appeared in 1682 in one of the last English witchcraft trials that resulted in an execution.[94] Sexual encounters figured in some accounts of the pacts that Scottish witches allegedly made with the Devil, the most notable being Isobel Gowdie's confession of 'carnal dealing' with the Devil in the shape of a very large black man in 1662.[95] Most accounts of demonic sex in Scotland appear in witchcraft trial records during the 1640s.[96]

Sexual encounters with demons appeared rarely if at all in Protestant accounts of the witches' sabbath. All the reports of promiscuous sexuality at such assemblies, in which witches allegedly copulated with demons and other witches, come from Catholic countries. The Protestant countries of England, Scotland, the Dutch Republic, Geneva, New England, and parts of Huguenot France were rarely the sites of alleged witch assemblies. In the first report of an assembly of witches in England, in 1612, the demons were depicted as enjoying an outdoor picnic of apparently tasty commodities with fully clothed witches.[97] The woodcut of this assembly gave no hint of sexual activity, which was explicit in some of the engravings of sabbaths on the continent, especially in German territories.

Jewish possessions

Jewish possessions in the sixteenth and seventeenth centuries provide further evidence for the cultural specificity of possession in early modern Europe. Relatively rare during the Middle Ages, Jewish possessions increased in number at the same time as they did among Catholics and Protestants.[98] These experiences were different both from Jewish possession by unclean spirits at the time of Christ and from those that occurred in either Catholic or Protestant communities in the sixteenth and seventeenth centuries. The distinguishing characteristic of Jewish possessions during this period was that the possessing agents were *dybbuks*, the spirits or disembodied souls of Jews' ancestors.[99] This belief, which originated in the twelfth-century cabbalistic doctrine of the transmigration of souls, provided a theological foundation for Jewish possessions that has continued to the present day. Since Christian theologians have repeatedly rejected the possibility of possession by the souls of the dead, the belief in *dybbuk* possession, which is especially strong in Hasidism, demonstrates the cultural specificity of demonic possession in yet another early modern religious context.

The Judaic tradition of *dybbuk* possession also illustrates the theatrical potential of such cases. S. Ansky's Yiddish play *The Dybbuk* (1914), which was translated into Russian and English and performed in Moscow, New York, and London as well as in Tel Aviv, exploited the theatrical potential of a female possessed body. The play, which was produced as a film in 1937, tells the story of Leah, who on the day of her wedding visits a graveyard and is possessed by the spirit of Hassan, a Talmudic scholar who had fallen in love with her and who had dropped dead when he learned of her plan to marry another man. Efforts of rabbis to exorcize Hassan's spirit failed, and the play ends with Leah joining Hassan in death. Ansky based the play on extensive research in Hasidic traditions in Russia and Ukraine, and the script incorporates many elements of traditional Hasidic belief regarding *dybbuk* possession, including Leah's speaking in the male voice of Hassan's spirit in Act II. The play reminds us that *dybbuk* possession scripts, like those of Catholics and Protestants in the early modern period, were encoded in religious cultures that had developed over the course of centuries.

CHAPTER 7

The Demoniac in Society

THE ARGUMENT OF THE last chapter is that possession reflected the specific religious culture in which it occurred. Demoniacs were following scripts that were encoded in their religious cultures. This was true regardless of whether these victims of diabolical torment were deliberately faking possession or had experienced a physiological, neurological, or psychic disorder. But possessions took place in, and were influenced by, the social environments in which they occurred. To extend the analogy with the theatre, religious culture provided the roles that demoniacs played in the sacred drama of possession, but their social relationships with family members and neighbours help to explain why demoniacs played these dramatic roles in the first place. If we take the position that religious anxiety was responsible for the early signs of possession, then we must study the social and cultural circumstances that helped to produce that stress. If possession was 'a disease of civilization', which is how Thomas Sydenham referred to hysteria, then we must look at how the structures of civilized society helped to spawn it.[1]

The social environments that most directly encouraged the onset of possessions were the close-knit communities in which the afflictions spread, sometimes with great rapidity, as a result of collective imitation or imagination. Convents were the classic example of such demonological hothouses, but orphanages, small villages like Mattaincourt, and pious households, such as those of Robert Throckmorton in Huntingdonshire and Nicholas Starkey in Lancashire, also provided appropriate social settings for these demonological psychodramas. In early seventeenth-century Geneva seventeen demoniacs lived on the same street, the rue de la Fontaine.[2] Group possessions, such as the one that took place at Eichstätt in the 1490s, require that we pay close attention to the social and cultural environment in which the possessions spread,[3] but individual possessions also occurred in a social matrix, and we cannot fully understand why they occurred without exploring the social relationships between the demoniacs and those with whom they interacted in their communities.

Since fraudulent possessions were voluntary and deliberate, they most readily lend themselves to a social analysis. The demoniac who faked her possession usually did so to achieve a specific social end, such as to attract attention or even fame, incriminate enemies or rivals by accusing them of witchcraft, or profit in one way another, such as by receiving alms from a sympathetic audience or municipal authorities.[4] There were, however, relatively few fraudulent demoniacs, despite the claims of Protestant propagandists. Only a small number of possessed people had the theatrical skill to fake the symptoms of possession. A social analysis of demonic possession, therefore, must also include the much larger category of demoniacs who experienced possession involuntarily.

Social analysis is essential to gaining a full understanding of why demoniacs acted the way they did. It appears that possessions, regardless of how one interprets them, were triggered when the demoniac experienced some sort of emotional or psychic crisis. Charcot held that the onset of hysteria, with which he identified demonic possession, was precipitated by traumas, such as the death of a loved one, an incapacitating accident, or a violent attack.[5] In his early work on hysteria in men, Freud argued that such traumas were physical, but in his later work he argued that emotions, ideas, and desires caused hysteria.[6] I argued in the two previous chapters that the crises or traumas that triggered possessions were almost always religious in nature. Yet no matter how one might classify them, such personal emotional experiences always occurred in a social context, and therefore the demoniacs' social relationships played an important part in causing them.[7] Identifying such circumstances has become one of the main objectives of modern psychotherapy, and the self-appointed task of social historians is to do the same for their far more elusive and often inscrutable historical subjects.

It is of course difficult to reconstruct the social relationships of these demoniacs, who with few exceptions left little evidence of their lives and their interactions with others. Any conclusions must be highly speculative. We can, however, acquire some clues by asking why certain types of people, living in certain social arrangements, were more likely to experience possession than others. This involves constructing a social profile of early modern European demoniacs and, using the limited amount of information on their possessions supplied by narratives and other accounts, speculating about the nature of their emotional crises.

One objection to conducting a social analysis of this sort is that early modern demoniacs did not conform to a clear-cut social profile; they included men and women, children and adults, and people from all economic brackets. They came from literate families but also from among the uneducated. Despite the claims of Michel Foucault and Michel de Certeau that possession, unlike witchcraft, was essentially an urban phenomenon, large numbers of demoniacs—probably a majority—lived in the countryside.[8] In this and in many other respects the social profile of demoniacs resembled that of witches. The complexity of the social profile of witches, however, has not deterred analysis relating to why most witches were women, why some witches were men, and why a smaller group of witches were children. Nor has it deterred historians from using case studies of witch-hunting in specific locations to determine how social relationships within towns and villages contributed to suspicions and accusations of witchcraft. This chapter will ask similar questions regarding demoniacs in the effort to develop a fuller picture of the social environments within which they exhibited their various symptoms.

Another objection to a social study of possession is that it encourages a crude functionalism in which the behaviour of demoniacs is attributed to their need to achieve certain ends. This objection presupposes that the possessed consciously used their condition as a means of saying and doing things that were otherwise prohibited, such as advancing their interests or criticizing superiors. There were very few situations, however, in which demoniacs deliberately initiated possession for such purposes. Even when possessions were fraudulent, demoniacs sometimes did not know, at least until they were well into their performances, that what they said and did served their own interests or those of family members who planned and stage-managed the entire production. To take just one example, in her possession, of Anne Gunter, who eventually confessed that she had faked the symptoms of her possession, apparently began when she contracted some sort of sickness, which her father then exploited by making her vomit pins and have seizures. At last Anne went along with this plan, deliberately feigning fits in the presence of many dons and students at Exeter College, Oxford, where her brother-in-law, the Regius professor of divinity, was principal.[9]

Female demoniacs

Most social analyses of demonic possession, like those of witchcraft, have focused on the observation that the majority of demoniacs were women. There is less statistical evidence to support this claim than there is for the proportion of female witches, which was about 75–80 per cent throughout

Europe.[10] The percentage of female demoniacs appears to lie in the same statistical range. Sixteen of the twenty-three, or 70 per cent, of individual demoniacs mentioned in Martin Del Rio's *Six Treatises on Magic* and twenty of the twenty-seven, or 74 per cent, of the demoniacs whom Johann Weyer referred to in *De praestigiis daemonum* were female. In his witchcraft treatise of 1580 the French demonologist Jean Bodin claimed that almost all demoniacs were women. The percentage of females in group posses-sions, which included nuns in convents, was of course much higher.[11] Of sixty-three English demoniacs identifiable by name, forty-five, or 71 per cent, were girls or women. All but two of the eighteen individual lay demo-niacs in France identified by Moshe Sluhovsky were female, while Pierre Fourier, the priest at Mattaincourt in Lorraine in 1631, observed that the eighty-five demoniacs in the village were 'almost all young girls and a few women'.[12] Girolamo Menghi's exorcisms always referred to demoniacs as female, and the Spanish Benedictine monk Benito Feijoo claimed that ninety-nine of every one hundred demoniacs in the early eighteenth century were female.[13] All the Russian shriekers since the beginning of the reign of Peter I were women.[14] It would not be unreasonable to estimate that at least three-quarters of demoniacs in early modern Europe were female. This rough estimate conforms closely to the more statistically reli-able percentages of female demoniacs in contemporary societies studied by cultural anthropologists. I.M. Lewis has noted the predominance of women in all instances of demonic or unsolicited possession.[15] Most of the individuals exorcized by the Catholic clergy today are female.

Early modern demonologists had greater difficulty explaining this gender imbalance among demoniacs than the corresponding imbalance among witches. The demonological argument that the Devil could pene-trate the female body more easily than that of men was easily refuted on the grounds that all human bodies, not just those of women, were viewed as porous in the early modern period. Moreover, as Feijoo observed, the Devil did not have difficulty penetrating any materials, including hard metals, so he certainly could not have been faced with a serious challenge when working his way through the stomach walls of a male demoniac. The alternative theory, which is similar to the demonological explanation of why most witches were women, was that women were intellectually or morally inferior to men. The French demonologist Rémy Pichard, for example, claimed that women, especially those who were weak-minded or of a dull and melancholic character, were more likely to be possessed, while the French physician Barthélemy Pardoux thought that demons preferred to possess women and children because of their 'fragile and infirm' condition.[16] This theory might have helped demonologists explain

why women were more likely than men to fall victim to demonic temptation, but it was of little use in explaining why morally innocent demoniacs
should be more vulnerable to demonic attack. The theory was persuasive,
as it was for Feijoo, only in cases where women *imagined* that they were
possessed.

Female spirituality

The new emphasis on female piety and the cultivation of female sainthood
in the late medieval and early modern periods, especially during the
Counter-Reformation, was one of the main reasons for the dramatic
increase in the number of possessions in these years. It is widely recognized
that the new spirituality affected women more than men, especially the male
clergy, who already had a long history of striving to attain moral perfection
in the monastery. The introduction of new interiorized spiritual exercises,
especially meditation and contemplation, in the early modern period led
many women also to aspire to sainthood. The new female spirituality flourished mainly in convents, but the publication of devotional materials in the
late sixteenth and seventeenth centuries also made it possible for literate
laywomen—admittedly a small group—to do the same. Many of the female
possessions of the early modern period, especially those that took place in
convents, originated in the difficulties such women encountered as they
submitted themselves to a spiritual discipline that made unrealistic demands
on them and led them to think they were possessed by demons.

The possession of the English nun Margaret Mostyn, who entered a
cloistered convent at Antwerp in 1644 and was exorcized seven years later
at a Carmelite convent at Lierre, illustrates how the religious culture of
the convent encouraged experiences that were interpreted as demonic
possessions. In her diary, Margaret of Jesus, the name she adopted as a nun,
explained how in her quest for moral perfection the performance of her
interior spiritual exercises fostered self-doubt, moral scruples, and spiritual
despair. She began to doubt her faith and found it difficult both to pray
and to obey her superiors. The belief that the Devil was responsible for her
inability to pray and for other moral lapses, coupled with her belief that
witchcraft was the source of her maladies, aggravated Margaret's spiritual
anguish. Her internal turmoil most likely caused or aggravated 'all sorts of
infirmities and pains', including an inability to digest many foods. During
her stay at Antwerp she experienced 'violent vomitings' and 'dreaded
convulsions' as often as twenty times in the space of twelve hours.

After transferring to the convent at Lierre in 1648, Margaret's condition
worsened, and her confessor there, the English priest Edmund Bedingfield,

came to the conclusion that the nun, who was at that time twenty-three years old, was possessed by demons. In 1651 he conducted an exorcism of Margaret and her sister, Elizabeth Mostyn, who had taken the name of Ursula of All Saints and had also migrated to Lierre. By this time Margaret had apparently become suicidal, a tendency that can be inferred from Bedingfield's claim that two of the demons he expelled from this afflicted woman (there were three hundred in all) specialized in making their victims eat broken glass, throw themselves from windows, or hang themselves. The case of Margaret of Jesus illustrates how the spiritual discipline of the convent could lead to the manifestation of symptoms that Catholics readily interpreted as demonic possession.[17] Her case also supports the argument of Cardinal Desiderio Scaglia, who in his handbook for inquisitors warned that nuns, especially those subjected to strict discipline, sometimes fell into desperation so deep that they began to doubt the tenets of their faith and often came to believe that they were bewitched or possessed by the Devil.[18]

The possession of the professed nun Margarita de San José in Mexico City in 1717 resembled that of Margaret of Jesus in its social and cultural context, but it involved a more serious rejection of religious faith. In her examination before the Mexican Inquisition, Sister Margarita explained that while trying to attain a state of sanctity she entertained constant doubts about the articles of the Christian faith and was tempted to take off her rosary, throw away her relics, and take the communion host from her mouth, stab it, and burn it in oil. She confessed to having committed sacrilege by receiving communion three times while in a state of mortal sin just to offend God, and on one of those occasions she actually took the host out of her mouth and trampled on it. She also admitted to having concluded a pact with the Devil, much in the manner of Jeanne Féry and Françoise Fontaine.[19]

Margarita's possession cannot easily be attributed to a subconscious rebellion against ascetic discipline, since she did not seem troubled by her daily spiritual regimen. Nor can her experience simply be reduced to a matter of repressed sexuality, although her guilt for not having confessed her sins against the sixth commandment shows that she, like many nuns her age, was dealing with erotic desires and urges. Margarita did not, like so many nuns in the early modern period, entertain fantasies of sexual intercourse with her confessor or actually have an affair with him. The most likely explanation of her possession was the belief promoted by Catholic demonologists that the Devil assaulted aspirants to sanctity with greater intensity and persistence than those who were less zealous in their pursuit of spiritual perfection.[20] The reason Margarita thought and acted the way she did was because she, as an aspirant to sanctity, was *expected* to endure far more demonic temptations than others. In her case, which was admittedly extreme, this expectation led to the belief that she was actually possessed by the Devil.

Margarita's case provides one of many examples of the narrow distinction contemporaries made between divine and demonic possession, especially among women. Many of the symptoms of these two types of spirit possession, most notably the trances, visions, and ecstasies, resembled each other closely. Possessions of both types also involved convulsions and the demonstration of preternatural strength.[21] Good possessions were, however, more likely to involve eating disorders, especially since fasting was one of the most common methods of achieving sanctity.[22] In any event, clerical authorities became increasingly involved in discerning the difference between the two types of spirit possession, and by the early seventeenth century they almost always determined that women who were apparently involved in good possessions were actually possessed by the Devil.

Female sexuality

Sexual desire and guilt for sexual transgressions, both of which impeded the achievement of female sanctity, lay at the root of many female possessions in Catholic areas, especially those that took place in convents.[23] The trances and visions of the demoniacs and the performance of exorcisms by male priests on writhing female bodies, which were very often lying on a bed during the rite, only served to accentuate the sexual dimension of the experience. Narratives of possession and exorcism, moreover, often used sexual metaphors of demonic penetration of the female body. The sexual dimension of possession and exorcism was not lost on contemporaries, many of whom criticized the female demoniacs rather than their male exorcists for their sexual propensities. The Italian demonologist Silvestro Mazzolini wrote in 1501 that clerics had to be especially cautious about exorcizing women, since some of them faked possession to get priests to touch their bodies.[24] Des Niau's account of the possession of the nuns at Loudun attributed their physical afflictions to sexual disease, while the eighteenth-century French priest Antoine Louis Daugis observed that demoniacs violated Christian standards of modesty.[25] In denying the authenticity of the possession of the German demoniac Elisabeth Lohmann, the theologian Johann Salomo Semler and his colleagues attributed this young woman's highly sexualized performance to nymphomania.[26] One effect of this early modern discourse on the sexuality of female demoniacs has been the belief, promoted by twentieth-century theatrical representations of demonic possession, that female demoniacs were sexually promiscuous, a belief for which there is little evidence.[27]

In dealing with the sexual dimension of female possession it is unnecessary, if not misleading, to have recourse to modern psychiatric theory to make sense of these women's internal turmoil. To claim that the guilt of a demoniac nun for her sexual anxieties or behaviour led to her detachment or dissociation of what was unacceptable in the form of an alternate personality posits an implausible and in any case an unverifiable process.[28] It is plausible, however, to argue that some female demoniacs might have been working out, or at least expressing, their sexual conflicts and anxieties through the idiom of possession. The view that their bodily convulsions resulted from an inability to express this inner turmoil linguistically, perhaps in the confessional, remains highly speculative, but the assignment of responsibility for their illicit expressions of sexuality to spirits was the only culturally available way of dealing with their sexual desires or guilt with impunity. Since most demoniacs had knowledge of other possessions through either reading or observation, they had a physical and mental script readily available by which they could express their anxiety.[29] One illustration of this was the way in which the 'lesbian' nun Benedetta Carlini represented her sexual activity with Sister Bartolomea as a symptom of possession, in which she was not responsible for her actions.[30]

The most well known examples of female possessions which appear to have been the product of sexual anxiety were those involving nuns and Catholic priests. The prototype for this clerical dynamic was the relationship between the nineteen-year-old Ursuline nun Madeleine Demandols of Marseille and Father Louis Gaufridy, the priest who was executed in 1611 for having caused this young woman's possession by means of witchcraft. It is impossible to determine whether a sexual relationship had ever existed between the two. Demandols claimed that Gaufridy had sexually abused her in her parents' home when she was a child and again after he seduced her into witchcraft. While it is not implausible that Gaufridy had in fact raped Demandols at a young age, the charge of having had sexual intercourse with her at the witches' sabbath, the orgiastic assembly of witches that was the product of overheated demonological imagination, calls into question the validity of her entire testimony.

In any event, the account of their alleged sexual affair, which was widely known through the publication of Sebastian Michaelis's *Histoire admirable*, provided a script for many other such sexually charged possessions, most notably those of Jeanne des Anges at Loudun in 1632, Madeleine Bavent at Louviers in 1643, and Marie-Catherine Cadière at Toulon in 1730. It also provided a template for other less well publicized possessions of Italian and Spanish nuns in the seventeenth century.

These sexual encounters, whether real or imagined, were the product of a distinctly Catholic culture in which aspirants to sanctity developed an intimate connection with priests who were also their confessors or spiritual advisers. Their spiritual intimacy with these clerics might very well have fostered sexual attraction by either or both parties, seduction by the confessor, or possibly even sexual assault.[31] What actually took place sexually in these relationships cannot be determined and does not greatly matter. The important consideration is the way that the women's guilt for their sexual attraction or for their consent to the priests' advances or their shame for having been raped might have found expression in the physical symptoms of their possessions and their accusation of some of these priests of having caused their possession by witchcraft.

The confession that Madeleine Bavent reputedly dictated to Charles Desmarets during her imprisonment between 1643 and 1647 suggests that Bavent's guilt for her sexual relationship with her former confessor, Mathurin Picard, who she claimed raped her on one occasion, caused the violent convulsions and 'animal howlings' night and day which she began to experience after Picard died in 1642. In her confession, Bavent admitted that she 'was tortured by scruples, by agonies of remorse' after Picard had sexually assaulted her in 1628, and that she was 'harassed and afflicted' when she went to confession after his death. The entire confession was filled with expressions of guilt for her many moral infractions, including attendance at the witches' sabbath and her sexual assault by an incubus demon in the convent.[32] There are problems with taking Bavent's confession at face value, but since its purpose was to exonerate her from responsibility for her real or imagined sexual transgressions with Picard and others, its expression of guilt appears to have been genuine.

The most striking of these possessions induced by sexual guilt was that of Marie-Catherine Cadière, the only laywoman of this group and the only one who had already acquired a reputation for sanctity in her community before she was possessed. The eighteen-year-old Cadière had yielded, either willingly or under pressure, to the advances of her spiritual adviser, Father Jean-Baptiste Girard. Whereas the nature of the sexual relationships of the other three demoniacs with their confessors lies mainly in the realm of the imagination, Cadière's guilt was probably deeper, her deviance from the high standard of probity she had set for herself more precipitate, and the embarrassment for her moral transgressions more public. One might even compare her sense of sinfulness with that of the small group of Protestant demoniacs who became possessed while in a state of spiritual desperation. Catherine had probably not given up hope of salvation, since the confessional was always available to her, just as it was to other Catholics. But her inner emotional turmoil, her sense that the Devil had literally possessed her, was probably just as strong as that of the English demoniacs Alexander Nyndge and Mistress Kingesfielde. Since her guilt was essentially sexual, the inner conflict may have been much greater than that of those spiritually desperate Calvinists. Like many other Catholic female demoniacs, Catherine succumbed to sexual temptation at the time in her life when she was battling with her recently awakened sexual desires. Most female demoniacs experienced possession at the age when they menstruated for the first time, married, or lost their virginity.[33]

One possession of a laywoman that originated in sexual guilt or shame but did not involve a putative relationship with a Catholic priest was that of Françoise Fontaine, a servant girl from Louviers, whose symptoms of possession in 1591 were so extreme that she twice attempted suicide by stabbing herself in the stomach. When interrogated by secular authorities, Françoise attributed her possession to having given herself sexually to the Devil, an admission that made her vulnerable to the charge of being a witch as well as a demoniac. The most revealing part of her testimony was that she had sexual intercourse with the Devil after having been raped three times by a soldier when the Protestants retook the city from the Catholic League in May 1591. Two other soldiers had attempted to rape Françoise at the same time, one of whom had threatened to have three hundred soldiers rape her if she did not yield to his demand.[34] It is fairly clear from this young woman's testimony that her symptoms of possession originated in the trauma she had suffered as a rape victim and in the guilt and shame that accompanied it. In her emotionally fragile state Françoise assumed two culturally prescribed roles—demoniac and witch—to cope with her profound guilt. By refusing to prosecute her as a witch the authorities confirmed her status as a demoniac.

The group possession of some twenty-five nuns in the convent of the Blessed Sacrament of San Plácido in Madrid in 1624 reveals even greater complexities of possessions involving female sexuality. It was widely known that the priest who was appointed prior, confessor, and spiritual director of the convent, Francisco García de Calderón, had had a sexual relationship with a living female saint in Seville before his arrival in Madrid. He was accused of justifying his illicit sexual activity on spiritual grounds, having claimed that the sexual act was a vehicle for attaining divine grace and was no sin when practised by a person seeking perfection.[35] This rationalization of illicit sex was often identified as an aspect of the heresy of illuminism (known as *alumbradismo* in Spain), which is a form of antinomianism—the rejection of the moral law on the grounds that 'to the pure all things are pure'.[36] Accusations of illuminism tended to be levelled against priests and nuns engaged in highly emotional devotional practices that were intended to achieve mystical union with the divine, resulting in the soul's indifference to the actions of the body.[37] The abbess of the Blessed Sacrament convent, Doña Teresa de Silva de Valle de la Cerde, apparently shared sexual intimacies with Calderón as well as with the patron of the convent, Don Jerónimo de Villanueva, although it is impossible to verify any such reports of sexual activity in the convent. It is unlikely that any other nuns had sexual relations with their confessors, but their guilt for their sexual desires could nonetheless have served as the main source of their possessions as well.

Originally Doña Teresa thought her possession was divine, but once it was labelled demonic, she and the other nuns underwent exorcism, which lasted three years. In the wake of this scandal the Spanish Inquisition prosecuted Doña Teresa for false illumination, pretence of sanctity, prophecy, witchcraft, and fraudulent possession. Condemned to four years of exile, she appealed for a new trial in 1642, in which she and the other nuns were liberated and Calderón was imprisoned for life in a monastery. Doña Teresa did not deny either her possession by the demon Peregrine or her relationship with Calderón, but she emphatically denied that she 'learned doctrines and dogmas of the *alumbrado* sect ... that lascivious contact between people and kisses were not a sin'.[38] The charges of participation in sexual orgies, which were often made against people suspected of heresy, were almost certainly groundless.[39]

Male demoniacs

Even if male demoniacs formed a distinct minority, we cannot ignore their presence among the possessed. Leaving aside for the time being children and adolescents, who belonged to a subgroup of demoniacs, we still must explain the possessions of a small but significant number of adult male demoniacs. Their prominence in the New Testament and in medieval texts suggests one possible explanation. Benito Feijoo argued that the male demoniacs in biblical antiquity were actually possessed, unlike the women in early eighteenth-century Spain, who imagined or pretended that they were demoniacs.[40] A more persuasive explanation is that the evangelists had no reason to select either men or women to illustrate Christ's miraculous power. Their main concern was to prove Christ's supernatural power by illustrating his authority over demons, and it is difficult to imagine that gender could have had any bearing on their selection of those examples.

The relatively large number of male demoniacs in the early Middle Ages can be explained mainly by the belief that the Devil preferred to assail members of religious orders, almost all of whom before the thirteenth century were male.[41]

In the late medieval and early modern periods gender became a major factor in determining which instances of possession attracted the attention of clerics, especially the exorcists whose main function was to identify and heal demoniacs. Suspicion of female sanctity and mysticism and a preoccupation with, and fear of, unbridled female sexuality all played a part in redefining the new group of demoniacs in the surge of possessions that began in the fifteenth century. An aspect of this shift was the replacement of monks with nuns as the preferred target of demonic temptation.

One reason why men formed a distinct minority in the early modern pool of demoniacs was that ecclesiastical authorities manifested little concern with *male* sexuality in either Catholicism or Protestantism. Their pressing concern was female seduction of holy men. None of the possession performances of sixteenth- and seventeenth-century male demoniacs, including that of the French exorcist Jean-Joseph Surin, who became 'possessed' while exorcizing Jeanne des Anges, were sexualized. Nor were there very many known instances in which men were possessed because a female witch had bewitched them for being unresponsive to their sexual overtures. One of the few such demoniacs was Eric of Lorraine, the bishop of Verdun, who attributed his possession to bewitchment by his nun lover.[42] Nor did Girolamo Menghi's claim that some demons preferred the companionship of men to that of women promote the belief that the Devil had a homosexual interest in penetrating the male body.[43] To the contrary, demonological theory held that men's bodies more closely represented the image of God than those of women and were therefore less vulnerable to demonic invasion and occupation.[44]

How then do we explain the significant if relatively small number of male demoniacs in early modern Europe? One clue is that their numbers were greater in Protestant than in Catholic territories. Half of identifiable adult demoniacs in England were male, and the number of possessed men in German Lutheran territories was proportionately higher than in Catholic German territories.[45] This relatively high concentration of Protestant male demoniacs can be partly attributed to the absence of convents in Protestant lands or to the discouragement of a distinctly female form of mysticism which convent discipline encouraged. More importantly, as discussed in Chapter 6, Protestants did not assign primacy to sexual transgressions in the hierarchy of human sins, choosing to condemn major and minor infractions equally. This meant that it was just as useful for Protestant ministers and moralists who wrote possession narratives for polemical purposes to focus on the moral transgressions and temptations of men as women. As in biblical antiquity, gender was not a factor in the selection or self-identification of Protestant demoniacs.

One striking difference between male demoniacs and their female counterparts is that the men tended to come from aristocratic or bourgeois society or were well educated, or both. This select diabolical fraternity included the nobleman's son who the French physician Jean Fernel became convinced was genuinely possessed; the English lawyer Robert Brigges; the English Puritan Alexander Nyndge, whose possession began after he attended a lecture by a godly minister; the mad German princes who were exorcized in an effort to cure them; the French Jesuit Jean-Joseph Surin, who became possessed (or obsessed) at Loudun; the seventeenth-century Frenchman who wrote an account of his possession in his own hand and whose full name was not divulged in the document (an indication of elite status); and Christoph Haizmann, the Bavarian painter who not only wrote an autobiographical account of his possession but also painted images of the Devil as he remembered his appearance at the time of their encounters.

The higher social status and literary abilities of these male demoniacs allowed them to maintain control of their own possessions and to represent them in positive terms. To be sure, these men were troubled souls, and they were aware of their moral imperfections, but none of them lost consciousness during their possessions, and none spoke in voices other than their own. A modern psychiatrist would find it extremely difficult to diagnose any of them as having suffered from a multiple personality disorder. Father Surin insisted that he was in fact blessed by his possession. None of these men, moreover, participated in a group possession. Their possessions were apparently involuntary, but with the exception of the mad princes, they were all able to maintain control of the symptoms of their possession.

As performers these male demoniacs followed very different scripts from those of female demoniacs and thereby reinforced the masculine gender stereotypes that prevailed in early modern European culture. Like other educated men they showed that they were more rational and more in control of their emotions than the women whose possession narratives they had read or whose possessions they had witnessed. One of their objectives was to demonstrate that they were not vulnerable to the demonic deceptions that female demoniacs fell prey to. It is also instructive that none of the adult male demoniacs were suspected of faking their possessions. The division between male and female demoniacs resembles the division between male ritual magicians who could command the demons they conjured and the female witches who were believed to be the Devil's sexual servants.

Children and adolescents

I have excluded children and adolescents of both sexes from the previous social analysis, since their age was far more important than their gender in understanding why large numbers of them became demoniacs. Adolescence in early modern Europe was thought to begin at about fourteen, the approximate age of puberty.[46] Some of the possessions of children and adolescents occurred in fairly large groups, such as the four episodes of demonic possession that took place in orphanages in the Dutch Republic between 1566 and 1672 and the possession of seventy girls at an orphanage in Rome in 1554.[47] Smaller groups of children, including the four Goodwin children in Boston, the five children of Robert Throckmorton together with seven of his maidservants in Huntingdonshire in 1589–93, and the ten possessed boys at St Annaberg in Saxony in 1712 belonged to domestic households. Two of the demoniacs cured by Christ—the epileptic boy and the daughter of the Syrophoenician woman—were young, while Paul the apostle also exorcized a number of young people, including the soothsaying slave girl at Philippi.[48] Five of the seven Lancashire demoniacs in 1595–7 were between the ages of nine and fourteen, and of those five only one was a boy.[49] Of the identifiable group of sixty-three English demoniacs, fifty-two were under the age of twenty-one.

The demonological explanation for the high number of child or adolescent demoniacs was the same as for as the high number of females: both groups were physically and psychologically more vulnerable than adult men to demonic attack. The French physician Barthélemy Pardoux wrote in 1639 that 'demons especially afflict women and children because of their fragile and infirm condition'.[50] A parallel interpretation that focused on the mental and spiritual weakness of demoniacs was that children, like women, were of weak mind and therefore easy prey for the Devil. This view of the moral weakness of children was much stronger in Protestantism, and especially in Calvinism, than in Catholicism. A culture that emphasized the depth of human sinfulness did not give free passes to children, who were born in a sinful condition and could escape it only by God's freely granted grace. In Protestant theology, baptism did not bestow God's grace on children. In his account of the possessed boy of Tocutt, whose father, a godly minister, had bewailed the lad's sins and sent him from Holland to New England, Cotton Mather claimed that the boy had constantly succumbed to temptation by the Devil, although he had not yet signed a pact with him. His possession narrative, which was modelled on that of the New England demoniac Elizabeth Knapp, was distinctly Calvinist in its claim that children from an early age could, like adults, make pacts with the Devil and be morally responsible for their actions. Like many Calvinist demoniacs, the Tocutt boy demonstrated 'the near affinity between witchcraft and possession'.[51]

One explanation for the relatively high incidence of possession among children, especially when they were living with others, is that they were highly suggestible and therefore more likely than adults to believe that they were possessed. Evidence of such juvenile suggestibility with respect to the presence of demons in the natural world comes from the confessions of more than 1,300 Basque children to having attended the witches' sabbath in the early seventeenth century.[52] Further evidence comes from the much more recent testimony of children in daycare facilities in the United States that they were the victims of Satanic ritual abuse.[53] It is reasonable to assume that some children, when prompted by priests or even by exorcists looking for demoniacs in their neighbourhoods, imagined that they were possessed. It was then only one easy step to follow the scripts that the published or orally transmitted performances of others had made available to them.

Child demoniacs and adolescent demoniacs engaged in different types of cultural performance. Demonic possession gave children the freedom to disobey their parents, violate the strict discipline enforced in the household, and refuse to conduct themselves politely and deferentially. When John, the ten-year-old son of Nicholas Starkey in Cleworth, Lancashire, experienced fits and seizures in 1595, he began to bite members of his household (including his mother), run from the adults in the household, sing and dance wildly, and ignore all efforts by adults to govern him. The possession of the Throckmorton children in Warboys, Huntingdonshire between 1589 and 1593 gave them 'the opportunity of inverting normality and chiding adults' especially Mother Sawyer, who was suspected of causing their possession by witchcraft.[54]

The demonic possessions experienced by adolescents or 'youth', defined here as those between the ages of fourteen and twenty-one, often differed from those of children.[55] Adolescent or young demoniacs, including many newly professed nuns, were at an emotionally fragile age, when they had to deal with both their recently discovered sexuality and the religious strictures of parents, pastors, or confessors. In this respect they shared many of the anxieties of unmarried demoniacs in their early twenties, especially the women in that slightly older age group.[56] The emotional turmoil that resulted from the conflict between these demands explains the large numbers of demoniacs in this age group both in Catholic and Protestant lands.

The possessed who had recently experienced the death of a parent or who had become orphans represent a distinct subgroup of young demoniacs whose possessions lend themselves to a social analysis. The recent loss of a parent, and especially both parents, at a young age certainly could induce the type of emotional trauma that apparently triggered many possessions, and demonologists recognized that orphans were the prey of the Devil. The death of Christoph Haizmann's father was the crisis that led to his encounter with the Devil and his belief that he was possessed. The outbreak of four mass possessions in orphanages in the Dutch Republic in the seventeenth century suggests how the emotional effects of parents' deaths could be aggravated in a small community of children and adolescents who had all experienced the same profound loss and consequently had fallen into a marginal social position.

Subordination, power, and status reversal

Combining the large number of female demoniacs with the smaller but significant number of children or adolescents supports the general observation that a large majority of the possessed belonged to subordinate groups in society. The women were subject to patriarchal control by fathers, husbands, or ecclesiastical superiors and were widely viewed as inferior to men physically, intellectually, and morally. The children were subjected to stricter parental control and discipline and suffered similar liabilities. Most scholars would agree that possession served the function of allowing demoniacs, either consciously or not, to violate moral norms with impunity. Thus child demoniacs were able to disobey their parents, while female demoniacs could express themselves sexually in ways that would not normally be permitted. The larger and more difficult question, however, is whether possession became a means of registering an oblique protest against their position in society. Did the young person's role as victim of possession provide an opportunity for at least temporarily subverting the age hierarchy in society?[57] Did adult female demoniacs contest their designated position in the public sphere? Was possession, like hysteria, an idiom of protest, a symbolic voice for those who were forbidden to verbalize their discontents and therefore create a language of the body?[58] Did their possessed bodies give them an agency that they otherwise did not possess in society?[59]

The inspiration for such a social analysis was Traugott Oesterreich's global study of possession and I.M. Lewis's seminal work on spirit possession in Africa. These scholars argued that possession gave at least temporary empowerment to women and other subordinate groups in society. Possession allowed them to assert themselves, to have their voices heard without risking social or political retaliation, since they were not responsible for their behaviour while under the Devil's control.[60] Adopting the role of the demoniac frequently brought a rise in social status, affording the possessed 'a degree of respect and social privilege that would have been unattainable in any other way'.[61] Possession thus became the site of conflict between the male and educated members of society and the socially inferior demoniacs who had this one opportunity to register a protest against their superiors.

The main attraction of this approach in the study of early modern possession is that it assigns a measure of agency to women whom contemporaries regarded as helpless victims of Satanic power and who were subject to the apparent control and occasional violence of their educated male exorcists.[62] The danger implicit in this approach, however, is that it can lead to an exaggeration of the demoniacs' empowerment and modernity.

Studies claiming that possessed nuns in the thirteenth and fourteenth centuries used their apparent access to the supernatural to gain a measure of privilege and authority otherwise denied them raise the question of whether early modern demoniacs might have benefited in similar fashion from possession. A comparison between medieval and early modern demoniacs in this regard is inappropriate, however, since the demoniacs of the thirteenth and fourteenth centuries were older and more aggressive in displaying their knowledge of the demonic world than the demoniacs who filled the ranks of the possessed in the early modern period.[63] It is difficult to see this latter group as having been as deliberate or successful in their efforts to gain prestige and respect. It is even more difficult to see them as agents of modernity.

Two studies of group possession reveal the problems in reading possession cases as challenges to the existing social order. The first is Ruth Harris's provocative study of a collective possession that took place in the remote, mountainous village of Morzine in the Savoy region that was annexed to France in 1860.[64] Although this episode occurred in the modern period of European history, the mental outlook of the participants was not very different from that of the people who lived in the area two centuries beforehand. Belief in witchcraft, the maleficent power of the Devil, and the reality of demonic possession remained strong in many Savoyard communes in the mid and late nineteenth century. The possessions began in 1857 when a group of young girls, after claiming to have seen the Virgin Mary, went into convulsive fits and started blaspheming the Holy Eucharist. The girls blamed witches for their condition, but by this time, more than sixty-five years after the statutory decriminalization of witchcraft in France, witchcraft accusations could not result in prosecutions. Hope for relief from their afflictions, therefore, depended completely on the prospect of exorcism. The local parish priest originally obliged them in this respect, but under instructions from his ecclesiastical superior he was forced to discontinue his efforts. Deprived of spiritual relief, the girls made more frequent public displays of their symptoms, and the number of the possessed increased to about two hundred. The demoniacs' claim to have been bewitched, their demand to be exorcized, and the public attention given to them all had early modern precedents. So too did the scepticism of physicians, the central government, and the ecclesiastical establishment.[65] As expected, a suspicion of fraud arose, as it had in many of the group possessions of French nuns, but there was little evidence to support such an interpretation of the girls' behaviour.

The predominance of young girls among the possessed and the conflicts between them and their male exorcists conform closely to the pattern of social relationships evident in many early modern possessions. Harris, however, goes further in arguing that the violent afflictions of these girls reflected aggressive fantasies that they harboured against the men in their village, whom they berated for being unable to drive the demons from their bodies. The girls' departure from the village in search of exorcists who were more powerful than those in their parish, just like their criticism of the doctors who were unable to cure them, is taken to reflect dissatisfaction with the men in their village. According to Harris, gender relations lie at the heart of the psychological drama that unfolded in Morzine. The fact that the people whom the demoniacs accused of causing their possessions by witchcraft were all men is offered as evidence to support this interpretation.[66]

It may have been that these troubled young girls entertained these negative fantasies about the men in their village, although using the girls' body language rather than the spoken word to provide evidence to support this claim moves the article into a higher speculative category of psychohistorical analysis than other studies of demonic possession. The more fundamental problem with this thesis, however, is its modern orientation. While rejecting earlier interpretations of the girls' behaviour as the last gasp of a traditional society struggling against the forces of secularization, Harris depicts these girls and women as agents of modernity.[67] In doing so she ironically sees the demoniacs, rather than their critics, as forces of secularization and interprets their afflictions in secular terms. Instead of analysing their collective religious anxiety on its own terms, by studying the demoniacs' inability to secure relief from inner torments that they believed were caused by the Devil, Harris interprets their religious demand for exorcism in terms of a gender conflict that can be applied to other societies. She does not argue that these demoniacs were proto-feminists, but her argument that they were agents of modernity rather than relics of a traditional Catholic past implies that their religious concerns were manifestations of deep-seated, mundane socio-economic tensions. In the final analysis Harris's thesis is just as reductionist as the medical categorization of such episodes as hysteria, which is exactly how Charcot and his followers interpreted the possessions at Morzine.[68] By refusing to take religion on its own terms Harris presents an anachronistic argument.

The second example of the danger of using modern social theory to analyse early modern demonic possession comes from Carol Karlsen's study of the 'possessed' accusers of the Salem witches. The overwhelming majority of these accusers were either women or adolescents, and they came almost entirely from the lower strata of society. Many of them were household servants. Karlsen argues that what these demoniacs said and did while possessed formed part of a power struggle in which they obliquely challenged both the religious and the social norms of their day. The power struggle took place between the possessed and the authorities who were culturally sanctioned to interpret their experience. The core issue was whether the claims of the possessed to be able to identify witches would continue to be acknowledged when they named powerful people in the colony as witches. In this way the possessed 'shaped the possession ritual to voice feelings that were proscribed by their faith' and expressed their 'rage at the world' by accusing wealthy and highly placed members of society of witchcraft. They also named persons whom the demoniacs themselves considered to be their personal enemies or oppressors. This 'status reversal ritual', which Karlsen argues 'won the day', represented an effort by these subordinate members of society to remedy their weak position in the social hierarchy and avoid consignment to a life of obscurity. Karlsen admits that their victory was transitory and that the demoniacs did not either confront or substantially alter the hierarchical structure of society. But by interpreting the words of the possessed as expressions of their anger at the world, she gives her subordinate demoniacs an agency they had not previously been accorded.[69]

There are a few problems with this argument. First, the social status of the possessed at Salem was far more diverse than Karlsen recognizes. Indeed the first girls to display their fits were members of the fairly substantial households of Samuel Parris and Thomas Putnam Jr.; they were therefore unlikely candidates for status elevation. The first people they accused, moreover, were those who conformed to the stereotype of the poor, old witch. Only later in the process did they name members of the colony establishment, such as Lady Phipps, the wife of the governor of the colony, and members of the wealthy Saltonstall family. This shifting pattern of accusations, which the historian Erik Midelfort has referred to as the breakdown of the witch stereotype, occurred in many witch-hunts that did not involve accusations by demoniacs.

A deeper problem is that Karlsen endorses a secular, socio-economic interpretation of possession in which the demoniacs were primarily concerned with changing their position in the social order. While promising to interpret the possessions in their proper religious context, she ultimately removes them from that framework and depicts them as protests against economic injustice. This is Karlsen's final answer to the question 'What was really happening?' when the girls experienced their fits and torments. In taking this approach Karlsen draws on Victor Turner's theory of status elevation and status reversal, which says a great deal about life crises but little about the religious context in which such crises sometimes take place.[70]

Karlsen relies almost exclusively on social scientific and psychiatric theory in concluding her book with an effort to make sense of the physical symptoms of the possessions, such as the convulsions, the inability to talk, trances, and paralysis. Here the challenge is even greater than in dealing with the linguistic statements and gestures of the possessed, since the demoniacs at Salem displayed very few of the physical symptoms of possession besides the fits they repeatedly fell into, and no contemporary claimed that the Devil actually occupied their bodies or spoke through them. In any event, Karlsen argues that the physical symptoms they manifested stemmed from the unbearable psychic tensions they experienced as they dealt with the simultaneous need to embrace social norms and rebel against them. In this turmoil they disengaged themselves from 'the socially constructed world of everyday life' and entered a state in which what was deemed socially dangerous within their psyches was allowed freer rein. In other words, these women entered an 'altered state of consciousness' in which they 'strove to communicate through these many physical disabilities what they so much wanted but so much feared to say: that their situation enraged them'.[71] This interpretation is in essence what Charcot and his disciples argued a full century before Karlsen wrote. Even though Karlsen recognizes that this type of reaction was most likely to occur in a Puritan household, her argument ultimately represents a secular, reductionist, psychiatric interpretation of demonic possession that raises more questions than it answers.

Even if early modern demoniacs were not involved in a status reversal ritual, they did acquire greater cultural authority than they had had before their afflictions began.[72] Ecclesiastical authorities and those who participated in or witnessed exorcisms often accepted the words spoken by demoniacs at face value. There were precedents for giving demoniacs this type of credibility. Some of the demoniacs in the Bible had recognized the divinity of Christ, and in the Middle Ages demoniacs were sometimes allowed to preach. By the sixteenth century, however, much of this respect for the words of demoniacs had dissipated. Threatened by their claims of access to the supernatural realm outside of prescribed ecclesiastical channels, wary of their relationship with the Devil, and suspicious because most of them were women, exorcists became more concerned with controlling demoniacs and discrediting their testimony than coaxing them to admit theological truths.[73] Exorcists therefore strove not only to control demoniacs physically but also to deny the truth of what they said while under demonic influence.

The only testimony by demoniacs that ecclesiastical authorities were sometimes willing to accept at face value was their identification of the witches who were afflicting them. Even this testimony became problematic when sceptics questioned whether the Devil had deliberately identified innocent people as the cause of their possession. Aside from the names of the demons occupying their bodies, this was the main type of information that ecclesiastical authorities tried to extract from them during their exorcisms. Naming the witches responsible for their afflictions also gave demoniacs, regardless of whether they were saints or sinners, the opportunity to prove their moral superiority over others in the community.

In naming witches demoniacs did not always act alone. In many cases family members, neighbours, or pastors suggested names of the people in their communities who were already suspected of witchcraft or were engaged in conflict with villagers of higher social status. Brian Gunter, for example, suggested that his daughter Anne accuse three women against whom he had a long-standing feud of having caused her possession.[74] Witches accused in this manner tended to come from lower strata of society than the demoniacs themselves, and the accusations served the purpose of ratifying the accusers' higher social status. In other cases of possession-cum-witchcraft, such as when nuns accused priests who were their confessors, the accusations travelled up the social ladder and were directed against clergymen who they claimed had impeded their own religious development. Those accusations, however, did not reflect strong anti-clerical sentiment. To most of priests the demoniacs remained deferential and respectful, especially when the priests succeeded in relieving them of their afflictions.

It would also be misleading to construe the blasphemies and revulsion from sacred objects as protests against either church doctrine or liturgical practice. Such irreverence may have represented reactions to the severity of the moral discipline enforced in the convent, the mission, or the holy household, but it can hardly be construed as a challenge to the authority of ecclesiastical superiors. The inability of two Dutch demoniacs to say their prayers or sing psalms in 1603, for example, was most likely a reaction against their strict religious upbringing, not a protest against the practices of the Dutch Reformed Church.[75] Such blasphemous outbursts were not in any way empowering. Quite to the contrary, they were the marks of emotional fatigue in response to a rigorous spiritual regimen.

Although the great majority of early modern European demoniacs, just like those in Africa in the twentieth century, occupied subordinate positions in society, they did not tend to exploit their moral or legal immunity to elevate their social status, protest about their economic condition, challenge leadership of their churches, or express unorthodox religious ideas. These demoniacs exercised their agency mainly in the naming of witches, and even that power was limited by the reluctance of legal authorities to prosecute or convict some of the witches they accused. If possession, like hysteria, was an idiom of protest against the established order, it was only a symbolic protest, and it was highly theatrical. The performances of the possessed can be compared in this respect to the charivari or the carnivals in the early modern period that symbolically turned the social order upside down but left that social order intact.[76] Like those cultural practices, possession was a form of escape from the constraints imposed by authority and social convention, but it was not an effort to abolish or even reform such conventions. Its transitory nature, and its resolution by means of dispossession, ensured that it would not have a systemic effect on society. In the theatre of possession and exorcism demoniacs could express their frustrations and anxieties, but as in all theatrical productions, they were unable and in many cases unwilling to change the social, political, or even the ecclesiastical order.

CHAPTER 8

The Demoniac and the Witch

Demonic possession and witchcraft, as they were understood in the early modern period, were two distinct but related activities. Possession was the alleged occupation of a human body by one or more demons that resulted in the person's loss of control over his or her physical and mental functions. Witchcraft was the infliction of harm or misfortune by means of a magical power that the witch was believed to have acquired from the Devil. In most cases it was believed that the witch had acquired this magical power by concluding a pact with the Devil. In some cases the witch was also believed to have worshipped the Devil together with other witches in nocturnal assemblies known as sabbaths (*sabbats* in French). The main difference between possession and witchcraft, at least according to demonological theory, was that demoniacs were not held criminally responsible for what they had done while possessed, whereas the witch was liable to vigorous prosecution by either ecclesiastical or secular authorities. While as many as fifty thousand individuals were executed for witchcraft during the early modern period, demoniacs were never prosecuted for what they did while under the influence of demons. A few of them were tried (but never executed) for faking their possessions, and a very small number were prosecuted for *becoming* witches, but prosecution for what they did while under the influence of the Devil would have been tantamount to prosecuting the Devil himself, and no secular or ecclesiastical court has ever claimed jurisdiction over supernatural beings.

Despite this fundamental difference, demonic possession and witchcraft were closely related activities. Since both involved the exercise of demonic power in human society, it is understandable why demonologists claimed that a relationship existed between the demoniac and the witch. The primary connection was that witches were often prosecuted for causing the possession of another person. According to contemporary demonological theory, possessions could be initiated either by the Devil himself or by a witch using demonic power. When the latter method of possession was employed, the afflictions suffered by the demoniac were regarded as the *maleficia*, or acts of harmful magic, performed by witches. The Dominican inquisitor Jean Vineti, writing in the 1460s, argued that demonic possession was the model for all other *maleficia*, since it was the simplest form of physical harm attributable to demonic power and had the deepest roots in the Christian tradition.[1] In the *Malleus maleficarum* Heinrich Kramer wrote that although demons could possess individuals directly with God's permission, they usually did so at the instance of witches. Witches, moreover, were morally responsible for the possession, since they guided the Devil's hand throughout the process.[2]

The belief that witches could send demons into the bodies of other human beings never commanded universal support. The main argument against this proposition was that witches did not have the power to perform the deeds attributed to them. In 1563 the sceptical Dutch physician Johann Weyer denied that witches could command demons to do anything, including sending them into the bodies of human beings.[3] Ironically, the Catholic demonologist Jean Bodin, who differed profoundly from Weyer on the prosecution of witches, agreed with him on this point, citing a Jesuit who in 1554 had argued that 'men did not have the power to send the Devil into a person's body, which is certainly true'.[4] The unclean spirits that possessed demoniacs in the Bible apparently did so directly, without human direction. The New Testament does not even hint that sorcery had anything to do with the afflictions of the demoniacs cured by Christ or the Apostles. As the English physician John Cotta wrote in the early seventeenth century, the possessions in the Bible were 'works of the Devil himself, solely wrought without the association of man'.[5]

In the late seventeenth century the English physician Richard Brinley attributed the symptoms of possession to either natural causes or the supernatural power of the Devil acting by himself, but denied that witches could mediate such supernatural power.[6] In 1694, fourteen years after Brinley wrote, Robert Calef, the Boston merchant identified by Increase Mather as 'a very wicked sort of Sadducee', took the same position in a disagreement with Cotton Mather regarding the possession of Margaret Rule. Calef could not see how witchcraft could cause a diabolical possession 'unless we ascribe the power to a witch, which is only the prerogative of the Almighty, of sending or commissionating the Devils to afflict her'.[7]

Nevertheless, the view that witches could in fact cause possessions commanded widespread support until the late seventeenth century, and it was frequently invoked in witchcraft prosecutions. A very large percentage of demonic possessions in Protestant kingdoms and territories were attributed to the activities of witches. Possession by means of a witch's spell was so common in England that the word 'possessed' came to be equated with the word 'bewitched'.[8] In Calvinist territories, most notably Scotland, the republic of Geneva, and the English colony of Massachusetts, almost all cases of possession (and there were relatively few in Calvinist jurisdictions) were linked to charges of witchcraft.[9]

The tendency to attribute cases of possession to witchcraft was less common in Catholic jurisdictions than in those that were Protestant, possibly because the wider availability of exorcism in Catholic countries offered an alternative explanation for the afflictions of the possessed.[10] A large majority of group possessions in European convents did not involve accusations of witchcraft.[11] Nevertheless, there were plentiful examples of possessions allegedly caused by witchcraft in Catholic regions. When the demons possessing a group of women in the French region of Galmier in 1452 were asked why and how they had entered these women's bodies, they explained that their followers, the witches, were responsible.[12] One of the first witch-hunts initiated by lay demoniacs in France, in 1582–3, led to the execution of six witches, while a wave of more than one hundred possessions in the Catholic German city of Paderborn in the late 1650s resulted in the execution of fifty people for witchcraft.[13] At Mattaincourt in Lorraine, some eighty-five possessions between 1627 and 1631 resulted in the execution of about fifty witches. One of the functions of exorcizing nuns at Louviers and Loudun in the early seventeenth century was to build a legal case against priests who were allegedly responsible for causing the demoniacs' afflictions by means of witchcraft.[14] In a late seventeenth-century possession in Mexico one of the demons that had possessed Francisca Mejía told the Franciscan exorcist that a group of witches had placed him and the other demons inside the woman's body. The same demon returned a few days later, saying that the witches had sent him back to 'service the maleficium' which had caused the young woman's violent convulsions, excruciating pains, and the expulsion of avocado stones, river pebbles, and a small toad from her body.[15]

A vivid illustration of the connection between witchcraft and possession in Catholic territories appears in the second edition of *Discours des sorciers* (A Discourse on Witches), by Henri Boguet, a lay judge in the county of Burgundy. Boguet began his treatise by discussing the prosecution of a witch, Françoise Secretain, for sending five demons into an eight-year-old girl, Loyse Maillat, in 1598. Boguet used this case, which he described at length, to support the general proposition that 'a person has the power to send demons into the body of another'.[16] In this discussion he referred to another six sixteenth-century cases of possession allegedly caused by witches and concluded that 'Every day in our own town we continually meet with large numbers of persons who, for the most part, impute their possession to certain Vaudois or sorcerers.' Boguet also cited the treatise by Claude Caron, *L'Antéchrist démasqué*, which reported that the witch Catherine Boyraionne sent a number of demons into one Madeleine, a woman of about twenty-two, and that another old woman commanded another demon to enter the body of one Marie.[17]

The connection between witchcraft and possession suggests that the increase in the number of possessions in the early modern period contributed to the rise in witch-hunting and, conversely, that the increase in the number of witchcraft accusations and prosecutions swelled the number of possessions. Certainly there is a close correlation between the two developments. Witch-hunting began in the early fifteenth century and reached a peak between the 1580s and the 1630s, before gradually declining. Although demonic possession was a feature of religious life in the Middle Ages, an abundance of literary evidence suggests that the number of episodes began to increase in the fifteenth century and reached a peak during the late sixteenth and early seventeenth centuries, the same decades when witch-hunting was at its most intense. Like witchcraft cases, instances of possession also declined after 1660, although, unlike witchcraft prosecutions, they continued into the modern period, long after witchcraft trials came to an end.

Two early modern Catholic works on exorcism offer further evidence for the connection between the rise of witch-hunting and the surge in demonic possessions. The first was Girolamo Menghi's *Compendio dell'arte essorcistica*, which was first published in 1572.[18] Menghi was convinced that an outbreak of possessions in Italy had been caused by the actions of witches. Believing that the world was under demonic assault and would soon end, he claimed that the entire population was in danger of demonic possession and that witches were assisting in this onslaught. The three books of the *Compendio* dealt successively with the nature and power of demons, witchcraft, and the remedies against both possession and witchcraft. Menghi became the most fervent promoter of the idea that possession was almost always caused by witchcraft.

The second treatise, *Histoire admirable de la possession d'une pénitente* (1612) by the Dominican inquisitor Sebastian Michaelis, did even more than Menghi's book to link possession to witchcraft and describe the demons that were believed to be possessing human beings in large numbers. Michaelis, a trained theologian, had already made a reputation as a successful witch-hunter when he became involved in the prosecution of Father Louis Gaufridy, a parish priest from Marseille, for causing the possession of Ursuline nuns in their convent at Aix-en-Provence in 1609. In his book on this episode, which involved repeated exorcisms of the nun Louise Capeau, Michaelis classified the numerous demons involved in the possession.[19] Like the treatises by Menghi and Boguet, Michaelis's book made Catholics aware of the extent of the rising threat from demons, which according to the chief demon Beelzebub, speaking through Capeau, numbered 6,600. Michaelis arrived at this number, which was slightly more than the 6,000 soldiers in an imperial Roman legion, by equating this possession with that of the New Testament demoniac who told Christ that his name was legion.

It is unsurprising that both possessions and witchcraft trials increased in number during the same period of time. Both developments reflected the demonization of European religious culture that began in the wake of the Black Death and gained strength during the age of the Reformation. Possession and witchcraft both involved a direct demonic assault on human society, and their prevalence in the early modern period owed much to the widespread belief that the world had entered the Last Days, in which an increase in demonic power would precede the Second Coming. It is no coincidence that the spate of possessions among the Jews at the time of Christ and among Christians at the time of the Reformation occurred in religious cultures suffused with apocalyptic expectations.

A further connection between possession and witchcraft was that growing scepticism regarding the authenticity of many possessions hastened the decline in witch-hunting. The revelation that some demoniacs had faked their symptoms contributed to greater caution in the handling of all witchcraft accusations, while the highly publicized exorcisms of possessed nuns in French convents led theologians, especially Protestants, to entertain and advance serious doubts about the extent of demonic interference in the world. The most direct effect of scepticism regarding the authenticity of possessions, however, was that it made judges uncertain whether the behaviour of demoniacs was sufficient to convict the witches whom they named as the proximate cause of their afflictions. The effective decriminalization of witchcraft in France in 1682 on these grounds led James Johnstone, the former Scottish secretary of state, to make a similar case for decriminalizing witchcraft in his country shortly after the condemnation of seven witches at Paisley for causing the possession of the young girl Christian Shaw in 1696. Johnstone observed that the *parlements* of France and other judicatories in Europe, even though they believed in the existence of witches, 'never try them now because of the experience they have had that it's impossible to distinguish possession from nature in disorder'.[20] There may have been other reasons why France and other countries had stopped prosecuting witches by the end of the seventeenth century, but Johnstone's explanation shows how the evidentiary problems associated with possession could result in a state of judicial paralysis in witchcraft cases.

The legal and moral standing of the demoniac

In the early 1970s the American comedian Flip Wilson did a routine called 'The Devil made me do it'. Confessing the inability of the characters he played to resist temptation, Wilson excused them by blaming their moral failings on the Devil. This mantra, 'The Devil made me do it', could easily have served as the conventional early modern demonological commentary on the guilt of demoniacs.[21] A broad consensus existed among theologians and jurists that people who were possessed by demons were not morally or criminally responsible for their behaviour, which could include blasphemy, violence, profanities, disobedience, and sexually suggestive postures.[22] The Devil, not the demoniac, was the agent of the person's offensive or sinful actions.[23] The only human being who might be held responsible for what the possessed person did while under the demon's influence was the witch who allegedly compelled the demon to enter the person's body.[24]

Legal culpability

There was no basis in Roman law, canon law, or English common law for the legal prosecution of a demoniac. As the Scottish jurist Lord Fountainhall wrote in 1712 regarding Janet Douglas's accusation against the witches of Pollock in 1677, 'if it be an unvoluntary possession . . . it can never be made criminal'.[25] As long as possession was involuntary, demoniacs could not be held responsible for the Devil's occupation of their bodies. In this respect demonic possession held a similar legal status to that of insanity, a medical condition with which possession was often identified. The main reason that demoniacs were not legally culpable was that they had not *intended* to perform the illegal deed; in other words, they had not given their wilful consent to the actions they had performed. The only circumstance in which a demoniac could be prosecuted was when that person deliberately faked the symptoms of possession to seek revenge on a personal enemy, engage in illegal, immoral, or otherwise unacceptable activity with impunity, or solicit charitable contributions. As discussed in Chapter 1, Anne

Gunter and Katheren Malpas were both prosecuted in the Court of Star Chamber for their malicious efforts to indict others for causing their possession by means of witchcraft. In the Spanish and Roman inquisitions counterfeit demoniacs could be prosecuted either for the dissimulation itself or for the activities they engaged in during the pretended possession, although such prosecutions were not common. For the most part, however, demoniacs were given a legal pass.

Legally knowledgeable individuals could use the non-culpability of demoniacs to their advantage. In July 1591 the English religious fanatic Henry Arthington denounced the Lord Chancellor and the archbishop of Canterbury as 'traitors to God and the realm' and pronounced his associate, the 'mad fool' William Hacket, to be Jesus Christ. Hacket was executed as a traitor despite claiming that he had been insane at the time of the incident, but Arthington avoided the same fate by claiming that Hacket, as Satan's minion, had seduced and demonically possessed him. This possession, so Arthington claimed, had been temporary; once Hacket had been executed, the possession ended. While in prison, Arthington wrote an account of this possession, *The Seduction of Arthington* (1592) in which he admitted that Hacket's brutal execution had freed him not only from Satan's control but from his own 'gross and palpable errors', which he now realized were so offensive. His contrition and the publication of his apology persuaded the members of the Privy Council, especially those with Puritan sympathies, to spare his life and modify the terms of his imprisonment.[26]

In eighteenth-century Spain, Benito Feijoo argued that the legal immunity of demoniacs to prosecution created a serious social problem, in that the falsely possessed enjoyed the freedom to commit as many crimes as they wished, including murder, theft, and arson because they knew that their deeds were 'cloaked with the imagination that the Devil did it all'.[27] Although Feijoo appears to have been genuinely concerned about this problem, he gave no evidence that counterfeit demoniacs had actually engaged in criminal activity under such false pretences. There may very well have been significant numbers of demoniac impostors in early modern Spain, even if they were not as numerous as those who pretended to be mystics, but it is unlikely that they were responsible for the crimes that Feijoo feared they were committing.

Moral culpability

The same logic that denied demoniacs criminal culpability because they did not intend to commit a crime also freed them from moral culpability for the acts they committed while under the Devil's influence. These might include cursing, blasphemy, displays of sexual desire, self-mutilation, and attempted suicide. Demoniacs could not be held morally responsible for the sins they committed while possessed because the commission of sin required intention and wilful consent. It did not matter whether the demoniacs were sinners or paragons of virtue at the time of their possession: some were known for their piety whereas others were notorious sinners.[28] In the *Malleus maleficarum* Heinrich Kramer enumerated five reasons why God allowed the Devil to possess a person: 'For sometimes a man is possessed for his own greater advantage; sometimes for a venial sin of another; sometimes for his own venial sin; sometimes for another's mortal sin; and sometimes for his own mortal sin.'[29] One French demoniac discussed by Boguet had actually been a witch before she became a demoniac, whereas none of the demoniacs cured by Christ was described as a sinner.[30]

Whether they were saints or sinners at the time of the possession, however, the Catholic Church did not hold demoniacs morally accountable for what they did while under the control of Satan. Indeed, the Catholic rite of exorcism was predicated on the assumption that the demon had invaded the demoniac's body of its own volition or at the command of a witch, even if the Devil had deliberately selected sinners as his victims. Unlike the sacrament of penance, exorcism was intended to expel the alien demonic intruder, not encourage the penitent to seek forgiveness for his or her sins.

This assumption of the moral innocence of the demoniac was reinforced by the Catholic belief, which dates from the early days of Christianity and which Bonaventure and Aquinas had most clearly articulated in the thirteenth century, that the Devil could only possess the body, not the soul.[31] He might control the will, thereby depriving the demoniac of moral freedom, but the soul itself was out of bounds.[32] Demoniacs were therefore never instructed to confess their sins. Even uneducated people could understand from the minimal instruction they received from their pastors that a demoniac 'was not even remotely responsible for the terrible things that the Devil might say or do' while inhabiting the possessed person's body.[33]

Sometimes demoniacs were viewed as valued sources of theological knowledge. The respect they commanded for this reason had nothing to do with their moral character. Rather it was based on the way theologians viewed the demons that possessed and spoke through them. Although the Church viewed the Devil as the implacable foe of Christ and the personification of evil, he was nonetheless God's creature, and the deity could therefore make him serve good purposes. The demoniacs in the New

Testament, for example, had been some of the first people to testify to Christ's sanctity and had often displayed greater knowledge of divine truth than the Apostles themselves. In the Middle Ages demoniacs were viewed as sources of theological knowledge and occasionally allowed to preach. The clergy took the prophecies of demoniacs as seriously as those of female saints.[34] The demons that allegedly possessed the nuns at Aix-en-Provence and Lille in the early seventeenth century defended the central elements of the Christian faith, including the Catholic belief in Purgatory and the Immaculate Conception of Mary. Nor did all these examples of theologically knowledgeable demons come from Roman Catholic exorcisms. During his long trance possession, the seventeenth-century Lutheran demoniac Hans Kurtshals from Brandenburg not only identified witches (as did many demoniacs) but also uttered prophecies and warned of God's impending justice.[35] The demon possessing a twelve-year-old Lutheran girl from Silesia engaged in lengthy discussions of theological points.[36] Most Lutheran demoniacs who preached, however, did so after their symptoms abated, conforming to the Protestant pattern in which demoniacs spoke with two voices, their own and that of the Devil.[37]

All these examples suggest that even in an age of unprecedented fear of the demonic, the Devil remained an ambiguous supernatural entity. In late seventeenth-century Mexico the demons that possessed a group of converts were described as docile servants of God who acted as his messengers, just as they had in the New Testament.[38] In Renaissance Italy there was a widespread belief, which had originated in classical antiquity, that demons were companions who conversed with human beings and served a variety of useful functions.[39] In Renaissance drama, which drew on many of these classical sources, demons were rarely represented as intrinsically evil.

The moral ambiguity of the Catholic demoniac

Although the Catholic Church did not hold demoniacs morally culpable for their behaviour while under the influence of demons, the possessed nonetheless aroused considerable suspicion when they transgressed moral codes. The widespread belief that demoniacs were being punished either for their own sins or those of their parents made them morally suspect, even if they were technically innocent of any offence committed while under the Devil's control.[40] Family members and neighbours who observed the demoniac's blasphemies, curses, and rejection of holy objects could not have been expected to rely on demonological theory to disabuse them of the plausible assumption that the demoniac had done something terribly wrong.

Demonologists added to this confusion by narrowing the gap between the demoniac and the witch. The Dominican theologian and inquisitor Johannes Nider established the basis for this ambiguity in his treatise, *Formicarius* (The Ant Heap), which he wrote in the mid 1430s during the early period of witch-hunting. Nider's treatise, which originated in the discourse on the discernment of spirits, led to an effort to distinguish not only the saint from the demoniac but the demoniac from the witch. He argued that because demonic possession involved a close relationship between human beings and demons, the possessed, who were predominantly female and therefore more prone to temptation, might be guilty of the newly defined crime of witchcraft.[41] In Book 5 of *Formicarius*, which dealt with witchcraft, Nider reported that some of the demons that had possessed nuns in the Dominican convent at Nuremberg were *incubi* and *succubi*, the sexual demons that pollute people with 'the sin of excess'.[42] Nider implied that these demoniac nuns had not only sinned but had also become witches.

If Nider, a trained theologian, could blur the categories of demoniac and witch in this way, it is certainly understandable how ecclesiastical authorities and other educated Europeans could have done the same. As Barbara Newman, Richard Kieckhefer, and Sarah Ferber have shown, the boundaries between the saint, the demoniac, and the witch could easily be crossed in late medieval and early modern Catholicism.[43] All it took was the suspicion that the demoniac had submitted to the Devil voluntarily rather than having been possessed against her will. The early sixteenth-century Spanish Franciscan Martín de Castañega claimed that a person might be possessed by the Devil by concluding 'an express or occult pact' with him, and thus become his disciple.[44] In popular culture the confusion between the witch and the possessed could be even more pronounced. This was true in the German communities studied by Erik Midelfort, where possessions sometimes began with temptation by the Devil and with the signing of a pact with him.[45] In Central and Eastern Europe, specialists in village magic, such as wizards and wise women, were often referred to as having been possessed. In the eastern parts of Hungary and in the Eastern Orthodox sections of the Balkans, witches were often believed to have been possessed by the Devil and sometimes by the spirits of the dead.[46]

The confusion between possession and witchcraft is evident today in Nigeria, where the Pentecostal preacher Helen Ukpabio has conducted hundreds of exorcisms of possessed children who have been accused of witchcraft. In her book *Unveiling the Mysteries of Witchcraft*, Ukpabio writes that 'if a child under the age of two screams in the night, cries and is always feverish with deteriorating health, he or she is a servant of Satan'.

The identification of these possessed children as 'witch children' shows how easily the two categories can be confused. Ukpabio's treatment of these possessed children, moreover, is more akin to the violence often inflicted on those accused of witchcraft than the violence involved in some exorcisms. Ukpabio has been accused of splashing the witch children with acid, burying them alive and dipping them in fire.[47]

One source of the confusion between the demoniac and the witch in early modern Europe was that authorities used the same technique of pricking for the Devil's marks to establish the authenticity of both witchcraft and possession. The theory that underlay this practice in witchcraft cases was that the Devil placed marks on the bodies of witches who had made pacts with him as signs of allegiance and that such marks, when pricked with a sharp object, were insensitive to pain and did not bleed. In defending the use of the procedure in the case of Father Louis Gaufridy in 1611, the French physician Jacques Fontaine argued that no one received the marks involuntarily.[48] This claim raised serious questions regarding the moral status of those demoniacs who also had such marks. Marthe Brossier, for example, was pricked for the Devil's marks, while Mary Glover was burned without showing pain.[49] It is important to recognize, however, that searching for spots insensitive to pain on the suspected witch and the demoniac served different purposes. Demonologists claimed that the Devil gave his mark to the witch at the time of the conclusion of the pact as a sign of the witch's allegiance to him. The insensitivity to pain manifested by demoniacs was seen as one of many manifestations of supernatural demonic power for which the demoniac was not responsible.

The claim of some demoniacs that they had made pacts with the Devil could also have added to the contemporary confusion between witches and demoniacs. In 1584 the possessed nun Jeanne Féry claimed to have made a number of such pacts, some of them written in her blood. Seven years later the young French demoniac Françoise Fontaine confessed that she had given herself to the Devil verbally and sexually and had received the Devil's mark as a sign of allegiance.[50] In 1600 Nicholas Prutenus, a twenty-two-year-old nobleman from Graz who 'spewed out blasphemous words full of despair against God' and lost his bodily strength as well as his sight, hearing, and speech, attributed his condition to his having made a pact with the Devil.[51] In 1676 the demonically 'possessed' Bavarian painter Christoph Haizmann also admitted to having concluded two pacts with the Evil One, and in the early eighteenth century a young German male demoniac described in detail the pact he too had made with Satan.[52]

It is surprising that none of these demoniacs was ever prosecuted for witchcraft, since many theologians and jurists considered a pact with the

Devil the essence of that crime. One reason for the failure to take legal action against them might have been that none of these individuals was suspected of committing *maleficia* or acts of harmful magic, which was how most witchcraft prosecutions originated.[53] Another is that the clergy, recognizing the spiritual anguish that plagued these troubled souls, were primarily concerned with giving them pastoral care and helping them break the pact. Prutenus, in a remark that his exorcists prompted or that Del Rio inserted in his narration of the possession, thanked his Jesuit exorcists and claimed that he could never have expected such treatment from the Lutherans. In any event these demoniacs' belief that they had made a pact with the Devil was probably the main reason that they manifested the symptoms of possession in the first place Their guilt for having succumbed to the Devil's temptation and rejected their faith was so extreme that it expressed itself somatically. Even in the late twentieth century the belief that a person has made a pact with the Devil has apparently 'caused' some demonic possessions.[54]

One Catholic demoniac who was suspected of witchcraft but in the end was not prosecuted for that crime was Françoise Fontaine of Louviers, who was arrested on suspicion of witchcraft in 1591. Louis Morel, the *prévôt* of Louviers who questioned Fontaine, could not understand how the young demoniac could also be a witch, since he knew that theoretically the categories were mutually exclusive. Françoise's insistence that she was in fact a witch made discernment even more difficult, but when the girl was successfully exorcized, Morel dropped all the charges against her.[55]

Despite the frequent confusion between the innocent demoniac and the culpable witch, very few demoniacs were actually convicted of witchcraft by either Catholic secular or ecclesiastical authorities. Not surprisingly, all of these demoniac witches were female. These prosecutions, which were initiated by Catholic judicial authorities, did not go unchallenged, and none of the possessed witches was executed. The first case was the prosecution of two female demoniacs as witches in the episcopal city of Bitonto in southern Italy in 1593–4. The episode began as a classic case of witchcraft in which two demoniacs, who claimed that the Devil had taken possession of them against their will, named a long list of people as the cause of their possession during their public exorcisms. The case took an unexpected turn, however, when the two demoniacs confessed to being witches themselves and started naming other witches as accomplices rather than as the cause of their possessions. It is not clear why these demoniacs confessed to being witches and implicated a host of others. It appears likely, however, that the suspicion that they were witches as well as demoniacs originated with local judicial authorities, who tortured the two women to secure their confessions.[56] The authorities may have been influenced by Girolamo Menghi's widely circulated exorcist manual, which established the close association between witchcraft and possession.

When one of the witches named by the two Bitonto demoniacs suffered fatal injuries while fleeing an angry crowd; when another accused witch suffered a miscarriage; when a third died in jail after severe torture; and when a fourth was found dead in a cistern in the bishop's palace, the Holy Office, which presided over the Roman Inquisition, intervened. The accused witches were released, the bishop and the local authorities who had tortured the accused were punished for violating due process, and the two demoniacs who had been charged with perjury, slander, and superstition were ordered to perform 'soul-saving penance'.

A second instance in which a Catholic demoniac was literally transformed into a witch occurred in 1610, when Louise Capeau, an Ursuline nun in Aix-en-Provence, accused the demoniac Madeleine Demandols of being a witch. The two nuns, nineteen and twenty years old respectively, had allegedly been possessed at the command of Father Louis Gaufridy, and they became the main witnesses against Gaufridy in his trial for having caused the possessions by means of witchcraft. The exorcism and the trial were directed by Sebastian Michaelis, author of the *Histoire admirable*, in which he established the close connection between witchcraft and possession. During their exorcism Capeau turned the tables on Demandols by accusing her of being a witch. She also accused Gaufridy of using witchcraft to seduce Demandols into joining him in the worship of the Devil.

Capeau's accusation of Demandols did not result in her prosecution for witchcraft at the time of Gaufridy's trial at Aix in 1611. In order to secure her testimony against the priest, the commissioners exempted her from prosecution. At the trial Demandols, speaking through her demon, Beelzebub, identified the places on Gaufridy's body where the Devil had made his marks when he had allegedly signed a pact with him. She also testified that he had sexually seduced her when she was a child, a charge of sexual abuse that may have been true, since Madeleine's father testified at the trial that Gaufridy had been a frequent visitor at his house when his daughter was a child. The charges against Gaufridy also included witchcraft, idolatry, and rape. Demandols testified that Gaufridy had not only caused her possession but had inducted her into witchcraft, forcing her to sign pacts with the Devil. He had also taken her to the witches' sabbath, where the participants had allegedly engaged in sexual orgies and had eaten the flesh of infants. These admissions helped to secure Gaufridy's confession, and although Demandols made them through Beelzebub, her testimony laid the basis for her reputation as a witch and her prosecution for that crime later in her life.[57]

Madeleine Demandols' prosecution for witchcraft did not occur until 1653, forty-two years after Gaufridy's execution. Often suspected of being a witch, she was accused of having caused the possession of one Madeleine Hodoul by sending her own demon, Beelzebub, into the bewitched demoniac. On the basis of this accusation Demandols was convicted and imprisoned for life in a monastery or hospital.[58] This was almost as lenient a sentence for the sixty-two-year-old nun as the penitential punishment assigned to the Bitonto demoniacs.

The case of Madeleine Bavent, one of the demoniacs in a group possession of fourteen nuns at Louviers, Normandy, in 1643–4, bears comparison with that of Demandols. Bavent, an orphan who at the age of eighteen had entered the convent of the Franciscan Tertiaries at Louviers, claimed during her exorcisms that between 1628 and 1648 Mathurin Picard and Thomas Boullé, two parish priests who served as chaplains at the convent, had taken her and other nuns from the convent to witch assemblies, where she had sexual intercourse with demons as well as the priests. These statements, together with the accusations of the other nuns who pinned responsibility for these transgressions on Bavent, led the charge that she was a witch. In March 1643 the bishop of Evreux, Monseigneur de Péricaud, declared Bavent guilty of apostasy, sacrilege, sorcery, attending the witches' sabbath, casting spells in various parts of the convent, signing pacts with the Devil, carrying the Eucharist to the sabbath to use in charms, and copulating with demons and witches. She was accordingly stripped of her nun's habit and veil and sentenced to imprisonment for life on rations of bread and water.[59]

Although Bavent confessed, almost certainly under duress, to these misdeeds, the *parlement* of Rouen, which conducted a four-year investigation of the incident, postponed a final sentence, and she died in prison one year later. Although the *parlement* sentenced Thomas Boullé to be burned alive as a witch, together with the illegally exhumed corpse of Father Picard, who had died in 1642, the *parlementaires* were reluctant to treat Madeleine Bavent in similar fashion. Pity for her harsh treatment or uncertainty regarding her guilt may have figured in this failure to take decisive action, but it is more likely that her atypical role as both innocent demoniac and guilty witch left the court in a quandary. Throughout the investigation the *parlement* accepted her testimony as a demoniac that others were responsible for the possessions, and they wanted to pursue the investigation of the former Mother Superior of the convent, Françoise de la Croix, whom Bavent had also implicated but who had taken refuge in

Paris.[60] Testimony by a demoniac was certainly being called into question at this time, but it still had far more evidentiary value than the testimony of a witch's accomplice. The court was in effect forced to prefer Bavent's status as a demoniac to that of witch.

Another example of the blurring of the boundary between the witch and the demoniac in early modern Catholicism occurred in the German prince-bishopric of Paderborn, when a group of demoniacs, mostly women, triggered a large witch-hunt between 1656 and 1659. When the women first manifested their symptoms, some authorities believed either that they were frauds, since they had failed the tests for genuine possession administered by Capuchin monks, or that they were actually witches. One of these counterfeit demoniacs was in fact executed as a witch in July 1657.[61] The rare claim that demoniacs were morally culpable was given a new twist when, at the request of the prince-bishop, the Holy Office in Rome sent an Italian Dominican exorcist, Father Michael Angelo, to determine the authenticity of the possessions. By the time he arrived, the number of demoniacs had grown to more than one hundred.

Michael Angelo, who was highly sceptical of the authenticity of these possessions, employed a new tactic that resolved the crisis. Having bound the violent demoniacs and secured them in a safe place, he explained that the demons could harm them only if they believed that the Devil had the ability to do so. The Devil, Angelo preached, 'harmed not by force but by persuasion'. If the demoniacs resisted him they would be freed from his assault upon them. The friar concluded that 'the possessed cannot actually be forced to speak or to do anything evil; rather they are persuaded and led into temptation'. In this way Michael Angelo was introducing the new concept, anchored in the Catholic doctrine of free will, that the possessed were not involuntary victims of the Devil's power but were responsible for their own possession. Demoniacs were morally culpable not because they had become witches but because, by failing to resist temptation, they were actually in agreement with evil spirits.[62] Angelo's position was not very different from that of the Lutheran physician Johann Weyer, who insisted that demoniacs were not helpless victims of demonic attacks but could put Satan in his place by trusting in God and leading a pious life.[63] The claim that demoniacs were responsible for their own possession was common in early modern Protestantism and was closely associated with the Protestant emphasis on the sinfulness of the demoniac.[64] In 1690 and 1708 two Lutheran women in Sweden were accused before the king's council 'for having let Satan take their body in possession'.[65]

Despite the novelty of Father Michael Angelo's claim, the conventional Catholic view of the demoniac's innocence prevailed well into the eighteenth century. Very few Catholic demoniacs were accused of witch-craft or tortured by local authorities to admit their guilt. In the over-whelming majority of Catholic cases, demoniacs were represented as the victims of witchcraft and did not become witches themselves. The occa-sional Catholic identification of the witch and the demoniac occurred almost exclusively at the popular level.[66] Suspicion of demoniacs would persist, but the theory of their innocence would continue to give counter-feit demoniacs licence to violate moral standards with impunity.

The moral status of Protestant demoniacs

Protestant possessions differed in many ways from those of Catholics. The scripts that Protestant demoniacs followed were different from those of Catholics, as were the Protestant methods of dispossession. Protestants and Catholics also had different views regarding the moral culpability of demo-niacs. These differences were rooted mainly in the Protestant, and especially in the Calvinist or Reformed, view regarding the prevalence of sin and the difficulty of overcoming it. This relentless emphasis on the prevalence and obduracy of sin in Calvinism led to the widespread belief that demoniacs were sinners, that it was more difficult for them to overcome demonic temp-tation, and that they might very well become witches themselves. Cotton Mather used the example of a possessed boy who had a long history of sinful behaviour, including lying and stealing since he was eleven years old, to demonstrate 'the near affinity between witchcraft and possession.'[67] Mather insisted, however, that this boy and others who were tempted by Satan in the same way could refuse to conclude a pact with the Devil. This task became much more problematic at the end of the seventeenth century, when the efflorescence of apocalyptic thought in Scotland and New England produced a surge in the number of possessions in both locations. In the sixteenth century Protestants had claimed that the spread of the Gospel had better equipped Christians to resist demonic temptation and that this had reduced the number of demoniacs, but the Devil's fury in the Last Days had made the task far more difficult than it had been in the previous century.[68]

The preoccupation of early modern Calvinism with sin found no parallel in either Catholicism or other Protestant denominations. Calvin and his followers stressed the total depravity of man, the intensity of spir-itual warfare that the Christian must wage against the Devil, and the difficulty of securing the assurance that they were recipients of God's grace and thus members of a very small elect. Acquiring God's freely granted grace was a much more difficult process than for Catholics, who could obtain it through good works and the sacraments.

Pierre Viret laid the basis for the Calvinist belief in the sinfulness of demoniacs by claiming that not only 'those whom we properly call possessed' but also the reprobate (who in orthodox or Calvinism comprised the majority of humankind) were possessed by the Devil; hence the title of his treatise, *The World Possessed with Devils*.[69] For Viret, therefore, the Devil possessed the soul as well as the body. The English Congregationalist minister Nathaniel Holmes agreed with this pessimistic commentary in 1650 when he claimed that the Devil possessed those who were 'entirely wicked', 'body and soul'.[70]

This Protestant position—that the Devil could possess the soul—stood at loggerheads with the prevailing Catholic position, articulated by theologians in the thirteenth century, that the Devil might possess the demoniac's body and mental facilities, including the will, but not the soul.[71] The demoniac's soul might very well become the target of the Devil's incursion into the body, but it was theoretically off limits during the actual possession. The struggle for the Catholic demoniac's soul—if it occurred at all—took place during the exorcism.[72] And even that struggle was problematic as long as the demoniac was not believed to have free will while under the Devil's power. The Protestant position can be seen in the fact that Protestant demoniacs rarely lost consciousness; like Mistress Kingesfielde, they usually spoke in two voices, indicating that the afflicted person was consciously struggling against the demon within.[73] Protestants were more reluctant than Catholics to absolve people from moral responsibility for their actions, even when they were not in their right mind.[74]

Calvinists might debate whether the possession was the result of natural causes, whether witchcraft was involved, or whether the malady should be labelled possession or obsession, but they never considered the possibility that the spirits who had invaded and occupied the body of the demoniac might be good spirits or whether the demoniac, before her dispossession, was engaged in some sort of ecstatic or mystical union with the divine.[75] The most that could be hoped for was that the Scottish Presbyterian, New England Congregationalist, Dutch Reformed, or French Huguenot demoniac could survive this spiritual warfare with the forces of evil and secure God's freely granted grace. This achievement of Calvinist 'sainthood' was far different from that of the Catholic nun, if only because the Calvinist demoniac had done nothing to achieve her election. In Calvinist theology, sin remained the natural state of mankind, the fundamental human condition, and the temptation to succumb to its pressures took centre stage in the theatre of Calvinist possession.

The difference between Calvinist and Catholic attitudes towards demonic possession emerges from a report drafted by William Ballentine, a Roman Catholic priest who in 1660 had served on the mission in Scotland for twelve years. Ballentine had been commissioned by his superiors in Rome to investigate and evaluate the state of Scottish religion. The subject of demonic possession came up in his discussion of the failure of Scottish Presbyterian ministers to give consolation to sinners. He reported that those ministers, unlike Catholic priests who provided solace through the sacrament of penance, told such demoniacs that their only hope of salvation lay in a public confession of their sins. This, according to Ballentine, led many of these troubled individuals to commit suicide rather than to subject themselves to 'public disgrace'.[76]

Ballentine then gave the example of three women troubled in conscience, two of whom 'had been falsely persuaded that they were possessed by the Devil'. Having gone to the minister for consolation, they were told that their only hope lay in 'a public manifestation of their whole life story'. All three women were on the point of committing suicide, when some of their friends brought them to Catholic households regularly visited by Catholic priests. According to Ballentine, this gave them peace of mind and they recovered from their suicidal despair.[77] This episode not only illustrates the Calvinist view that demoniacs had far greater difficulty than Catholics in overcoming their sinfulness but also the psychological burden placed on these afflicted souls who were being asked to confess their sins publicly.

The greater difficulty Protestants had in resisting temptation explains why Protestant possession narratives devoted much more attention to the spiritual anguish of the demoniacs as they struggled to resist the enticements of Satan.[78] Catholic demoniacs, to be sure, might also experience demonic temptations and struggle to resist them. These temptations became apparent in the exorcisms of French nuns in the seventeenth century and the possession experiences of the demoniacs in the Franciscan mission at Querétaro in Mexico in the eighteenth century.[79] Even those Catholic demoniacs, however, did not reach the same level of spiritual despair as Protestants, mainly because it was much easier for Catholics to obtain salvation by means of the sacraments.

Because of the Protestant preoccupation with sin there was considerable concern in Protestant communities that demoniacs would become witches. Cotton Mather argued that the possessed might very well make covenants with the Devil.[80] During the Salem witchcraft trials in 1692, at least six individuals identified as demoniacs were publicly accused of witchcraft.[81] There is no evidence that these or any other Protestant demoniacs were actually prosecuted for the crime, as Madeleine Demandols was in 1653, but the fear that demoniacs would become witches was far more pervasive in Protestantism than in Roman Catholicism. Demoniacs in Sweden,

Germany, England, Scotland, and New England all were considered to have been in danger of crossing the moral boundary and becoming witches themselves. What was a rarity in Catholicism became a common feature of Protestantism. In 1597 the English demoniac William Somers lived in fear that an alderman in Nottingham would name him as a witch.[82]

Further evidence of the dominant role played by sin in Protestant possessions came from the statements of personal guilt that Protestant demoniacs made when they were supposedly possessed. These admissions of sinfulness were not attributed to the Devil, as was often the case in Catholic exorcisms, but to the person herself. Catholic exorcists occasionally had to struggle to determine whether the speech of a demoniac was that of the person herself or that of the invasive demon, as they did with Madeleine Demandols and the demon Beelzebub, but in Protestant possessions there was no problem making such a distinction. In these possessions, which Oesterreich had labelled as lucid rather than somnambulistic (in which the person has no memory or consciousness of the possession), it appeared that the original personality coexisted with that of the demon, which compelled the person to have thoughts, ideas, and actions that were repugnant to her.[83] In such circumstances it was relatively easy to determine when the demoniac was speaking and when the voice was that of a demon. The Scottish demoniac Margaret Lumsden made this determination even easier when, in responding to the minister's announcement that her audience would now hear the spirit speaking, she said in Latin 'You hear him speaking.'[84] The thirteen-year-old Thomas Darling, who aspired to be a Puritan preacher, actually conducted a dialogue between himself and the Devil during his possession, reporting Satan's response in his own voice.[85] In a number of Lutheran possessions in Germany the demoniac also spoke in two distinct voices. The Devil delivered his usual blasphemous invective in a deep, coarse voice, while the demoniac herself praised God and spoke of repentance in a sweet, reasonable voice, thereby reflecting the inner conflict the person was experiencing.[86] The conclusion that the demoniac was struggling with demonic temptation is difficult to avoid. In such situations the demoniac obviously could not plead moral innocence.

There is little doubt that when the wife of Edmund Kingesfielde, a London innkeeper, proclaimed during her possession in 1564 that she was damned to Hell, the voice that observers heard was recognized as that of Kingesfielde herself, not the demon who had invaded her body. The initial incident that allegedly triggered this woman's possession was that her husband had posted a sign outside the inn depicting the Devil in a jocular fashion. The local community viewed this action as irreverent and offensive to God. Punishing Mistress Kingesfielde rather than her husband for this offence by allowing the Devil to possess her was not unusual. Catholics as well as Protestants were often subjected to possession to atone for the sins of relatives. Nicole Obry's possession, for example, was interpreted as punishment for her mother's sins.[87] But Mistress Kingesfielde was not a completely innocent victim of the Devil's invasion. She may not have been the 'worst of that family', but her infection 'with the disease of the rest' was partially her fault, since she had allowed her household 'to lapse into great negligence in attending church and receiving communion'.[88]

Mistress Kingesfielde's sense of her own responsibility for her husband's moral delinquency explains why she became 'troubled in mind and assaulted with continual temptations'. In this state she suddenly cried out in church one morning that she was destined for eternal damnation. The congregation tried to assure her that this was not the case, but she explained that this revelation had occurred when 'a smoke or mist came before her eyes with an extreme air of brimstone in her nose', an experience that led her and her husband to believe that she was possessed by the Devil. It was widely believed that a foul smell, especially that of brimstone, the odour of Hell, was a sure sign of possession, just as a sweet smell was a sign of sanctity. The important consideration here, however, is that Mistress Kingsfielde's sense of anxiety about her moral status and her consequent proclamation of her damnation were her words, not those of a demon. At this point in the possession a demon had not even been identified and had not been engaged in a dialogue.

One possible explanation of the preoccupation with the sinfulness of the demoniacs in Protestantism is that the afflicted persons were engaged in a conversion experience. These exercises were most common among Calvinists, especially English Puritans, Scottish Presbyterians, and New England Congregationalists. These experiences, which young people engaged in to determine whether they were numbered among the elect, involved a recognition of one's sinfulness, the resistance to demonic temptation and the search for signs that God had chosen them (from all eternity) for salvation. Conversion experiences also involved a persistent questioning of whether they were authentic or delusions caused by the Devil, who might either deceive the person into a false sense of sanctity or alternatively might encourage the person to give in to a life of sin since damnation was foreordained. The fact that these experiences were most common among girls and boys in their early teens—the same groups that were disproportionately represented among the pool of demoniacs—suggests that some Protestant possessions might have originated in conversion experiences. Overwhelmed with a sense of one's sinfulness, which was a prerequisite for the bestowal of God's grace, the demoniac could easily have become convinced that the Devil had taken control of his or her body. Members of the person's family and community might just as easily have come to the same conclusion.

Just as some Protestant youth could experience a happy outcome to their experiences, so some Protestant demoniacs had happy endings to their possessions. The path to this was difficult, since, unlike Catholic demoniacs, Protestants could not enlist the assistance of exorcists. They could (theoretically) only pray and fast in the hope that God would remedy their plight. But by steadily resisting Satan's temptations they could give signs of their sanctity and thus either claim or reclaim their position in their communities. They could also forestall the danger that they might become witches. This was the case with Mistress Kingesfielde in London in 1564, Christian Shaw in Scotland in 1696, and Catharina Fagerberg in Sweden in 1700, who was possessed by demons but then was visited by a good spirit and became a healer.

The main issue in Protestant possessions, therefore, was whether the demoniac would succumb to demonic temptation. This was not a major theme of Catholic possessions because they rarely focused on human sinfulness. Quite to the contrary, many of the most spectacular Catholic possessions arose when pious nuns or laywomen attempted to achieve religious ecstasy and when suspicious authorities discerned that the spirits possessing them were evil rather than divine. Catholics were mainly concerned with the narrow boundary between the saint and the demoniac, whereas Protestants were concerned with a more invidious distinction: whether the demoniac, whom they always considered morally suspect, might be a witch. One indication of this different approach to demonic possession is that the Roman Catholic art of discernment of spirits did not develop within Protestant congregations. Lutherans might occasionally consider the possibility that a possession was divine or angelic rather than demonic, but even for them such a positive experience was interpreted as a divine call for repentance, not an indication of sanctity.[89]

Calvinist demoniacs and witches

One example of the fine line that Calvinists drew between possession and witchcraft comes from Rev. Samuel Willard's narrative of the exceptionally long possession of Elizabeth Knapp, his sixteen-year-old maidservant, in Groton, Connecticut in 1671 and early 1672. Many of the symptoms that Knapp manifested were those that demoniacs in different European religious cultures, including that of Catholicism, were reported to have experienced: fits so violent that it took six men to restrain her, the extrusion of the tongue, stiffening of the limbs, the loss of speech, and uncontrolled screaming. Other symptoms, however, betrayed the cultural specificity of her deeply Calvinist upbringing, such as her 'self condemnation', i.e. her catalogue of personal sins at the beginning of her possession; the horrible temptations to murder, suicide, theft, idleness, and blasphemy; her falling into fits on the Sabbath; her violation of unspecified church ordinances; and disobedience to her parents.[90] The script that Knapp followed therefore was distinctly Calvinist, as was the response of Willard, who observed and questioned Knapp on many occasions to assess the source of her afflictions.

After the earliest manifestation of her possession Knapp impeached some unnamed people as responsible for her affliction. Attributing the cause of a demoniac's afflictions to a witch was more common in Protestantism than in Catholicism. Most of the possessions in Scotland, England, Denmark, the Dutch Republic and in New England led at least to accusations of, if not prosecutions for, witchcraft. But when Knapp learned that the individuals whom she had accused of witchcraft were some of the most righteous members of the Groton congregation, she abandoned this line of argument, claiming that the Devil had deceived her by assuming the appearance of these honest people, thus anticipating the critique of spectral evidence that emerged at the time of the Salem witchcraft prosecutions twenty years later.[91] At this point Knapp herself fell under the suspicion that she was a witch.

Elizabeth Knapp's confession that she had signed the Devil's book in which the names of witches were recorded led Willard to focus almost exclusively on the question of whether she was in fact a witch. The frequent appearance of the Devil to his servant in the guise of a man or a dog, his temptation of her with money and power, and his persistent efforts to have her make a covenant, i.e. a pact, with him all made her suspect on these grounds.[92] When she made contradictory statements, however, Willard questioned the authenticity of her confession, and he grew to doubt that his servant had actually agreed to a diabolical pact. He claimed that the Devil had gained control of the girl's body but not her soul, and he treated her mainly as a victim rather than a culprit.[93] By a circuitous route therefore Willard endorsed the standard Catholic line that demoniacs were for the most part morally and legally innocent.

Knapp's response to questions regarding the Devil's overtures to her also reveals another dimension of Calvinist religious culture. During her possession, which lasted three months, she vacillated between denying that she had made a pact and confessing that she had either wanted to negotiate such an arrangement or that she had actually done so. Her vacillation suggests either that she was struggling with demonic temptation or that Willard and his associates were interpreting her testimony in this way. Knapp, like so many Puritans in New England, was engaged in the spiritual warfare that occurred during Calvinist conversion experiences. A central motif in this struggle was temptation by the Devil.[94] Willard's narrative does not reveal whether Knapp succumbed to or conquered this demonic temptation to commit the worst possible sin, since the account breaks off while Knapp was still struggling with her moral condition. But there it little doubt that this possession narrative was being reshaped to fit those of both witchcraft and Puritan conversions.

Another possession narrative, that of Christian Shaw in Scotland twenty-five years later, suggests that some members of Reformed congregations could successfully resist the type of demonic temptations that beset Elizabeth Knapp. In August 1696 Christian, the eleven-year-old daughter of the laird of Bargarran in Renfrewshire, began to experience fits and bodily contortions, her body became stiff and motionless, and her tongue extruded at great length. She experienced temporary deafness, blindness and an inability to speak. She regurgitated hair, straw, coal cinders the size of chestnuts, gravel, pins, feathers of wild fowl, and bones of various sorts. At times her head twisted as if her neck bone had been dissolved. Her stomach 'swelled like a drum, as like a woman with child'.[95] At times she had difficulty breathing and felt as if she was being choked. During some of her fits she took off all her clothes.[96] She also conversed with invisible spectres.

Unlike the possession of Elizabeth Knapp, Christian Shaw's possession resulted in the formal accusation of some twenty-four persons for having caused her afflictions by witchcraft. Seven of these accused witches were executed at Paisley in 1697.[97] Shaw's possession, no less than Knapp's, bore a distinctive Calvinist stamp, for it also involved a struggle against demonic temptation, thoughts of suicide, and the danger that she would likewise become a witch. It is also plausible to argue that Shaw's possession originated in the terrors that she, like many Calvinist youth, was experiencing as she sought and then struggled through a conversion experience. The fact that she lived in a pious Calvinist household and that she was at an age when many Calvinist youths began to tremble at the thought of going to Hell makes this interpretation even more plausible. Louise Yeoman argues that Shaw's possession was a conversion experience that had gone seriously wrong.[98] The hallmark of that experience, it needs to be emphasized, was recognition of one's natural sinfulness. It is no wonder, therefore, that such experiences, like that of the Scottish schoolmaster John Livingston, involved blasphemous thoughts, self-loathing and the temptation to commit suicide. This young man also claimed that he was possessed by the

Devil, using the term, as did Pierre Viret, to describe the reprobate rather than those who displayed the symptoms of demoniacs.[99]

Christian Shaw's case occupies a special place in the small pantheon of Calvinist possession cases in that this young girl successfully resisted temptation and her afflictions abruptly stopped. Whether she faked her symptoms, as some contemporaries claimed, or whether they were caused by a conversion disorder, a transient psychotic disorder, or childhood epilepsy, as three psychiatrists have argued, does not really matter.[100] The important consideration is that Shaw, her family, the local clergy, and the community all willingly participated in a sacred drama that involved her struggle against Satan and her eventual recognition that she had entered into the covenant of grace. In this case at least the demoniac was able to maintain the distinction, often lost in Calvinism, between the demoniac and the witch.

Two cases of demonic possession in Utrecht—one in the last decade of the sixteenth century and the second in the following decade—conformed to this distinctly Calvinist view of possession, exorcism, and witchcraft. The first, that of David Wardavoir in 1595, had a similar outcome to that of Christian Shaw, at least according to the Calvinist author of the pamphlet describing his deliverance. According to this source the young man struggled against temptation and succeeded in casting out the demon by the unwavering strength of his faith in Jesus Christ.

The second case, in 1603, revealed the recurrent suspicion that Calvinist demoniacs might actually be witches. When two Calvinist sisters-in-law displayed the traditional physical symptoms of possession, a major debate erupted in the city, which was the centre of European scepticism, regarding the cause of their distress. The case engendered a public debate on the nature of their affliction. Two options discussed in the debate—that the women were truly possessed, or that they were faking their symptoms—often arose in cases of demonic possession in both Catholic and Protestant countries. But the third option—that the two demoniacs were witches who had made pacts with the Devil—could only have surfaced in a culture that had collapsed the boundary between the demoniac and the witch. The two women responded to this possible reclassification as witches by insisting that they were in fact possessed by the Devil and accused the Calvinist minister of blasphemy for denying that they were.[101] In order to protect themselves from prosecution and public opprobrium for being witches, the two women, just like Henry Arthington, understood that as long as they were considered to be possessed, they would not be legally or morally culpable for their behaviour. It was far more advantageous to be a demoniac than a witch.

CHAPTER 9

Possession in the Age of Reason

UNTIL ABOUT 1700, THE number of cases of demonic possession and the number of witchcraft prosecutions tracked each other fairly closely. They had risen hand in hand, especially as witches were increasingly held responsible for sending the demons into the bodies of the possessed. In the seventeenth century, when witchcraft prosecutions entered a long period of decline, the number of possessions also began to shrink. Growing scepticism regarding the authenticity of many instances of demonic possession, especially those in convents at Loudun and Louviers, contributed to this decline in witchcraft prosecutions, most notably in France.[1] In Catholic Germany a new phase in the history of demonic possession also began around 1650, as scepticism among elites regarding possession led to the placement of demoniacs in hospitals on the assumption that they were mentally ill.[2] This new attitude to demonic possession in Germany was linked to, if it did not actually help to cause, the decline in witchcraft prosecutions. The same pattern was also evident in England, where both possessions and witchcraft trials entered a noticeable decline in tandem in the 1620s.[3] After the last large witch-hunt in the 1640s, witch trials in England became relatively uncommon, and the number of reported possessions dropped accordingly. As the seventeenth century wound down, it appeared that the great European witch-hunt and the wave of reported demonic possessions, both of which had peaked in 1590s and maintained a brisk pace through the first half of the seventeenth century, would soon be over.[4]

Surprisingly, demonic possession and witch-hunting did not remain on the same trajectory after 1700. Witchcraft prosecutions continued their decline, except in Poland and Hungary, where they peaked in the eighteenth century, but demonic possessions continued to occur, although in significantly reduced numbers, throughout the eighteenth and nineteenth centuries. Very few of these possessions led to prosecutions for witchcraft, and only a handful of those resulted in conviction. To be sure, illiterate peasants and townspeople sometimes accused people in their communities of causing possessions by witchcraft. Occasionally the author of a possession narrative would endorse such popular beliefs, indicating that witchcraft had not completely disappeared from the belief systems of the educated. But charges that witches caused such possessions never became central to these narratives or the polemical pamphlets that were published in support of them. Such a focus was unlikely to have served any practical purpose, since the possibility of prosecuting, much less convicting a witch after 1700 was increasingly slim, even in Germany, where a few isolated prosecutions took place in the first half of the eighteenth century.

Possessions unrelated to witchcraft, however, could serve a significant polemical purpose by proving that the Devil could exercise considerable power in the natural world.[5] This explains why narratives of possession continued to be published long after the last European witch had been executed. This possession literature was indicative of a broader change in the discourse regarding spirits in the eighteenth century that had begun with Joseph Glanvill and Richard Baxter's responses to the neo-Sadducees in the 1680s and 1690s. Instead of focusing on witchcraft, an activity for which there was no empirical evidence, those who defended the existence of a spiritual world (and their numbers increased rather than decreased in the nineteenth century) focused on incidents that could be observed. These included both divine and demonic possessions, the activities of convulsionaries in France in the 1730s, reports of miraculous occurrences in Protestant as well as Catholic territories, and the claims of spiritualists that they could commune with the spirits of the dead. All these efforts were made in order to find empirical evidence that spirits not only existed but could influence the course of events in the natural world. They formed part of a counter-offensive against the scepticism and the secularism of the Age of Reason.

The men who described possessions and used them for polemical purposes did not have to look very far for good material. Possessions have always occurred in societies that believe in evil spirits that can interact with human beings. Those beliefs continued to flourish in both Catholic and Protestant communities in the eighteenth and nineteenth centuries. The main determinant in whether they would come to the attention of the broader community was whether ecclesiastical authorities would lend credence to them or, at the very least, take no steps to discredit them. The crucial step in this process would be an exorcism, which had the capacity to aggravate the symptoms of possession, accentuate its theatrical elements, and attract a public audience—one potentially larger than the audience at a witch trial and execution. An exorcism moreover, unlike a trial for witch-craft, could take place as long as a priest or minister was willing to perform one and as long as the exorcist's ecclesiastical superior allowed him to proceed. One of the main reasons why Catholic possessions in the eight-eenth century continued to exceed the number of Protestant possessions by a large margin was that it was relatively easy to find a Catholic priest to conduct the ritual and, despite the Vatican's prohibition of unlicensed exor-cism, the papacy was unwilling to ban them, simply because they believed that some possessions were authentic. Despite the scepticism of the Vatican, the exorcism rite in the *Rituale Romanum* was grounded in the confident Catholic belief that demons did in fact invade *some* human bodies and could be expelled.

Eighteenth- and nineteenth-century possessions

The possessions that took place in Europe during the eighteenth and nine-teenth centuries conformed to three dominant patterns: spontaneous possessions that afflicted single individuals and often became the centre of controversy; medical possessions treated by exorcists conducting healing campaigns; and group possessions that involved scores of demoniacs whose symptoms appeared to be contagious. All three types of possession had precedents in the early modern period. What distinguished them from the thousands of possessions that had originated in the age of the Reformation was their failure to result in witchcraft prosecutions.

Spontaneous possessions

These possessions, in which individuals displayed many of the classic physiological and behavioural symptoms of possession, tended to attract considerable public attention and led to controversies regarding their authenticity. The possessions of this sort that attracted the most national and international interest occurred in France, Germany, and England.

France

The most famous of these eighteenth-century possessions was that of Marie–Catherine Cadière, an illiterate eighteen-year-old girl in the southern French city of Toulon in 1730. Marie-Catherine's possession began as a case of divine possession and resembled many of those of

French, Spanish, and Italian nuns who displayed similar symptoms in the
late sixteenth and early seventeenth centuries. Although not a nun herself,
Marie-Catherine had been raised by her widowed mother in an environment of 'obsessive religiosity' and intense moral discipline.[6] During her
adolescence she came under the tutelage of Jean-Baptiste Girard, a forty-
eight-year-old Jesuit priest in Toulon, who became the girl's confessor and
spiritual adviser. During this period of tutelage the young woman began to
display some of the symptoms of divine possession, which reportedly
included clairvoyance, divination, levitation, and stigmata. Consequently
Marie-Catherine soon acquired a reputation among the people of Toulon
as a living saint.

During this period of tutelage Cadière's relationship with Father Girard
became sexual, and it was later rumoured, although never proved, that she
had become pregnant by him and that he had arranged an abortion for her.
It is uncertain whether the 'astonishingly beautiful' Catherine resisted the
priest's initial sexual advances, but at some point she acquiesced in the
relationship and probably experienced profound guilt regarding her participation in it.[7] It is reasonable to assume that her guilt about the affair
contributed to her display of the initial symptoms, especially the convulsions, which were interpreted as signs of her possession.

Catherine's possession led to an unauthorized exorcism by her brother,
François Cadière, a novice priest, in November 1730. Although the exorcism was performed over the young woman's body in an upstairs bedroom,
it was nonetheless a semi-public ritual, in that large crowds who revered
Cadière as a saint knew it was taking place and gathered outside the house.
As in many cases of possession, the exorcism itself aggravated the symptoms of the demoniac. Cadière alternated between periods of unconscious-
ness and violent convulsions, her face became contorted, she screamed
blasphemies and obscenities, and she spat on the crucifix in her brother's
hand. When asked in Latin (a language she did not know, although obviously her brother did) who had caused her possession, she replied in a
mixture of Latin and Provençal that Father Girard was the guilty party.

At this stage Catherine's possession began to bear a close resemblance
to the three most famous French possession cases in the seventeenth
century: that of Madeleine Demandols at Aix, which led to the execution
of Father Louis Gaufridy for witchcraft in 1611; that of Jeanne des Anges
at Loudun, which resulted in the burning of Urbain Grandier at the stake
for witchcraft in 1634; and that of Madeleine Bavent at Louviers, for
which Father Thomas Boullé was executed as a witch in 1647. In all three
of these cases the female demoniacs allegedly had had sexual relations
with, or at least entertained sexual fantasies about, their priest-confessors.

In all three cases, moreover, the possession had resulted in the execution of the priest for witchcraft. It appeared therefore that the dynamic of possession-cum-witchcraft was being revisited once again in the eighteenth century, almost fifty years after the edict of Louis XIV had put an end to most witchcraft prosecutions in the kingdom.[8]

The outcome of Catherine's possession reveals that the relationship between demonic possession and witchcraft had changed during the eighty years since Father Boullé had been burned at the stake. Although investigations by ecclesiastical and secular authorities resulted in charges that Girard was guilty of sorcery, bewitchment, 'spiritual incest', Quietism, and the procurement of an abortion, the charge of witchcraft never even reached the deliberative stage. When the case was referred to the *parlement* of Aix, which had ratified the conviction of Gaufridy more than a hundred and twenty years before, the judges refused even to consider the charge of witchcraft, for which there was no reliable evidence. Instead the charges which the judges considered were those relating to priestly malfeasance. To be sure, these were serious charges, and twelve of the judges voted for the conviction and execution of Girard. The same number, however, voted to acquit Girard and convict Cadière of faking her possession and sentence her to two years in prison. These differences within the *parlement* reflected the fierce controversy that had raged for more than a year between the Jansenists (French Catholics who subscribed to some Calvinist doctrines), who took Cadière's side and initiated the charges of witchcraft, and the Jesuits (with whom the Jansenists were often at odds), who defended one of their own and introduced the charges against Marie-Catherine. The judicial impasse was resolved when the president of the *parlement* voted to acquit both parties.

The possession of Marie-Catherine Cadière reveals the striking segregation of demonic possession from witchcraft prosecutions that had emerged by the second decade of the eighteenth century. Cadière's possession had become a *cause célèbre* and had ignited a major controversy over the authenticity of demonic possession, but very little was said, except in the polemical accounts of the affair, about Girard's alleged witchcraft. Possession continued to be a live topic in France, whereas witchcraft gradually disappeared from the mental world of eighteenth-century French elites.

Germany

As in other parts of Europe, reported cases of possession in German territories declined notably in the early eighteenth century, but the few

German cases that attracted public attention showed that belief in the connection between possession and witchcraft persisted longer than in France. It is not surprising that the possession of a group of young boys in the Saxon town of St Annaberg in 1712 led to allegations that witches caused their afflictions.[9] But three possessions in the middle of the eighteenth century showed that the issue continued to simmer. The first was the possession of a group of Norbertine nuns, eventually numbering ten, in the cloistered convent of Unterzell near Würzburg in 1744. After a series of intermittent exorcisms lasting three years, Maria Renata Singer, the senile sub-prioress of the convent who came from a family in the lower nobility, confessed under pressure to having caused the nuns' possessions by means of witchcraft. The beheading of Singer for this crime in 1749—the last witchcraft execution in Würzburg—went forward only after a heated debate between the sceptical administrators of the bishop of Würzburg and more credulous members of the city council and an assortment of clerical allies. The difference between her treatment and the acquittal of Jean-Baptiste Girard at Toulon eighteen years earlier had a great deal to do with the much slower decriminalization of witchcraft in German territories than in France. Singer's execution actually emboldened some overly zealous clerics to call for further witchcraft prosecutions, leading to the last public dispute regarding witchcraft in south-east Germany.[10]

The possession of the twenty-one-year-old Lutheran woman Anna Elisabeth Lohmann from Anhalt-Desau in 1759 reveals that while individual possessions continued to occur among Lutherans, the link between possession and witchcraft in Lutheran territories had become more tenuous than in Catholic Würzburg. It is difficult to tell whether Elisabeth's possession was originally divine or demonic. When this young pious woman began falling into paroxysms on a daily basis, she had visions first of the Devil and then of three angels. Gottlieb Müller, the Lutheran pastor of Kemberg to whom she appealed for help, diagnosed her as a demoniac and tried unsuccessfully to exorcize her on two separate occasions. The apparent reason for his interest in the case was his intention to use the possession to inspire a religious revival in the community, an undertaking that associated him with the reformist programme of Pietism, a movement that tried to breathe life into the official Lutheranism of the day. Most cases of possession in Protestant Germany in the eighteenth century originated in Pietest communities, and Pietist ministers took the lead in arguing for their reality.[11]

Sceptical Lutheran authorities in Dresden were not sympathetic to either Lohmann or her exorcist, and they suppressed a pamphlet that Müller published recounting the episode, while the superintendent in

Wittenberg recalled recent 'scandals' that had resulted when other Protestant girls in Erfurt, Quedlinburg, Halberstadt, and Württemberg had feigned possession.[12] Although Lohmann avoided imprisonment in Wittenberg by escaping to Anhalt, her case sparked a major debate on the reality of possession in which the Protestant biblical scholar Johann Salomo Semler assumed a leading role.[13]

It is significant that this incident of possession did not lead to accusations of witchcraft from ecclesiastical or secular authorities. By this time secular authorities in German Lutheran territories had stopped prosecuting witches. Nor did the people of Kemberg, who witnessed Elisabeth's paroxysms in great numbers, initiate witchcraft accusations. The only charge of witchcraft came from Elisabeth herself, who accused Johann Christian Tietze, a huntsman with whom her brother-in-law had quarrelled, of having caused her possession. In a novel twist to the theory of possession, Lohmann claimed that the spirit which had spoken through her in a deep voice was that of Tietze, not that of Satan or of one of his demonic underlings. But witchcraft in this case was given no credence in elite circles. Even the German scholars who took issue with Semler regarding the authenticity of demonic possession rejected any connection between possession and witchcraft. This scepticism can be attributed to a Lutheran tradition regarding witchcraft which rejected the possibility that God would allow a human being to exercise supernatural power. The Devil might possess a person by his own power with God's permission, as Johann Weyer had conceded, but a witch could not command demonic spirits to do anything at her behest. That would have been no different from the practice of necromancy.

The conviction of Anna Maria Schwägelin for having caused the possession of a young girl in Upper Swabia in 1775 showed that the link between possession and witchcraft in some Catholic circles persisted well into the age of the Enlightenment. Schwägelin was a poor, crippled woman, who was plagued by feelings of guilt for having abandoned her Catholic faith to marry a Protestant from Memmingen. When a five-year-old girl living in the same poorhouse as Schwägelin began to display some of the signs of possession, a local pastor accused the old woman of having caused the child's afflictions by witchcraft. After another inmate beat her severely, she confessed to having made a pact with the Devil. Although she retracted that confession, the master of discipline reported her to the authorities in the prince-abbotship of Kempten. There she voluntarily confessed to having made a pact with the Devil, a claim that her guilt for having abandoned her Catholic faith had probably prepared her to make. On the basis of that confession she was convicted, although apparently not executed, as has long been believed.[14] Schwägelin's was clearly an isolated case, but it does provide evidence that in Catholic Germany the once axiomatic link between possession and witchcraft still had life, although it may be more accurate to say that it was on life-support.

England

England had relatively few witchcraft prosecutions in the late seventeenth and early eighteenth centuries, and it also had relatively few cases of demonic possession that received significant public exposure. Traditional English scepticism regarding demonic possession and the apparent triumph of Sadducee sentiment in the early years of the eighteenth century discouraged the publication of possession narratives. The reductions in the number of English witchcraft prosecutions in the early eighteenth century, followed by its statutory decriminalization in 1736, guaranteed that any possessions that took place after that date would not result in legal action against individuals for causing possession by means of witchcraft.

Nevertheless, a few possessions did occasionally come to the attention of the English reading public. At the same time, however, these possessions show that suspicion of witchcraft as a cause gained no traction. In 1761 the two daughters of Richard Giles, an innkeeper in Bristol were repeatedly pinched, bitten, and scratched on their arms and breasts by an 'invisible power' later identified as the demon Malchi. The two girls. Molly and Dobby, also suffered repeated piercings by pins, nails, and glass. According to the pamphlet that described their afflictions, they were choked and beaten, incurred large wounds, and lost pieces of flesh. They were dragged around the house and thrown as much as five feet in the air. These attacks took place only at night and when the girls were praying. Because the assaults were external, and because the girls did not vomit any foreign objects, their initial afflictions would have been technically classified as obsession rather than possession.[15]

The appearance of additional symptoms, however, complicated the diagnosis, making the girls' afflictions an apparent case of demonic possession. These symptoms included the girls' barking four or five times and crowing like a cock, repeatedly turning their heads from the right to the left shoulder as well as backwards and forwards, and falling into convulsions. The tongue of one girl was pulled 'out of her mouth very long, then doubled down her throat'.[16] Their bodies became so rigid that no one could bend them, and three able-bodied people could not prevent the girls from being pulled up to the ceiling. As one girl was hoisted in this manner (it is unclear whether this was considered to be levitation), the other would 'lie in a senseless state, trembling with hands and feet'.[17] The girls suffered paralysis for short periods of time. Efforts to communicate with the demon in Latin and Greek elicited unspoken responses that took the form of scratching. Since the demon refused to answer in a voice, this aspect of the Giles girls' possession did not conform to the usual pattern in which the Devil spoke through the demoniac. The narrative claimed that the demon spoke only once, and he was reported to have spoken to the girls rather than through them. Nevertheless the spirit's indication that it had infected six other persons, four of them in Bristol, made this case appear similar to those in the previous two centuries, in which the symptoms had spread to other individuals in the community.[18]

There were two notable features of this eighteenth-century case of demonic possession. The first is that it occurred in Protestant England, where scepticism was deeply ingrained in both secular and religious culture. The fact that Henry Durbin, the 'eye and ear witness' of the possession who wrote the narrative, believed in the authenticity of the possession leads one to question the extent of scepticism regarding possession among educated eighteenth-century Englishmen. (It also raises a question about the level of Durbin's education.) It is important to note, however, that Bristol had become a centre of Methodism, an enthusiastic religion that continued to profess a belief in witchcraft and possession.[19]

The second notable feature of this possession is that although the published title of the narrative claimed that the tormenting of the Giles children was 'supposed to be the effect of witchcraft', Durbin mentioned witchcraft only three times in his account. The first was the report that the demon told Molly that an unnamed man had 'employed a witch' apparently to threaten the girls with their lives. The second was when Richard Giles met a woman dressed in a cloak who he thought was the person who troubled his family. Finally, there was the suggestion that a witch had caused the death of Richard Giles, the girls' father.[20] In no place did Durbin claim that witchcraft had been the cause of the girls' possession. The two phenomena had been segregated in England just as much as they had in Lutheran Germany. With the exception of John Wesley and possibly some of his associates, educated Englishmen did not believe that witchcraft caused demonic possession.[21]

The possession of George Lukins, a tailor of Yatton in Somersetshire, in 1787, had even less to do with witchcraft than that of the Giles children, but it led to a more extensive debate regarding the authenticity of the possession.[22] Lukins's symptoms, which included recurrent fits, howling, bodily distortions, and insults hurled at clergymen, began in 1769 but did not attract widespread attention until eighteen years later, when he was brought to Bristol for an exorcism. Efforts of the Rev. Joseph Easterbrook to enlist members of the Anglican clergy to join him in exorcizing Lukins failed, since participation in the ritual would have violated the prohibition on exorcisms without episcopal authority that had been included in the canons of the Church of England in 1604. Accordingly, Lukins was exorcized by a committee of seven Methodist ministers, who acted under no such ecclesiastical restraints. The exorcism, which consisted of adjurations and commands for the demon to depart, accompanied by the prayers and hymns of the faithful, succeeded in the final expulsion of the Devil amidst wild howling. In many respects this Methodist exorcism resembled the Catholic rituals that the Church of England and other Protestant denominations had rejected outright.

The possession of George Lukins exposed the weakness of the connections between possession and witchcraft in late eighteenth-century England. The only person to raise the issue of witchcraft was Lukins himself, who had accused local witches of causing his afflictions when they began. By the time of his exorcism, however, he held the Devil himself entirely responsible for his fits and distortions. He also claimed to have been possessed by seven demons, just like Apolonia Geisslbrecht in 1582, Jeanne Féry in 1584, Madeleine Bavent in 1643, Jeanne des Anges in 1632, and Anna Mayer in 1695. Like Féry and other early modern demoniacs, Lukins probably learned that part of his possession script from the New Testament, which says that Mary Magdalene was possessed by seven demons. The reason for enlisting seven clerics to conduct the exorcism was to have one exorcist assigned to each demon.

The pamphlets published in the wake of this possession and exorcism resembled many of those that had been published in response to possessions at the height of the 'epidemic' in the late sixteenth and early seventeenth centuries. Easterbrook's claim that the possession was authentic was based on the argument that to deny its reality would be to claim that the power of the Lord had been diminished since biblical times, an argument that conveniently ignored the Protestant doctrine of the cessation of miracles.[23] The sceptics, most notably the Yatton physician Samuel Norman, claimed not only that Lukins was an impostor but also that he and other advocates of religious enthusiasm were threatening a return to Roman Catholicism.[24]

English possessions continued to take place in the late eighteenth and early nineteenth centuries. Only some were recorded in pamphlets or books, but the relative sparseness of those narratives does not mean that the number of cases was inconsequential. Quite to the contrary, there is evidence that in some locations, such as Bristol, Methodists conducted many exorcisms during their revival meetings. The Catholics, although a small minority of the English population, also continued to perform exorcisms, as they had consistently done (and in larger numbers) in the seventeenth century. The exorcism of a Birmingham woman performed by a Catholic priest, Edward Peach, ignited a controversy that recalled those of the sixteenth century.[25] Possessions within Anglican communities also continued into the nineteenth century. These possessions, like that of the ten-year-old boy John Evans of Plymouth Dock in 1820, who experienced convulsions, insensitivity to pain, and temporary loss of speech and who also exhibited hostility to the Bible or any religious book, often closely resembled those that had taken place two centuries earlier.[26] The main difference between these and their early modern counterparts was that they made only passing reference, if any at all, to witches as the alleged cause of the demoniacs' afflictions.

Medical possessions

A second broad category of eighteenth-century possessions can be classified as medical. There were far more of these than the spontaneous possessions that occurred at such locations as Toulon, Würzburg, and Bristol. They differed from spontaneous possessions in that almost all of the symptoms were physiological, and most were the products of ailments that had readily identifiable natural causes. Very few of the physiological symptoms of medical possessions could be classified as pathological, and those that could became apparent only during the exorcism. For this reason the psychoanalyst Henri Ellenberger classified such possessions as 'latent'.[27] These demoniacs rarely exhibited the verbal and behavioural symptoms of possession, such as blaspheming and spitting on sacred objects or speaking in unknown languages. They sought out exorcists to find a supernatural cure since both they and their exorcists shared the belief that all illnesses, even those of a relatively minor nature, were caused by the Devil. Thus the role of the exorcist in these cases was essentially that of a spiritual healer. Indeed, it was only because the exorcist had a reputation for curing medical ailments that hundreds of people flocked to them. These exorcisms did not last very long, and because they were so numerous, they were handled in a routine fashion.

Another distinctive feature of these medical possessions and routine exorcisms is that they rarely if ever identified a witch as their cause. This was clearly the case with the hundreds of exorcisms performed by Giovan Battista Chiesa in Piedmont in the last decade of the seventeenth century. Chiesa compiled an impressive record in curing various illnesses, including blindness, lameness, sciatica, and paralysis, by using what today would be described as primitive techniques of psychotherapy. In traditional fashion this parish priest attributed all illnesses to the Devil, thus giving a cosmic, metaphysical explanation of misfortune instead of attributing it to the active evil intent of another person in the community.[28] At the same time he rarely placed blame on the afflicted person; the source of the malady was both external and supernatural. It was relatively easy for Chiesa to explain illness in this way to his Piedmontese clients since belief in *maleficium* was never very strong in Italy. Witchcraft in Italy was essentially a crime of diabolism, not the infliction of misfortune on another person by magical means.[29]

The hundreds of exorcisms performed by the German Catholic priest Johann Joseph Gassner in the 1770s provide further evidence of the persistence of demon possession with little or no reference to witchcraft in the eighteenth century. Gassner's exorcisms, which took place about eighty years after Chiesa's, are even more telling than those of the Piedmontese parish priest. Unlike Chiesa, Gassner cured illnesses that were known to have natural causes, including not only epilepsy, leprosy, blindness, and paralysis, but more prosaic maladies such as fevers, headaches, and infections. The marital impediment that he treated by exorcism was probably erectile dysfunction. The inclusion of madness in his healing repertory shows that the ailments he cured were not exclusively somatic in nature, but like the illnesses that Chiesa cured, they did not include any of the verbal or behavioural symptoms of early modern possessions. The evidence for the apparent effectiveness of Gassner's cures was even more compelling than for those of Chiesa.

Gassner's healing campaign appealed to both Catholics and Protestants, especially to Pietists. As Erik Midelfort has shown, most of the Protestant writers who supported Gassner in the controversy engendered by his healing campaign were Pietists, who were attracted by charismatic figures such as this exorcist priest. Pietists were also the promoters of the four 'scandalous' possessions of young girls that embarrassed Lutheran authorities in the 1740s.[30]

The connection between Pietism and possession became even more pronounced in 1842–3, when the Pietist minister Johann Christoph Blumhardt conducted a large number of exorcisms in the remote Black Forest village of Möttlingen in Württemberg. Blumhardt's methods bore a distinctly Protestant stamp. Unlike Gassner, Blumhardt used only the scripturally warranted methods of dispossession; commentators observed no trace of the Catholic ritual in the exorcisms he staged. One of his demoniacs, Gottlieben Dittus, manifested more of the traditional behavioural signs of possession than any of Gassner's clients, claiming she was possessed by thousands of demons, uttering blasphemies, losing consciousness, and reporting an earthquake in the West Indies before it became known in Germany.[31] In other respects, however, the two exorcists were similar. Both believed in the reality of witchcraft, as did many of their clients, and none of Gassner's or Blumhardt's demoniacs accused others of having caused their possession by that means. Both exorcists, moreover, can be considered practitioners of a form of primitive healing that resembled some of the techniques used in psychotherapy in the twentieth century.

Group possessions

The mass possessions in various parts of Europe in the nineteenth century resembled those of the sixteenth and seventeenth centuries that had taken place villages like Mattaincourt and Belmonte and in the Catholic convents of France, Italy, and Spain. These collective or group possessions sometimes involved popular accusations of witchcraft, but those charges were quickly dismissed by ecclesiastical authorities and did not result in prosecutions.

The first of these mass possessions took place in the small Aragonese village of Tosos in 1812 during the Spanish revolution that occurred in the wake of Napoleon's armed intervention in the country in 1808. The possessions began when eight women began to manifest some of the traditional symptoms of possession during a procession on the feast of Corpus Christi.[32] Within a few days the symptoms had spread to more than thirty-two women. Unnamed people soon accused a hated resident of the village, Joaquina Martinez, of having caused all the possessions by means of witchcraft. With no possibility of a prosecution for witchcraft, a few men in the village took justice into their own hands, going to Martinez's house with the stated intention of killing her but resorting in the end to breaking in and throwing her furniture and jewellery into the street. This violence, which was hardly unprecedented in the treatment of suspected witches after prosecutions had come to an end, forced Martinez and her family to leave the village. The accusation that she was a witch reflected a growing divide between educated elites and the illiterate public regarding the existence of witchcraft that has continued to the present day. To the clerical authorities the notion that God had put at this woman's disposal 'a host of devils, to be passed on to anyone she wishes' was not consistent with sound religious belief.

There was also a division between the clerical establishment and the people of Tosos regarding the authenticity of these women's possession.

The vehemence with which the bishop and other commentators insisted that the possessions were either fraudulent or caused by 'perturbed imagination, invaded by melancholic notions' should not, however, be taken as a rejection of the authenticity of all possessions. Their insistence applied only to this particular group possession, which in light of the limited symptoms manifested by the women even the most credulous person might have difficulty accepting as genuine. In taking their stance the clergy were simply following a long tradition in Spanish inquisitorial practice that attributed many but by no means all possessions to natural causes, imagination, or fraud.

The mass possession of at least 290 women in the small Savoyard commune of Morzine between 1857 and 1863 bears some resemblance to the possessions at Tosos earlier in the century. Like the possessed in Aragon, the demoniacs of Morzine believed that they had been possessed as a result of a *mal donné*, or a witch's curse, and they demanded to be exorcized. In 1857 the parish priest had been willing to oblige the demoniacs in the village in this way, but by 1861 he had reversed his position, probably as the result of pressure from his ecclesiastical superiors. This left the women with little relief from their religious anxiety. With no specific witch to blame, the demoniacs and their families employed a variety of traditional measures against witchcraft to put an end to their afflictions. When these had little effect, the number and intensity of their symptoms increased. The group possession ended when both ecclesiastical and secular authorities, determined to rid the population of such superstitious beliefs and practices, hospitalized some of the afflicted and called in the infantry to restore order in the village. These measures, buttressed by the dominant medical diagnosis of the women's symptoms, led to a reduction and eventually the elimination of the demoniacs' symptoms. The prevalence of secular power and a secular diagnosis had apparently triumphed.[33]

Some scholars have seen this episode as evidence of how powerful elites controlled and suppressed the epidemic, thereby leading to the further secularization of French society. Others, as discussed in Chapter 7, have seen the episode as evidence of social conflicts, especially between the demoniacs and the men in the village. For the broader purposes of this study the episode confirms the hypothesis that the peasants' religious anxieties, which were aggravated when the bishop visited the town and denounced the demoniacs' behaviour, lay at the source of their possession. It also shows that although the local population attributed the possessions to witchcraft, there was no possibility that this episode would lead to a witch-hunt or even an illegal lynching such as had been attempted at Tosos. Finally, the incident raises questions about the persistence of beliefs in the authenticity of possession. In this case physicians, clergy and secular authorities all agreed that these possessions were not genuine. As in Tosos, however, the ecclesiastical authorities never addressed the broader question of whether *any* possessions were real. It is quite likely that Bishop Magnin believed that some possessions, although not these, were authentic and that exorcisms were necessary to end them. This after all had been the official policy of the Vatican since the publication of the relatively sceptical *Rituale Romanum* of 1614.

The group possession at Morzine occurred at a surprisingly late date, but it was not an isolated occurrence. Similar episodes of collective demonic activity took place at Verzegnis in the Friuli in 1878, at Plédran near Saint Brieuc in France in 1881, and at Jaca in Spain in the same year. All of these episodes followed the same pattern as the possessions at Morzine, and they appear to have had similar causes. In none, moreover, did clerical authorities (as opposed to villagers) give serious consideration to witchcraft as their possible cause.

A group possession of Russian shriekers in 1898 and the failure of secular authorities to take action against witches for causing their possessions provides further evidence of the separation of possession from witchcraft in the nineteenth century. Shriekers acquired their name because they were known to shout out the names of the witches they believed had caused their possessions. This ritualistic behaviour developed at the same time that Russian witchcraft prosecutions began.[34] There was therefore a close link between witch-hunting and demonic possession during the period of Russian witchcraft trials, just as there was in other parts of Europe in the early modern period. But as in other European countries, possession and witchcraft in Russia began to follow different paths in the late seventeenth and eighteenth centuries, when witchcraft prosecutions declined and the belief in a causal relationship between witchcraft and possession gradually died out among the educated elite and the nobility. The clergy also began to believe that many such possessions had natural medical causes and therefore referred the demoniacs to physicians, although they continued to believe that religious institutions, such as monasteries and shrines, could still heal shriekers by traditional spiritual means.

Scepticism and authority

There are two closely related reasons for the persistence of demonic possession in an age of declining witchcraft prosecutions. The first is that while an increasingly large number of intellectuals and members of the reading public became sceptical regarding the authenticity of some or most possessions, a consensus on this never materialized, especially within the clergy. The second is that ecclesiastical authorities, especially those of the Catholic faith, were reluctant or perhaps unwilling to ban all exorcisms. Scriptural support for the reality of possession had much to do with both explanations.

The limits of scepticism

There is plenty of evidence for the gradual emergence of a sceptical mentality regarding possession and all other manifestations of the supernatural in the late seventeenth and eighteenth centuries. This evidence can be found in the writings of the Sadducees of the late seventeenth century who denied the existence of spirits; in the emerging consensus among physicians, especially in England, that incidents of possession had natural causes; and in scathing ridicule of the superstitious beliefs of the uneducated in English and French literature.[35] This sceptical tradition reached its most vigorous expression in the works of the *philosophes* of the Enlightenment, especially Voltaire and Denis Diderot, who conducted a crusade against superstition and all other irrational expressions of religious belief.[36]

Scholars often cite this growing body of sceptical literature as evidence of the banishment of such beliefs from the mental landscape of educated Europeans. They use this literature to document the 'disenchantment' of the world and celebrate the inexorable triumph of rationalism and secularism in European intellectual life. This thesis is fundamentally flawed. Secular, rational thought regarding possession developed much more slowly than most historians are willing to admit, and it never achieved a consensus among educated Europeans. In particular the clergy, the group most directly responsible for dealing with possessions in the first instance, have never adopted an unqualified scepticism regarding demonic possession.

One of the main reasons why the emergence of a sceptical consensus did not develop in the eighteenth century is that the arguments of sceptics encountered challenges at every turn. Even within the medical profession, where naturalist interpretations of supernatural phenomena had found expression ever since the Middle Ages and which continued to grow in the seventeenth and eighteenth centuries, belief in the reality of demonic possession continued into the eighteenth century. This was especially true in Germany, where Friedrich Hoffmann and many members of the medical faculty at the University of Halle in the mid eighteenth century tenaciously clung to the belief that the Devil could possesses human beings.[37]

The fact that controversies erupted in connection with almost all the cases of possession discussed above shows that the designation of the eighteenth century as the Age of Reason must be qualified. The publication of the narrative of the possession of the Giles children in 1761, with its spirited defence of the reality of possession and its appendix written by a Hereford cleric earlier in the century, shows that scepticism had hardly triumphed, especially in a city that was the centre of the Methodist revival. Peter the Great of Russia (r. 1682–1725) subscribed to the Enlightenment credo when he denied the validity of possession, but he did not find support among his advisers or even from his own sister.[38] Voltaire's attack on religion and superstition, including demonic possession, and the similar position taken by Diderot and Jean d'Alembert in the *Encyclopédie* did not win universal support among the educated. Belief regarding possession was not confined to the uneducated, 'superstitious' masses for whom the English Whigs and French *philosophes* had deep contempt.

The most significant challenges to the scepticism among the educated came from within the clergy, who found it difficult to accommodate the new spirit of rationalism and scepticism with their religious beliefs. One of the most credulous works on demonic possession was the eight-volume study of the supernatural by the French priest Alphonse Costadeau, who believed in possession and other supernatural interventions in the natural world and even warned exorcists not to spend too much time conversing with demons.[39] In 1732 the French priest Antoine Louis Daugis responded to a sceptical treatise by the royal physician to Louis XV, François de Saint-André, which denied the power of the Devil to intervene in the natural world. Daugis defended his belief in the reality of possession by citing all the customary references to Scripture and the evidence that exorcisms were effective.[40] In 1746 the prolific French Benedictine scholar Augustin Calmet published a two-volume study of the 'philosophy of apparitions and spirits' in which he not only proved the reality of possession and obsession by citing Scripture but also accepted fully the authenticity of the possession of Nicole Obry, Marthe Brossier, Elizabeth de Ranfaing, and the nuns at Loudun, all of whom had been suspected of fraud. Calmet's nineteenth-century English Protestant translator commented that the author's 'simplicity and credulity' in recounting these cases of possession was 'very remarkable'.[41]

A more qualified clerical defence of demonic power appeared in Abbé Nicolas Lenglet Dufresnoy's multi-volume collection of treatises on the supernatural, which was published in 1751. Only one treatise in the second volume, *Dissertation sur la possession du corps* (1746) by the Dominican professor of theology Charles-Louis Richard, dealt specifically with possession. In this work Richard had taken a moderate position, arguing for the possibility of authentic possession while recognizing the difficulty of believing in it.[42] In commenting on Richard's work, Lenglet combined scepticism with a reluctance to question God's plan, noting that Father Richard had not been able to produce any examples of possession in the city where he published his treatise.[43] Lenglet's commentary on the entire set of treatises in his collection revealed the difficulties a cleric who was sympathetic to current rationalist critiques of superstition had in reconciling faith and reason.[44] The only French priest who seems to have come down heavily on the side of scepticism in the mid eighteenth century was the country priest Jean Pierquin, who in *Conjectures sur les effets de l'obsession naturelle* explained possession as the product of continuously preoccupation with visions that were caused by an overactive nervous system. Even Pierquin, however, could only attribute *most* of the possessions that took place in his day to fraud or lunacy.[45]

The only cleric who categorically denied the possibility of possession in the late seventeenth or early eighteenth century was the Calvinist minister and biblical scholar Balthasar Bekker, whose book, *De betoverde weereld*, was published in Dutch in 1691 and 1693 and was soon translated into French, German, and English (The Enchanted World). Bekker argued, mainly on the basis of biblical scholarship, that the Devil could not exercise power in the material world, since God had consigned him to Hell, where he would remain until Judgement Day. In this way Bekker challenged the contemporary belief in the reality of both witchcraft and possession.

The commercial success of this book led eighteenth-century commentators to exaggerate Bekker's influence on Dutch and European beliefs regarding the Devil and his powers. In 1713 the English freethinker Anthony Collins clearly had Bekker in mind when he celebrated the banishment of the Devil in the Dutch Republic and satirized the belief that the Devil 'obsesses some, possesses others, and enters into confederacy with others'.[46] In 1800 the anonymous editor of Henry Durbin's possession narrative of the Bristol girls credited Bekker with undermining the entire diabolical 'system' by making the Devil a 'nonentity'. His claim not only misrepresented Bekker's position on the existence of the Devil, which Bekker never denied, but grossly overstated the Dutch scholar's influence on eighteenth-century intellectual life. Bekker's book was published too late to have any significant impact of the number of witchcraft prosecutions, which had long since ended in his own country and had entered their final stage in the north-west German territories nearby. The work was even less likely to have undermined the belief of educated Europeans in demonic possessions, about which he said comparatively little in this massive tome.

No other Protestant theologian in the eighteenth century endorsed Bekker's categorical denial of the reality of possession. The English biblical scholars Thomas Woolston and Arthur Ashley Sykes, who denied that the demoniacs exorcized by Christ were in fact possessed by demons, said nothing about possessions in their own day. Nor did they deal with the broader theological problem of the nature and extent of demonic power. Their apparent objective was to make a contribution to biblical scholarship, thereby strengthening the latitudinarian agenda of reconciling faith with reason. They might have believed that the Devil could not possess a human body, but they certainly did not state that case in their publications.

Lutheran scholars were even more non-committal on this issue than doctrinal Calvinists like Bekker or latitudinarians like Sykes and Woolston. Lutherans' reluctance to challenge the reality of possession is understandable, since they did not, like Calvinists, believe in the cessation of miracles, and they had always been more willing than Calvinists to accept the reality of possessions in their communities. No Lutheran scholar, not even Johann Semler, took such an unequivocal position in the eighteenth century. Unlike Woolston and Sykes, Semler had been drawn to the subject after discrediting a possession in his own day—that of Elisabeth Lohmann in 1759. His critique of Pastor Müller's pamphlet was so devastating that one might have readily inferred that he denied the authenticity of all possessions. There is, however, no evidence that Semler took such a position, and the fact that he based his analysis of the Lohmann case on the absence of the classic signs of possession set down in the *Rituale Romanum* of 1614—a curious recognition of Catholic authority for a German Protestant to make—suggests that he, no less than the Vatican authorities that drafted the Roman ritual, made an allowance for some genuine possessions.

Among Catholic scholars, the Spanish Benedictine monk Benito Feijoo, who was arguably the most sceptical Catholic scholar on this issue during the eighteenth century, did not go as far as Semler, much less Bekker, in his treatment of demonic possession. In a long essay titled 'Demoniacos', first published in 1739, Feijoo, who is considered a leading figure in the early Spanish Enlightenment, contended that the overwhelming majority of demoniacs either imagined that they were possessed or faked their symptoms. But Feijoo, who unlike Bekker, Woolston, and Sykes subscribed to a literal interpretation of Scripture, would not deny the authenticity of either those that had taken place in biblical times or a small number of demoniacs in his own day who were 'really possessed'.[47] In this respect Feijoo anticipated the position of the Catholic Church in modern times. Always sceptical of the cases that have come to its attention, the Vatican has nonetheless always accepted the objective reality of those possessions that pass the traditional tests to determine whether the demoniac was in fact possessed.

Without being able or willing to deny the reality of all demonic possessions, the clergy unwittingly made possible the perpetuation of new cases. By keeping open the possibility of possession, clergymen gave implicit permission to people to play the role of demoniacs in the hope that their experiences would be taken seriously by their priests or pastors. As long as the clergy continued to believe that even a few cases of possession might be authentic, they could not end the spread of the convulsions, contortions, and blasphemies. In such circumstances, it was left to secular authorities, such as the magistrates and police forces that intervened at Morzine, to stop the spread of the possessions.

The persistence of exorcisms

The second explanation of the persistence of demonic possessions into the eighteenth century and beyond was the difficulty ecclesiastical authorities faced in their efforts to eliminate or restrict unauthorized exorcisms. As discussed in Chapter 4, the papacy took steps in the early seventeenth century to prevent exorcisms by unlicensed practitioners as well as the use of 'superstitious' exorcism rites. Despite these efforts, unauthorized exorcisms by parish priests continued to take place throughout Europe in the seventeenth and eighteenth centuries, and the papacy found it necessary to place them on the Index of Prohibited Books in the early eighteenth century.

Popular demand for exorcism, encouraged by unlicensed exorcists, helps to explain why many possessions continued to take place in the eighteenth century. Feijoo admitted as much, claiming that such exorcisms were in large part responsible for a surge in the number of possessions in Spain in the first half of the century. But the difficulty in prosecuting such offenders, especially in the face of widespread popular support, made it hard to suppress them. Chiesa was not tried for misconduct until after he had exorcized hundreds of demoniacs in his village. It is also unclear how determined ecclesiastical officials were to clamp down on such practices. All Catholic authorities, one might assume, believed in at least the possibility of demonic possession and the necessity of expelling demons from the bodies of the possessed when such an invasion actually occurred. The *Rituale Romanum* had, after all, prescribed an official exorcism ritual, and new editions of that manual have continued to do so until the present day. Some ecclesiastical authorities were probably ambivalent about denying parishioners the services of exorcists, even if they did operate without official approval. Prosecution of an exorcist, which was an administrative action rather than a punishment for immoral or unethical behaviour, was probably a fairly low priority for an eighteenth-century Catholic; even for a reform-minded bishop.

Protestant churches, especially the Church of England, were more successful than the Vatican in restricting unauthorized exorcisms. The prosecution and deprivation of John Darrell and his associates by the Court of High Commission in 1602 and the provision in the canons of 1604 requiring that all exorcisms have prior episcopal approval made it especially difficult for freelance preachers to flourish in seventeenth- and eighteenth-century England. The canons were clearly the reason (or the excuse) for the Anglican clergy's refusal to accept the invitation to exorcize George Lukins in 1788. Demonic possession had, moreover, never been as widespread in England as it was in Catholic Europe, and scepticism regarding the authenticity of possessions had long been the dominant attitude of Anglican churchmen. The few possessions that did occur after 1700 took place in Nonconformist or Methodist communities, as in the case of the Giles children in 1761. That episode, moreover, had not involved an attempt to exorcize the child. Official prohibition, reinforced by ecclesiastical scepticism, prevented such remedial treatment from taking place.[48] Indeed, one of the many ways in which the incident was exceptional was the absence of significant clerical involvement. The anonymous publisher of Durbin's narrative indicated in the Preface that several learned clergy had also observed the Giles children and were convinced that they were not impostors, but Durbin had not mentioned these clergymen in his account.

Lutheran authorities were no less sceptical than were Anglicans of the authenticity of demonic possessions, but they had even greater difficulty suppressing exorcisms that took place in their territories. When the Lutheran Gottlieb Müller exorcized Elisabeth Lohmann twice in 1759, Lutheran authorities in Dresden suppressed the pamphlet that Müller had written on the affair and ordered Lohmann's arrest, but they took no action against Reverend Müller.[49] The problem was the relative weakness of ecclesiastical discipline of the German Lutheran clergy, especially when compared with the control of the activities of Calvinist ministers in a Presbyterian system or in the hierarchical structure of church government in the Church of England.

Possession, exorcism and secularization

The persistence of possessions and exorcisms in the Age of Reason and the reluctance of clerical authorities to deny that possessions could take place in the modern world have provided support for the claims of some historians and social scientists that by the end of the eighteenth century, if not earlier, secularism had triumphed over religion. The word secular in this context is taken to denote the absence or rejection of either religious belief or ecclesiastical authority as the basis for human behaviour and collective social and political activity.[50]

Now, it requires little historical knowledge to appreciate the fact that religious belief and ecclesiastical authority matter much less in the present day, at least in the West, than they did in the Middle Ages. The replacement of churches and monasteries with non-ecclesiastical buildings; the reduction in the size of the clerical profession; the separation of scientific, economic, political, and historical thought from theology and from the academic control of theological faculties at the universities; the replacement of religious by non-religious motifs in works of visual art; the dramatic reduction in church attendance; and the reliance on human reason alone, devoid of religious preconceptions, in solving human problems all point to the fact that modern Western societies are far more secular than they were some five hundred years ago.[51]

The difficulty with the scholarly discussion of such developments is in large part the result of efforts by historians and social scientists to identify a process of *secularization* in this complex transformation of human thought and action over the course of centuries.[52] Such an analysis can easily lead to the belief that the emergence of a more secular society has followed a linear, progressive path and that at some particular juncture a secular age dawned. It can also lead to the Whiggish tendency to celebrate and exaggerate the modernity of individuals (such as Edward Jorden or Balthasar Bekker) or movements (such as the Protestant Reformation or the Enlightenment) that have supposedly contributed to this process of secularization, making those individuals or movements out to be more secular and therefore more modern than they really were.

The key concept in this proclaimed process of secularization with respect to demonic possession is the 'disenchantment of the world', the phrase coined by the German sociologist Max Weber to describe the abandonment of magical, supernatural, and religious explanations in favour of the broader process of rationalization that inspired Weber's oversimplified view of Western history. The growth of scepticism regarding the authenticity of demonic possession, the willingness of many writers to accept natural explanations of demoniacs' symptoms, the eighteenth-century ridicule of the superstition of the ignorant masses, the denial that the Devil could intervene in the natural world, and the assignment of demoniacs to medical doctors rather than exorcists have all been seen as contributions to this inexorable process of secularization. The most heralded achievement of all was the triumph of psychiatry over demonology, a victory epitomized by the work of the committed rationalist and secularist Jean-Martin Charcot and his associates in late nineteenth-century France.[53]

But when did this process of secularization begin and when was it complete? From the early years of the Renaissance many physicians, relying in large part on the writing of their Greek and Hellenistic predecessors, claimed that demonic possession had natural, somatic causes. They did so without claiming that the Devil worked through nature and thus was indirectly responsible for the afflictions of demoniacs. But these secular views always competed with strong beliefs in the supernatural causes of possessions, and those supernatural interpretations became more common than their naturalist alternative during the age of the Reformation. The banishment of the demonic and the supernatural from the world has never been a steady process; at times it made deep inroads into educated opinion, as in early eighteenth-century England, and then retreated in the face of a spiritual revival or a romantic reaction.[54] This is apparently what happened when, after a period of growing scepticism in the late seventeenth and early eighteenth centuries, Methodists, Pietists, and Jansenists contributed to a revival of the belief in the reality of demonic possession. This revival occurred at the time when such groups also gave new life to a variety of emotional or ecstatic religious experiences. The two processes were closely related. This period also witnessed the revolt of the Camisards in southern France, the Great Awakening in America, and the birth of the Shakers. All these groups participated in an effort to bridge the gap between the spiritual and the natural worlds. They thereby not only challenged the advance of secularism and rationalism in eighteenth-century Europe but actually contributed to a re-enchantment of the world in places where belief in the supernatural and magical appeared to be on the decline.

Resistance to disenchantment was not restricted to remote areas such as Tosos and Morzine, where the population had remained largely 'superstitious'.[55] The publication of possession narratives in Bristol, Würzburg, and Leipzig show that the belief in the reality of possession could exist in places where the Enlightenment had made considerable headway. For this reason it is problematic to follow Henri Ellenberger in claiming that after 1700 possessions took place only in isolated areas that had not been influenced by the Enlightenment.[56] That was not true then, nor is it true today.

The most forceful expressions of secularism and rationalism in the eighteenth century came from the *philosophes* of the Enlightenment, and they flourished in the predominantly urban, cosmopolitan environments where

Enlightenment thought found its most fertile ground. But even in these contexts secularism did not always triumph in the eighteenth century.[57] In the Dutch medical profession, for example, where the naturalist ideas of Spinoza and the radical Enlightenment flourished, opposition to naturalist theories of the causes of diseases found significant support.[58] They also found surprising support in 'sceptical' England, perhaps because most English physicians received their medical education in the Netherlands.[59]

The emergence of a secular approach to healing provides a different set of cautions regarding the secularization of possession and exorcism in Europe. Just as many Renaissance physicians adopted a naturalist interpretation of possession, so too a natural, secular approach to healing demoniacs emerged during the early modern period and gradually became the reigning orthodoxy in medical circles in the late seventeenth and early eighteenth centuries.[60] It took many decades, however, for this secular approach to win the support of the clerical establishment in both Catholic and Protestant territories, and their reluctance to agree with an emerging consensus of medical practitioners allowed popular belief in spiritual healing to continue well into the age of the Enlightenment. Spiritual healing also enjoyed a long life because it seemed to work. It was especially effective among Catholics, who could heal by means of exorcism, but it also registered success among English Puritans and Methodists. These Protestant healers employed the traditional methods of prayer and fasting but also adopted the Catholic procedures of engaging in a dialogue with the Devil. This allowed Protestant spiritual healing to rival that of the Catholic exorcism in its theatrical appeal.

Because spiritual healing persisted, there was a long period in which spiritual and medical healing coexisted in the treatment of demoniacs.[61] Even the Church of Scotland in its report on parapsychology in 1996, while dismissing exorcism in a manner consistent with the Protestant tradition, reserved a place for spiritual remedies for the possessed. The report states, 'We believe that it [exorcism] effects nothing that cannot be accomplished by expeditious use of medical skills, *the latter including prayer, blessing and such healing procedures as the pastoral agent may have at his disposal*.'[62] In charismatic Protestant communities the practice of faith healing testifies to the persistent belief that illnesses have supernatural causes and can be relieved by means of spiritual remedies. The same attitude to spiritual healing prevailed in Russian Orthodox circles throughout the imperial period.[63] All this makes it difficult to talk about the progressive secularization of healing, much less the triumph of secularism.

The most powerful forces that have contributed to the disenchantment of the world are temporal governments that have sought to limit the social disruption which often accompanies both possessions and exorcisms. They were driven by the same considerations as they had been in bringing witch-hunts to an end.[64] To secular governments manifestations of religious enthusiasm represented a threat to civil order, a concern that Hobbes had expressed in the middle of the seventeenth century.[65] Absolutist rulers like Peter the Great of Russia took the lead in debunking the traditional Christian interpretation of possession. David Lederer has argued that the practical impetus behind the end of religious madness was the pragmatic victory of political concerns over confessional strife.[66] In Bavaria the construction of the first asylum for the mentally ill in 1803 marked the turning point in this process. The state could also use its military and police forces to restore order when episodes of possession threatened public order, as the French government did at Morzine. In the final analysis the modern bureaucratic state has proved to be the most effective restraint on ecclesiastical authorities who allowed possessions and exorcisms to proceed. Those authorities might have wished to limit them at various times, but their efforts were undermined by their reluctance to discredit the entire phenomenon.

CHAPTER 10

Possession: Past and Present

Tₕₑ mass possessions at Morzine, Verzegnis, Plédran, and Jaca in the late nineteenth century were the last of their kind. These epidemics resembled much more the large contagious possessions of the seventeenth century than the smaller, individual possessions that had taken place throughout the history of Christianity. In the twentieth century individual possessions still took place, although in significantly reduced numbers. They continued to resemble the possessions that had taken place since early modern times. The only difference between the two most widely publicized cases in the early twentieth century is that they took place in locations where few if any possessions had ever been reported. In other respects the narratives of these possessions conformed closely to those of demoniacs in early modern Europe.

Possessions in the twentieth century

The narrative of the first of these—the possession of Clara Germana Cele, a sixteen-year-old orphan of mixed race at a mission school in Natal in South Africa in 1906–7—could have been written three centuries earlier. Her symptoms included understanding of 'Polish, German, French and all other languages', clairvoyance, speaking in a savage, animal voice never heard before, hurling nuns around the convent rooms, and levitating five feet in the air. During her exorcism by two Catholic priests, she knocked the Bible out of one priest's hands and tried to choke him with his stole. She was healed after being sprinkled with holy water on the second day of the exorcism. Clara's age and sex, her status as a member of a marginal and powerless segment of the population, and her Roman Catholicism made her more vulnerable to demonic possession than others in her community. The occasion of her possession, like that of Françoise Fontaine and Christoph Haizmann, was that she claimed to have made a pact with the Devil.[1]

The possession of Anna Ecklund and her exorcism in Earling, Iowa in 1928 shared only a few common features with that of Clara Germana Cele, but her experience nonetheless resembled closely those of many demoniacs in early modern Europe.[2] Anna's possession began in 1896, when she was fourteen years old. Its main symptoms were an aversion to sacred objects and an inability to enter a church. The proximate cause of her possession was sexual guilt or anxiety, which manifested itself as an obsession with sexual acts. Whether or not sexual abuse by her father, Jacob, was the source of this preoccupation cannot be determined, but in either case Anna's anxieties regarding her sexuality recall those of many nuns and pious laywomen in early modern France. Like many of those women, Anna reportedly led 'a religious, fervent and blameless life'.[3]

Anna's possession lasted for many years, and it was not until she was twenty-six that Father Theophilus Riesinger, a Capuchin monk from Wisconsin, exorcized her. Despite the apparent initial success of this dispossession, Anna was repossessed by many demons, including Lucifer, Beelzebub, Judas Iscariot, and the spirits of both her father and his mistress, whom she suspected of being the cause of her repossession. She was also possessed by countless silent devils. After an unexplained passage of another sixteen years, Father Riesinger performed another exorcism that lasted twenty-three days but was ultimately successful.

During the exorcism Anna manifested many of the traditional signs of possession, including preternatural strength, levitation, blasphemous speech, vomiting tobacco leaves, swelling of her lips and body, bulging eyes, speaking in unknown languages, and clairvoyance. All this was reminiscent of early modern possessions, with which Father Riesinger, a veteran exorcist, was familiar. Like many early modern exorcists, Riesinger also interpreted the possession as evidence that the Antichrist would be arriving shortly, directing his furious rage against the Church of God.[4]

When individual possessions like that of Anna Ecklund took place, they invariably became sources of controversy, as in the past. Claims that the demoniacs had faked their possessions and were experiencing some sort of dissociative disorder were proposed in such cases. The possessions also attracted publicity, just as in the early modern period, although knowledge of these modern cases became far more widespread in an age of mass communication. Despite this publicity, the total number of reported possessions in Christian communities remained very small during the first half of the twentieth century, and there was no talk of a new epidemic of possessions, such as had occurred in early modern times. Scholarly interest in the phenomenon of possession, mainly among anthropologists, focused almost entirely on African and Caribbean societies whose religious cultures were strikingly different from those of twentieth-century Christianity, even in societies where a measure of syncretism had taken place between Christian and non-Christian beliefs, as in the Haitian religion known as Voodoo.

Only in the 1960s and 1970s did the number of reported cases of demonic possession rise dramatically, and possession and exorcism once again became topics of widespread interest in the Christian West. The popularity of William Peter Blatty's novel, *The Exorcist,* and the even greater worldwide success of the movie based on it did a great deal to bring the subject to the attention of the literate and movie-going public. The publication in 1976 of *Hostage to the Devil,* a non-fictional account of five cases of possession and exorcism in modern America by Malachi Martin, a former Jesuit priest, made some of those who dismissed *The Exorcist* as fiction recognize the reality, if not of possession itself, at least of the exorcisms undertaken to cure troubled souls.

During the last decade of the twentieth century and the first decade of the twenty-first century interest in the subject reached new heights. A series of botched exorcisms, in most cases by amateur exorcists or family members, and even cruder and more violent efforts to drive demons from children who manifested signs of physical or emotional illness, contributed to this heightened awareness.[5] Many of these cases resulted in criminal charges, and their trials raised public awareness of possession to a level unprecedented in modern times. *The Exorcism of Emily Rose* (2005), a film based on the trial of two German parish priests in 1973 for killing a twenty-three-year-old woman, Anneliese Michel, after exorcizing her sixty-seven times, beginning when she was only sixteen, was especially instrumental in increasing public awareness of a disturbing criminal development.[6]

Even more instrumental in heightening public awareness of possession was the publication of a new exorcism ritual by the Roman Catholic Church in 1999. This was the first significant updating of the Catholic rite since its original publication in 1614; earlier editions had only made minor changes of wording.[7] The publication of the new ritual was not intended to encourage the performance of exorcisms. The Second Vatican Council (1962–5) had called for the updating of all the rituals of the Church, and the exorcism rite was in fact the last to be revised. Like the original of 1614 and its many editions over the course of nearly five centuries, the exorcism rite was intended to be used only after the exorcist could establish that the possession was not the result of natural causes. It was also intended to provide a standardized alternative to the many improvised exorcisms that were being performed, especially in Italy. The publication of the revised text, therefore, represented an effort to reduce rather than expand the number of exorcisms. It provided that an exorcism would not be authorized until the afflicted person had seen a medical doctor and until ecclesiastical authorities had decided whether medical or pastoral care would be more likely to effect a cure. As in the seventeenth century, the Church faced a challenge from unofficial lay exorcists who were taking advantage of troubled souls, whom they promised to cure for a fee. Today the Italian population still provides a ready supply of people who are susceptible to overtures by such unauthorized exorcists, many of whom are hucksters.

The Catholic Church's training of more exorcists has been represented as another effort to contain the number of exorcisms. In 2004 the Pontifical Regina Apostolorum, a university on the outskirts of Rome with close ties to the Vatican, began offering a four-month course, 'Exorcism and the Prayer of Liberation'. One purpose of the course was to teach priests 'how to discern between demonic possession and psychological problems'.[8] Hundreds of priests from around the world, including the American priest Gary Thomas, the main subject of Matt Baglio's book, *The Rite*, took the course and used the training it gave to begin careers as exorcists. Also in 2004, the Congregation for the Doctrine of the Faith, the official doctrinal arm of the Vatican, sent letters to bishops throughout the world, starting with the United States, asking them to appoint an official exorcist in each of their dioceses.[9] At the time there were only seventeen exorcists in the United States.[10]

In the United States this Vatican training programme has achieved mixed results. There has not been a significant increase in the number of official exorcists, but the bishop of Springfield, Illinois organized a conference of priests and bishops in November 2010 to help them meet what they claimed to be an increased demand for exorcism.[11] The bishop insisted, just like the promoters of exorcism in the Vatican, that their main purpose was to distinguish between authentic possessions and those that can be explained in natural terms.

The Vatican's exorcist training programme has achieved its most notable success outside Italy in the staunchly Catholic country of Poland, where the number of exorcists increased from thirty in 1999 to more than one hundred in 2010. At the same time that American exorcists convened in Springfield, the Polish National Congress of Exorcists met in Warsaw. As in the United States, the Polish exorcists claimed that in recognition of the advances of modern social science, they wanted to work with psychologists to distinguish between the truly possessed and those who had serious psychiatric problems. One of the exorcists in attendance, Father Andrzej Greftowicz, also said that the congress wanted to counter the Hollywood image of cross-wielding exorcists engaged in dramatic conflicts with the Devil. Taking a page out of the Protestant tradition, he said that most of the more mundane exorcisms in which he was involved required only common prayer.

It is unclear how receptive modern Catholic exorcists have been to the diagnoses of psychologists when demoniacs have presented themselves to be cured. Father Greftowicz, for example, considers individuals to be genuinely possessed when they are unable to enter a church or, if they do manage to make it through the door, feel faint or breathless or, more dramatically, scream, shout, or throw themselves to the ground. Father Gabriele Amorth, the exorcist of the diocese of Rome, disagrees with Greftowicz in that he thinks the performance of Linda Blair in *The Exorcist* a 'substantially exact' representation of an authentic possession. Father Amorth, who is also the honorary president of the International Association of Exorcists, has said that the patients whom he treats scream, utter blasphemies, spit, and vomit sharp objects. All this suggests that few Catholic exorcists today have been willing to refer many demoniacs to psychiatrists.

Catholic authorities claim that the increase in the number of exorcisms has resulted from heightened demand from people who believe, or who have been told, that they are possessed. That may be true, but the eagerness of exorcists to conduct these rituals, and in many cases their appetite for fame, may actually have created or at least swelled that demand. The question is analogous to the problem of whether the legal profession has expanded in response to the demands of a more litigious society or whether the lawyers have encouraged clients to bring lawsuits. There is probably an element of truth in both propositions. We have seen how exorcists, especially those with charismatic appeal, have encouraged people to believe they are possessed. Certainly the fame of Giovan Battista Chiesa and Johann Joseph Gassner led prospective clients to claim they were possessed so that they might be cured. In the eighteenth century Benito Feijoo claimed that only on rare occasions did 'there appear to be any possessed person in places where no one starts exorcizing'.[12] The careers of two twentieth-century Roman Catholic exorcists would seem to support this contention. The first is that of Father Amorth, who claims to have performed 70,000 exorcisms over the course of his long career.[13] Amorth may have been responding to a popular demand for exorcisms, but he himself helped to fuel that demand. The second was the Latin American exorcist Padre Fortea, a charismatic priest whose exorcism campaigns have attracted thousands of participants and whose career is the subject of a Norwegian documentary film.[14]

In any event, the efforts of the Roman Catholic Church to train a new corps of exorcists cannot provide a full explanation of the increase in the number of possessions in the past fifty years. For one thing, possessions began to increase in the 1960s, long before the Vatican published its new exorcism ritual and the pontifical university in Rome began training exorcists. What is more, many of the possessions in the 1960s and 1970s took place among Pentecostals, often known as charismatics, who were seeking more emotional religious experiences than mainstream Christian denominations offered.

Pentecostalism originated in the late nineteenth century, and by the late twentieth century it had become the third-largest force in Christendom, after Catholicism and Protestantism.[15] Pentecostals believe that at their baptism they receive the Holy Spirit, giving them the ability to speak in tongues, a ceremonial re-enactment of the original Pentecost when the Holy Spirit descended on the Apostles. Thus divine possession, in this case by the third person in the Blessed Trinity, lies at the core of the Pentecostal belief system. So too does the belief in demonic possession. Pentecostals believe that the modern world is infested with demons—not merely the metaphorical demons equated with evil but real supernatural beings with their own identities and missions, just like the demons of medieval and early modern Roman Catholicism.[16] The Pentecostal belief in demonic presence in the world is grounded in the apocalyptic belief that the world is in its Last Days, when the Book of Revelation foretold that the power of the Devil would be greater than in the past. As discussed in Chapter 3, the same type of apocalyptic expectation contributed to the large number of possessions at the time of Christ and again in the early modern period.[17]

This belief in the possibility of demonic possession explains the Pentecostal tradition of performing exorcisms.[18] In keeping with the Protestant tradition, laypeople perform these ceremonies. There are no prescribed scripts for these exorcisms, nor have any manuals been published. But the circulation of reports of other rituals for casting out demons has provided scripts that others have followed in their own sacred dramas of possession and exorcism. All Pentecostal exorcisms stress the importance of the faith of the participants, placing them in a long tradition of Protestant faith healing.

Two other features of Pentecostal exorcisms recall the possessions that took place in Protestant communities in the early modern period. The first is that the Pentecostals are in a certain sense heirs of the 'enthusiastic'

Protestant sects, especially Methodists in England and Pietists in Germany, who maintained a belief in possession and dispossession when the mainstream Protestant denominations, most notably Presbyterians, Anglicans, and Lutherans, had rejected them.[19] Felicitas Goodman has argued that charismatics represent a persistent strain in Christianity which, ever since its inception, has sought an experiential as opposed to an abstract, theological religion and which therefore makes trances or some form of ecstatic experience central to its ritual.[20] The difference between modern Pentecostals and eighteenth-century Methodists and Pietists is that the Pentecostals have not had to negotiate their position vis-à-vis mainstream ecclesiastical organizations. They have been able to develop their emotional religion without institutional restraints.

The second feature of Pentecostal possessions that is reminiscent of those that occurred in the sixteenth and seventeenth centuries is that they focus on the sins of the demoniac, in a manner similar to those in early modern Protestantism and especially Calvinism. Michael Cuneo's narrative of the possession and exorcism of a man in his mid-twenties who had joined a Pentecostal prayer group and was eventually exorcized by two lay ministers in Kansas City recalls the spiritual turmoil of Alexander Nyndge and Robert Brigges in late sixteenth-century England. The man, Paul, who had been sexually abused as a child, was plagued by sexual fantasies, which included violent sexual assaults both on women who were strangers and on young children. At the same time he was coping with his own sexual urges, which had resulted in compulsive masturbation as many as five times a day, self-sodomy, bestiality, and unsuccessful efforts at self-fellatio. When referral to psychologists and the healing prayers of his Pentecostal community failed to redeem this troubled soul, he agreed to exorcism as a last resort. After binding the spirits not to interfere with their prayers, and forbidding them to manifest themselves (a tactic radically different from that of early modern Catholicism), the two exorcists—a man and a woman—cited both Psalm 34: 17 and the passage from the Gospel of Luke regarding the power of 'treading upon' serpents and scorpions. Then the female exorcist, Ellen, began speaking in tongues and claimed that she identified the 'demons' of guilt and shame, rejection, and unforgiveness, sexual perversion, masturbation, and hatred of women' that inhabited this man. She asked Paul if he was prepared 'to renounce this sin and renew his commitment to Jesus Christ as Lord and Savior'. When Paul agreed, she led him in silent prayer and commanded the 'spirit of guilt' to leave him and send him to the Creator, who would decide what to do with him.[21] Despite the occasional lapses into the Roman Catholic tradition of exorcism, the possession and exorcism of Paul conformed to a tradition of

Protestant possession that emphasizes the power and pervasiveness of sin and the difficulty in freeing demoniacs from its grasp.

When the Pentecostal movement began, its highly emotional religious gatherings, suffused with apocalyptic expectation, appealed mainly to people on the margins of society, including the poor, blacks, and drug addicts. In the 1960s, however, the movement, sometimes referred to as neo-Pentecostalism, developed a much broader appeal to mostly white, middle-class Americans, especially those living in the heartland of the United States. It was among this new group of neo-Pentecostals, many of whom styled themselves charismatics, that exorcism became a frequently performed ritual. This power of driving out demons derived from the special gift or *charism* that Pentecostals claim to have acquired, together with the gifts of prophecy, wisdom, and speaking in tongues, from the transformative experience of baptism.[22] Somewhat paradoxically, the movement won most of its new recruits in the 1980s among Episcopalians and Catholics, the two denominations that had continued to authorize official possessions but had always tried to limit the type of impromptu exorcisms that these self-appointed lay exorcists were performing at prayer meetings in their living rooms.[23]

As the charismatic movement grew and eventually accounted for as many as 20 per cent of practising Christians in the United States, the performance of these ceremonies was reclassified as a *deliverance ministry*, a term that carefully avoided the term exorcism that had always been associated with Roman Catholicism. During the 1970s and 1980s deliverance ministries were established within the mainstream Protestant denominations, thereby distinguishing them at least in name from the overly exuberant forms of religious experience associated with independent charismatic prayer groups. By 1980 there were hundreds of such ministries in the United States.

Even more indicative of this trend in modern religion was the establishment of deliverance ministries in about a third of all parishes in the Church of England. Most exorcisms in England are undertaken under the auspices of Ellel Ministries, the largest healing and deliverance ministry in England, which was founded by the Rev. Graham Dow, the bishop of Willesden and author of *Those Tiresome Intruders* (1990). These dispossessions or deliverances, which have a presence in Anglican parishes, represent a direct challenge to the long-standing tradition of scepticism regarding demonic possession in Anglicanism that dates back to the efforts of Samuel Harsnett, John Deacon, and John Walker to debunk the exorcisms of both Jesuit missionaries and Puritan ministers like John Darrell.[24] That sceptical tradition still finds strong support among mainstream theologians in the Church of England, who are highly critical of these ministries on the grounds that they can be psychologically and spiritually harmful to the people who seek their help.

Comparisons with early modern possessions

In what ways does the surge in the number of possessions in the late twentieth and early twenty-first centuries resemble that which occurred in early modern Europe? It is of course impossible to measure the number of possessions or exorcisms with any degree of accuracy, either in real terms or as a percentage of the Christian population. Even if we had some figures, we would have to discount the exaggerations of contemporary commentators and the exorcists themselves. We can, however, venture some general comparisons between the two periods.

The most striking difference is that in the modern period the belief in and fear of the Devil, while possibly increasing within certain religious cultures, has been confined to a smaller percentage of the population than in the early modern period. This was almost inevitable in light of the fact that secularism, defined generally as a subscription to non-religious values, has been far more pervasive in all European and Western societies—even in Italy and Poland—in the twentieth and twenty-first centuries than in the early modern period. This secular outlook has been especially evident in America, where approximately one fifth of the population in 2010 identified themselves as atheists, and where the notion of a Devil with power in the natural world has met with increasing ridicule, even within established religious congregations. Having been raised a Catholic in the 1950s and 1960s, I cannot recall any discussion of the Devil or of possession in my religious education by Sisters of Charity in grammar school and Jesuits in prep school and college. My own religious education therefore would support Andrew Delbanco's claim in 1996 that Satan was dead in contemporary America.[25]

Once we concede the point that ours is a more secular age than that of the sixteenth and seventeenth centuries and recognize that the increase in possessions and exorcisms occurred only in certain types of religious communities, it is instructive to compare the possessions that took place in early modern Europe with those that have occurred in both Catholic and Protestant communities in more recent years. The first and most obvious of these comparisons is that possessions in both periods have taken place in religious cultures that believe strongly in the interpenetration of the natural and the supernatural. The efflorescence of possession in both historical periods could not have taken place if people had not tried to engage in ecstatic and mystical experiences, whether nuns aspiring to sanctity or neo-Pentecostals believing in the infusion of special gifts at baptism. Demonic possession is just one manifestation of the belief of members of 'enthusiastic' religious denominations that the boundaries between the natural and supernatural realms can be crossed. Other ways of crossing those boundaries include mystical experiences, participation in religious revivals, and prophesying. In all these contexts enthusiastic Christians have displayed similar somatic symptoms of their religious anxieties or aspirations.

As in the early modern period, the lion's share of possessions in modern times has taken place in Roman Catholic communities. The main reasons for this have been the ready availability of the ritual of exorcism, the belief within Catholic communities that such exorcisms work, and the prominence of celebrity exorcists—those who have achieved great fame in predominantly Catholic countries, especially in Italy and Latin America. The epicentre of the late twentieth-century wave of possessions was Italy, where according to one source about 500,000 people still see an exorcist annually.[26] There are no estimates for Latin America, but there is ample evidence that exorcism flourishes in that region, especially in rural communities. To be sure, possession has become more common in Protestant cultures than in the past, especially among evangelicals. But Protestant exorcisms are administered locally, and consequently there is scant opportunity for a Protestant to become a travelling celebrity like Gabriele Amorth in Italy or Padre Fortea in Latin America. And although Protestant dispossessions have taken a page or two from the manuals of exorcists like Girolamo Menghi, they are still relatively simple rites that seek spiritual healing and the elimination of sin rather than the relief from physical pain which still characterizes most Catholic exorcisms.

The differences between Catholic and Protestant possessions in both periods provide evidence for the argument that possessions reflect the particular religious cultures in which they take place. As discussed in Chapter 6, Catholic, Lutheran, and Calvinist possessions all reflected different ideas regarding soteriology and sacramentalism. Jewish possessions, which like those in Christianity increased greatly in frequency during the same period, reflected the cabbalistic Jewish belief in the transmigration of the souls of the dead. In similar fashion, modern Protestant possessions reflect the beliefs of the charismatic and evangelical cultures in which most of them take place. In the case of Paul, who was exorcized by two Pentecostal ministers, the cause of the possession was the demoniac's sinfulness, and the ceremony was intended to rescue him from that state and save his soul. The exorcism of charismatics like Paul was relatively simple, consisting of a few short prayers. Most modern-day Catholic possessions, on the other hand, retain the features that set such ceremonies apart from those in the Protestant world four hundred years ago. Catholic demoniacs display far more physiopathological symptoms than their Protestant counterparts; they are far more likely to vomit alien objects; and they utter blasphemies and exhibit horror at sacred objects much more frequently. The exorcisms are far more complicated than those of the deliverance ministries, and they take much longer. In a proper exorcism the priest recites the ritual prescribed in the *Rituale Romanum*, invokes the name of the Virgin Mary and the saints, employs the traditional sacramentals, especially holy water and making the sign of the cross, and engages in conversations with the demon. These encounters often involve physical violence.

A comparison of an Italian exorcism witnessed by Father Gary Thomas and discussed in *The Rite* provides a striking contrast to the possession and exorcism of the charismatic demoniac Paul, discussed above. The Catholic demoniac, identified as Sister Janica, who had been born in Austria, displayed physical symptoms that were far more pathological than those manifested by the charismatic Paul. In this regard she also differed from the many self-proclaimed demoniacs who manifested few if any of the classic signs of possessions but who had sought out the exorcist, Father Carmine De Filippis, for a blessing or a brief exorcism.[27] Sister Janica screamed, shook her head violently, spoke in a deep rasping guttural voice, banged her head against the wall, and physically attacked Father Carmine. Her limbs did not, like those of another client of Carmine, become completely rigid, nor did she vomit pins, as had one of the demoniacs whom a colleague of Father Carmine had exorcized,[28] but the physical symptoms were far more extreme than those displayed by charismatic demoniacs. In exorcizing this woman, who had been his client or patient for nine years, Father Carmine employed the rite in the *Rituale Romanum*, adjured the demon, tried to get him to identify himself, invoked the protection of St Michael the Archangel, and appealed to God to hear the prayers of *all* the saints who had conquered the Evil One. In keeping with the Catholic tradition that demoniacs were not responsible for their actions during the possession, he claimed that the Devil had prevented her from confessing her sins.

Another example of the cultural specificity of modern possessions in America comes from an account of possession performances in a Haitian community in Brooklyn, New York, in the 1980s. The religious culture in which these possessions took place was that of Voodoo, the traditional religion of Haitians that represents a synthesis of Christianity and West African religion. The singular and supreme god in Haitian Voodoo is Bondye, who resembles both the Christian deity and the high gods of West Africa. Much more involved in people's lives are the spirits, who represent a fusion of Christian angels and the spirits in West African traditional religion. Much of Voodoo religion is based on the relationship between individuals and their spirits, who select them, provide them with protection, and help them direct their lives. They often perform these services in possessions, during which they explore all the potential constructive and destructive choices that the possessed person can make in a particular situation.[29] The role of the priest and priestess is to preside over these possessions and, in cases where the spirits possess children, drive them away.[30] Alourdes, a Voodoo priestess who emigrated from Haiti to the United States, describes her fear when she was first possessed at the age of thirteen, but she no longer fears the trance experiences that took place when her spirits took possession of her body.[31]

Scepticism

One common feature of early modern and modern possessions is that they have invariably generated scepticism regarding the authenticity of possessions, not only in religions different from their own but also within their own denominations. We have seen that such scepticism prevailed in both Catholicism and Protestantism in the early modern period, although it never became so absolute that authorities in either confession denied the possibility of demonic possession. In the late twentieth century such scepticism also found committed proponents, especially among theologians who criticized the work of the healing ministries. Nowadays even some Pentecostals and charismatics have abandoned their healing ministries, reserving their most severe criticism for the practice of exorcism within their own communities. They also insist that if authentic possessions do occur, they are very rare. None of this should surprise us. The belief in demonic possession has been contested throughout the history of Christianity, and it has never acquired the status of doctrine. Denying it has never led to the labelling of a sceptic as a heretic or resulted in his or her excommunication.

Media

In both periods the media have played important roles in raising the consciousness of the Devil, offering empirical evidence that such possessions actually took place, and providing scripts for demoniacs to follow. In early modern Europe the printing press and sermons that recounted such episodes or used them as moral *exempla* served as the main means by which such knowledge was disseminated to a broader audience. We have seen how crucial the publication of possession narratives was in this regard, and the publication of sermons as well as theological treatises, while appealing to a smaller audience, supplemented the graphic accounts of the torments of the possessed. It is reasonable to argue that without the invention of printing the dramatic increase in the number of possessions in the sixteenth century would not have taken place and that the scale of the phenomenon would have remained as it had been in the fifteenth century. The same argument has been made regarding the intensification of prosecutions for witchcraft during the same period, and the two developments were closely related.

In the modern period the new media of television and film, as well as the popular press and the proliferation of mass-market paperbacks, have played a role analogous to that of the printing press four centuries earlier in making audiences aware of a phenomenon that had remained relatively obscure in the nineteenth and early twentieth centuries. The media have promoted belief in the Devil and his powers and also provided scripts for the new crop of demoniacs to imitate. The emergence of the internet in the 1990s, with its demonstrated capacity of reaching a theoretically inexhaustible and insatiable market efficiently and cheaply, made it possible for information on possession and the demonic world to reach an even broader audience than television, film, newspapers, and paperbacks had in the previous three decades.

It would certainly be going too far, however, to claim, as has Michael Cuneo in his valuable study of American exorcism, that the entertainment industry bears primary responsibility for the startling increase in the number of possessions in the late twentieth and early twenty-first centuries.[32] There is no discounting the role played by *The Exorcist, Hostage to the Devil*, and television shows on the subject of possession and exorcism in promoting belief in, and perhaps even fear of, the Devil in modern religious culture. It is more questionable whether media representation of the subject actually led to the apparent increase in the number of late twentieth-century possessions. Then and now, possessions have been rooted in the spiritual anxieties of Christians, their apocalyptic beliefs and expectations, their belief in the pervasiveness of sin in the world, and their need to heal. People do not need the entertainment industry to suggest that either they or others are possessed by the Devil. Their religious education and their conversations with ministers and other members of their congregations have already made that option known to them. The possibility of demonic possession, with all its fears and hazards, is deeply rooted in the belief systems of these communities, whether Protestant, Catholic, or Pentecostal.

Cuneo also argues that the entertainment industry is responsible for promoting the belief in the occult, and specifically modern Satanism. That may be true, but it is difficult to show how the representation of Satanism in television and film has led to an increase in possessions and exorcisms. Publicity regarding Satanic ritual abuse and black masses may have given the impression to conservative Christians that the Devil is active in the world during the Last Days, but the attention given to Satanic worship, which in any case was a passing phenomenon in the 1980s, has nothing to do with the experience of possession. The link between possession and witchcraft was broken in the eighteenth century, and there has been no effort to reconnect these two forms of diabolical activity in the recent past. What is more, only a small portion of current witches define themselves as Satanists, while criminal investigations of charges of Satanic ritual abuse, such as the highly publicized prosecution of the owner and six staff members of the McMartin Pre-School in Manhattan Beach, California in the 1980s, have yielded no reliable evidence that such rituals ever took place.[33]

The only possible connection between modern Satanism and demonic possession is that some modern demoniacs may have participated in such practices, as a result of which they may have developed feelings of sinfulness and self-loathing. For example, Father Carmine claimed that Sister Janica's father had performed Satanic rituals on her when she was a child and that this experience led to her possession.[34] In similar fashion, the Italian exorcist Father Francesco Bamonte claimed that the possession of a woman named Anna, whom he had exorcized in 2006, was caused by a Satanic ritual performed by members of her family in which the participants sacrificed an infant to a demon. Not surprisingly, Father Bamonte was never able to verify this account.[35] Even if the ritual had taken place, exposure to or participation in Satanic rituals was not sufficiently widespread in the 1980s and 1990s to account for the dramatic surge in the number of possessions throughout the Western world.

One final comparison between the early modern and modern periods of demonic possession is that in both periods demoniacs, whether deliberately or not, participated in a form of sacred theatre. Like early modern Catholics and Protestants, latter-day demoniacs have followed scripts encoded in their particular religious cultures. They have also assumed roles that were assigned to them by their religious communities. Just like the possession of French nuns, German Lutherans, and English Puritans in the sixteenth and seventeenth centuries, modern possessions and exorcisms are religious psychodramas, in which the response of the audience has been just as important as the relief of the demoniac from his or her afflictions.

CHAPTER II

Conclusion

ALTHOUGH WE SHALL NEVER know how many European men and women were possessed during the early modern period, by the end of the sixteenth century possession had reached very large and possibly unprecedented proportions. Possessions became so frequent in these years that William Monter called the seventeenth century 'the golden age of the demoniac'.[1] Even if we exclude the possessions that occurred in the context of large healing campaigns, on the grounds that those demoniacs did not display many of the classic signs of their affliction, we know that the number of demoniacs reached into the thousands. Further evidence that this period witnessed an exceptionally large number of possessions comes from Catholic demonologists who commented on their frequent occurrence and Catholic priests who proudly noted how many exorcisms they had performed. Even some Protestants admitted that possessions increased in the seventeenth century. In 1605 Heinrich Riess argued disapprovingly that the multiplying of exorcisms was a sign of the Last Days, and at the end of the century Cotton Mather made the same argument.[2]

Was the early modern explosion of possessions in Europe and its colonies unique in the history of Christianity? Was this period the only golden age of the demoniac? There are two possible competitors for this distinction: the period of Christian antiquity and the late twentieth and early twenty-first centuries. The prevalence of exorcists in Palestine at the time of Christ, the possible historical identity of Christ as an exorcist, and the reliance on exorcism as the primary method of conversion to the new religion all point to the first four centuries of Christianity as a time when possession was a widespread phenomenon.[3] Writing around 150 CE, Justin Martyr claimed that there were large numbers of demoniacs among both Christians and non-Christians throughout the Roman Empire.[4] Widespread apocalyptic thought in anticipation of the arrival of the Messiah in Palestine provided fertile ground for possessions and exorcisms during the life of Christ, while apocalyptic enthusiasm in the early years of Christianity helps to explain why they continued to occur in large numbers during that period. The belief of early Christians that 'the devil, prowls around like a roaring lion, seeking someone to devour' (1 Peter 5: 8–9) and that his 'furious rage' would signal the arrival of the Antichrist created a fear of the demonic that had no parallel until the early modern period.

In the absence of reliable statistical evidence, it is impossible to determine whether possessions were as common during Christian antiquity as in the early modern period. The real number of demoniacs was probably not as high, but as a proportion of the Christian population, which was fairly small during the first two centuries after the death of Christ, the number may have equalled or surpassed that of the early modern period. In 1600, at the height of the early modern epidemic, there were almost eighty million Christians in Europe, whereas the entire population of the Roman Empire around 250 CE was probably little more than half that, and the number of Christians living within its borders was even smaller. The main reason for arguing that possessions were more frequent in the early modern period is that only during those years did possessions spread rapidly, appearing almost as if they were contagious, within in small communities. There is no evidence of large group possessions in Christian antiquity, and hence they have never given the impression of being an epidemic.

The second period in the history of Christianity that has witnessed a surge in the number of possessions is that of the late twentieth and early twenty-first centuries. The attention that modern media have given to possession has given it wider exposure than it had during the early modern period, and the reports of thousands of exorcisms by priests in Italy and Latin America suggest that possession has once again become a prominent feature of modern Christian culture. Whether it has become as prominent or as widespread as it was in the early modern period is difficult to determine. The confinement of the modern phenomenon to certain types of Christian communities makes it unlikely that the number of possessions and exorcisms can match the number of such incidents in early modern Europe, especially if we take the relative size of the Christian populations during the two periods into account. There are more than one billion Christians in the world today, and a large number of them are either sceptical regarding the reality of possession or have no direct knowledge of instances of it in their parishes.

Even in the Christian communities where possessions have occurred, very few demoniacs have manifested the classic symptoms associated with the phenomenon. Few of the possessed have fallen into convulsions, demonstrated preternatural strength, vomited alien objects, lost their sight and hearing, uttered blasphemies, or recoiled in the presence of holy objects. In this respect the symptoms of most late twentieth-century demoniacs are different from those of Clara Germana Cele and Anna Ecklund in the early twentieth century. Even clergy who have expressed concern about the recently increased demand for exorcisms admit that genuine possessions are rare. In 1974 the French priest and exorcist Henri Gesland claimed that only four of some three thousand individuals who had come to him to be exorcized were possessed by demons.[5] Even in countries where Christian exorcisms are relatively common, such as Italy, instances in which the demoniacs have exhibited such classic signs of possession are rare.[6] In writing about the recent training of exorcists in the Catholic Church, Matt Baglio admits that the number of possessions among Catholics can still be counted in double digits. The Devil may not be dead, as Andrew Delbanco argued in 1996, but in most Christian communities the belief that Satan can actually invade human bodies and control their physiological and mental functions is on life-support.[7]

Causes of the early modern wave of possessions

How do we explain the distinct and perhaps unprecedented rise in the number of demonic possessions during the early modern period? In the most general terms, the flood of possessions was the product of efforts by both Catholics and Protestants to bring about religious reform between 1400 and 1700. The intensification of these efforts in the late sixteenth century resulted in a corresponding increase in the number of possessions, giving birth to the so-called 'golden age of the demoniac'. Confessional conflict between Catholics and Protestants during these years inspired the use of exorcism as a tool of Catholic propaganda, thereby placing a premium on detecting, curing, and publicizing instances of demonic possession.

Demonism

One of the changes that occurred within Catholicism and Protestantism during this broadly defined age of reform was the demonization of European culture. This process, which traced its origin to the Black Death in the late fourteenth century, included the development of demonology among the educated and a growing awareness of demonic presence in the world by all segments of society. The Devil was never accorded the power that Cathars and other dualist heretics attributed to him in the Middle

Ages; Protestants as well as Catholics consistently proclaimed the sovereignty of God. But the prevalence of nominalist theological thought in the fifteenth century, which accorded the Devil more freedom than did scholastics writing in the Thomistic tradition, and the revival of the belief that God had allowed the Devil to cause harm and chaos in the days before the Second Coming, made Satan and his subordinate demons a much more frightening presence in people's lives than in the past.

The intense fear of demonic power in the world affected the experiences of demoniacs as well as those who attributed their acute physiological symptoms to the Devil. Many Catholic and Protestant possessions originated in the efforts of demoniacs to resist demonic temptation. Some individuals became possessed because they believed they had made a pact with the Devil, a view that belief in witchcraft encouraged. For the families, pastors, and neighbours of the afflicted the awareness of the Devil's presence and power in the world offered an explanation of the demoniacs' symptoms, especially when they could not, even with the help of a physician, identify a likely natural cause of the person's pathological behaviour.

Witchcraft

The close chronological correspondence between the rise of witch-hunting and the increase in the number of demonic possessions suggests that the two developments were closely related. Possession had a longer history than witchcraft, and possessions continued long after the last witches had been executed, but witchcraft prosecutions and the incidence of possessions reached a peak at the same time—in the years between 1580 and 1630. The connection was by no means hard and fast. Many but not all demoniacs claimed that witches had caused their possession, while many but not all witchcraft prosecutions included the afflictions of the demoniacs in their enumeration of the witches' *maleficia*. Witchcraft and possession were also linked by a common demonology: both were predicated on the assumption that the Devil could, with God's permission, actively intervene in the operation of the natural world and human affairs. This explains why most demonological literature in the early modern period dealt with both witchcraft and possession.

Female and lay piety

The promotion of piety among women, both within and outside the convent, inspired many of the possessions of the early modern period. This undertaking began in the thirteenth century, achieved broader success in the fifteenth century, and became central to both Catholic and Protestant programmes of reform in the sixteenth and seventeenth centuries. It led directly to the efforts of women, mainly nuns but also laywomen in the towns, to aspire to sanctity and, as part of their spiritual regimen, to achieve mystical union with the divine. The similarities between the symptoms of divine possession that these women cultivated and those attributed to the Devil, coupled with the misogynistic assumption that women were more likely than men to have commerce with demons, aroused suspicion among clerical authorities that divine possession was of demonic origin. This reclassification of divine possessions as demonic became almost routine by the early seventeenth century.

The promotion of piety among the female and lay population led more directly to an increase in the number of demonic possessions when both Catholics and Protestants encountered difficulties or even a sense of failure in their efforts to achieve sanctity. The profound religious anxiety that accompanied their guilt or despair often expressed itself somatically in convulsions, contortions, and vomiting. The reaction against the rigours of their spiritual regimen, especially in Catholicism, also found expression in their aversion to sacred objects.

The printing revolution

Printing played a crucial role in allowing the number of possessions to reach unprecedented proportions. The dissemination of demonological texts, sermons, possession narratives, bibles, reports of witchcraft prosecutions, and the printed versions of plays featuring demoniacs provided scripts for demoniacs to follow, precedents for those who diagnosed the symptoms of the possessed as demonic in origin, apocalyptical predictions to make the Devil's fury seem plausible, and rituals for exorcists to use in their efforts to publicize the possession.

Contemporaries were aware of the role of print in swelling the number of possessions. English ecclesiastical authorities took steps to prevent the circulation of possession narratives and took action against unlicensed printers who published accounts of fraudulent demoniacs.[8] In order to prevent isolated cases of possession at Avignon from developing into an epidemic in the wake of the possessions at Loudun, Cardinal Mazarin, Richelieu's successor as chief minister, ordered that the demoniacs should receive no publicity.[9] A century later the Spanish inquisitor Benito Feijoo, who was troubled by the surge in the number of possessions in his country in the early eighteenth century, wrote that if it were not for the publicity that surrounded exorcisms, the number of demoniacs would have been much lower.[10] His observation echoed the assessment by the sceptical Spanish inquisitor Alonso Salazar de Frias in the early seventeenth century that large witch-hunts, such as that in the Basque country between 1609 and 1614, did not occur until people started writing about them.[11]

Catholic and Protestant possessions

Although we can never obtain an accurate count of the number of possessions in early modern Europe, there is little doubt that a large majority of cases occurred in Catholic territories. Even if we take into account the relative size of the Catholic and Protestant populations, roughly 75 and 25 per cent respectively at the beginning of the seventeenth century, Catholic demoniacs outnumbered their Protestant counterparts by significant margins. One reason for this was that most group possessions took place in Catholic communities, especially in French, Spanish, and Italian convents. The large group possessions in the Italian region surrounding Belmonte in Italy in 1595, the rural village of Mattaincourt in 1627–33, and the German town of Paderborn in 1656 all took place in Catholic territories. There were, to be sure, a number of group possessions in Lutheran Germany, especially in Saxony and Brandenburg, but there were only three group possessions in Protestant England, the largest being of the five children and seven maidservants in the Throckmorton household between 1589 and 1593.

The contrast between Protestant and Catholics demonic possessions becomes even sharper if we compare the number of demoniacs in Calvinist, that is, Reformed, communities and those that took place in Catholic areas. The number of Lutheran possessions certainly needs to be taken into account in the broader comparison of Protestant and Catholic demoniacs, especially since there were significant numbers of possessions in German Lutheran territories and in Denmark. But the Lutheran position regarding exorcism, as on many other liturgical and ecclesiastical practices, fell between the Catholic and Reformed positions. The exorcism of a pious Lutheran girl from Platten in 1559 who manifested many of the classic signs of possession, including the expression of blasphemies, reflected Lutheran accommodation of Catholic practice. Although the demon was driven out by the congregational prayers and singing of some one thousand people, in accordance with prescribed Protestant practice, the pastors who managed the exorcism violated one of the rules of Protestant dispossession by conversing with the Devil. In these conversations the Devil, who reportedly flew out the window like a swarm of flies, claimed, in keeping with Catholic belief, that he had come to possess the girl's body but not her soul.[12]

Nor did Lutheran demonologists exhibit the same degree of scepticism regarding the authenticity of demonic possessions as did a number of Calvinist demonologists, from Reginald Scot to Balthasar Bekker. The Lutheran physician Johann Weyer has won recognition as an early sceptic regarding the reality of witchcraft, but he did not deny the authenticity of cases of demonic possession in which the Devil acted alone without the assistance of a witch. Lutherans were quick to suspect that Catholic exorcisms were fraudulent, but they were far more cautious in dismissing cases that came under their purview. Even in their treatment of the Catholic demoniac Anna Mayer at Stuttgart in 1695, at a time when scepticism regarding demonic possession was growing throughout Europe, the Lutheran ministers who examined her would not dismiss the possibility that her possession had supernatural causes.[13] Systematic Lutheran scepticism began only with Johan Salomo Semler in the second half of the eighteenth century, and Semler relied greatly on earlier Dutch and English scholarship on the subject. What is more, Lutherans did not subscribe to the Calvinist doctrine of the cessation of miracles, and they disagreed with Calvinists on the use of exorcism in baptism.[14] When the Catholic clergy tried to determine whether Clara Germana Cele was possessed in 1906, they consulted Johann Hartmann's *Lutheran Pastoral Handbook*, published in 1678, since its recommendations regarding exorcism differed little from those of the Vatican's *Rituale Romanorum* of 1614.[15] In 2009 the Lutheran Church of South Australia denied that it permitted exorcisms after three men tried forcibly to exorcize a teenage boy at a Lutheran church camp. This disclaimer, coupled with the excommunication of charismatic members of the Lutheran Church in Victoria, Australia, for 'going too far' in their beliefs about exorcism not long before they accidentally killed a woman during an exorcism in 1994, exposed the historical ambivalence of the Lutheran Church on this issue.[16]

Compared to the thousands of Catholic possessions and the more modest number in Lutheran communities, the number of Calvinist demoniacs was exiguous. In Scotland, which boasted the most fully Reformed church in early modern Europe, no more than eleven possessions were recorded in contemporary sources, and almost all of these took place between 1696 and 1705. In the small Calvinist principality of Montbéliard in the Holy Roman Empire, the historian Alexander Tuetey could find only one demoniac, who he claimed was 'really' suffering from hysteria.[17] In the Dutch Republic the names of fewer than twenty-five demoniacs have found places in the historical record. One reason that Balthasar

Bekker devoted more effort to discrediting witchcraft than demonic possession (he denied the reality of both for similar reasons) was that he had so few examples of the latter at hand.

The only state where there were significant numbers of Calvinist demoniacs in proportion to the population was the tiny Republic of Geneva, where more than twenty-five demoniacs accused witches of causing their possessions in the early seventeenth century.[18] In England, with a population of about four million people in 1600, it is possible to identify only twenty-five demoniacs that lived in Puritan or Dissenting communities, where Calvinism, considered as a lived religion, flourished. This number of Calvinist demoniacs pales in comparison with the five hundred or more Catholic demoniacs that Jesuit missionary priests claimed to have exorcized in Essex in 1585–6 or the sixty they dispossessed in Lancashire in 1626.[19] These demoniacs belonged to a Catholic population that had shrunk to about 2 per cent of the entire English population by the turn of the seventeenth century.

In Puritan New England the number of demoniacs remains a subject of academic disagreement, since some contemporaries and modern scholars have considered the accusers of witches during the Salem witchcraft trials as demoniacs.[20] But these afflicted individuals gave no indication that the Devil inhabited their bodies or spoke through them. They went into fits not because the Devil controlled their movements but because they reacted to seeing the spectres of the witches they claimed were responsible for their afflictions. Whether or not these spectres were considered to be demons or the product of demonic illusion—an issue that contemporaries debated—is beside the point. In neither case did the Devil possess the girls or even control their imagination, as he allegedly did in many other possessions. If we decertify these Salem possessions, we are left with a very small number of seven New England demoniacs in the late seventeenth century, and, as in Scotland, their possessions occurred long after the peak period of European demonic possessions had passed. The similarity between the pattern of possessions in New England and Scotland was due not only to a shared Calvinist culture but also to a brisk transatlantic book trade that allowed them to read each other's accounts of demonic possession shortly after they took place.

How then do we explain the vast discrepancy between the number of Catholic possessions on the one hand and those of Reformed Protestants on the other? The answer lies not so much in differences between the intensity of the religious experiences of these zealous Christians; both confessions were capable of fostering the deep religious anxiety that triggered the initial, somatic symptoms of possession. Rather it lies in the way that the clergy interpreted those symptoms. Catholic priests—even those of a sceptical bent—were much more willing than Calvinist ministers to identify the Devil as the cause of the demoniacs' afflictions and call in exorcists to cast out the invasive demons.

Protestant scepticism

One reason for the reluctance of Calvinist clergy to diagnose people in their communities as possessed was the scepticism of Protestant theologians, ministers, and physicians regarding the authenticity of many possessions. Most Calvinist theologians believed that possession was possible but did not think it occurred very frequently. In 1599 the Catholic polemicist and scholar Pierre de Bérulle argued, contrary to Calvinist demonologists, that demonic possessions had actually increased rather than decreased since biblical times. So too had authentic exorcisms, which Calvinists claimed had ceased at the end of the Apostolic Age.[21] This conviction that possessions took place infrequently predisposed Calvinists to consider most Catholic possessions fraudulent.

One illustration of Calvinist scepticism comes from Geneva, where in 1610 the consistory examined a cluster of proclaimed demoniacs to determine whether they were possessed.[22] Another comes from Scotland, where in 1628 the Privy Council refused to take seriously the belief that a poor illiterate woman from Duns in Berwickshire who had reportedly conversed with a minister in Latin was actually possessed.[23] In a public dispute in the Dutch city of Utrecht over the reality of the possession of two women in 1603, three ministers took the negative side, claiming that the possessions were fraudulent. The magistrates who presided over the debate did not declare outright fraud, but they commanded the husbands of the two women to keep them indoors and threatened to put the women in a madhouse if they were to appear once again on the streets.[24]

Catholics rarely exercised this type of scepticism. To be sure, the Vatican insisted in 1614 that natural causes be ruled out before bishops authorized exorcisms, and Catholic authorities were known occasionally to apply the prescribed tests, especially that of language and preternatural strength, to determine whether the possessions were authentic. But with a variety of exorcism rites in print, and with an army of unofficial exorcists looking for business, the exorcism of Catholic demoniacs became routine in the late sixteenth and early seventeenth centuries. Only towards the end of this period did some members of the Catholic ecclesiastical hierarchy make serious efforts to restrict the number of exorcisms. But these efforts did not prevent exorcists like Giovan Battista Chiesa and Johann Joseph Gassner from conducting healing campaigns that used exorcism as their main therapeutic instrument. Consequently exorcism was available to those who were diagnosed as demoniacs in the eighteenth century, and the availability of exorcism in turn encouraged diagnoses of possession by demons.

The continued availability of Catholic exorcisms, and their apparent success in casting out demons, led many Catholics suffering from various pathological disorders to seek the services of exorcists. This demand continued into modern times. In the 1850s the young female demoniacs in Morzine actually demanded that they be exorcized, and when they were refused, their symptoms became more acute. Plans to increase the number of Catholic exorcists in the first decade of the twenty-first century have been made in large part to meet the increased demand for their services.[25] Exorcists themselves have contributed to that demand by cultivating their own reputations, much in the way Girolamo Menghi and his colleagues did in sixteenth-century Italy. Like Menghi and Chiesa, modern-day Catholic exorcists have become celebrities, and their reputations have served to expand their healing ministries.

There was no comparable demand for exorcism in early modern Calvinist communities. Neither the demoniacs themselves nor their families actively sought dispossession. Nor did Calvinist ministers create a demand for their services as exorcists. There were few Calvinist counterparts to Menghi and Valerio Polidori. One possible exception was the scandal-plagued Dutch minister Johannes Mauritius Bergerus, whose use of Catholic methods of dispossession was a source of embarrassment to Protestants in Utrecht.[26] Another was the English minister John Darrell, who achieved a measure of fame for his exorcisms but whose career was shorter than that of Bergerus. But even these Calvinist ministers were unable to build popular demand for their services. The main reason for this was that the role of the Protestant exorcist was essentially that of community prayer leader. He was never considered responsible for the demoniac's dispossession. Deliverance was believed to be completely in the hands of God, whose will was inscrutable.

Calvinists were reluctant to identify people as demoniacs because the identity carried a great deal of spiritual baggage. As we have seen, Calvinist demoniacs, while technically not responsible for their actions, were nonetheless regarded as sinners and potential witches. While the demoniacs themselves might have admitted to their sinful condition as part of a conversion experience, their families, friends, and pastors were much more reluctant to reach this conclusion. Such a spiritual diagnosis would have raised the possibility that their kin were not predestined to salvation, which in turn might have raised concerns about their own faith and piety.

Calvinists therefore usually came to the conclusion that a person in their family or community was possessed by the Devil only as a last resort. Once they had reached that painful conclusion, they joined the local minister in praying to God for the deliverance of the possessed while trying to discern God's holy purpose behind the possession. This response contrasted dramatically with the eagerness of Catholic priests and relatives of the possessed to seek the assistance of an exorcist as soon as possible, knowing that this strategy had the greatest chance of relieving morally innocent demoniacs from their afflictions.

At the root of these different attitudes were different views regarding the attainment of sanctity. The Catholic belief that the will remained free to receive or reject God's grace and that one could play an active role in the quest for salvation provided the foundation for the belief that one could cultivate a mystical union with the divine. When mystics reached this ecstatic state, they sometimes displayed the pathological signs of divine or good possessions. Catholic ecclesiastical authorities developed techniques for distinguishing these good possessions from those that were demonic in origin. But both types of possession were predicated on the same belief that the boundary between the supernatural and natural realms, between body and spirit, could be crossed, at the initiative of either a human being or a demonic spirit.

Protestants, and especially Calvinists, had a very different view regarding the attainment of sanctity. For them human beings had no control over their predestined salvation. They were able only to provide the preconditions for the reception of God's freely granted grace. To become a Calvinist saint meant that one recognized one's predetermined justification, usually by means of a conversion experience, not that one had achieved mystical union with the divine. This was even true of Thomas Darling, whose aspiration to sainthood led to the suspicion that he was demonically possessed, and for a youth like Christian Shaw, whose demonic possession apparently originated in her conversion experience. There were very few good or positive possessions in early modern Calvinism, and when they did take place they usually involved angelic visions, not the ecstatic raptures that Catholic mystics cultivated. Calvinist ministers and theologians did not engage in the art of discerning between divine and demonic possessions. When possessions occurred—and they took place infrequently in Calvinist communities—they were always interpreted as demonic, and the only way to relieve them was to pray to God to liberate the demoniacs by helping them overcome temptation. The boundary between the supernatural and natural realms could be crossed in early modern Calvinism, but not very frequently and only when God decided it should happen.

The contrast between the frequency of possessions among Catholics and Protestants of all denominations became more marked in the eighteenth and nineteenth centuries, as Protestant authorities reacted strongly against the religious enthusiasm that members of their denominations manifested. The discouragement of emotional forms of religious experience was most evident in the growing influence of latitudinarianism within the Church of England, a movement that emphasized the role of reason, natural theology, and toleration. But the same trend can be seen in the English Nonconformist sects, the Dutch Reformed Church, and in Lutheranism.[27] This change in the outlook of mainstream Protestant churches helps to explain why Protestant possessions in the eighteenth and nineteenth centuries almost always occurred among groups that rejected the formalism of the religious establishment and encouraged a more experiential form of Protestantism. There were relatively few Protestant possessions in these centuries, and the majority occurred among English Methodists, German Pietists, and the members of various evangelical sects. In the twentieth century most non-Catholic possessions took place in charismatic congregations and evangelical healing ministries. Charismatics are the only Christians besides Catholics who have continued to practise exorcism in significant numbers. Like Catholics, they have refused to accept the Calvinist doctrine, developed in the early modern period, that miracles have ceased.

Notes

Chapter 1. Making Sense of Demonic Possession

1. Hartmann Schedel, *Liber chronicarum* (Nuremberg, 1493), fol. 1080; Cornelius Gemma, *De naturae divinis characterismis seu raris et admirandis spectaculis causis indiciis* (Antwerp, 1575), 174–5; *Dove Speculum Anni, or, an almanac for the year of our Lord God 1678* (London, 1678), sig. C1ᵛ; Nathanael St Andre, *A Short Narrative of an Extraordinary Delivery of Rabbets, Perform'd by Mr John Howard Surgeon at Guilford* (London, 1726).
2. Pierre Boaistuau, *Histoires prodigieuses et memorables, extraictes de plusieurs fameux autheurs, Grecs et Latins, sacrez et prophanes* (Paris, 1566); idem, *Certaine Secrete Wonders of Nature*, trans. Edward Fenton (London, 1569).
3. Simon Goulart, *Histoires admirables et memorables de notre temps* (Paris, 1600); idem, *Admirable Histories, Containing the Wonders of Our Time*, trans. Edward Grimelston (London, 1607), 161–82.
4. On changing attitudes towards such preternatural occurrences see Katharine Park and Lorraine J. Daston, 'Unnatural Conceptions: The Study of Monsters in Sixteenth- and Seventeenth-century France and England', *Past and Present* 92 (1981): 20–54.
5. For a comprehensive analysis of prodigies and wonders in late medieval and early modern Europe see Lorraine Daston and Katharine Parks, *Wonders and the Order of Nature, 1150–1750* (Cambridge, Mass., 1998).
6. Increase Mather, *An Essay for the Recording of Illustrious Providences*, in *Narratives of the Witchcraft Cases 1648–1706*, ed. George Lincoln Burr (New York, 1914), 17, argued that it was rare for preternatural occurrences not to be caused by the Devil.
7. Jean Bodin, *De la démonomanie des sorciers* (2nd edn, Paris, 1587), Bk. 2, ch. 3., fol. 76ᵛ.
8. Henri Boguet, *An Examen of Witches*, trans. E. Allen Ashwin (London, 1929), xxxiii.
9. William Monter, *A Bewitched Duchy: Lorraine and its Dukes, 1477–1736* (Geneva, 2007), 111–12; Robin Briggs, *The Witches of Lorraine* (Oxford, 2007), 83–4, 188, 372. An unspecified number of the afflicted were obsessed rather than possessed.
10. Rainer Decker, *Witchcraft and the Papacy: An Account drawing on the Formerly Secret Records of the Roman Inquisition*, trans. H.C. Erik Midelfort (Charlottesville, 2008), 158–64. It is unlikely that there were two thousand inhabitants of this village, as the inquisitor claimed. Either he deliberately inflated the number of victims, or the possessions spread to the surrounding area, as happened in many other group possessions.
11. Fernando Cervantes, 'The Devils of Querétaro: Scepticism and Credulity in Late Seventeenth-century Mexico', *Past and Present* 130 (1991): 55.

12. Robert Burton, *Anatomy of Melancholy*, ed. Thomas C. Faulkner, Nicolas K. Kiessling and Rhonda L. Blair, vol. 1 (Oxford, 1989), 194. Burton's source was the physician and astronomer Cornelius Gemma, *De naturae divinis characterismis*, Bk. 2, ch. 4.

13. Peter Brown, *The Cult of the Saints: Its Rise and Function in Latin Christianity* (Chicago, 1981), 106. Nicetius of Trier reported that the possessed 'floated in the air.' Ibid.,107.

14. Edward Nyndge, *A Booke Declaringe the Fearfull Vexasion of One Alexander Nyndge* (London, 1573); idem, *A True and Fearefull Vexation of One Alexander Nyndge* ...(1615).

15. Stuart Clark, *Thinking with Demons: The Idea of Witchcraft in Early Modern Europe* (Oxford, 1997), 392.

16. H.C. Erik Midelfort, 'The Devil and the German People: Reflections on the Popularity of Demon Possession in Sixteenth-century Germany', in *Religion and Culture in the Renaissance and Reformation*, ed. Steven Ozment. Sixteenth Century Essays and Studies 11 (1989): 118–19.

17. John Swan, *A True and Breife Report, of Mary Glovers vexation and of her deliverance by the meanes of fastinge and prayer* (London, 1603).

18. Tobias Seiler, *Daemonomania: Uberaus schreckliche historia von einem besessenen zwelffjährigen jungfräwlein zu Lewenberg in Schlesien in diesem 1605 jahr* (Wittenberg, 1605); H.C. Erik Midelfort, *A History of Madness in Sixteenth-century Germany* (Stanford, 1999), 57.

19. Clark, *Thinking with Demons*, 410.

20. On Kingesfielde, see Kathleen R. Sands, *Demon Possession in Elizabethan England* (Westport, Conn., 2004), ch. 3. The demonologist Nicolas Rémy argued that the appearance of the Devil was always accompanied by 'a loathsome stench', which was a demonstration of his filthiness. Nicolas Remy, *Demonolatry*, trans. E. A. Ashwin; ed. Montague Summers (London, 1930), ch. 10. On the 'extraordinary smells' in the place where the demoniac William Somers slept see Philip C. Almond, *Demonic Possession and Exorcism in Early Modern England: Contemporary Texts and their Cultural Contexts* (Cambridge, 2004), 263. In Augsburg a loathsome smell was emitted when the demon left a body. Lyndal Roper, *Oedipus and the Devil: Witchcraft, Sexuality and Religion in Early Modern Europe* (London, 1984), 176.

21. See the symptoms listed in Zacharia Visconti, *Complementum artis exorcisticae* (1600), in P.G. Maxwell Stuart, ed. and trans., *The Occult in Early Modern Europe: A Documentary History* (New York, 1999), 47–9; Almond, *Demonic Possession and Exorcism*, 34.

22. Nicolas Aubin *The Cheats and Illusions of Romish Priests and Exorcists, Discovered in the History of the Devils of Loudun* (London, 1703), 203.

23. Thomas Jolly, *The Surey Demoniack: or, An Account of Satan's Strange and Dreadful Actings in and about the Body of Richard Dugdale of Surey, near Whalley in Lancashire* (London, 1697), 3–8.

24. Johann Weyer, *Witches, Devils and Doctors in the Renaissance: Johann Weyer, De praestigiis daemonum*, ed. George Mora. (Medieval and Renaissance Texts and Studies, 73, Binghamton, NY, 1991), 304.

25. Guido Ruggiero, *Binding Passions: Tales of Magic, Marriage, and Power at the End of the Renaissance* (New York, 1993), 162.

26. National Archives of Scotland, JC 10/4, precognitions taken at Paisley, 19–21 April 1699.

27. The young English demoniac Margaret Muschamp was described as 'wringing her hands, weeping bitterly, as if she could have torn her flesh from the bones'. [Mary Moore], *Wonderfull News from the North, or, a True Relation of the Sad and Grievous Torments Inflicted on the Bodies of the Three Children of Mr George Muschamp* (London, 1650), 11–12. In nineteenth-century France demoniacs hurt themselves when demons allegedly mutilated them with axes. Ruth Harris, 'Possession on the Borders: The "Mal de Morzine" in Nineteenth-century France', *Journal of Modern History* 69 (1997): 466. In a sermon given in the 1690s Cotton Mather claimed that bewitched or possessed people often contemplated suicide, but reports of actual suicides by demoniacs were rare. Mather gave a sermon on one such occasion. Cotton Mather, 'A Discourse on the Power and the Malice of the Devils', in *Memorable Providences regarding Witchcrafts and Possessions* (Boston, 1697), 64.

28. Tobias Seiler, *Daemonomania* (Halle, 1679), 3.
29. Cervantes, 'The Devils of Querétaro', 54.
30. François Hédelin, abbé d'Aubignac, 'Relation de M. Hédelin, abbé d'Aubignac, touchant les possédées de Loudun au mois de Septembre 1637', in Robert Mandrou, ed., *Possession et sorcellerie au XVIIᵉ siècle* (Paris, 1979), 163. Hédelin observed that this feat was 'painful but not impossible'.
31. Sands, *Demon Possession*, 22–3. See Carol Karlsen, *The Devil in the Shape of a Woman. Witchcraft in Colonial New England*, (New York, 1987), 232–3; Anita M. Walker and Edmund H. Dickerman, '"A Woman under the Influence": A Case of Alleged Possession in Sixteenth-century France', *Sixteenth Century Journal* 22 (1991): 549.
32. Benoît Garnot, *Le Diable au couvent: les possedees d'Auxonne (1658–1663)* (Paris, 1995), 35.
33. Jeffrey R. Watt, *The Scourge of Demons: Possession, Lust and Witchcraft in a Seventeenth-century Italian Convent* (Rochester, NY, 2009), 117.
34. Roper, *Oedipus and the Devil*, 176.
35. Samuel Garnier, *Barbe Buvée, en religion Soeur Sainte-Colombe et la prétendue possession des Ursulines d'Auxonne (1658–1663)* (Paris, 1895), 66.
36. Cotton Mather, *Memorable Providences regarding Witchcrafts and Possessions* (Boston, 1697), 3.
37. *Procès verbal, fait pour délivrer une fille possédée par le malin esprit à Louviers*, ed. Armand Bénet; introduction by B. de Moray (Paris, 1883), 59. Anita Walker and Edmund H. Dickerman, 'The Haunted Girl: Possession, Witchcraft and Healing in Sixteenth-century Louviers', *Proceedings of the Annual Meeting of the Western Society for French History* 23 (1996): 211.
38. [Des Niau], *The History of the Devils of Loudun: The Alleged Possession of the Ursuline Nuns and the Trial and Execution of Urbain Grandier*, ed. and trans. Edmund Goldsmid. Collectanea Adamantea 21 (Edinburgh, 1887), vol. 1: 43.
39. *A True Narrative of the Sufferings and Relief of a Young Girle* (Edinburgh, 1698); reprinted in *A History of the Witches of Renfrewshire* (Paisley, 1877), 84.5; Robert Calef, *More Wonders of the Invisible World*, in *Narratives of the Witchcraft Cases*, 337–8.
40. The incident was recorded by François Hédelin, the abbé d'Aubignac, who had visited Loudun to confirm his own sceptical view and had invited the more credulous duchess, his patron, to see for herself. 'Relation de M. Hédelin', 165–6.
41. Sands, *Demonic Possession*, 82.
42. *A Breife Narration of the Possession, Dispossession, and, Repossession of William Sommers* (Amsterdam, 1598), sig. C2ᵛ.
43. George More, *A True Discourse concerning the certaine possession and dispossession of 7 Persons in One Familie in Lancashire* (Middelburg, 1600), 44, 54.
44. Cervantes, 'Devils of Querétaro', 54.
45. Roper, *Oedipus and the Devil*, 176.
46. National Archives of Scotland, JC 10/4, 19–21 April 1699, precognitions 1. 3. 39, 3, 56, 59, 66.
47. Armando Maggi, *Satan's Rhetoric: A Study of Renaissance Demonology* (Chicago, 2001), 108.
48. Almond, *Demonic Possession and Exorcism*, 251.
49. *Scottish Diaries and Memoirs*, vol. 2: *1746–1843*, ed. J. D. Fyfe (Stirling, 1927), 44.
50. Richard Bernard, *A Guide to Grand-Jury Men* (London, 1630), 16–17.
51. Denis Crouzet, 'A Woman and the Devil: Possession and Exorcism in Sixteenth-century France', in *Changing Identities in Early Modern France*, ed. Michael Wolfe (Durham, NC, 1997), 191–215. In 1689 the English demoniac Richard Dugdale alternated between fits of frenzy and paralysis. M.F. Snape, '"The Surey Impostor": Demonic Possession and Religious Conflict in Seventeenth-century Lancashire', *Transactions of the Lancashire and Cheshire Antiquarian Society* 90 (1994): 102
52. Caroline Walker Bynum, *Holy Feast and Holy Fast: The Religious Significance of Food to Medieval Women* (Berkeley, 1987), 138.

53. *The Hartford-shire Wonder, or Strange News from Ware* (London, 1669), title page, 5, 9.
54. Cotton Mather, 'A Brand Pluck'd out of the Burning,' in *Narratives of the Witchcraft Cases,* 265–6.
55. *Gründlicher Bericht und Anzaig einer Warhafften Histori welcher massen zu Schmidweyler . . . ein Meydlein siben Jar lang weder gessen noch getruncken . . . (*Augsburg, 1585).
56. The sixteenth-century nun Benedetta Carlini claimed that Jesus had ordered her to abstain from meat, eggs, and milk products and drink only water. Judith Brown, *Immodest Acts: The Life of a Lesbian Nun in Renaissance Italy* (New York, 1986), 64.
57. Bynum, *Holy Feast and Holy Fast,* 125.
58. Thomas Browne, *Religio medici* (London, 1642), 57; G. Woledge, 'An Allusion in Browne's *Religio Medici*', *Modern Language Review* 16 (1921): 65.
59. Rudolph M. Bell, *Holy Anorexia* (Chicago, 1985). John Putnam Demos, *Entertaining Satan: Witchcraft and the Culture of Early New England* (New York, 1982*)*, 164. On Protestant evangelical anorexia nervosa in America see Julius H. Rubin, *Religious Melancholy and Protestant Experience in America* (New York, 1994), ch. 3.
60. Erika Bourguignon, *Possession* (San Francisco, 1976), 3.
61. On the change in the nature of the symptoms at this time, which is probably related to the increased attention given to demoniacs, see Barbara Newman, 'Possessed by the Spirit: Devout Women, Demoniacs and the Apostolic Life in the Thirteenth Century', *Speculum* 73 (1998): 733.
62. See Thomas Sanchez, *In Praecepta Decalogi* (Lugduni, 1661), 312. See Bodin, *Démonomanie*, fol. 76^v and Menghi, cited in Watt, *Scourge of Demons*, 257, n. 75.
63. Michel de Certeau, *The Possession at Loudun*, trans. Michael B. Smith (Chicago, 1996). 41–3. For the belief that the Devil could speak perfect Latin, even while using the tongue of a beast, see Maria Tausiet, 'From Illusion to Disenchantment: Feijoo versus the "Falsely Possessed" in Eighteenth-century Spain', in *Beyond the Witch Trials*, ed. Owen Davies and Willem de Blécourt (Manchester, 2004), 49.
64. Richard Baxter, *The Certainty of the Worlds of Spirits and, consequently, of the immortality of souls of the malice and misery of the devils and the damned* (London, 1691), 85.
65. Paul Ladame, *Les Possédés et les démoniaques à Genève au XVIIe siècle* (Geneva, 1892), 28–9.
66. H.C. Lea, *Materials toward a History of Witchcraft*, ed. A. C. Howland. 3 vols. Philadelphia, 1939), 1041; Eberhard David Hauber, ed., *Bibliotheca sive acta et scripta magica*, vol. 2: 711–15.
67. Euan Cameron, *Enchanted Europe: Superstition, Reason and Religion, 1250–1750* (Oxford, 2010), 182. Bernard, *Guide to Grand-Jury Men*, 50–1.
68. David Lederer, *Madness, Religion and the State in Early Modern Europe. A Bavarian Beacon* (Cambridge, 2006), 235.
69. [Des *Niau*], *Devils of Loudun*, vol. 2: 27; Certeau, *Possession at Loudun*, 121. Michel Marescot, *A True Discourse upon the Matter of Martha Brossier of Romorantin, Pretended to be Possessed by a Devil*, trans. Abraham Hartwell (London, 1599), 23. Moshe Sluhovsky, 'A Divine Apparition or Demonic Possession? Female Agency and Church Authority in Demonic Possession in Sixteenth-Century France', *Sixteenth Century Journal* 27 (1996): 1041.
70. More, *A True Discourse*, 41.
71. Heinrich Kramer, *The Hammer of Witches: A Complete Translation of the* Malleus Maleficarum, trans. Christopher S. Mackay (Cambridge, 2009) 348; Maggi, *Satan's Rhetoric*, introduction.
72. Robert Mapes Anderson, *Vision of the Disinherited: The Making of American Pentecostalism* (New York, 1979), 16–17.
73. *An account of the strange and wonderful manner in which John Fox, who some time ago lived near Nottingham, was sorely afflicted with an Evil Spirit* (Glasgow, n.d.). Fox's speaking without moving his lips was offered as proof of his possession. See the report of the sixteenth-century ventriloquist Petrus Brabantius, who 'could speak from the lower part of his body, his mouth being open, but his lips not moved'. John Webster, *The Displaying of Supposed Witchcraft* (London, 1677), 122.

74. Sands, *Demon Possession*, 156–7, 184. According to St Jerome, St Paula heard demoniacs howling like dogs and wolves before the graves of saints, roaring like lions, and hissing like snakes. Jerome, *Letters*, 108, 13, cited in Adolf Rodewyk, *Possessed by Satan: The Church's Teaching on the Devil, Possession, and Exorcism*, trans. Martin Ebon (Garden City, NY, 1975), 12.
75. Decker, *Witchcraft and the Papacy*, 18.
76. Pierre de Lancre claimed that God and Job named the devil Behemoth because this monster alone combined many animals in one. *On the Inconstancy of Witches: Pierre de Lancre's Tableau de l'inconstance des mauvais anges et démons (1612)*, ed. Gerhild Scholz Williams (Tempe, Ariz., 2006), 19–20. Job did not, however, identify Behemoth as either a demon or the Devil.
77. Henri Boguet, *An Examen of Witches*, 2.
78. Midelfort, 'Devil and the German People', 113.
79. National Archives, London, STAC 8/4/10, fol. 201.
80. Letter from Thomas Marsden in Zachary Taylor, *The Devil Turn'd Casuist or the Cheats of Rome* (London, 1696), Epistle Dedicatory.
81. Fernando Cervantes, *The Devil in the New World: The Impact of Diabolism in New Spain* (New Haven and London, 1994), 104.
82. John Darrell, *An Apologie, or Defence of the possession of William Sommers, a yong man of the Towne of Nottingham* [1599], sig. B4.
83. See for example John Barrow, *The Lord's Arm Stretched out in an Answer to Prayer*. (London 1664), 8.
84. Decker, *Witchcraft and the Papacy*, 163.
85. [Des *Niau*], *Devils of Loudun*, vol. 2: 31, 44.
86. Richard Meade, *Medica sacra; or, a Commentary on the Most Remarkable Diseases, Mentioned in the Holy Scriptures* (London, 1755), pp. 74–5.
87. *A Breife Narration of the Possession, Dispossession, and, Repossession of William Sommers* (London, 1598), sig. B3ᵛ.
88. See J.H. Chajes, *Between Worlds: Dybbuks, Exorcists, and Early Modern Judaism* (Philadelphia, 2003), 5.
89. Ernst Benz, 'Ergriffenheit und Besessenheit als Grundformen religiöser Erfahrung'. In Jurg Zutt, ed., *Ergriffenheit und Besessenheit: ein interdisziplinäres Gespräch über transkulturell-anthropoligishe und psychiatrische Fragen* (Bern and Munich, 1972). See also Oesterreich, *Possession*, 77; Augustin Poulain, *Des grâces d'oraison: Traité théologie mystique*, 5th edn (Paris 1906), 423.
90. J. Le Breton, *La Deffense de la vérité touchant la possession des Religieuses de Louviers* (Evreux, 1643), 27. Certeau, *Possession at Loudun*, 38 claims that on the basis of these criteria nine of the nuns at Loudun were declared to be possessed, with the remaining eight simply being obsessed.
91. Bell, *Holy Anorexia*, 73.
92. *A True and Most Dreadfull discourse of a woman Possessed with the Devill, who in the Likeness of a Headlesse Beare Fetched her out of her Bedd . . .* (London, 1584).
93. Oesterreich, *Possession*, 50ff. claims that Surin was obsessed but not possessed. See Sarah Ferber, 'Possession and the Sexes,' in Alison Rowlands, ed., *Witchcraft and Masculinities in Early Modern Europe* (Basingstoke, 2009), 226, who refers to it as a case of possession by transference, and Cervantes, *Devil in the New World*, 101ff.
94. See for example Karlsen, *Devil in the Shape of a Woman*, 11–12, 35, 135–6. Karlsen, 222–6, extends this analysis to include all seventy-eight 'convulsed accusers' of witches at Salem, who she says described themselves as 'possessed by witches'.
95. David Harley, 'Explaining Salem: Calvinist Psychology and the Diagnosis of Possession', *American Historical Review* 101 (1996): 307–30, also denies that the Salem girls were possessed but goes too far in claiming that seventeenth-century Calvinists made a clear distinction between possession and the effects of witchcraft. See below, Chapter 8.

96. Lederer, *Madness, Religion and the State*, 206–14; Sluhovsky, *Believe Not Every Spirit*, 50–1; Tomasz Wislicz, 'Talking to the Devil in the Early Modern Popular Imagination', in *Faith and Fantasy in the Renaissance: Texts, Images, and Religious Practices*, ed. Olga Zorzi Pugliese and Ethan Matt Kavaler (Toronto, 2009), 135–46; Éva Pócs, 'Possession Phenomena, Possession-Systems: Some East-Central European Examples,' in *Communicating with the Spirits*, ed. Gábor Klaniczay and Éva Pócs (Budapest, 2005), 124–5. Peter Brown, *Society and the Holy in Late Antiquity* (Berkeley, 1982), 18, argues that in late antiquity many demoniacs did not go to a shrine 'in a state of acute possession' but went there 'so as to become possessed'.

97. Nancy Caciola, *Discerning Spirits: Divine and Demonic Possession in the Middle Ages* (Ithaca, NY, 2003), 235–6, notes that exorcisms at such sites declined in the late Middle Ages. It is arguable, however, that they were as dramatic or as public as she suggests.

98. On this issue see Sarah Ferber, *Demonic Possession and Exorcism in Early Modern France*, pp. 2–3; Lederer, *Madness, Religion and the State*, 200. The exceptionally high number of exorcisms at the Bavarian shrine in the monastery of Benediktbeuren during an eleven-year period in the seventeenth century leads Lederer to make this distinction.

99. See for example Garnier, *Barbe Buvée*, 6; Henri Bouchet, *Relation sur l'épidémie de Morzine* (Lyon, 1899).

100. Pierre Viret, *The World Possessed with Devils, conteinying three dialogues* (London, 1583) 2nd dialogue, sig D4ᵛ.

101. Andrew Boorde, *The Breviary of Helthe* (London, 1547), fols. iv–vii; Clark, *Thinking with Demons*, 420. The Cambridge scholar John Greene used the word in this sense when he claimed that a woman was 'possessed of the Devil' when she went to a play. John Greene, *A Refutation of the Apologie for Actors* (London, 1615), 42.

102. Burton, *Anatomy of Melancholy*, vol. 1:194.

103. See Caciola, *Discerning Spirits*, 41–8 for a description of this bodily invasion. Lyndal Roper, *Oedipus and the Devil*, 176, describes the demonic body as 'the glass within which its demonic inhabitants cavorted'. One graphic illustration of the permeability of the body to demonic attack was the testimony of a young Catholic gentleman to Sir William Cecil in 1586 that one 'could actually see the devils gliding and moving under the skin' of a demoniac. 'There were immense numbers of them, and they looked just like fishes swimming here, there and everywhere.' William Weston, *The Autobiography of an Elizabethan*, trans. Philip Caraman (London, 1955), 25. On the permeability of the skin in the early modern period see Barbara Duden, *The Woman Beneath the Skin: A Doctor's Patients in Eighteenth-century Germany*, trans. Thomas Dunlap (Cambridge, Mass., 1991), 123, 142. The skin was viewed as a fragile surface on which the inside of the body revealed itself, 'a sheath of the inside' that was everywhere open to the outside. John Jeffries Martin, *Myths of Renaissance Individualism* (Basingstoke, 2004), 84, refers to the skin as 'not a barrier but rather a frontier across which spirits, whether benevolent or demonic, could cross (entering or exiting) with relative ease'.

104. Watt, *Scourge of Demons*, 115, 121.

105. See Louise Nyholm Kallestrup, '"Da kom den onde ånd ind i mit knae"': i kulturhistoisk undersøgelse af djaevlebesaetttelser i Danmark efter Reformationem', in *Religios tro og praksis i den dansk-norske helsat fra reformatasjonen til opplysningstid ca. 1500–1814*, ed. Arne Bugge Amundsen and Henning Laugerud (Oslo, 2010), 192, on the dialogue between Church and people, theology and folklore.

106. Certeau, *Possession at Loudun*, 90–1. Demoniacs were often possessed by seven demons, the same number that possessed Mary Magdalene. There were also believed to be seven Princes of Hell.

107. Clark, *Thinking with Demons*, 424.

108. Georg Scherer, *Christliche Erinnerung bey der Historien von jüngst beschehener Erledigung einer Junckfrawen* (Ingolstadt, 1584), 19–21. Cotton Mather made the

same estimate in his sermon on Revelation 12: 12. See *Wonders of the Invisible World* (Boston, 1693), 5.

109. The statement by D.P. Walker, *Unclean Spirits* (London and Philadelphia, 1981), 15 that 'Historians should not ask their readers to accept supernatural phenomena' is on the face of it unobjectionable. Stuart Clark, *Thinking with Demons*, 396 argues that there is an implicit realism in Walker's statement, but I do not see how either Walker's position or mine endorses 'the view that we cannot understand the actions or beliefs of others without accepting them as true and valid ourselves'. Mary Keller, *The Hammer and the Flute: Women, Power, and Spirit Possession* (Baltimore and London, 2002), 122, addresses the related question of how a scholar 'can assess the agency of a possessed body, given that it is epistemologically impossible to verify a possession'.

110. Webster, '(Re)possession of Dispossession', 110.

111. Sluhosky, *Believe Not Every Spirit*, 190 argues that the primary concern with simulation shows that the crucial distinction in matters of spirituality was no longer between the divine and the diabolic but between sincerity and deception.

112. Andrew W. Keitt, *Inventing the Sacred: Imposture, Inquisition, and the Boundaries of the Supernatural in Golden Age Spain* (Leiden, 2005), 55.

113. In commenting on the possessions at Loudun, Des Niau, *History of the Devils of Loudun*, vol. 2: 27, wrote that it was only necessary for the demoniac to pass one of these four tests for the public exorcism to proceed.

114. Certeau, *Possession at Loudun*, 36.

115. Lynn Thorndike, *A History of Magic and Experimental Science* (New York and London, 1958), vol. 8: 542.

116. Claude Pithoys, *A Seventeenth-century Exposure of Superstition: Select Texts of Claude Pithoys (1587–1676)*, ed. P.J.S. Whitmore (The Hague, 1972), 3–44. Pithoys distinguished between insufficient proofs of possession and more certain ones. The latter included speaking strange languages, discovering secrets, and acquiring knowledge without previous instruction. On the failure of Pithoys to win support for his arguments see Briggs, *Witches of Lorraine*, 82–3.

117. In the Middle Ages, as early as the ninth century counterfeit demoniacs were subject to severe beatings but were not prosecuted. Rodewyk, *Possessed by Satan*, 45.

118. On the Spanish Inquisition's prosecution of false mystics see Stephen Halliczer, *Between Exaltation and Infamy: Female Mystics in the Golden Age of Spain* (Oxford, 2002), chs 5 and 6. The Inquisition apparently prosecuted more false mystics than demoniacs, but the punishments for feigned sanctity were relatively light. Ibid., 144–5. On the prosecution of false sanctity by the Roman Inquisition, which began later than in Spain, see Anne Schutte, *Aspiring Saints: Pretense of Holiness, Inquisition, and Gender in the Republic of Venice, 1618–1750* (Baltimore and London, 2001), 63–72. One Venetian visionary, Maria Sparano, was sentenced to seven years in prison for her pretended sanctity in 1611. For a comparison between the crime of feigned sanctity in the Spanish Inquisition and the more specifically defined Italian crime of 'pretense to holiness' in the Roman Inquisition see Keitt, *Inventing the Sacred*, 78–86.

119. Nancy Caciola, *Discerning Spirits*, 317. Rodewyk, *Possessed by Satan*, 45, claims that the fraudulently possessed demoniacs at Paderborn in 1656 were also beaten.

120. Samuel Harsnett, *A Declaration of Egregious Popish Impostures* (London, 1603); idem, *A Discovery of the Fraudulent Practises of John Darrel* (London, 1599).

121. Walker, *Unclean Spirits*, ch. 4. In the late seventeenth century the Anglican minister Zachary Taylor, chaplain to the bishop of Chester, made the same claims as Harsnett in dealing with both Catholic and Protestant demoniacs in Lancashire. See Taylor, *The Devil Turn'd Casuist*.

122. National Archives, London, STAC 8/4/10. For the account of this trial see Brian P. Levack, 'Possession, Witchcraft and the Law in Jacobean England'. *Washington and Lee Law Review* 52 (1996): 1613–40.

123. Richard Raiswell, 'Faking It: A Case of Counterfeit Possession in the Reign of James I', *Renaissance and Reformation* 23 (1999): 29–48; National Archives, STAC 8/32/12.
124. Webster, *Displaying of Supposed Witchcraft*, 273–5.
125. See for example Walker, *Unclean Spirits*.
126. Stuart Clark, 'The Scientific Status of Demonology,' in *Occult and Scientific Mentalities in the Renaissance*, ed. Brian Vickers (Cambridge, 1984), 351–74.
127. More, *True Discourse*, 41–8.
128. Sands, *Demon Possession*, 76. See also Lea, *Materials*, 1047; Otto Snell, *Hexenprozess und Geistesstorung* (Munich, 1901), 119–20.
129. Oesterreich, *Possession*, 376 argues although possessions the world over differ in detail, 'at bottom they are all identical'. Although Morton Klass, *Mind over Mind: The Anthropology and Psychology of Spirit Possession* (Lanham, Md., 2003), 111, proposes a category of *patterned dissociative identity* that opens up the possibility of different types of possession, he nonetheless contends that the set of psychological categories he proposes are not 'culture bound' and in the final analysis are 'etic', a term coined in the late twentieth century to describe social scientific phenomena that have universal applicability.
130. For a modern historical endorsement of this argument see Edward Bever, *The Realities of Witchcraft and Popular Magic in Early Modern Europe: Culture, Cognition and Everyday Life* (Basingstoke, 2008), 87–92.
131. See David Ingelby, 'The Social Construction of Mental Illness,' in *The Problem of Medical Knowledge: Examining the Social Construction of Medicine* (Edinburgh, 1982), 123–43.
132. For an interpretation of all rituals as theatre see Victor Turner, *From Ritual to Theatre: The Human Seriousness of Play* (New York, 1982), 89–101.

Chapter 2. Possession and Exorcism in Christian Antiquity

1. Erik H. Erikson, *Young Man Luther: A Study in Psychoanalysis and History* (New York, 1962), 23. It is uncertain whether this incident ever occurred. Even if it was a Catholic fabrication, however, it testifies to the power of the biblical exorcism texts in the sixteenth century.
2. The exorcism stories in the New Testament support the argument that one of Jesus's historical roles was that of an exorcist, but there is widespread acceptance of the fact that these stories did not portray actual historical events. See Eric Sorensen, *Possession & Exorcism in the New Testament and Early Christianity* [Wissenschaftliche Untersuchungen zum Neuen Testament 2: 157] (Tübingen, 2002), 131, n. 17.
3. These were the most frequently consulted versions of the Bible and the ones used by the biblical scholars discussed in this chapter. For a discussion of the manuscript and printed bibles in circulation in the fifteenth and early sixteenth centuries see Andrew Gow, 'Challenging the Protestant Paradigm: Bible Reading in Lay and Urban Contexts of the Later Middle Ages', in *Scripture and Pluralism*, ed. Thomas J. Heffernan and Thomas E. Burman (Leiden and Boston, 2005), 161–91.
4. All quotations in this chapter are from the Revised Standard Version.
5. Mark 1: 32–4.
6. One of the ironies of this story is that by performing this miracle Jesus not only permitted the possession of the pigs but actually caused it. If a human being had performed such an act he would have been liable to a charge of *maleficium*. Walter Stephens, *Demon Lovers: Witchcraft, Sex and the Crisis of Belief* (Chicago, 2001), 327. Paul sent Satan into the body of the Corinthian fornicator and into the heretics Hymenaeus and Alexander, but in doing this Paul was consigning them to Satan, not ordering their possession.
7. Mark 9: 29
8. Matthew 12: 22–30; Mark 3: 22–7; Luke 11: 14–23.

9. The Pharisees made the same charge against Jesus in Matthew 9: 32, when he exorcized another mute demoniac.

10. Mark 3: 24–5. This was not a statement regarding the strength of Satan's kingdom. Christians believed that Satan's kingdom had been weakened since his expulsion from Heaven but would gather strength before its final defeat at Armageddon.

11. Johannes Dillinger, 'Beelzebulstreitigkeiten: Besessenheit in der Bibel', in *Dämonische Besessenheit: zur Interpretation eines kulturhistorischen Phänomens*, ed. Hans de Waardt et al. (Bielefeld, 2005), 57.

12. The Greek word used by Matthew is *seleniazetai*. The Vulgate and the English Bibles of the early modern period translated the word as lunatic or frantic, while the German Bible of 1534 renders it as *mondsüchtig* or moonstruck. The Greek word for epileptic is *epiliptikos*. For the modern translation of *seleniazetai* as as 'epileptic' see the Revised Standard Version.

13. Early modern demonologists, following Petrus Chrysologus, argued that it was only the spirit, not the boy, who was mute and deaf. Chrysologus, *Sermo 52*, cited in Maggi, *Satan's Rhetoric*, 108, n. 31.

14. Zacharia Visconti, *Complementum artis exorcisticae*, 771–4.

15. Maggi, *Satan's Rhetoric*, 108.

16. On suicide in early modern Europe see Lederer, *Madness, Religion and the State*, and R. A. Houston, *Punishing the Dead? Suicide, Lordship, and Community in Britain, 1500–1830* (Oxford, 2010).

17. Walker, *Unclean Spirits*, 39. Marescot, *True Discourse*, 25 wrote that if one were only looking for signs of possession set down by the evangelists, every epileptic and every melancholic would be a demoniac. Almond, *Demonic Possession and Exorcism*, 27, notes that all but two signs of possession in the New Testament texts appeared in the possession narratives of the early modern period. The more significant comparison is with the exceptionally large number of symptoms of early modern possessions that cannot be found in Scripture.

18. E.g. Luke 7: 17–18. Mark, however, used different verbs to distinguish the two. Sorensen, *Possession and Exorcism*, 135. Graham Twelftree, *Jesus the Exorcist: A Contribution to the Study of the Historical Jesus* (Tübingen, 1993), 55. Christ did not address Satan when he cured the sick. See Luke 13: 12–13. On the relationship between exorcism and specific acts of healing in the New Testament see Richard A. Horsley, *Jesus and the Spiral of Violence* (New York, 1987), 181.

19. See for example *A Breife Narration*, sig. E.

20. Raiswell, 'Faking It', 33.

21. Dillinger, 'Beelzebulstreitigkeiten', 62.

22. Ferber, *Demonic Possession and Exorcism*, 77.

23. Walker, *Unclean Spirits*, 5–6.

24. See Sorensen, *Possession and Exorcism,* 136.

25. Johann Weyer quoted Melanchthon as saying 'I have no doubt that this malady can be ended, and the Devils expelled, by the sincere prayers of pious men.' *Witches, Devils and Doctors,* 470.

26. Acts 19: 13.

27. Jane Shaw, *Miracles in Enlightenment England* (New Haven and London, 2006), 21–2.

28. See Cameron, *Enchanted Europe,* 205. Jean-Louis, Quantin, *The Church of England and Christian Antiquity: The Construction of a Confessional Identity in the 17th Century* (Oxford, 2009), 133, claims Harsnett hinted that the power to exorcize had died many centuries before.

29. D.P. Walker, 'The Cessation of Miracles', in *Hermeticism and the Renaissance: Intellectual History and the Occult in Early Modern Europe*, ed. Ingrid Merkel and Allen G. Debus (Washington, DC, 1988), 111–24. Calvin extended the doctrine to include his rejection of the sacrament of extreme unction, a 'gift of healing' that Christ allowed for a certain period of time but had not willed to continue to allow for the new preaching of the Gospel. Calvin explained that the Apostles, acting on the basis of the command

they had received from the Lord, 'raised up the dead, cast out demons, cleansed lepers, healed the sick, and in curing the sick used oil', but the work of the Apostles 'now has nothing to do with us, to whom the administering of such powers has not been committed'. *Institutes*, Bk. 4, ch. 18. Nevertheless, Luther and Calvin displayed some ambivalence on this question. See Cameron, *Enchanted Europe*, 206–8. Shaw, *Miracles in Enlightenment England*, shows that many Protestants, especially those who were not theologians, contested the doctrine.

30. On the scriptural basis of this mission see Matthew 10: 1, Mark 6: 7 and Luke 9: 1. These passages refer to the disciples' acquisition of power over unclean spirits, but they do not specify by what means. Mathew 10: 1 for example reads, 'He gave them the power against unclean spirits, to cast them out'.

31. John Hooper, *A Brief and True Confession* (London 1550), 9. See Cameron, *Enchanted Europe*, 388, n. 61.

32. See also William Perkins, *A Discourse on the Damned Art of Witchcraft* (Cambridge, 1608), 232–9.

33. John Deacon and John Walker, *Dialogicall Discourses of Spirits and Devils, Declaring their Proper Essence* (London, 1601), 334. Deacon and Walker also proposed that the biblical accounts of possession should be interpreted metaphorically. Ibid., 17–21.

34. [Richard Baddeley], *The Boy of Bilson: or, a true discovery of the late notorious impostures of certain Romish priests in their pretended exorcisme* (London, 1622), 2–7; quote at 2.

35. Deacon and Walker, *Dialogicall Discourses*, 333–6, cites Augustine, Chrysostom, and Lyra as well as the medieval theologians Hugo and Isidore and the Protestants Beza, Calvin, Cooper, Fulke, and Dearing as the authorities for the doctrine. In a sermon on the Thessalonians Chrysostom referred to miracles 'iam olim cessarint'.

36. 'For those that are baptized do not now receive the Spirit on the imposition of hands, so as to speak in the tongues of all the peoples; neither are the sick healed by the shadow of the preachers of Christ falling on them as they pass; and other such things as were then done, are now manifestly ceased.' Augustine, *Retractions* 1.13. 7. See also Augustine, *De verbis Domini secundum Matthaeum*, sermon 28, cited in Reginald Scot, *The Discoverie of Witchcraft*, ed. M. Summers (London, 1930), 89, and *De vera religione*, in Augustine, *Earlier Writings*, trans. J.H.S. Burleigh (Louisville, 1953), 220, 224. Augustine, however, reported extensively on a revival of miracles in his later ministry, and in his discussion of miraculous healing he claimed that demonic seizures could be cured only by miracles. *City of God*, 22. 8. See Ilza Veith, *Hysteria: The History of a Disease* (Chicago, 1965), 47–9. See Augustine, *Earlier Writings*, 286, for the explanation that he only meant to deny that *great* miracles still happened.

37. [Harsnett], *Discovery of the Fraudulent Practises*; [idem], *A Declaration of Egregious Popish Impostures* (London, 1603).

38. Keitt, *Inventing the Sacred*, 179–80.

39. Joseph Mede, *The Apostasy of the Latter Times . . . or the Gentiles Theology of Daemons* (London, 1644). The anonymous pamphlet, *The Doctrine of Devils: proved to be the grand apostacy of these later times, an essay tending to rectifie those undue notions and apprehensions men have about dæmons and evil spirits* (London, 1676), written by the sceptical humanist and physician Thomas Ady, made some of the same points as Mede and incorporated Mede's title into its own; see especially pp. 34–41.

40. On Hobbes's religious beliefs see Aloysius Martinich, *The Two Gods of Leviathan* (Cambridge, 2002). Hobbes's endorsement of the cessation of miracles and his belief that Christ gave 'faith, piety and all manner of moral virtues . . . to some only and not to all' provides strong evidence for this theological orientation.

41. Thomas Hobbes, *Leviathan* (London, 1651), ch. 34. Hobbes believed that most references to angels in the Old Testament were to images raised supernaturally, but that in the New Testament angels were real. The argument that angels were corporeal found support in Webster, *Displaying of Supposed Witchcraft*, ch. 10. Like Hobbes, Webster was critical of scholastic demonology, especially the idea that demons could assume bodies, and the support this belief provided for witch-hunting.

42. Hobbes, *Leviathan*, ch. 45. This was the idea of biblical *accommodation* to an ignorant audience for pedagogical purposes, an idea that had first been proposed in the fourteenth century but did not acquire any traction until this period.

43. George Sinclair, *Satan's Invisible World Discovered* (Edinburgh, 1685), 'The Preface to the Reader', sig, A4ᵛ, attacks Hobbes, who was 'too well known by his atheistical writings', for slighting religion and undervaluing Scripture 'because there is such an express mention of spirits and angels in it' and for claiming that everything in the universe 'comes under the notion of things material and bodies only'.

44. Sinclair was inferring this position from Spinoza's denial of the existence of the Devil and his claim that the Bible was fallible and was not intended to convey religious doctrine. If its truth could not be demonstrated rationally, it must be interpreted philologically, historically, or psychologically. For Spinoza's denial of the power of the Devil see Spinoza, *God, Man and His Well-Being*, ch. 25 in *The Collected Works of Spinoza*, ed. Edwin Curley (Princeton, 1985), 145. On his approach to biblical criticism, see Andrew Fix, 'Bekker and Spinoza', in *Disguised and Overt Spinozism around 1700*, ed. Wiep van Bunge and Wim Klever (Leiden, 1996), 30–1; Richard Popkin, 'Cartesianism and Biblical Criticism,' in *Problems of Cartesianism*, ed. Thomas M. Lennon, John M. Nicolas and John W. Davis (Kingston and Montreal, 1982), 66–7.

45. The first two books were published separately in one volume in 1691 and the third and fourth books in 1693. In that year the complete work, *De betoverde weereld . . . in vier boeken ondernomen* was also published in Amsterdam. Bekker's discussion of demonic possession appears in Bk. 2, chs 26–8. See Andrew Fix, *Fallen Angels: Balthasar Bekker, Spirit Belief, and Confessionalism in the Seventeenth-century Dutch Republic* (Dordrecht, 1999), 65–75.

46. German translation: *Die bezauberte Welt* (Amsterdam, 1693); French translation: *Le Monde enchanté* (Amsterdam, 1694); English translation (Book 1 only): *The World Bewitch'd* (London, 1695).

47. Fix, 'Bekker and Spinoza', 23–40.

48. G.J. Stronks, 'The Significance of Balthasar Bekker's *The Enchanted World*', in *Witchcraft in the Netherlands: From the Fourteenth to the Twentieth Century*, ed. Marijke Gijswijt-Hofstra and Willem Frijhoff (Rotterdam, 1991), 152.

49. 2 Peter 2: 4. On the descent into Hell in English theology see Quantin, *The Church of England and Christian Antiquity*, 115–29.

50. Bekker, *De betoverde weereld*, Bk 2, ch. 29.

51. Wiep van Bunge, 'Eric Walton (1663–1697): An Early Enlightenment Radical in the Dutch Republic', in *Disguised and Overt Spinozism*, 41.

52. Thomas Woolston, *A Discourse on the Miracles of our Saviour: in view of the present controversy between infidels and apostates* (London, 1727), 3.

53. Ibid., 31.

54. More than a century earlier a Dutch Protestant preacher in Brandenburg at the time of the mass possessions at Spandau and Friedeberg claimed that the Gadarene swine represented the dissolute people in these towns. Claiming that there was 'nothing but gluttony and drunkenness' among them, he attributed the possessions to Satan's fearful execution of God's just judgement. Goulart, *Admirable Histories*, 182.

55. Woolston, *A Discourse on the Miracles of our Saviour*, p. 35.

56. Midelfort, *History of Madness*, 134. See also Hobbes on the possession of Judas in *Leviathan*, ch. 45.

57. The conviction for blasphemy fulfilled the threat made by the French Calvinist demonologist Lambert Daneau in 1575 that anyone who claimed that the demoniacs exorcized by Christ were melancholic, which was the medical interpretation of possession as insanity advanced by sceptics such as Johann Weyer, should be considered blasphemous. Lambert Daneau, *A Dialogue of Witches*, trans. R.W. (London, 1575), fol. 22.

58. Arthur Ashley Sykes, *Enquiry into the Meaning of Demoniacks in the New Testament* (London, 1737), 2–6.

59. Samuel Pegge, *An Examination of the Enquiry into the Meaning of Demoniacs in the New Testament* (London, 1739), esp. 9–20.

60. Burton, *Anatomy of Melancholy,* vol. 1: 175 traces this 'foolish opinion' to Maximus Tyrius, the Greek rhetorician in the second century CE who believed that the soul became a demon when it left the body and became an intermediary between God and man.

61. Yoram Bilu, 'The Taming of the Deviants and Beyond: An Analysis of Dybbuk Possession and Exorcism in Judaism', in *Spirit Possession in Judaism: Cases and Contexts from the Middle Ages to the Present,* ed. Matt Goldish (Detroit, 2003), 42. See also H.C. Erik Midelfort, *Exorcism and Enlightenment: Johann Joseph Gassner and the Demons of Eighteenth-century Germany* (New Haven and London, 2005), 180, n. 16 (k); Chajes, *Between Worlds.*

62. See Armando Maggi, *In the Company of Demons: Unnatural Beings, Love and Identity in the Italian Renaissance* (Chicago, 2006), 10. The ghost of Nicole Obry's grandfather, which appeared to her in a vision, claiming he was in Purgatory, did not possess her, but once the friar Pierre de la Motte identified the ghost, first as an angel and then as a demon, he claimed that the demon had in fact taken possession of her. See Sluhovsky, 'Divine Apparition', 1040–1; Walker, *Unclean Spirits,* 22. For the Catholic condemnation of the belief that the souls of the dead could possess human beings, see Girolamo Menghi, *Compendio dell'arte essorcista* (Bologna, 1579), 406–8.

63. Laura de Mello e Souza, *The Devil and the Land of the Holy Cross: Witchcraft, Slavery, and Popular Religion in Colonial Brazil,* trans. D.G. Whitty (Austin, Tex., 2003), 167. The belief was clearly of African origin. On the belief in eastern Hungary and the Orthodox regions of the Balkans that witches could be possessed by the spirits of the dead, see Pócs, 'Possession Phenomena', 108, 116. Most of the possessing spirits in the modern cases treated by the clinical psychologist Adam Crabtree have been the spirits of deceased blood relatives. Adam Crabtree, *Multiple Man: Explorations in Possession and Multiple Personality* (New York, 1985), 147.

64. Keller, *The Hammer and the Flute,* 17.

65. Sykes, *Enquiry,* 53.

66. Acts 8: 7

67. Sykes, *Enquiry,* 70.

68. Nor was there a change of opinion among Catholic biblical scholars. Augustin Calmet, the French Benedictine scholar who has been credited with introducing a new critical approach to biblical studies, insisted upon a literal interpretation of the scriptural references to Christ's exorcisms in his treatise on apparitions and spirits, first published in 1746. See Augustin Calmet, *The Phantom World: or the philosophy of spirits, apparitions etc., etc.,* trans. Henry Christmas (Philadelphia, 1850), 107–8.

69. Richard Meade, *Medica sacra* (1755), 73–92.

70. Jeannine Blackwell, 'Controlling the Demoniac: Johann Salomo Semler and the Possession of Anna Elisabeth Lohmann (1759)', in *Impure Reason: Dialectic of Enlightenment in Germany,* ed. W. Daniel Wilson and Robert C. Holub (Detroit, 1993), 425–42.

71. Johann Salomo Semler, *Abfertigung der neuen Geister und alten Irrtümer in der Lohnmannischen Begeisterung zu Kemberg* (Halle, 1760); idem, *Dissertatio theologico-hermeneutica de daemoniacis quorum in Evangeliis fit mentio* (Halle, 1760).

72. On the irony of Protestants abandoning literalism see Midelfort, *Exorcism and Enlightenment,* 102.

73. The Septuagint used the word *daimonion* mainly to describe idols, as in Psalms 96: 5 and Is. 65: 11. Psalm 106: 36–9 likens the idols of Canaan to demons.

74. On the difficulty of identifying direct Hellenistic influences on Jewish literature see Martin Hengel, *Judaism and Hellenism: Studies in their Encounter in Palestine during the Early Hellenistic Period,* 2 vols. (Philadelphia, 1974), esp. 107.

75. Sorensen, *Possession and Exorcism,* 80, 117.

76. Daniel 7. The mid-seventeenth-century English millenarian and revolutionary sect known as the Fifth Monarchy Men took its name from this prophecy, identifying the fifth kingdom as that of Jesus after the Second Coming.

77. The oldest section, known as the Book of Watchers, dates from about 300 BCE, while the latest, the Book of Parables, was probably composed at the end of the first century BCE. The writers of the New Testament were familiar with its thought regarding demons.

78. Mark 9: 25.

79. Philo of Alexandria, 'On Giants', in *Philo*, vol.2, trans. F.H. Colson and G.H. Whitaker (London, 1929), 441–79.

80. The confluence of these influences in the early years of Christianity can be seen in the *Testament of Solomon*, a non-canonical book of the Hebrew Bible that claims to be a first-hand account of Solomon's construction of the Temple but was written in Greek between the first and third centuries CE and was probably written by a Christian. The book deals extensively with demons and reflects Jewish, Greek, and early Christian understandings of such evil spirits.

81. Twelftree, *Jesus the Exorcist*, 106. For scepticism regarding the identification of Beelzebul and Satan see Meinrad Limbeck, 'Satan und das Böse im Neuen Testament', in Herbert Haag, *Teufelsglaube* (Tübingen, 1974), 297.

82. *Diabolos* was derived from the Greek verb *diaballein*, to slander (literally 'to hurl across'). This explains why the name Satan has been translated as 'accuser' in most modern versions of the Bible.

83. See Bekker, *De betoverde weereld*, Bk. 2, chs 26 and 27, on the translation of *daimon* as *diabolus*.

84. See e.g. Luke 10: 17 in *The Bible: Authorized King James Version with Apochrypha* (Oxford, 1997), 89 (NT). See also Willis Barnstone, *The Restored New Testament: A New Translation with Commentary, including the Gnostic Gospels Thomas, Mary, and Judas* (New York, 2009), 145, n. 45 on the translation of demon as devil in the King James Version.

85. William Whiston, *An Account of the Daemoniacks and of the Power of Casting out Demons both in the New Testament and in the First Four Centuries* (London, 1737), 2–3.

86. In 1602 the Catholic demonologist Henri Boguet described the five spirits that possessed Loyse Maillat as *démons*, not *diables*. Henri Boguet, *Discours execrable des sorciers*, ed. Nicole Jacques-Chaquin (Paris, 1980), 12. The modern English translation, however, perpetuated the early modern practice of calling them devils. Boguet, *An Examen of Witches*, 5.

87. For a discussion of Justin's Martyr's demonology see Everett Ferguson, *Demonology of the Early Christian World* (New York and Toronto, 1984), ch. 4.

88. The seven Princes of Hell that Peter Binsfeld identified in 1579—Satan, Lucifer, Beelzebub, Asmodeus, Leviathan, Mammon, and Belphegor—all traced their origin to the Hebrew Bible. None of them could claim a Greek or Hellenistic pedigree. The seven princes corresponded to the seven archangels before the Fall and were also identified with the Seven Deadly Sins.

89. See Weyer, *Witches, Devils, and Doctors*, 66–71.

90. For examples of possession only by Satan in Protestantism see *A Breife Narration*, sig. E, and Seiler, *Daemonomania*, 2. One of the few Protestant possession narratives that referred to Beelzebub and Lucifer as well as Satan and described demoniacs having 'two spirits at the least' was More, *True Discourse*, 42.

91. The initial construction of this demonic hierarchy was mainly the work of fourth-century Neoplatonists, most notably Iamblichus of Syria.

92. Jean Boulaese, *L'Abregee histoire du grand miracle par nostre Sauveur & Seigneur Jesus Christ en la saincte Hostie du Sacrament de l'Autel, faict à Laon* (Paris, 1573), 3.

93. The two names refer to the same god, Baal, which is Hebrew for Lord. The King James Version substituted Beelzebub for Beelzebul in the exorcism controversy.

94. *The Confessions of Madeleine Bavent*, trans. and ed. Montague Summers (London, [1933]), lii–liii, 96–8.

95. Cécile Ernst, *Teufelaustreibungen: Die Praxis der Katholischen Kirche im 16. und 17. Jahrhundert* (Bern, 1972), 83.

96. [Harsnett], *Declaration of Popish Impostures*, 239–43.
97. *Les Sorciers du carroi de Marlou: un procès de sorcellerie en Berry (1582–1583)*, ed. Nicole Jacques-Chaquin and Maxime Préaud (Grenoble, 1996), 96–7.
98. Nicky Hallett, *Witchcraft, Exorcism and the Politics of Possession in a Seventeenth-century Convent: 'How Sister Ursula was Once Bewitched and Sister Margaret Twice'* (Aldershot, 2007), 92–106.
99. Johann Weyer listed sixty-nine of these demons in *Pseudomonarchia daemonum*, which he appended to the 1577 edition of *De praestigiis daemonum*. Reginald Scot included an English version of Weyer's description of these demons in *The Discoverie of Witchcraft*, ed. M. Summers (London, 1930), Bk. 15, ch. 1. On the names used in ritual magic see Richard Kieckhefer, *Forbidden Rites: A Necromancer's Manual of the Fifteenth Century* (University Park, Pa., 1997), 155–6.

Chapter 3. Possession in Christian Demonology

1. Aquinas, *Summa theologica*, Pt. I. question 50, articles 1 and 2.
2. Richard P.H. Greenfeld, *Traditions of Belief in Late Byzantine Demonology* (Amsterdam, 1988), esp. 310–12. For references to material demons in fifteenth-century ritual magic, see Kieckhefer, *Forbidden Rites*, 154–6. On the apparent corporeality of demons in the fifteenth-century manuscript and artistic tradition, see Stephens, *Demon Lovers*, 108–24.
3. Burton, *The Anatomy of Melancholy*, vol. 1: 176. See also Webster, *The Displaying of Supposed Witchcraft*, 203–4.
4. Deacon and Walker, *Dialogicall Discourses*, 17–28. The position taken by the literary character Orthodoxus in this dialogue, which represents that of the authors, argues that demons, which are finite (i.e. not eternal) creatures of God, are 'substances invisible and spiritual'. Nyndge, *A True and Fearfull Vexation*, sig. A3.
5. On the Renaissance view that the bodies of spirits were 'visible metaphors' see Maggi, *In the Company of Demons*, viii–xii, 5–6.
6. *Summa theologica*, Pt. I, question 114, article 4.
7. For an attack on the scholastic idea that spirits can assume aerial bodies see Reginald Scot, *A Discourse of the Nature and Substance of Devils and Spirits*, appended to the 1665 edition of *The Discoverie of Witchcraft*, 15.
8. See for example Bernard, *Guide to Grand Jury-Men*, ch. 1. See Mary Beth Norton, *In the Devil's Snare: The Salem Witchcraft Crisis of 1692* (New York, 2002), 31–2, on the effect of this on Calvinist responses to possession.
9. See below, Chapter 8. Midelfort, *History of Madness*, 134. One Vatican authority actually used the Catholic doctrine of free will to reach the same conclusion as the Protestants, claiming that the demoniac had free will to resist the Devil's temptations. See Decker, *Witchcraft and the Papacy*, 161–7.
10. Newman, 'Possessed by the Spirit', 738 and sources cited in n. 20.
11. Bonaventure, *Commentaries on the Four Books of Sentences*, Bk. 2, Distinction 8, Pt. 2, art. 1, question 2; Rainer Jehl, 'Melancholie und Besessenheit im gelehrten Diskurs des Mittelalters,' in Waardt et al., *Dämonische Besessenheit*, 64–5. Jeffrey Burton Russell, *Lucifer: The Devil in the Middle Ages* (Ithaca, NY and London, 1984), 180. On the role played by Peter Lombard's *Sentences* in the 'professional study of angels' at the universities see David Keck, *Angels and Angelology in the Middle Ages* (New York, 1998), 87–92.
12. J. Ribet, *La mystique Divine* 3 vols (Paris, 1883), 109ff. See Midelfort, 'Devil and the German People,' 112–13 on the Devil's saying in the voice of a pious young demoniac that God sent him to plague the girl's body but not her soul. In the early modern period the medical opinion that melancholy, with which possession was closely associated or identified, could affect the rational soul was considered heretical. Angus Gowland, 'The Problem of Early Modern Melancholy', *Past and Present* 191 (2006): 97.
13. Kramer, *Hammer of Witches*, 343–53.

14. Ibid., 43–4. A few paragraphs later in the *Malleus* Kramer explains that the Devil can 'work on' the soul from the outside and thus be a source of temptation by imposing images on the intellect.
15. Ibid., 343–4.
16. Andreas Cesalpinus, *Daemonum investigatio peripatetica* (Florence, 1580); Jason Pratensis, 'De mania', in *De cerebri morbis* (Basel, 1549).
17. Nathan Johnstone, 'The Protestant Devil: The Experience of Temptation in Early Modern England', *Journal of British Studies* 43 (2004): 173–205.
18. Nyndge, *A True and Fearefull Vexation*, sig. B1. One of the few Calvinist descriptions of their appearance occurs in More, *True Discourse*, 79–80.
19. On the question of whether Luther really believed that he struggled physically with the Devil see Mark U. Edwards, Jr., *Luther's Last Battles: Politics and Polemics 1531–46* (Ithaca, NY and London, 1983), 18.
20. The condemnation appears in the preface to Bodin, *Démonomanie*. An English translation of the condemnation appears in Brian P. Levack, ed., *The Witchcraft Sourcebook* (London, 2004), 48–50. On Gerson's importance in discernment see Caciola, *Discerning Spirits*, 284–312 and Keitt, *Inventing the Sacred*, 56–65.
21. See above, p. 200.
22. Caciola, *Discerning Spirits*, 315–19.
23. Sluhovsky, *Believe Not Every Spirit*, 174–5, 212–13.
24. Johnstone, 'The Protestant Devil'. For an example of this Protestant emphasis on temptation see Cotton Mather's sermon, 'A Discourse on the Power and the Malice of the Devils'.
25. On the composition of the book and its challenge to the Roman Empire see Elaine Pagels, *Revelations: Visions, Prophecy, and Politics in the Book of Revelation* (New York, 2012), ch. 1, esp. 7–13.
26. Mark 13; Luke 17: 20–37; Luke 21: 8–36; 2 Tim. 3: 1–5; 1 Peter 4: 7–11. See also the apocryphal *Apocalypse of Peter* and the surviving fragments thereof.
27. Clark, *Thinking with Demons*, 339. Joseph Mede, the seventeenth-century Cambridge theologian, proposed a millenarian version of the Apocalypse by placing the thousand-year reign of Christ entirely in the future rather than in the past, in *Apostasy of the Latter Times*. See also John Rogers, *Ohel or Beth-shemess: A Tabernacle for the Sun* (London, 1653).
28. Clark, *Thinking with Demons*, 409.
29. Menghi, *Compendio dell'arte essorcistica*. The first edition of 1572 is not extant.
30. The book was published in the vernacular so that it could assist pastors in their work, Later editions of this and his other exorcist manuals reflected Menghi's desire to reach the widest popular audience in Europe.
31. Petrus Anusius Synesius [Guillaume Postel], *De summopere consyderando miraculo victoriae corporis Christi, quod Lauduni contigit 5566 a creatione mundi anno deque eius fructu Opusculum* (Paris, 1566); Jean Boulaese, *Le Miracle de Laon en Lannoys*, ed. A.H. Chambard (Lyon, 1955). On this literature see Irena Backus, *La Miracle de Laon: le déraisonnable, le raisonnable, l'apocalyptique et le politique dans les récits du miracle de Laon (1566–1578)* (Paris, 1994).
32. Jean Boulaese, *La Thrésor et entière histoire de la triomphante victoire de corps de Dieu sur l'esprit maling Beelzebub* (Paris, 1578), fol.8.
33. On the contemporary apocalyptic interpretation of these exorcisms see Clark, *Thinking with Demons*, 423–34. At Lille the lay promoter of exorcism, Jean le Normant, inspired by Sébastien Michaelis's *Histoire admirable* (1613), made even more explicit connections between the possessions of the nuns at Lille and the Apocalypse. Jean Le Normant, *Histoire veritable et memorable de ce qui c'est passé sous l'exorcisme de trois filles possedées és pais de Flandre* (Paris 1623). On the publication of this book see Ferber, *Demonic Possession and Exorcism*, 86. Part 2 of the book specifically linked the possessions at Lille with those at Aix.
34. Clark, *Thinking with Demons*, 411. On the importance of the Apocalypse for exorcisms in the Dutch Republic see Marc Wingens, 'Political Change and Demon Possession in

the South of the Dutch Republic: The Confrontation of a Protestant Bailiff and a Catholic Priest in 1650', in Waardt et al., *Dämonische Besessenheit*, 255–7.

35. Robert B. Barnes, *Prophecy and Gnosis: Apocalypticism in the Wake of the Lutheran Reformation* (Stanford, 1988). On the Catholic side, however, the Jesuit preacher and exorcist Georg Scherer worked the Apocalypse into his sermon on the exorcism of Anna Schlutterbäurin in 1584. *Christliche Erinnerung*, 21–3.

36. Weyer, *Witches, Devils and Doctors*, 470.

37. Seiler, *Daemonomania*. A second edition appeared in 1679.

38. Midelfort, 'Devil and the German People', 106. On the possessions in Spandau and Frieburg see Goulart, *Admirable Histories,*181–2; Jacob Horst, *De aureo dente maxillari pueri Silesii* (Lipsy, 1595).

39. Andreas Celichius, *Notwendige Erinnerung: Vonn des Sathans letzten Zornsturm und was es auff sich habe und bedeute, das nun zu dieser Zeit so viel Menschen an Leib und Seel vom Teuffel besessen werden* (Wittenberg, 1594).

40. Daniel Schaller, *Herolt* (Magdeburg, 1595), sig, N2ᵛ, quoted in Clark, *Thinking with Demons*, 411.

41. Clark, *Thinking with Demons*, 404.

42. See Sorensen, *Possession and Exorcism* 128–9 on the apocalyptic context of Mark. See also Twelftree, *Jesus the Exorcist*, ch. 20; Dillinger, 'Beelzebulstreitigkeiten', 57 for the apocalyptic reading of the exorcism of the epileptic boy.

43. The one exception was the rash of possessions—all linked to witchcraft accusations— in Geneva in the early seventeenth century. See William E. Monter, *Witchcraft in France and Switzerland: The Borderlands during the Reformation* (Ithaca, NY and London, 1976), ch. 2.

44. J.D., 'To the Reader', in *The Most Wonderful and True Storie of a Certaine Witch Named Alse Gooderige* (London, 1597); Almond, *Demonic Possession and Exorcism*, p. 152.

45. Willem Frijhoff, *Wegen van Evert Willemsz: een Hollands weeskind op zoek naar zichzelf, 1607–1647* (Nijmegen, 1995) 284. On both possessions see Bekker, *Die bezauberte Welt*, Bk. 4, ch. 25, pp. 219–27.

46. The sermon was included in Mather's book of the same name, *Wonders of the Invisible World* (Boston, 1693), 2–40. The sermon was intended to show that the Devil was exceptionally active during the Last Days. A specific reference to demoniacs appears on p. 11.

47. See Philip M. Soergel *Wondrous in His Saints: Counter-Reformation Propaganda in Bavaria* (Berkeley, 1993) on the relative strength of apocalyptic thought in the northern, Lutheran German territories.

48. Jean Vineti, *Tractatus contra demonum invocatores* (Cologne, 1487); Stephens, *Demon Lovers*, 324–31.

49. Sydney Anglo, 'Reginald Scot's *Discoverie of Witchcraft*: Scepticism and Sadduceeism', in *The Damned Art: Essays in the Literature of Witchcraft*, ed. Sydney Anglo (London, 1976), 111. In *A Discourse of the Nature and Substance of Devils and Spirits*, which was appended to the 1665 edition of *The Discoverie of Witchcraft*, Scot insisted that although demons had spiritual bodies, they possessed human bodies only in the sense that the spirit of evil entered a person. See *Discourse*, 14–15.

50. James VI, *Daemonologie* (Edinburgh, 1597), xii, 55. On whether James had the *Discoverie* burned upon his accession to the English throne in 1603 see Kallendorf, *Exorcism and its Texts*, 210, n. 7 and James Estes, 'Reginald Scot and his *Discoverie of Witchcraft*', *Church History* 52 (1983): 455.

51. Meric Casaubon, *Of Credulity and Incredulity in Things Natural, Civil and Divine* (London, 1668). On Casaubon see Michael Heyd, *'Be Sober and Reasonable': The Critique of Enthusiasm in the Seventeenth and Early Eighteenth Centuries* (Leiden, 1995), ch. 3.

52. J. Glanvill, *Saducismus triumphatus* (London, 1681); Sinclair, *Satan's Invisible World Discovered*. The translation of François Perreaud, *L'Antidemon de Mascon* (1653) as F. Perrault, *The Devill of Mascon, or, a True Relation of the Chiefe Things which an*

Unclean Spirit Did, and Said at Mascon (Oxford, 1658) can be considered part of this discourse. Robert Boyle was responsible for having Perreaud translated. On Boyle and witchcraft see Clark, *Thinking with Demons*, 308.

53. Henry More, *An Antidote against Atheism* (London, 1655), 278.
54. Mather, *Memorable Providences*, 2–3.
55. Ibid., 'To the Reader' and p. 28.
56. Deodat Lawson, *A Brief and True Narrative of Some Remarkable Passages relating to Sundry Persons Afflicted by Witchcraft* (Boston, 1693); Mather, *Wonders of the Invisible World*.
57. Thomas Jolly, *The Surey Demoniack: or, An Account of Satan's Strange and Dreadful Actings in and about the Body of Richard Dugdale of Surey, near Lancashire* (London, 1697), Preface.
58. Zachary Taylor, *The Surey Impostor, being an Answer to a Late Fanatical Pamphlet entituled The Surey Demoniack* (London, 1697). Jolly responded with *A Vindication of the Surey Demoniack* (London, 1698). Taylor compares the incident with that of William Somers, whom John Darrell exorcized in 1597.
59. *Rituale Romanum Pauli V. Pont. Max. iussu editum* (Antwerp, 1635), 363.
60. Mather, *Memorable Providences*, 3.
61. McLachlan, Hugh and Kim Swales. 'The Bewitchment of Christian Shaw: A Reassessment of the Famous Paisley Witchcraft Case of 1697', in *Twisted Sisters: Women, Crime and Deviance in Scotland since 1400*, ed. Yvonne Galloway Brown and Rona Ferguson (East Linton, 2002), 54–83, argue that the main authors were Andrew Turner, minister at Erskine, and James Brisbane, minister at Kilmacolm.
62. *A True Narrative of the Sufferings and Relief of a Young Girle*, 64. Grant also cited the trial of the atheist Thomas Aikenhead, who was executed at Edinburgh in 1696, to show what happened when someone denied the existence of spirits and a demon that tormented sinners.
63. On the authorship of this pamphlet see Christina Larner, 'Two Late Scottish Witchcraft tracts; *Witch-Craft Proven* and *The Tryal of Witchcraft*,' in Anglo, ed., *The Damned Art*, 230–2.
64. *Witch-Craft Proven, Arreign'd and Condemned in its Professors, Professions and Marks* (Glasgow, 1697), 2.
65. Ibid., 5.
66. *A True and Full Relation of the Witches at Pittenweem* (Edinburgh, 1704).
67. Weyer, *Witches, Devils, and Doctors*, 304–7.
68. Whiston, *An Account of the Daemoniacks*.
69. Cervantes, 'The Devils of Querétaro', 62.
70. *Collected Works of Spinoza*, 145.
71. Bekker had published a treatise on Cartesian philosophy in 1668, and he belonged to the Cartesian faction within the Dutch Reformed Church. His criticism of Spinoza's biblical scholarship was based on Descartes' insistence that theology and philosophy should remain separate disciplines. He showed his subscription to the mechanical philosophy in a treatise on comets in 1683, in which he rejected the traditional interpretation of signs and wonders as indicators of supernatural disapproval and as portents of the future.
72. This claim is supported mainly in Bk. 2, chs 26–30.
73. Balthasar Bekker, *The World Bewitched, or, An examination of the common opinion concerning spirits: their nature, power, administration and operations* (London, 1695).
74. On the radicalism of Bekker's work in redefining superstition, see Cameron, *Enchanted Europe*, 268. Instead of arguing that learned demonology defined and corrected popular superstition, Bekker argued that learned demonology and popular superstition were identical, in that both believed that the Earth was full of spirits. For a more general assessment of Bekker's radicalism see Jonathan Israel, *Radical Enlightenment: Philosophy and the Making of Modernity* (Oxford, 2001), 377–405.

75. In particular, Simon de Vries, *De Satan in sijn weesen, aert, bedryf, en guychel-spel* (1692), which presented a comprehensive study of the properties of Satan and his acts and sorceries, complete with historical examples of his interventions in the natural world.
76. Edward Nyndge recognized this ultimate divine source of his brother Alexander's possession in 1573. In Edward's view, however, God allowed the possession to remind Alexander of his religious duty to lead a moral life. Almond, *Demonic Possession and Exorcism*, 44. Nyndge, *A True and Fearfull Vexation*, sig. A3.
77. Cervantes, 'The Devils of Querétaro', 60–6.

Chapter 4. Expelling the Demon

1. Wingens, 'Political Change', 249.
2. The Catholic Church retains the use of exorcism in adult baptism, but in 1969 it replaced the exorcism of infants with a statement of their deliverance from original sin.
3. Jean Vineti sanctioned the exorcism of animals, and he cited the exorcism of pigs by Christ to support the practice. Stephens, *Demon Lovers*, 327. Saint Hilarion, the famous exorcist-saint, reputedly drove a demon out of a camel. See St Jerome's Vita of Hilarion in *Patrologia Latina*, ed. J.P. Migne, vol. 23: 29–54. Martín Del Rio reports that a skilled exorcist burned and exorcized various magical materials found in the bedding of a bewitched girl. Del Rio, *Investigations into Magic*, ed. and trans. P.G. Maxwell-Stuart (Manchester, 2004), 252.
4. The Spanish exorcist Pedro Ciruelo condemned all such exorcisms as superstitious. *Pedro Ciruelo's A Treatise Reproving All Superstitions and Forms of Witchcraft*, trans. Eugene A. Maio and D'Orsay W. Pearson (Cranbury, NJ and London, 1977), chs 9 and 10.
5. Jorge Cañizares-Esguerra, *Puritan Conquistadors: Iberianizing the Atlantic, 1550–1700* (Stanford, 2006), ch. 4. Demonologists usually denied the Devil dominion over nature, but in the New World he was assigned power over a world that appeared to be replete with preternatural phenomena. In the 1920s the Anglican priest Donald Ormand exorcized not only human beings but also animals, places, and objects.
6. 'Exorcism, or the Specter', in *The Colloquies of Erasmus*, trans. Craig R. Thompson (Chicago, 1965), 230–7.
7. Scot, *Discoverie of Witchcraft*, saw no difference between the methods of Catholic exorcisms and 'popish conjurations', Bk. 15, ch. 22. See also ch. 29.
8. See Kieckhefer, *Forbidden Rites*, 14. Compare the seventeenth-century definition of a conjuror as 'he that by the holy and powerful names of Almighty God invokes and conjures the Devil to consult with him, or to do some act' in Sir Edward Coke, *Institutes of the Laws of England*, Pt. 3, ch. 6, with the definition of an exorcist as one who uses 'the name of God with a design to drive Devils out of the places or bodies, which they possess' in Augustin Calmet, *An Historical, Critical, Geographical and Etymological Dictionary of the Holy Bible* (London, 1732), vol. 1: 541.
9. See Stephens, *Demon Lovers*, ch. 12 on Jean Vineti's discussion of exorcism and necromancy in the fifteenth century.
10. Twelftree, *Jesus the Exorcist*, 13.
11. Mark 1: 34.
12. David Lederer draws a distinction between public and private exorcisms in Bavaria, with the latter having been performed at shrines. But there is no way to determine how many people observed these 'routine' exorcisms. Lederer, *Madness Religion and the State*, 206–14. Heinrich Kramer reports that he spent two weeks or more taking a possessed priest to 'various shrines of the saints', *Hammer of Witches*, 348.
13. Norman Cohn, *Europe's Inner Demons: The Demonization of Christians in Medieval Christendom* (Chicago, 1993), 22–3.
14. On the use of exorcism by Jesuits to win converts to Christianity in China in the sixteenth century see Qiong Zhang, 'About God, Demons, and Miracles: The Jesuit Discourse on the Supernatural in Late Ming China', *Early Science and Medicine* 4 (1999): 4–36.

15. Pierre de Bérulle, *Traité de energumenes*, in *Les Oeuvres*, ed. F. Bouroing (Paris, 1644), 7–13. This treatise was originally published under the pseudonym of Leon d'Alexis and attached to Bérulle's *Discourse sur le possession de Marthe Brossier* (Troyes, 1599). For a full discussion of this treatise see Walker, *Unclean Spirits*, 39–42 and Ferber, *Demonic Possession and Exorcism*, 54–7.

16. Henry Holland, *A Short Discourse*, appended to *A Treatise against Witchcraft* (Cambridge, 1590), 2.

17. Ernst, *Teufelaustreibungen*, 83.

18. See for example Jean Benedicti, *La Triomphanti victoire de la vierge Marie, sur sept malins esprits, finalement chassés du corps d'une femme, dans l'Eglise des Cordeliers de Lyon* (Lyon, 1611).

19. Jonathan Pearl, *The Crime of Crimes: Demonology and Politics in France, 1560–1620*. (Waterloo, Ontario, 1999), 43; Henri Weber, 'L'Exorcisme à la fin du XVIe siècle: instrument de la contre réforme et spectacle baroque', *Nouvelle revue du seizième siècle* 1 (1983): 79–101.

20. See Marc Venard, 'Le démon controversiste' in *La controverse religieuse (XVIᵉ–XIXᵉ siècles)*, ed. Michel Peronnet (Montpelier, 1979), 45–60.

21. On the possessions at Laon, Soissons, and Paris and their connection with religious conflicts see Walker, *Unclean Spirits*, 1–42 and Ferber, *Demonic Possession and Exorcism*, 30–58.

22. Crouzet, 'A Woman and the Devil', 211 argues that the vigorous preaching and provocative processions at Laon provided a model for the tactics of the fanatical Holy League in the 1580s and 1590s.

23. The pamphlets written in the wake of the Miracle of Laon served as prototypes for many of these later works. On this literature see Backus, *Le Miracle de Laon*. The most important work written at the time of the possessions at Soissons was Charles Blendecq, *Cinq Histoires admirables, esquelles est monstré comme miraculeusement pas la vertu et puissance du sainct sacrement de l'Autel a esté chasse Beelzebub prince des diables* (Paris, 1582).

24. On the relative dearth of possessions, especially those of a collective nature, in the southern territories see Midelfort, 'The Devil and the German People', 118. The one large possession in the south, moreover, occurred in the 1490s, before the Reformation.

25. Roper, *Oedipus and the Devil*, ch. 8; quote at 180.

26. Martin Eisengrein, *Unser liebe Fraw zu Alten Oetting* (Ingolstadt, 1571). On Eisenbrein and the exorcism at Altötting see David Lederer, '"Exorzieren ohne Lizenz …": Befugnis, Skepsis, und Glauben in frühneuzeitlichen Bayern', in Waardt et al., *Dämonische Besessenheit*, 213–32; Midelfort, *History of Madness*, 318.

27. On these exorcisms see Lederer, *Madness, Religion and the State*, 230–9.

28. *Erschroeckliche gantz warhafftige Geschicht welche sich mit Apollonia Hannsen Geisslbrechts Burgers zu Spalt inn dem Eystaetter Bistumb Haussfrawn so den 20 Octobbris Anno 82. Von dem boesen Feind gar hart besessen …* (Ingolstadt, 1584).

29. Ernst, *Teufelaustreibungen*, 81–5.

30. Ibid., 84.

31. Ursula-Maria Krah, '"Von boesen Feindt / dem Teuffel / eingenommen …".': Das Motiv der Besessenheit in Flugschriften der Frühen Neuzeit', in de Waardt et al., *Dämonische Besessenheit*, 165–7.

32. Scherer, *Christliche Erinnerung*, 28–9. The grandmother, who was harshly tortured, confessed that she made a pact with the Devil and had intercourse with him in the shape of a goat or cat and often as a ball of thread.

33. Willem Frijhoff and Marijke Spies, *Dutch Culture in a European Perspective* (New York, 2004), 350–4. Protestantism made its most significant gains in the provinces of Groningen, Friesland, Drenthe, and Zeeland, where 85 per cent of the population was Protestant by 1650, but in Overijssel, Gelderland, Utrecht, and North Holland, about half the population was still Catholic. Within these provinces there were differences between the cities and the countryside, where as much as 75 per cent of the population was Catholic.

34. Hans de Waardt, *Toverij en Samenleving, Holland, 1500–1800* (The Hague, 1991), 148–9.

35. Benjamin J. Kaplan, 'Possessed by the Devil? A Very Public Dispute in Utrecht', *Renaissance Quarterly* 49 (1996): 742–3.

36. Wingens, 'Political Change', 249–62.

37. An Act against Jesuits and Seminarists (27 Elizabeth, cap. 2) declared it to be treason just to be a seminary priest or Jesuit in England. Priests were given forty days to leave England or be liable to prosecution for treason. On the basis of this statute 123 Catholic priests were executed.

38. Weston, *Autobiography of an Elizabethan*, 24–7; Walker, *Unclean Spirits*, 43–9. Walker speculates that the reason the government allowed the public exorcisms to go on for so long was that it needed informants on the Babington Plot against the government. On the inflated number of conversions in 1585–6 see Clive Holmes, 'Witchcraft and Possession at the Accession of James I: The Publication of Samuel Harsnett's *Declaration of Egregious Popish Impostures*', in *Witchcraft and the Act of 1604*, ed. John Newton and Jo Bath (Leiden, 2008), 73–4.

39. Harsnett, *Declaration of Egregious Popish Impostures*, in Brownlow, *Shakespeare, Harsnett, and the Devils of Denham*, 191–413. The Court of High Commission conducted the investigation in 1602. Harsnett dealt only with the six exorcisms performed at Denham, Buckinghamshire in 1586. On the publication of Harsnett's book see Holmes, 'Witchcraft and Possession', 69–90.

40. Harsnett, *Declaration*, 300–1, 356–7, 365–7, 407–8.

41. John Bossy, *The English Catholic Community, 1570–1850* (London, 1975), 266; Clark, *Thinking with Demons*, 390n. On the religious divisions in Lancashire, which also had the largest percentage of Nonconformists, see Jonathan Westaway and Richard D. Harrison, '"The Surey Demoniack": Defining Protestantism in 1690s Lancashire', in *Unity and Diversity in the Church*, ed. R.N. Swanson (Oxford, 1996), 264–5.

42. Taylor, *The Devil Turn'd Casuist*, 1–7.

43. Ferber, *Demonic Possession and Exorcism*, 32.

44. More, *True Discourse*, 5–6.

45. Darrell and his supporters insisted that dispossession by means of prayer and fasting was no miracle. In this respect their dispossessions differed from the miraculous exorcisms of Christ. See *A Breife Narration*, sig. E1ᵛ.

46. On Harsnett's theological orientation see Nicholas Tyacke, *Anti-Calvinists: The Rise of English Arminianism, c. 1590–1640* (Oxford, 1987), 164–5.

47. Michael MacDonald, *Witchcraft and Hysteria in Elizabethan London*, xix–xxvi.

48. Gabriele Amorth, the Vatican's chief exorcist in the late twentieth century, claims that this scriptural warrant gave a 'general power, based on prayer and faith' to all Christians. These prayers of deliverance, however, are not to be confused with actual exorcisms, which only the Church can authorize. Gabriele Amorth, *An Exorcist Tells His Story*, trans. Nicoletta V. MacKenzie (San Francisco, 1999), 43.

49. D.P. Walker argues that the main purpose of exorcism in the Middle Ages, aside from curing the demoniac, was to demonstrate the sanctity of the exorcist. 'Demonic Possession Used as Propaganda in the Later Sixteenth Century,' in *Scienze, credenze occulte livelli di cultura*, ed Leo S. Olschki (Florence, 1982), 237.

50. Scherer, *Christliche Erinnerung*, 10, cites Hieronymus, Ambrosius, and Epiphanius as the sources of this legend.

51. On the decline in the number of exorcisms at shrines in the fifteenth century see Caciola, *Discerning Spirits*, 235–6. In Modena, the tomb of the town's patron saint, Germiniano, who was renowned for his exorcisms, was the site of many exorcisms. See Matteo Duni, *Under the Devil's Spell: Witches, Sorcerers, and the Inquisition in Renaissance Italy* (Florence, 2007), 65–6.

52. See Muriel Laharie, *La Folie au moyenage XIᵉ–XIIIᵉ siècles* (Paris, 1991), 26–7.

53. See Sluhovsky, *Believe Not Every Spirit*, 51, 56.

54. Del Rio, *Investigations into Magic*, 264.

55. Heinrich Kramer claimed that one reason for the failure of exorcisms was that the faith of the exorcist was flawed. *Hammer of Witches*, 454–6.
56. Scherer, *Christliche Erinnerung*; H.C. Erik Midelfort, 'Sin, Melancholy, Obsession: Insanity and Culture in Sixteenth-century Germany', in *Understanding Popular Culture: Europe from the Middle Ages to the Nineteenth Century*, ed. Steven L. Kaplan (Berlin, New York and Amsterdam, 1984), 135.
57. Mark 16: 17.
58. More, *True Discourse*, 77.
59. Ibid., 6.
60. *Hammer of Witches*, 445. Kramer was citing the thirteenth-century exorcist William Durand's commentary on St Raymond. The preference for a 'regular priest', i.e. one in monastic orders, reflected his suspicion of the lower secular clergy, who were often uneducated and criticized for having performed superstitious exorcisms. Hence his demand that the exorcist, if not a monk, be a 'discreet' priest or a layperson 'of outstanding way of life and proven discretion'.
61. Newman, 'Possessed by the Spirit', 737; Sluhovsky, *Believe Not Every Spirit*, 41–2.
62. *Pedro Ciruelo's A Treatise Reproving All Superstitions*, ch. 8.
63. The wife of one of the Teufelsbanner who had run a thriving business in Osnabrück cut off an exorcist's head and his arm. 'Der ungluckseelige Teufels-Banner zu Osnabrück', in Hauber, *Bibliotheca*, vol. 1: 493–8.
64. Lederer, '"Exorzieren ohne Lizenz"', 231.
65. Watt, *Scourge of Demons*, 108.
66. *Rituale Romanum*, 363.
67. 'The Roman Ritual of Exorcism', in Malachi Martin, *Hostage to the Devil* (San Francisco, 1992), 460.
68. Wingens, 'Political Change', 256.
69. Ibid., 255.
70. Lea, *Materials*, 1054.
71. Keitt, *Inventing the Sacred*, 193–201.
72. Protestants had made similar claims for Queen Elizabeth of England. See William Tooker, *Charisma or the Gift of Healing* (London, 1597). Martín Del Rio challenged this claim of Protestant thaumaturgy, arguing that only Catholic monarchs had such power: *Investigations into Magic*, 81. English monarchs continued to practise 'the royal touch' until the early eighteenth century, although this gift did not specifically include the power to cast out demons.
73. Gerald Bray, ed., *The Anglican Canons, 1529–1947* (Woodbridge, Suffolk, 1998), 362–4.
74. See Thomas Freeman, 'Demons, Deviance and Defiance: John Darrell and the Politics of Exorcism in Late Elizabethan England', in *Conformity and Orthodoxy in the English Church, c. 1560–1660*, ed. Peter Lake and Michael Questier (Woodbridge, 2000), 37–43.
75. Almond, *Demonic Possession and Exorcism*, 193.
76. Souza, *Devil and the Land of the Holy Cross*, 166–7.
77. Harsnett, *Declaration of Popish Impostures*, 350, 356. The exorcists also had a woman 'squirt something by her private parts into her body, which made her very sick'. Ibid. 357; Sands, *Demon Possession*, 119.
78. Ferber, 'Possession and the Sexes', 226.
79. Watt, *Scourge of Demons*, 122–3.
80. See for example Decker, *Witchcraft and the Papacy*, 161.
81. Kieckhefer, *Forbidden Rites*, 149. One reason for the improvisation is that exorcism never became a sacrament. Maggi, *Satan's Rhetoric*, 105.
82. See [Baddeley], *The Boy of Bilson*, 34–7.
83. See for example the excerpt from the ninth-century West Frankish manuscript in Kieckhefer, *Forbidden Rites*, 144.
84. Perkins, *Damned Art of Witchcraft*, 246.
85. Peter Martyr, *Epistola Demonologica*, cited *in A Breife Narration*, sig. E1^v.

86. Kieckhefer, *Forbidden Rites*, 149; idem, *Magic in the Middle Ages* (Cambridge, 1990), 166–9.
87. Charging Satan to leave a demoniac in response to prayers was marginally more conformable to Protestant practice. In William Shakespeare, *The Comedy of Errors*, Act IV, scene iv, lines 55–6, the character Pinch says 'I charge thee, Satan, housed within this man, /To yield possession to my holy prayers.'
88. Nyndge, *A True and Fearefull Vexation*, sig. A4. In other respects the dispossession conformed to Protestant practice, with the main emphasis on prayer to God for relief.
89. Éva Szacsvay, 'Az ördög"uzés református szabályozása 1636-ban (I.)'(The Calvinist Regulation of Exorcism in 1636), in *Test, lélek, természet: Tanulmányok a népi orvoslás emlékeiből*, ed. Gábor Barna and Erzsébet Kótyuk (Budapest and Szeged, 2002), 79–92, with English summary at 92.
90. The formulae also began to get longer in the fifteenth century. Caciola, *Discerning Spirits*, 235–43. The readings, incantations, and prayers ranged from three to 135 pages. Watt, *Scourge of Demons*, 256, n. 42.
91. On the desomatization of the spiritual in Protestantism see Roper, *Oedipus and the Devil*, 177.
92. Michel de Certeau, *The Writing of History*, trans. Tom Conley (New York, 1988), 244–68. For a development of this point see Maggi, *Satan's Rhetoric*, ch. 3.
93. Even some Protestants interrogated demons. The English Dissenting minister Thomas Jolly justified the interrogation of Satan in the exorcism of Richard Dugdale by appealing to Scripture. Jolly, *The Surey Demoniack*, 24–5. Zachary Taylor argued against Jolly that there was no biblical example of conversing with demons. *The Surey Impostor*, 4–5.
94. See for example Martín Del Rio, *Disquisitionum magicarum libri sex* (Mainz, 1617), 1051–3.
95. This reluctance to trust the words of the Devil was also evident in Denmark. See Louise Nyholm Kallestrup, 'Lay and Inquisitorial Witchcraft Prosecutions in Early Modern Italy and Denmark', *Scandinavian Journal of History* 36 (2011): 269.
96. Brown *Cult of the Saints*, 108–13. The same argument was used to justify such violence in the early modern period. See Petrus Thyraeus, *Daemoniaci, hoc est: de obsessis a spiritibus daemoniorum hominibus liber unus* (Cologne, 1603), Pt. 3, ch. 46, p. 165; Lea, *Materials*, 1054.
97. Before the revival of judicial torture in the thirteenth century the violence against demoniacs was moderate and largely symbolic, such as when seven exorcists in 1169 struck the afflicted person on various parts of her body with a rod symbolizing the rod of Moses.
98. Sanchez, *In Praecepta Decalogi*, 314–15.
99. *The Journal of Montaigne's Travels in Italy by Way of Switzerland and Germany in 1580 and 1581*, ed. W.G. Waters (London, 1903), vol. 2: 111.
100. Ferber, 'The Abuse of History', 39.
101. Ferber, *Demonic Possession and Exorcism*, 101.
102. Ibid., 1.
103. For a list of such cases see http://whatstheharm.net/exorcisms.html
104. References to the torments inflicted on English demoniacs such as Margaret Muschamp recall John Foxe's *Book of Martyrs*, in which he describes the torture and torments of the martyrs who suffered for the true faith. Foxe made a specific connection between martyrdom and possession. See Diane Purkiss, 'Invasions: Prophecy and Bewitchment in the Case of Margaret Muschamp', *Tulsa Studies in Women's Literature* 17 (1998): 237–8.
105. Popular healing rituals of witch-induced possession generally did not use demonological theory to justify their violence, and they used violence against the witch, not the demoniac. Owen Davies, *Witchcraft, Magic and Culture, 1736–1951* (Manchester, 1999), 27.
106. Maggi, *Satan's Rhetoric*, 107 n. 29.

107. Decker, *Witchcraft and the Papacy*, 163.
108. Wingens, 'Political Change', 260.
109. Ernst, *Teufelaustreibungen*, 83.
110. Kramer, *Hammer of Witches*, 451–2.
111. Soergel, *Wondrous in His Saints*, 45.
112. Ernst, *Teufelaustreibungen*, 82.
113. Marescot *True Discourse*, 4.
114. Taylor, *The Devil Turn'd Casuist*, 2.
115. Kieckhefer, *Forbidden Rites*, 148–9.
116. Cameron, *Enchanted Europe*, 206, 388, n. 54.
117. Ibid., 235–7 on the proximity of such exorcisms to orthodox practice.
118. Valerie Flint, *The Rise of Magic in Early Medieval Europe* (Princeton, 1991), 154.
119. Walker, *Unclean Spirits*, pp. 46–7.
120. Giovanni Romeo, *Inquisitori, esorcisti e streghe nell'Italia della Controriforma* (Florence, 1990), 141–3.
121. Andrew Cambers, 'Demonic Possession, Literacy and "Superstition" in Early Modern England', *Past and Present* 202 (Feb. 2009): 3–10. For the argument that New England Puritans treated the Bible as a charm or a 'preternatural physical object' see Cañizares-Esguerra, *Puritan Conquistadors*, 117.
122. Roper, *Oedipus and the Devil*, 177. See also the medieval exorcism formula that commands the unclean spirit 'on account of the prayers of the Virgin Mary' to withdraw from the demoniac in the name of Jesus Christ. Claire L. Sahlin, *Birgitta of Sweden and the Voice of Prophecy* (Woodbridge, 2001), 128.
123. Wingens, 'Political Change', 255–6.
124. Maxwell-Stuart, *Occult in Early Modern Europe*, 51. Ferber, 'Cultivating Charisma', 64.
125. See Matt Baglio, *The Rite: The Making of a Modern Exorcist* (New York, 2010), 3.
126. Manfred Probst, *Besessenheit, Zauberei und ihre Heilmittel* (Münster, 2008), chs 2 and 3, gives German translations of *Flagellum daemonum* and *Fustis daemonum* with commentary.
127. The two manuals in the *Thesaurus* previously published by Polidori were *Practica exorcistarum* (Padua, 1585) and *Dispersio daemonum* (1584).
128. Polycarpus Leysern, *Vom exorcismo. Ein Christliche nötiger und in Gottes Wort wohlgegründter Bericht* (Jena, 1592), quoted in Maggi, *Satan's Rhetoric*, 121, n. 67.
129. Kramer, *Hammer of Witches*, 446–7.
130. Maggi, *Satan's Rhetoric*, 103.
131. Lederer, ' "Exorzieren ohne Lizenz", ' 213–32.
132. Souza, *Devil and the Land of the Holy Cross*, 166. The titles of the two books were *Mestre da vida* and *Opus de maleficiis*.
133. Erich Klingner, *Luther und der deutsche Volksaberglaube* (Berlin, 1912), p. 35. The account of this incident came from Frederich Staphylus, a Catholic convert, who claimed to have been present at the event. The account appears in Johann Rabus, *Christlicher und wohlgegründeter Gegenbericht yon Mirackeln und Wunderzeichen* (Dillingen, 1572), fol. 157ᵛ. See Soergel, *Wondrous in His Saints*, 141. See also Ludwig Dunte, *Decisiones mille et sex casuum conscientiae* (Lübeck, 1664), 100–3. Luther claimed that his method of dispossession was one of prayer and contempt for the Devil. He showed that contempt when he kicked a demoniac who had been brought to him. Oesterreich, *Possession*, 186–7. Lea, *Materials*, 1045; Snell, *Hexenprozess und Geistesstörung*, 116.
134. Scot, *Discoverie of Witchcraft*, 72–3. Mildred later confessed to having faked her possession and received 'condign punishment'.
135. *An account of the strange and wonderful manner*. The author claimed that Fox lost his speech and did not recover it until three years after his deliverance.
136. Thomas Jolly justified the interrogation of Satan in the exorcism of Richard Dugdale by appealing to Scripture. Jolly, *The Surey Demoniack*, 24–5.

137. See Reginald Scot's report of the exorcism of Mildred Northington at Westwell, Kent, in October 1574. *Discoverie of Witchcraft*, 72–3.
138. *The Private Diary of John Dee*, ed. James Orchard Halliwell (London, 1842), 35. On this exorcism, Dee's Catholic past, and his ordination as a Catholic priest see Glyn Parry, *The Arch-Conjuror of England. John Dee* (New Haven and London, 2011), 1–15, 28–9. It is unknown whether the nurse displayed the pathological symptoms of possession, but she had attempted to commit suicide and succeeded on the second try by cutting her throat. Cotton Mather gave a sermon on demonic power to his Boston congregation on the occasion of a suicide by a possessed woman in his neighbourhood. *Memorable Providences*, 50, 64.
139. Monter, *Witchcraft in France and Switzerland*, 59.
140. See Kaplan, 'Possessed by the Devil?', 744, on Protestant concern with failure.
141. Bodin, *Démonomanie*, Bk. 2, ch. 3. The Devil had allegedly possessed these women, most of whom were Jewish converts, because they had been baptized; Lederer, *Madness, Religion and the State*, 233.
142. For the failures of a Catholic parish priest to exorcize demoniacs in late sixteenth-century Italy, see Decker, *Witchcraft and the Papacy*, 161–2. The Dominican friar assigned to the case by the Vatican eventually succeeded in liberating those who were possessed. Ibid., 164. For a similar failure in nineteenth-century France see Harris, 'Possession on the Borders', 471–2.
143. Louis Richeome, *Trois discours pour la religion catholique et miracles et images* (Bordeaux, 1598), 193, 199, 211–12. See also Scherer, *Christliche Erinnerung*, 55–63 on Luther's exorcism and the question of whether Lutherans could effectively drive out demons.
144. Kaplan, 'Possessed by the Devil?' 742; Soergel, *Wondrous in His Saints,* 144–5; Thomas, *Religion and the Decline of Magic*, 479.
145. Giovanni Levi, *Inheriting Power: The Story of an Exorcist*, trans. Lydia G. Cochrane (Chicago, 1988), 25–8. On this point see also Harris, 'Possession on the Borders' and Mart Bax, 'Women's Madness in Medjugorje: Between Devils and Pilgrims in a Yugoslav Devotional Centre', *Journal of Mediterranean Studies* 1 (1992): 42–54.
146. Midelfort, *Exorcism and Enlightenment*, 104–5.
147. Henri F. Ellenberger, *The Discovery of the Unconscious: The History and Evolution of Dynamic Psychiatry* (New York, 1970), 13.
148. See Shaw, *Miracles in Enlightenment England*, 41–4, on the exorcisms conducted by Baptists and Independents in the second half of the seventeenth century. The restrictions imposed by the Church of England in 1604 had no authority over Dissenters.
149. Michael MacDonald, 'Religion, Social Change, and Psychological Healing in England, 1600–1800', in *The Church and Healing*, ed. W.J. Sheils (Oxford, 1982), 101–25.
150. Harris, 'Possession on the Borders', 452.

Chapter 5. Demonic Possession and Illness

1. Although the terms *illness* and *disease*, both of which bear negative connotations, are sometimes used interchangeably, they should be distinguished on the grounds that disease has traditionally referred to a somatic or organic condition, whereas illness is a broader term that can also refer to non-organic or psychological conditions. It is customary therefore to speak of *mental illness* rather than *mental disease*. The word *disorder*, also a value-laden term, is even broader than *illness*. It is the term used in the American Psychiatric Association's *Diagnostic and Statistical Manual* of 1994. See Ian Hacking, *Rewriting the Soul: Multiple Personality and the Sciences of Memory* (Princeton, 1995), 17.
2. This idea arose in Christian antiquity, giving Christians an opportunity to make war on Satan by curing disease or exorcizing the demons that caused it.

3. Early modern writers made this point frequently. See for example Bernard, *Guide to Grand-Jury Men*, 25. On Paracelsus, who in most cases attributed the deprivation of reason to natural rather than supernatural causes, see H.C. Erik Midelfort, *History of Madness*, 132–3.

4. Levi, *Inheriting Power*, 25.

5. Hippocrates, *On the Sacred Disease*, in *The Genuine Works of Hippocrates*, trans. Charles Darwin Adams (New York, 1886), vol. 2: 327–46; <http://classics.mit.edu/Hippocrates/sacred.html>

6. Owsei Tempkin, *The Falling Sickness: A History of Epilepsy from the Greeks to the Beginnings of Modern Neurology*, 2nd edn (Baltimore, 1971), 21.

7. Jean Taxil, *Traicté de l'épilepsie, maladie vulgairement appellée au pays de Provence, la gout-tete aux petits enfans* (Tournon, 1602).

8. Marescot, *True Discourse*, 14.

9. Riolanus, who attributed possession to the natural disease of melancholy, wrote in response to Fernel, arguing, 'it is not necessary for us to have recourse to a demon as the last refuge of ignorance, since we have a natural cause'. Riolanus, *Ad libros Fernelii de abditis rerum causis commentarius*, in *Opera omnia* (Paris, 1610), 134. Edward Jorden, *A Briefe Discourse of a Disease called the Suffocation of the Mother* (London, 1603).

10. Jean Fernel, *De abditis rerum causis libri duo* (Paris, 1548), Bk. 2, ch. 16. On Fernel see Charles Sherrington, *The Endeavor of Jean Fernel* (Cambridge, 1946).

11. John Cotta, *The Triall of Witchcraft* (London, 1616), 71–2.

12. *The most wonderful and true storie of a certaine witch named Alse Gooderige of Stapenhill ... As also a true report of the strange torments of Thomas Darling, a boy of thirteen years of age, that was possessed by the Devill, with his terrible fittes and terrible Apparitions by him uttered at Burton upon Trent in the County of Stafford and of his marvellous deliverance* (London, 1597).

13. For a rare diagnosis of possession as epilepsy in late seventeenth-century Lancashire see Taylor, *The Devil Turn'd Casuist*, Epistle Dedicatory.

14. Gowland, 'The Problem of Early Modern Melancholy', 77–8.

15. Roger Bartra, *Melancholy and Culture: Essays on the Diseases of the Soul in Golden Age Spain* (Cardiff, 2008), 34.

16. MacDonald, 'Religion, Social Change, and Psychological Healing' 102. Gowland, 'Problem of Early Modern Melancholy', 80, refutes the belief that the melancholy was a distinctively English disease. It was pervasive throughout Europe in the early modern period, and the authorities cited by Burton were German, French, and Italian as well as English. Nor was it restricted to Protestantism. For its influence in Spanish culture, see Bartra, *Melancholy and Culture*.

17. On the more favourable interpretation of melancholy as a source of genius see Lawrence Babb, *The Elizabethan Malady: A Study of Melancholia in English Literature from 1580 to 1642* (East Lansing, Mich., 1951), 58–60. Babb attributes this positive interpretation, which flourished in the Renaissance, to Aristotle, who viewed the condition much more favourably than Galen. The term melancholy was also used loosely or even metaphorically to describe any kind of passion or mental disturbance. André Du Laurens, the physician to Henri IV of France, distinguished between the disease of melancholy and the melancholic condition that gave rise to 'a kind of divine ravishment, commonly called *Enthousiasma*, which stirreth men up to plaie the Philosophers, Poets, and also to prophesie, in such manner, as that it may seeme to containe in it some divine parts'. Du Laurens, *A Discourse of the Preservation of the Sight: of Melancholike Diseases, of Rheumes, and of Old Age* (London, 1599; reprinted Oxford, 1938), 86. This occurred when the melancholic humour grew hot with the vapours of the blood. In 1605 the Spanish physician Alonso de Freylas distinguished between the melancholic humour that produced the good temper possessed by Plato and Socrates and the 'black melancholy caused by adustion and burning up of choler.' Bartra, *Melancholy and Culture*, 89.

18. *Rituale Romanum*, 363–96. In 1952, the wording was changed to 'those who suffer from illness, particularly mental illness'.

19. Bartra, *Melancholy and Culture*, 79.

20. The French name for hysteria was *mal de mère*.

21. Marescot, *True Discourse*, 29–30.

22. Riolanus, *Ad libros Fernelii*, 134; Mandrou, *Possession et sorcellerie*, 195–218.

23. Scot, *Discoverie of Witchcraft*, 33. Physicians claimed that melancholy mainly affected the internal mental faculty of the imagination. Gowland, 'Problem of Early Modern Melancholy', 90.

24. Scot, *Discoverie of Witchcraft* (1930 edn), 31–3. Scot denied the reality of possession but did not specifically attribute possession to melancholy. He implied the connection, however, when he explained that melancholy makes persons imagine that they are witches, adding that 'others troubled with this disease imagine many strange, incredible and impossible things'. Ibid., 30.

25. Each of the four humours was believed to have the same qualities as one of the four elements with which it was analogous. Blood, like air, was hot and moist; phlegm, like water, was moist and cold; choler, like fire, was hot and dry; and melancholy or black bile, like earth, was cold and dry. While depression was often attributed to melancholy, mania was sometimes linked to choler, madness to blood, and dementia to phlegm.

26. See for example *The Firebrand taken out of the fire, or, the Wonderful History, Case and Cure of Mrs. Drake* (London, 1654).

27. Kallendorff, *Exorcism and its Texts*, 201–2.

28. Maggi, *Satan's Rhetoric*, 108.

29. *The Great Biblical Commentary of Cornelius à Lapide*, quoted in Rodewyk, *Possessed by Satan*, 110–11.

30. Guazzo, *Compendium maleficarum*, 105.

31. Burton, *Anatomy of Melancholy*, vol. 1: 172.

32. Pietro Pomponazzi, *De naturalium effectuum causis, sive de incantationibus* in *Opera* (Basel, 1567), 6–327. This is essentially a demonological treatise. See especially pp. 6–20 on the nature of demons and 225–6 on demoniacs. For a French translation see *Les Causes des merveilles de la nature, ou les enchantements*, ed. H. Bussom (Paris, 1930).

33. Midelfort, *History of Madness*, 158. On the naturalist interpretation of Spanish physicians at the time see Bartra, *Melancholy and Culture*. See also Sluhovsky, *Believe Not Every Spirit*, 80.

34. Andrew Cunningham, '"Where There Are Three Physicians, There Are Two Atheists"', in *Medicine and Religion in the Enlightenment Europe*, ed. Ole Peter Grell and Andrew Cunningham (Aldershot, 2004), 1–4.

35. See Oskar Diethelm, 'The Medical Teaching of Demonology in the 17th and 18th Centuries,' *Journal of the History of the Behavioural Sciences* 6 (1970): 3–15. Gowland, 'Problem of Early Modern Melancholy', 92, argues that it was common for physicians to take the middle ground in the debates between naturalistic and supernatural interpretations of melancholy when they dealt with hallucinations. See also Heyd, *'Be Sober and Reasonable'*, 63–4. For the views of Italian physicians on possession see Oscar di Simplicio, *Inquisizione stregoneria medicina: Siena e il stato (1580–1721)* (Siena, 2000), 39–46.

36. *Diálogos filosofía natural y moral* (1558), Bk. 6: *De melancolía*. See Bartra, *Melancholy and Culture*, 75–6. Mercado himself identified with the naturalist position of the physician Joanicio in the dialogue, who was modelled on a medieval Arab physician.

37. Michael MacDonald, *Mystical Bedlam, Madness, Anxiety, and Healing in Seventeenth-century England* (Cambridge, 1981), 155–6, 199–200.

38. Levinus Lemnius, *De miraculis occultis naturae* (Frankfurt, 1593), 573; translated as *The Secret Miracles of Nature* (London, 1658), 86–92, 385–6, 391. In discussing the cures for

these natural disorders Lemnius also wrote that patients needed to be freed from 'poisonous vapours, *or the Devil* or fantasy'.

39. See the chapter titled 'De mania' in Pratensis, *De cerebri morbis*. This book is recognized as the first textbook on neurology.

40. Weyer, *Witches, Devils, and Doctors*, 183–9, 315. John Cotta and Girolamo Cardano agreed with Weyer that the confessions of witches were the product of melancholy. In Cardano's view the taciturn and demented women who confess to witchcraft 'differ little from those who are believed to be possessed by an evil spirit'. *De varietate rerum* (Basel, 1557), Bk. 15, ch. 80, quoted in Maxwell-Stuart, *Occult in Early Modern Europe*, 176.

41. Francisco Vallés, *De sacra philosophia* (1587).

42. Joseph Glanvill, *A Blow at Modern Sadducism* (London, 1668), 20. Glanvill was apparently echoing Burton in making this statement.

43. Burton, *Anatomy of Melancholy*, vol. 3: 330–3.

44. Jeremy Schmidt, *Melancholy and the Care of the Soul: Religion, Moral Philosophy and Madness in Early Modern Europe* (Aldershot, 2007), 47–81.

45. Sluhovsky, 'Divine Apparition', 260–1.

46. Jean Delumeau, *Sin and Fear: The Emergence of a Western Guilt Culture, 13th–18th Centuries*. trans. Eric Nicolson (New York, 1990).

47. Angus Gowland has argued that the main reason for the wide usage of melancholy as a diagnostic category in early modern Europe (and not just in cases of possession) was the development of the spiritual aspect of the ability to disturb the emotions, 'Problem of Early Modern Melancholy', 103.

48. Jean Bodin, *Démonomanie*, fol. 76v.

49. Hippolyte-Jules Pilet de Ménardière, *Traité de la mélancholie, sçavoir si elle est la cause des effets que l'on remarque dans les possédées de Loudon* (La Fleche, 1635). He wrote this credulous treatise in response to the sceptical work of Marc Duncan.

50. Certeau, *Possession at Loudun*, 129–30.

51. Diethelm, 'Medical Teaching', 6. Johann Lange, *Medicinalium epistolarum miscellanea* (Basel, 1554).

52. Gowland, 'Problem of Early Modern Melancholy', 99

53. Browne, *Religio medici*, 57. Browne did not suggest that the Devil worked through melancholy.

54. *History of the Witches of Renfrewshire*, 118.

55. On a medical revival of the theory of temperaments and therefore a version of humoral theory in modern-day pharmacology see Bartra, *Melancholy and Culture*, 15.

56. Rodewyk, *Possessed by Satan*.

57. A further inconsistency in this diagnosis was that mania, which was attributed to possession, was supposed to come from yellow bile and was associated with the choleric personality, which was also more likely to be found in men.

58. Andrew Skull, *Hysteria: The Biography* (Oxford, 2009), 7. The idea that hysteria imitates or mimics other maladies originated in Sydenham. See G. S. Rousseau, '"A Strange Pathology": Hysteria in the Early Modern World, 1500–1800', in *Hysteria Beyond Freud*, ed. Sander L. Gilman (Berkeley, 1993), 91–223.

59. It was suggested, although not by name, as a possible diagnosis of the possession of the English girl Katherine Wright in 1586.

60. Jorden *A Briefe Discourse*, title page.

61. Samuel Harsnett, however, did claim that the Catholic demoniac Richard Mainey, who had just returned from France, had long suffered from attacks of suffocation of the mother. Harsnett made this claim in the same year that Jorden published his treatise. Harsnett, *Declaration of Egregious Popish Impostures*, 237 ff.

62. National Archives, STAC 8/4/10, fol. 57; Levack, 'Possession, Witchcraft and the Law', 1629.

63. Of the three classic diseases that affected personality and/or behaviour, melancholy offered the best contemporary explanation of pathological swallowing, since it was believed that it could cause depressed people to swallow alien objects.

64. Antonio Benivieni, *De abditis nonnullis ac mirandis morborum et sanationum causis*, (Florence, 1507) ch. 8; Benivieni, *The Hidden Causes of Disease*, trans. Charles Springer (Springfield, Ill., 1954), 37. The woman also prophesied and did other things 'which went further than any violent symptoms produced by disease and even passed human power'. For Richard Baxter's reference to this case see *Certainty of the Worlds of Spirits*, 93.

65. In 1595 the demonologist Nicolas Rémy argued that the swallowing and extrusion of large objects was in fact possible in nature but did not in any way foreclose the possibility that the Devil, whose power was capable of exceeding the course of nature, could do the same. Remy, *Demonolatry*, 139–42.

66. MacDonald, *Witchcraft and Hysteria*, viii–ix.

67. On Browne's testimony at this trial see Gilbert Geis and Ivan Bunn, *A Trial of Witches: A Seventeenth-century Witchcraft Prosecution* (London, 1997), 150–5. See also Kevin Killeen, *Biblical Scholarship, Science and Politics in Early Modern England: Thomas Browne and the Thorny Place of Knowledge* (Aldershot, 2009), 143–54.

68. Cotton Mather, 'Another Brand Pluckt Out of the Burning, or More Wonders of the Invisible World', in *Narratives of the Witchcraft Cases*, 312–14.

69. Veith, *Hysteria*, 123 gives Jorden credit for transferring the seat of all hysterical manifestations to the brain. Skull, *Hysteria*, 20–1 and Rousseau, '"A Strange Pathology"', 114–15, make far less grandiose claims regarding Jorden's importance or novelty.

70. Thomas Sydenham, *Dr Sydenham's method of curing almost all diseases*, 3rd edn, (London, 1697).

71. Skull, *Hysteria*, 39–40.

72. Mark S. Micale, *Approaching Hysteria: A Disease and its Interpretations* (Princeton, 1995), 111, argues that throughout the greater part of its history hysteria has been interpreted as a wholly somatic derangement, a physical infirmity caused by a physio-pathological mechanism, whereas the current view is that it is essentially a psychological condition.

73. Rousseau, '"A Strange Pathology"', 99. Skull, however, refers to some modern cases of what was earlier called hysteria that have been diagnosed as having had physiological causes. *Hysteria*, 8.

74. Mark S. Micale, *Hysterical Men: The Hidden History of Male Nervous Illness* (Cambridge, Mass., 2008), 244. Charcot emphasized the neurological nature of hysteria, and when he died in 1893 he was still searching for the brain lesion that caused his patients' symptoms. In his obituary of Charcot, Freud took issue with his former teacher, claiming that hysteria was the result of repressed memories and ideas. Towards the end of his career Charcot admitted that hysteria could have psychic (i.e. psychological) origins. Both Freud and Pierre Janet recognized that the master had not thought only of nerve fibres in his analysis of hysteria and that he acknowledged the role played by imagination. See A.R.G. Owen, *Hysteria, Hypnosis and Healing: The Work of J.M. Charcot* (New York, 1975), 62; Sarah Ferber, 'Charcot's Demons: Retrospective Medicine and Historical Diagnosis in the Writings of the Salpêtrière School', in *Illness and Healing Alternatives in Western Europe*, ed. Marijke Gijswijt-Hofstra, Hilary Marland and Hans de Waardt (London 1997), 120–40.

75. Skull, *Hysteria*, 15. One of the implications of the view that hysteria had psychological rather than organic origins was the recognition that many cases of hysteria had in fact been misdiagnosed as organic disorders, such as epilepsy. Hence epilepsy, which clearly had neurological causes, had to be decoupled from hysteria shortly after Charcot had synthesized them. Micale, *Approaching Hysteria*, 111.

76. In 1887 Charcot and Paul Richer collaborated in the production of *Les Démoniaques dans l'art*, a retrospective study to show that hysteria was not a sickness exclusive to the nineteenth century. The images of epileptics, ecstatics, and demoniacs in the volume were also intended to show that hysteria attacked both males and females. Owen, *Hysteria, Hypnosis and Healing*, 69.

77. Paul Marie Louis Pierre Richer, *Études cliniques sur la grande hystérie ou hystéro-épilepsie*, 2nd edn (Paris, 1885). One of the recent outbreaks was the collective possession at Yaca, Spain in 1881. Ibid., 851–65.

78. D.M. Bourneville, ed., *La Possession de Jeanne Féry, religieuse professe du couvent des soeurs noires de la ville de Mons (1584)* (Paris, 1886). Bourneville included this in an introductory note to the reissue of François Buisseret's possession narrative of the case, *Histoire admirable et veritable des choses advenues a l'endroict d'une religieuse professe du couvent des Soeurs noires . . . possédée du malign espirit, & depuis delivrée* (Paris, 1586).

79. On Bourneville's role in reissuing these tracts see Sarah Ferber, 'Charcot's Demons', 120–40, and Jan Goldstein, *Console and Classify: The French Psychiatric Profession in the Nineteenth Century* (Cambridge, 1987), 370–1. Bourneville also wrote the preface to the medical doctor Samuel Garnier's account of the possession of the nuns at Auxonne: Garnier, *Barbe Buvée*. B. du Moray wrote the introduction to the reissue of the possession narrative of Françoise Fontaine in 1591: *Procès verbal fait pour délivrer une fille possédée par le malin esprit à Louviers*. (Paris, 1886).

80. Alexandre Tuetey, *La Sorcellerie dans le pays de Montbéliard au XVIIᵉ siècle* (Dole, 1886), 26.

81. Ladame, *Les Possédés et les démoniaques à Genève*, 35–41.

82. Snell, *Hexenprozess und Geistesstörung*, 118.

83. Lea, *Materials*, 1041–9.

84. See for example Emmanuel Le Roy Ladurie, *Les Paysans du Languedoc*, (2nd edn, (Paris, 1966), vol. 1: 614–56; Chadwick Hansen, *Witchcraft at Salem* (New York, 1969), 22–3, 38–40; Geis and Bunn, *A Trial of Witches*, 232; Jacqueline Carroy-Thirard, *Le Mal de Morzine: de la possession à l'hystérie (1857–1877)* (Paris, 1981), 30–40; Judith Devlin , *The Superstitious Mind: French Peasants and the Supernatural in the Nineteenth Century* (New Haven and London, 1987), ch. 5.

85. See Klass, *Mind over Mind*, 89.

86. Alfred Métraux, *Voodoo in Haiti*, trans. Hugo Charteris (New York, 1959), 120.

87. For a recent application of this retrospective diagnosis of cases of possession in early modern Württemberg see Edward Bever, *The Realities of Witchcraft and Popular Magic in Early Modern Europe: Culture, Cognition and Everyday Life* (Basingstoke, 2008), 87–92. But neither of the two cases of apparent demonic possession that Bever identified in his research serves as an example of multiple personality syndrome. A forty-three-year-old crippled woman who manifested some of the signs of possession in Stuttgart in 1695 was by Bever's admission only 'half-possessed' and did not display any signs of alternative consciousness. The more 'full-blown' case of the possession of Maria Wurster in 1642 referred to the invasion of an evil spirit but in no place identified the spirit as the Devil. Bever admits that the case had much more to do with witchcraft than diabolical possession.

88. On these lucid possessions see Oesterreich, *Possession*, 40–89.

89. For this general criticism of psycho-history see Robert Dawidorff, *The Education of Edmund Randolph* (New York, 1979), 15.

90. Onno Van der Hart, Ruth Lierens and Jean Goodwin, 'Jeanne Féry: A Sixteenth Century Case of Dissociative Disorder', *Journal of Psychohistory* 24 (1996): 1.

91. On the weakness of the boundaries of the conceptual and bodily self in early modern Europe see Natalie Zemon Davies, 'Boundaries and the Sense of Self in Sixteenth-century France', in *Reconstructing Individualism: Autonomy, Individuality, and the Self in Western Thought*, ed. Thomas C. Heller, Morton Sosna, David E. Wellbery et al. (Stanford, 1986), 53–63; Martin, *Myths of Renaissance Individualism*, 83–102.

92. Luke 8: 2; Mark 16: 9.

93. The most thorough account of this episode is Richard A. Hunter and Ida Macalpine, *Schizophrenia 1677* (London, 1956). It includes colour reproductions of the nine paintings. See also Certeau, *The Writing of History*, ch. 8.

94. Freud's paper is included in *The Standard Edition of The Complete Works Psychological Works of Sigmund Freud*, ed. James Strachey (London, 1975), vol. 19: 67–105.

95. On Freud's 'rediscovery' of sexuality in diagnosing hysteria and all other forms of neurosis see Veith, *Hysteria*, 164–8; Skull, *Hysteria*, ch. 7. On his differences with Charcot on this issue see Owen, *Hysteria, Hypnosis and Healing*, 62–3. Freud did, however, refer to Haizmann's loss of his father as an example of melancholy, thereby subscribing to the emotional, as opposed to the somatic, view of melancholy. 'Neurosis', 87.

96. Freud, 'Neurosis,' 72.

97. See Blackwell, 'Controlling the Demoniac', 437–8.

98. For a critique of Freud see Gaston Vandendriessche, *The Parapraxis in the Haizmann Case of Sigmund Freud* (Louvain and Paris, 1965), 36–43.

99. Freud did, however, suggest that the idea of the Devil as a father-substitute could be applied to 'cultural history'. Freud, 'Demonological Neurosis', 87, n. 1.

100. On Freud's ahistorical interpretation of the female breasts in Haizmann's paintings see Certeau, *The Writing of History*, 292–3. The biblical foundation for this motif was the multi-breasted statue of Diana of Ephesus that Paul confronted in his preaching to the Ephesians. Depictions of the Devil as multi-breasted were not restricted to Catholicism. See for example the engraving in *The Devill's Tryumph over Rome's Idoll* (London, 1680), facing p. 112.

101. See Vincent Crapanzano, 'Introduction', in *Case Studies in Spirit Possession*, ed. Vincent Crapanzano and Vivian Garrison (New York, 1977), 7, for the use of the term *altered states of consciousness* to define rather than analyse possessions. Adam Crabtree refers to the 'alternate consciousness paradigm' in making the distinction between possession, in which the alternate consciousness comes from a Devil that invades the body from the outside, and awareness of a second consciousness that is intrinsic to the human mind. Crabtree, *From Mesmer to Freud: Magnetic Sleep and the Roots of Psychological Healing* (New Haven and London, 1993), 86–7.

102. For the similarity between the symptoms of demoniacs and a larger group of early modern people reputedly suffering from similar psychopathological phenomena see Albrecht Burkardt, 'Besessenheit, Melancholie, und *mal de mère* in Wunderberichten fränzosischer Heiligsprechungsprozesse des frühen 17. Jahrhunderts', in Waardt et al., *Dämonische Besessenheit*, 125.

103. Erik Midelfort has argued that mentally ill patients, with whom he compares demoniacs, may not display all the symptoms of a mental illness until they are diagnosed as such. At that point they make their illnesses conform to cultural expectations. H.C. Erik Midelfort, 'Madness and the Problems of Psychological History in the Sixteenth Century', *Sixteenth Century Journal* 12 (1981): 11.

104. Many of these are included in Louis-Florentin Calmeil, *De la folie, considérée sous le point de vue pathologique, philosophique, historique et judiciaire*, 2 vols (Paris, 1845). Moshe Sluhovsky, '*Devil in the Convent*', 1382–5, has identified more than fifty episodes in Catholic convents. For mass possessions in sixteenth-century Germany see Midelfort, 'Devil and the German People', 124.

105. Garnier used the term in his account of the possession of the nuns at Auxonne between 1658 and 1663. See Garnier, *Barbe Buvée*, vi.

106. The anonymous French doctor who submitted a medical brief to Philibert de la Marre regarding the possessions at Louviers in 1647 made this point forcefully. Mandrou, *Possession et sorcellerie*, 211–12.

107. Hacking, *Rewriting the Soul*, 187.

108. Scholars sometimes use the term mass hysteria to describe such epidemics, but in so doing they are using it to designate what are often referred to as moral panics, not the medical disease of hysteria that Jorden, Willis, Sydenham, Charcot, Janet, and Freud made the subject of their research. See Rousseau, '"A Strange Pathology"', 98, on the invention of the term mass hysteria in the nineteenth century. For the use of the term 'collective hysteria' in the medical sense of the word see Devlin, *Superstitious Mind*, 129.

109. Crabtree, *Multiple Man*, ch. 11.

110. The possessed behaviour of the Camisards inspired similar manifestations of spirit possession among Pietists in Germany, Methodists in England, Calvinists in Scotland, and various groups of Protestants, most notably the Shakers, in North America. Camisard influence, which reached Sweden and Finland in the 1760s, formed part of what Clarke Garrett calls a 'prophetic diaspora' after the suppression of the Camisard Revolt in Lower Languedoc in 1710. Clarke Garrett, *Spirit Possession and Popular Religion: From the Camisards to the Shakers* (Baltimore, 1987), ch. 2.

111. George Rosen, 'Psychopathology in the Social Process: Dance Frenzies, Demonic Possession, Revival Movements and Similar So-called Psychic Epidemics: An Interpretation', *Bulletin of the History of Medicine* 36 (1962): 13–44; Garrett, *Spirit Possession, passim*. See also Rubin, *Religious Melancholy*. On the dancing manias in Germany see Midelfort, *History of Madness*, 32–49. Some commentators argued that demoniacs were really victims of chorea or St Vitus Dance, which was the naturalist explanation for the dancing manias.

112. Dekker, *Witchcraft and the Papacy*, 163.

113. Christine D. Worobec, *Possessed: Women, Witches, and Demons in Imperial Russia* (DeKalb, Ill., 2001), 3–7.

114. Midelfort, *History of Madness*, 132.

115. Marc Duncan, *Discours sur la possession des Religieuses ursulines de Loudun* (Saumur, 1634), 13–15. Duncan was principal of the college of Saumur at the time. He told the duke of Lauderdale how he discovered that one of the nuns was faking her possession by holding a demoniac's arm and challenging the devils in Hell to wrest it from his hand. See Baxter *Certainty of the Worlds of Spirits*, 91.

116. Duncan, *Discours*, 14. See also Michel Certeau, *Possession at Loudun*, 135–7. Father Jean-Joseph Surin, the exorcist at Loudun, claimed that demons Leviathan and Iscaaron and others leapt from Sister Jeanne to him during exorcism. Ferber 'Possession and the Sexes', 224–6 and n. 56; Webster, '(Re)possession of Dispossession', 101.

117. Pomponazzi, *Les causes des merveilles de la nature*, 222–5. Pomponazzi developed his theory of imagination (*phantasia*) in his treatise on the immortality of the soul. For Pilet de la Ménardèrie's claim in *Traité de la mélancholie* (1635) that 'the philosophers of the sect of Pomponazzi' were responsible for the 'ridiculous' claim that the nuns at Loudun were melancholic see Certeau, *Possession at Loudun*, 129–30.

118. Benito Jerónimo Feijóo, 'Demoniacas,' in *Teatro Critico Universal* (Madrid, 1779), vol. 8: 76–151.

119. Kaplan, 'Possessed by the Devil.'

120. Maria Tausiet, 'The Possessed of Tosos (1812–1814): Witchcraft and Popular Justice during the Spanish Revolution', in Waardt et al., *Dämonische Besessenheit*, 263–80.

121. Samuel Pfeifer, 'Belief in Demons and Exorcism in Psychiatric Patients in Switzerland,' *British Journal of Medical Psychology* 67 (1994): 247–58. See also idem, 'Psychopathologie und Kausalattribution: Besessenheit als Metapher für psychisches Leiden', in Waardt et al., *Dämonische Besessenheit*, 293–305.

Chapter 6. The Performance of the Possessed

1. Peter Brown, *Society and the Holy*, 122 argues that exorcisms in late antiquity were duets between the possessed and the non-possessed in which each side had a role and each unconsciously followed a score.

2. L. Michael White, *Scripting Jesus: The Gospels in Rewrite* (New York, 2010).

3. Brown, *Cult of the Saints*, ch. 6.

4. Newman, 'Possessed by the Spirit', 734.

5. Certeau, *Possession at Loudun*, 85–9.

6. Weber, 'L'Exorcisme à la fin du XVIe siècle', 79, 101.

7. Walker, *Unclean Spirits*, 23. Inside the cathedral at Laon, a scaffold was erected at the intersection of the transept. Distinguished spectators were seated in the upper gallery

of the rood screen and in the side galleries of the transept while the common people were accommodated down below in the transept. Weber, 'L'Exorcisme', 85.

8. Walker, *Unclean Spirits*, 29.
9. On the role of the audience playing parts in the possession see Roper, *Oedipus and the Devil*, 175.
10. Foucault, *Abnormal Lectures*, 211. For the argument that the human body became the focal point of political and cultural activity in the early modern 'somatic society' see Bryan Turner, 'Theoretical Developments in the Sociology of the Body', *Australian Cultural History* 13 (1994): 27.
11. *A Breife Narration*, sig. B.
12. Snape, '"The Surey Impostor"', 101–2.
13. H.C. Erik Midelfort, 'Catholic and Lutheran Reactions to Demon Possession in the Late Seventeenth Century', *Daphnis* 15 (1986): 643–8. Mayer was a forty-three-year-old Catholic.
14. MacDonald, 'Religion, Social Change, and Psychological Healing', 105.
15. Demos, *Entertaining Satan*, 128.
16. Darrell claimed that sixty people witnessed the dispossession of William Somers. John Darrell, *A True Narration of the Strange and Grevous Vexation by the Devil* (1600), 18. See Ferber, *Demonic Possession and Exorcism*, 36, on the exorcism of two Celestine nuns before hundreds of people with the purpose of supporting the league during its rise.
17. Nyndge, *A True and Fearefull Vexation*, sig. B1. The depiction of male actors in female dress on the title page may have reflected the claim by the Cambridge Puritan John Greene that the Devil instituted plays, that the Bible forbade transvestitism of male actors, and that a woman in Christian antiquity left the theatre 'possessed of the devil'. The Devil justified his entrance into this woman's body because 'he found her in his own house'. I. G., *A Refutation of the Apology for Actors* (London, 1615), 44.
18. Stephen Greenblatt, 'Loudun and London', *Critical Inquiry* 12 (1986): 330; idem, *Shakespearean Negotiations: The Circulation of Social Energy in Renaissance England* (Berkeley, 1988), 106–11, 116.
19. See Jan Frans van Djkhutzen, 'Theatricality, Inwardness and the Demonic in Ben Jonson', in Waardt et al., *Dämonische Besessenheit*, 145–62.
20. *The Devil is an Ass*, Act V, scene V: 25–8.
21. Ibid., Act V, scene iii: 1–8.
22. *King Lear* (Folio text) Act III, scene iv: 108–33.
23. Greenblatt, *Shakespearean Negotiations*, 118.
24. *Twelfth Night*, Act III, scene iv: 101, 127–8; Act IV, scene ii: 5–6; Greenblatt, *Shakespearean Negotiations*, 115. Kallendorf, *Exorcism and its Texts*, 33–5, 216, n. 70.
25. Midelfort, 'Catholic and Lutheran Reactions to Demon Possession', 642.
26. Kallendorf, *Exorcism and its Texts*, 52–6.
27. Métraux, *Voodoo in Haiti*, 126–9. Métraux admits that those frightened hysterics in the past who thought themselves victims of devils 'certainly drew the devilish part of their personality from the folklore in which they lived' but their circumstances differed from those of the possessed in twentieth-century Haiti.
28. See however Michel Leiris, *La Possession et ses aspects théâtraux chez les Éthiopiens de Gondar* (Paris, 1958), on the theatrical dimension of exorcisms of evil spirits who had possessed the Ethiopians of Gondar.
29. On belly speech see Scot, *Discoverie of Witchcraft*, Bk. 7, ch. 1 and Thomas Ady, *A Candle in the Dark* (London, 1655), 78. In *Gargantua and Pantagruel*, Bk. 4, 58, François Rabelais calls those referred to as *ventriloqui* as 'soothsayers, enchanters, cheats, who gulled the mob, and seemed not to speak and give answers from the mouth, but from the belly'. On taking drugs to induce convulsions see *The Case of Mrs. Mary Catharine Cadiere against the Jesuit Father John Baptist Girard* (London, 1732), vi.
30. Hédelin's book on dramatic theory, *La Pratique de théâtre*, was published in 1657. On Hédelin's visit to Loudun and the duchesse d'Aiguillon's defence of him against the

charge that he was a magician, see Amy Wygant, *Medea, Magic, and Modernity in France: Stages and Histories, 1553–1797* (Aldershot, 2007), 151–61.

31. Walker, *Unclean Spirits*, 33–7.
32. One of the ironies of this episode is that Holland, whose sceptical views on demonic possession and exorcism were similar to those of Samuel Harsnett and John Deacon, refused to testify on behalf of his sister-in-law at her trial in the Star Chamber. Levack, 'Possession, Witchcraft and the Law', 1635.
33. National Archives, STAC 8/4/10, fol. 21. Both Harding and Holland were members of the commission that prepared the King James Version of the Bible, so they were fully familiar with the episodes of possession in the New Testament.
34. Huntington Library, EL MS 5955/2. Examination of Murray by Lord Ellesmere, 29 July 160.
35. For those audiences that accepted the reality of the possession they witnessed, the theatrical production was of course not fictional but one that they themselves lived. See Leiris, *La Possession et ses aspects théâtraux*, 89–96.
36. [Jesse Bee et al.], *The Most Wonderful and True Storie of a certaine Witch named Alse Gooderige . . . As also a true report of the strange torments of Thomas Darling, a boy of thirteen years of age, that was possessed by the Devill, with his terrible Fittes and terrible Apparitions by him uttered at Burton upon Trent in the County of Stafford and of his marvellous deliverance* (London, 1597). Denison wrote the preface. On the composition of this pamphlet see Samuel Harsnett, *A Discovery of the Fraudulent Practises*, sig. Mm^v–Mm2^v.
37. Two other Protestant demoniacs who displayed uncharacteristic holiness were Mary Glover and Margaret Muschamp. See Purkiss, 'Invasions: Prophecy and Bewitchment in the Case of Margaret Muschamp', 236.
38. For two different analyses of this case see Almond, *Demonic Possession and Exorcism*, 150–4 and Walker, *Unclean Spirits*, 52–6; quote at 56.
39. Brown, *Immodest Acts*. The investigation eventually determined that the Devil had deceived her.
40. Ibid., 126–7.
41. B.J. Biddle and E.J. Thomas, eds, *Role Theory: Concepts and Research* (New York, 1966); R. H. Turner, 'Role Taking, Role Standpoint, and Reference Group Behavior', *American Journal of Sociology* 61 (1956): 316–28.
42. *The Most Strange and Admirable Discoverie of the three witches of Warboys, arraigned, convicted and executed at the last assises at Huntington, for the bewitching of the five daughters of Robert Throckmorton, esquire, and divers other persons, with sundry Divellish and grievous torments* (London, 1593). See Walker, *Unclean Spirits*, 49–52 and Almond, *Demonic Possession and Exorcism* 71–4 for commentary on this case of possession.
43. The girls were apparently responsible for naming these spirits. Samuel confessed that their names were Pluck, Catch, and White.
44. Garnier, *Barbe Buvée*. See also Garnot, *Le diable au couvent*.
45. Asti Hustvedt, *Medical Muses: Hysteria in Nineteenth-century Paris* (New York, 2011), 89–94. See also Elaine Showalter, *Hystories: Hysterical Epidemics and Modern Media* (New York, 1997), ch. 7; Georges Didi-Huberman, *Invention of Hysteria: Charcot and the Photographic Iconography of the Salpêtrière*, trans. Alisa Hartz (Cambridge, Mass., 2003), 241–3.
46. Walker, *Unclean Spirits*, 34.
47. Certeau, *Possession at Loudun*, 138–9.
48. For Anne Gunter's use of the Throckmorton possession narrative see James Sharpe, *The Bewitching of Anne Gunter* (London, 1999), 7–8, 62. In the trial of the witches accused of causing his daughter's possession, Brian Gunter objected to a procedural decision of the judge on the grounds that it denied his daughter 'that justice which Mr Throckmorton's children had'. National Archives, STAC 8/4/10, fol. 9v.
49. *A Breife Narration*, sig. A3^v. Somers had also read the tract on the possession of the Throckmorton children.

50. Lederer, *Madness, Religion and the State*, 233.
51. Norton, *In the Devil's Snare*, 52.
52. See Cambers, 'Demonic Possession', 3–35.
53. Harsnett, *Declaration of Egregious Popish Impostures*, 185, 213, 217.
54. *An Answer of a Letter from a Gentleman in Fife to a Nobleman* ([Edinburgh] 1705); *A Just Reproof to the False Reports and Unjust Calumnies Dropt in Two Late Pamphlets* (Edinburgh, 1705).
55. Baddeley, *The Boy of Bilson*, 61–2.
56. Raiswell, 'Faking It', 29–30.
57. *An Answer of a Letter from a Gentleman in Fife to a Nobleman*; *A Just Reproof to the False Reports and Unjust Calumnies Dropt in Two Late Pamphlets*; Levack, *Witch-hunting in Scotland*, 146–9.
58. Certeau, *Possession at Loudun*, 36.
59. *The Case of Mrs. Mary Catharine Cadiere*.
60. Midelfort, 'The Devil and the German People', 110, 118.
61. Ethan Watters, 'The Americanization of Mental Illness', *New York Times Magazine*, 10 Jan. 2010: 40–5. See also Ethan Watters, *Crazy Like Us: The Globalization of the American Psyche* (New York, 2010).
62. Robert W. Scribner, *Popular Culture and Popular Movements in Reformation Germany* (London, 1987), 13.
63. Corporation Act of 1661 and Test Act of 1673.
64. *Spinoza: The Letters*, trans. Samuel Shirley (Indianapolis, 1995), letter 76, December 1675.
65. On the novelty of this technique see Walker, *Unclean Spirits*, 23.
66. Darrell, *A True Narration*, 9.
67. Barrow, *The Lord's Arm Stretched*, 8.
68. Mather, *Memorable Providences*, 23–4, par. 28.
69. Ibid., 16–17 par. 20. The books she could not read included a catechism, named *Milk for Babes*, once owned by Cotton Mather's grandfather, and the *Assembly's Catechism*.
70. Roper, *Oedipus and the Devil*, 178–9.
71. Nyndge, *A True and Fearefull Vexation*, fol. A4
72. Swan, *A True and Breife Report, of Mary Glovers Vexation*. See also *An account of the strange and wonderful manner in which John Fox, who some time ago lived near Nottingham, was sorely afflicted with an Evil Spirit*.
73. Nathaniel Holmes, *Plain Dealing* (London, 1652). See also the account of the possession of Hannah Crump, of Warwick, appended to Barrow, *The Lord's Arm Stretched Out*, 17–20. In his possession dialogue with Satan, however, the young aspiring Puritan saint Thomas Darling reportedly said, 'Do your worst, Satan, you cannot touch our soul.' Almond, *Demonic Possession and Exorcism*, 190.
74. Sophie Houdard, 'Mystics or Visionaries? Discernment of Spirits in the First Part of the Seventeenth Century in France', in Klaniczay and Pócs, *Communicating with the Spirits*, 74–5.
75. In response to the charge of being possessed by Beelzebul, Christ claimed that he who blasphemes against the Holy Spirit is guilty of an eternal sin. The blasphemy in this case was the claim that Christ had an unclean spirit. For a Puritan discussion of this blasphemy see Darrell, *An Apologie, or Defence of the Possession of William Sommers*, sig. Aii^v.
76. John Foxe's narrative of this possession, titled 'Mr Brigges Temptation', is included in British Library, Harley MS 590, fols. 6–63. Kathleen Sands, *An Elizabethan Lawyer's Possession by the Devil: The Story of Robert Brigges* (New York, 2002), provides a full account. Brigges misunderstood the lecture, thinking that all sins were unforgivable.
77. Mather, *Memorable Providences*, 48. Italics mine.
78. *The Zurich Letters*, ed. Hastings Robinson, vol. 1 (Cambridge, 1842), 303.
79. Kaplan, 'Possessed by the Devil?', 742–3. For Willemsz's reading of this pamphlet a century later see Frijhoff, *Wegen van Evert Willemsz*, 287–9.
80. *A True Report of the Strange Torments of Thomas Darling*, in Almond, *Demonic Possession and Exorcism*, 187.

81. Ellenberger, *Discovery of the Unconscious*, 18–19.
82. Benedicti, *La Triomphanti victoire de la vierge Marie*.
83. Cervantes, *Devil in the New World*, 98–102.
84. Ibid., 101–2.
85. Margo Todd, *The Culture of Protestantism in Early Modern Scotland* (New Haven and London, 2002), 291–5; Brian P. Levack, 'The Prosecution of Sexual Crimes in Early Eighteenth-century Scotland', *Scottish Historical Review* 89 (2010): 172–93.
86. Thomas N. Tentler, *Sin and Confession on the Eve of the Reformation* (Princeton, 1977), 100–1, 141–8.
87. University of Nottingham, MS MiF 10/4. 'A note of the syght in Nottingham by one possessed the 5th of November 1597'. Darrell arrived at Nottingham on 5 Nov. and met Somers for the first time that day. The Throckmorton girls and maidservants, who during their possession repudiated any sign of Protestant holiness, had no problem engaging in the Puritan vice of playing cards.
88. Marion Gibson, *Possession, Puritanism and Print: Darrell, Harsnett, Shakespeare and the Elizabethan Exorcism Controversy* (London, 2006), 86–7.
89. Jolly, *The Surey Demoniack*, 210; Taylor, *The Surey Impostor*.
90. *The Confessions of Madeleine Bavent*, 1–2. This is a translation and edition of Charles Desmarets, *Histoire de Magdelaine Bavent, religieuse du Monastère du St Louis de Louviers* (Paris, 1652), which included what Desmarets claimed was Bavent's autobiographical account of the entire episode.
91. Desmarets, *Histoire*, 66.
92. Almond, *Demonic Possession and Exorcism*, 193.
93. For the centrality of this theme in Catholic demonology see Stephens, *Demon Lovers*, *passim*.
94. *A True and Impartial Relation of the Informations against Three Witches* (London, 1682), 29.
95. Gowdie also confessed that the youngest and lustiest women had more pleasure copulating with the Devil than with their husbands. Emma Wilby, *The Visions of Isobel Gowdie: Magic, Witchcraft and Dark Shamanism in Seventeenth-century Scotland* (Sussex, 2010), 46–7.
96. See for example the confession of Janet Barker to sex with the Devil in the National Archives of Scotland, JC 2/8, pp. 347–9.
97. See Thomas Potts, *The Wonderfull Discoverie of the Witches in the County of Lancaster* (London, 1612).
98. C. H. Chajes, 'Judgments Sweetened: Possession and Exorcism in Early Modern Jewish Culture', *Journal of Early Modern History* 1 (1997): 124–69.
99. The claim of Keller, *The Hammer and the Flute*, 200 that the belief was as old as the Hebrew Bible is not supported by the reference to 1 Samuel 18: 10, which says that God rushed an unidentified evil spirit upon Saul.

Chapter 7. The Demoniac in Society

1. Rousseau, 'A Strange Pathology', 94, 98, 109.
2. Ladame, *Les Possédés et les démoniaques a Genève*, 30–1.
3. Midelfort, 'The Devil and the German People', 118.
4. At Utrecht the municipality gave two demoniacs weekly alms. Kaplan, 'Possessed by the Devil?', 750. In France the alms were paid voluntarily, as in the case of Marthe Brossier. A poor Swedish demoniac who was convicted of fraud in 1708 pretended to be possessed so that she might receive food and shelter from sympathetic villagers. Olli, 'The Devil's Pact', 112.
5. Charcot believed, however, that a predisposition to hysteria was acquired by heredity. There is a consensus in modern medicine that a neurological or biochemical abnormality, which is usually inherited, provides the precondition or predisposing cause of

mental illness or some other psychosomatic disorder. Ian Hacking, *The Social Construction of What?*, 118.

6. Micale, *Hysterical Men*, 239–40, 245–7.
7. Modern medical scholars also think that a social or possibly a socio-organic condition provides the trigger or precipitant of mental illness.
8. Foucault, *Abnormal Lectures*, 205; Certeau, *Possession at Loudun*, 4. Their argument was shaped by their primary focus on the group possessions in French convents.
9. Levack, 'Possession, Witchcraft and the Law'.
10. Levack, *Witch-Hunt in Early Modern Europe*, 141–2.
11. Midelfort, 'Sin, Melancholy, Obsession', 139–40. Eleven of the sixteen group possessions were exclusively female, two were male, and three were mixed.
12. Sluhovsky, 'Divine Apparition', 1044. For the testimony of one lay French male demoniac, Bernard Girault, a boy of twelve or thirteen, against witches in Berry in 1582 see Jacques-Chaquin and Préaud, *Les Sorciers du carroi de Marlou*, 55–62.
13. Watt, *Scourge of Demons*, 256, n. 40; Feijoo, 'Demoniacos', 142–5.
14. Worobec, *Possessed*, 10–11. At this time the gender neutral word for shrieker, *klikusha* was replaced by the female *klikushi*, indicating that possession was a feminine trait.
15. I.M. Lewis, *Ectastic Religion: An Anthropological Study of Spirit Possession and Shamanism* (Baltimore, 1971), 30–5.
16. Rémy Pichard, *Admirable vertu des saincts exorcism sur les princes d'enfer possédants réellement vertueuse demoiselle Elisabeth de Ranfaing* (Nancy, 1622); Barthélemy Pardoux, *De morbis animi liber* (Lyon, 1639), 34.
17. Hallett, *Witchcraft, Exorcism and the Politics of Possession*, 1–20, 49–92.
18. Schutte, *Aspiring Saints*, 68–9. Scaglia also criticized the 'simple and ignorant' confessors and spiritual directors of these aspiring saints for fostering and publishing their revelations and prophecies.
19. Cervantes, *Devil in the New World*, 102–6.
20. Ibid. See also Sluhovsky, *Believe Not Every Spirit*, ch. 5.
21. For some of these common symptoms see Joseph von Görres, *Die Christliche Mystik*, vol. 4 (Graz, 1960), 138–298.
22. Demos, *Entertaining Satan*, 164–5; Bynum, *Holy Feast and Holy Fast*; Bell, *Holy Anorexia*, 148–50.
23. Watt, *Scourge of Demons*, 6.
24. Sluhovsky, *Believe Not Every Spirit*, 110. On the sexual dimension of exorcism see Roper, *Oedipus and the Devil*, 188–92.
25. Des Niau, *The History of the Devils of Loudun*, in Levack, *Sourcebook*, 253; Antoine Louis Daugis, *Traité sur la magie, le sortilege, les possessions, obsessions et maleficies* (Paris, 1732), 158.
26. Jeannine Blackwell, 'German Narratives of Women's Divine and Demonic Possession and Supernatural Vision 1555–1800: A Bibliography', in *Women in German Yearbook: Feminist Studies in German Literature & Culture*, 16 (2000): 244.
27. See Karlsen, *Devil in the Shape of a Woman*, 336, n. 19. Arthur Miller's play, *The Crucible*, and Ken Russell's film, *The Devils*, have contributed to this misconception.
28. See Ferber, 'The Abuse of History?', 29–41.
29. For a similar sexual dimension in Jewish possessions at the same time see Bilu, 'The Taming of the Deviants', 45–55.
30. Brown, *Immodest Acts*, 202, explains how psychologists might interpret Benedetta's experience as a manifestation of multiple personality disorder but does not subscribe to such an interpretation. The fact that Benedetta relieved her guilt by claiming that it was either an angel or Jesus Christ rather than she herself who was having sexual relations with Sister Bartolomea makes an interpretation based on multiple personality disorder highly unlikely. Attributing the possession to Jesus, however, does reflect Benedetta's immersion in the religious culture the convent, in which it was believed that nuns became brides of Christ.

31. See Giovanni Romeo, *Esorcisti, confessori e sessualità femminile nell'Italia della Controriforma* (Florence, 1988), 86–127, 192–4.

32. *Confessions of Madeleine Bavent*, 27, 67. For other expressions of guilt see for example 14–15, 21, 56, 94. Her account of the rape, which Bavent claimed was the only time the two had sexual intercourse, appears on p. 18.

33. Sluhovsky, *Believe Not Every Spirit*, 261.

34. *Procès verbal fait pour délivrer une fille possédée*, 32–5; Walker and Dickermann, 'The Haunted Girl'.

35. The new road to mysticism was based on the premise that passive contemplation led to perfection. The danger implicit in this approach was that by becoming passive the soul became empty and therefore was vulnerable to demonic possession, while the body, which was detached from the soul, could perform sinful acts, especially those of a sexual nature, which did not affect the soul.

36. In seventeenth-century England the antinomians who attracted the most attention, consternation, and opprobrium were known as Ranters, who also declared their freedom from all moral laws. See A.L. Morton, *The World of the Ranters* (London, 1970). As with the Spanish *alumbrados*, authorities greatly exaggerated their numbers, their religious radicalism, and the level of their sexual deviance. Jules Michelet claimed that illuminism taught that 'You must kill sin by being made humble and lost to all sense of pride through sin.' Michelet, *La Sorcière: The Witch of the Middle Ages*, trans. L.J. Trotter (London, 1863), 280.

37. On the changing and complex nature of illuminism in Spain see Keitt, *Inventing the Sacred*, 78–86. See Ferber, *Demonic Possession and Exorcism*, 92–4 for accusations of illuminism made against Madeleine Bavent and her spiritual advisers during the possessions at Louviers in 1643–7.

38. Julio Caro Baroja, *The World of the Witches* (Chicago, 1965), 136–7. Doña Teresa also said that she had never heard Calderón say such things, which raises the question whether he too was falsely accused. The different accounts of the possessions at San Plácido recommend that one exercise caution in attributing possessions in convents to the influence of illuminist or pre-quietist ideas. For speculation on this issue see Sluhovsky, *Believe Not Every Spirit*, 139. See also Calmeil, *De la Folie*, vol. 2: 3ff. and Oesterreich, *Possession*, 41.

39. Alison Weber, 'The Inquisitor, the Flesh, and the Devil: Alumbradismo and Demonic Possession', in Waardt et al., *Dämonische Besessenheit*, 177–91.

40. Benito Feijoo's argument that the male demoniacs in biblical antiquity, unlike their female counterparts in the eighteenth century, were genuinely possessed made unwarranted assumptions about the authenticity of both sets of possessions. Tausiet, 'From Illusion to Disenchantment', 54.

41. Sluhovsky, *Believe Not Every Spirit*, 138.

42. Ferber, 'Possession and the Sexes', 218–23, 232–3.

43. Maggi, *In the Company of Demons*, 2. The belief that some demons preferred the companionship of men was grounded in the literature of classical antiquity.

44. Caciola, *Discerning Spirits*, 137–9.

45. Midelfort, 'The Devil and the German People', 110. The number of witches was also higher in the Catholic territories.

46. There was some disagreement as to when adolescence ended, especially since it was usually referred to as 'youth', which could last until twenty-five or twenty-eight. See Paul Griffith, *Youth and Authority: Formative Experiences in England, 1560–1640* (Oxford, 1996), 19–34; Ilana Krausman Ben-Amos, *Adolescence and Youth in Early Modern England* (New Haven and London, 1994), 9, 11, distinguishes between adolescence in the early teens and youth in the later teens and twenties.

47. Waardt, *Toverij en Samenleving, Holland*, 236–7. The possessions occurred in Amsterdam in 1566, Enkhuizen between 1617 and 1619, Delft in the early seventeenth century, and Hoorn in 1670 or 1672. All the demoniacs were boys except in Hoorn, where the sexes were mixed. Instead of the orphans in Amsterdam and Hoorn

being exorcized, they were placed in foster homes. See Weyer, *Witches, Devils, and Doctors*, 301–2 on Amsterdam and Rome, and Bekker, *Die bezauberte Welt*, vol. 4: 219–27 on Amsterdam and Hoorn. On the orphan demoniacs at Rome see also Johann Lange, *Medicinalium epistolarum miscellanea*.

48. Acts 16: 16–18.
49. Webster, '(Re)possession of Dispossession', 99. The remaining two demoniacs were aged thirty and thirty-three respectively. Since both of the older demoniacs were female, the profile of this group supports the generalization that the large majority of demoniacs were subordinate members of society. The site of the possessions was the household of a gentry family, but the older women were a poor kinswoman of the family and an unmarried servant.
50. Quoted in Ferber, 'Possession and the Sexes', 222.
51. Mather, *Memorable Providences*, 48.
52. Gustav Henningsen, *The Witches' Advocate: Basque Witchcraft and the Spanish Inquisition (1609–1614)* (Reno, Nev., 1980), ch. 10; Lawrence Wright, *Remembering Satan* (New York, 1994).
53. Susan E. Devine, *Out of Darkness: Exploring Satanism and Ritual Abuse* (New York, 1992).
54. J.A. Sharpe, 'Disruption in the Well-ordered Household: Age, Authority and Possessed Young People', in *The Experience of Authority in Early Modern England*, ed. Paul Griffiths, Adam Fox and Steve Hindle (Basingstoke, 1996), 200.
55. In England references to youth were far more common than to adolescence. There was, however, no consensus regarding the chronological boundaries of youth. See Paul Griffiths, *Youth and Authority: Formative Experiences in England 1560–1640* (Oxford, 1996), 19–34.
56. Italian ecclesiastical authorities were especially concerned about the sexuality of young novices and for this reason objected to their sleeping together in the same bed. See Craig A. Monson, *Nuns Behaving Badly: Tales of Music, Magic, Art, and Arson in the Convents of Italy* (Chicago, 2010), 136.
57. Sharpe, 'Disruption in the Well-ordered Household', 191.
58. Skull, *Hysteria*, 7.
59. See Keller, *The Hammer and the Flute*, for a discussion of how such an agency can be achieved in modern cases of possession.
60. Oesterreich, *Possession*; I.M. Lewis, 'Spirit Possession and Deprivation Cults', *Man*, n.s. 1 (1966): 307–29; idem, *Ecstatic Religion*. See also Lesley A. Sharp, *The Possessed and the Dispossessed: Spirits, Identity and Power in a Madagascar Migrant Town* (Berkeley, 1993); idem, 'The Power of Possession in Northwest Madagascar: Contesting Colonial and National Hegemonies', in *Spirit Possession, Modernity and Power in Africa*, ed. Heike Behrend and Ute Luig (Oxford, 1999), 3–19.
61. Nicholas P. Spanos and Jack Gottlieb, 'Demonic Possession, Mesmerism, and Hysteria: A Social Psychological Perspective on their Historical Interactions', *Journal of Abnormal Psychology* 88 (1979): 535.
62. On the agency of demoniacs, especially during their exorcisms, see Robert Rapley, *A Case of Witchcraft: The Trial of Urbain Grandier* (Montreal, 1998), 155 and Sluhovsky, 'Divine Apparition,' 1044–6.
63. Newman 'Possessed by the Spirit', 760.
64. Harris, 'Possession on the Borders'.
65. See Catherine-Laurence Maire, *Les Possédées de Morzine, 1857–1873* (Lyon, 1981) for the narrative of the entire episode.
66. Harris, 'Possession on the Borders', 466.
67. Ibid., 453–4.
68. See Henri Bouchet, *Relation sur l'épidémie de Morzine* (Lyon, 1899); Maire, *Les Possédés de Morzine*, 21–2.
69. Karlsen, *Devil in the Shape of a Woman*, 244–9.
70. Victor Turner, *The Ritual Process: Structure and Anti-Structure* (Chicago, 1969), ch. 5; Karlsen, *Devil in the Shape of a Woman*, 341, n. 66.

71. Karlsen, *Devil in the Shape of a Woman*, 249.
72. Kaplan, 'Possessed by the Devil?', 742.
73. Ferber, *Demonic Possession and Exorcism*, 122.
74. Sharpe, *The Bewitching of Anne Gunter*, ch. 2.
75. Kaplan, 'Possessed by the Devil,' 749.
76. See Devlin, *Superstitious Mind*, 130–1 for a similar analysis of the nineteenth-century French possessions.

Chapter 8. The Demoniac and the Witch

1. Vineti, *Tractatus contra demonum invocatores*, Pt. 4; Stephens, *Demon Lovers*, 326.
2. Hans Peter Broedel, *The* Malleus Maleficarum *and the Construction of Witchcraft: Theology and Popular Belief* (Manchester, 2003), 56–7. The story in the *Malleus* of a priest possessed as a result of a witch's spell reveals how, according to Kramer, 'demonic possession becomes an aspect of witchcraft, almost unrelated to the demon himself'. *Hammer of Witches*, 347–53.
3. Weyer, *Witches, Devils, and, Doctors*, Bk. 3; See also Sir George Mackenzie, *The Laws and Customs of Scotland in Matters Criminal* (Edinburgh, 1678), 99 (section 15 of the chapter on witchcraft), for the debate among Protestants on this issue.
4. Bodin, *Démonomanie*, Bk. 2, ch. 3. The Jesuit had used this argument to dissuade Pope Paul V from prosecuting Jews for having caused the possession of eighty-two female demoniacs, most of whom were converts from Judaism.
5. Cotta, *The Triall of Witchcraft*, 28–30.
6. Richard Brinley, *A Discovery of the Impostures of Witches and Astrologers* (London, 1680), 58–61.
7. Calef, *More Wonders of the Invisible World*, 293, 339. On the distinction between bewitchment and possession in New England see Harley, 'Explaining Salem', 307–30.
8. Thomas, *Religion and the Decline of Magic*, 478. On the popular perception that demonic possession was similar to malevolent magic in Denmark see Kallestrup, 'Knowing Satan from God', 179.
9. On possessions attributed to witchcraft in Geneva in the early seventeenth century, see Monter, *Witchcraft in France and Switzerland*, ch. 2.
10. For a comparison between England and Spain in this regard see Kallendorf, *Exorcism*, xvi–xvii.
11. Sluhovsky, 'The Devil in the Convent', 1380 claims that of forty-five mass possessions in European convents, only five involved charges of witchcraft. The number is at least marginally larger. On Santa Chiara's exclusion from Sluhovsky's tally see Watt, *Scourge of Demons*, 5–9. On witchcraft and possession in the convent of Oisy-Verger in Artois between 1613 and 1619 see Lottin, 'Sorcellerie, possessions diaboliques et crise conventuelle', 112–16.
12. Martine Ostorero, *Le Diable au sabbat: Littérature démonologique et sorcellerie (1440–1460)* (Florence, 2011), 7.
13. Jacques-Chaquin and Préaud, *Les sorciers du carroi de Marlou*, 45–62; Decker, *Witchcraft and the Papacy*, 157–73.
14. Ferber, *Demonic Possession and Exorcism*, 102.
15. Cervantes, 'Devils of Querétaro,' 55; idem, *Devil in the New World*, 116–17.
16. Boguet, *An Examen of Witches*, ch. 5.
17. Claude Caron, *L'Antéchrist démasqué* (Tournon, 1589), 67–8.
18. The earliest extant edition is 1576.
19. The book was translated by William Aspley as *The Admirable History of Possession and Conversion of a Penitent Woman* (1620).
20. *The Manuscripts of the Duke of Roxburghe* (Historical Manuscripts Commission, Fourteenth Report, Appendix 3 London, 1894), 132. On the events in Paisley see *History of the Witches of Renfrewshire*.

21. On the rare use of this argument in suicides in early modern Scotland see Houston, *Punishing the Dead?*, 288–300. In 1756 Agnes Crockat, accused of a capital crime, claimed 'it was the Devil that made her do it.' Ibid., 294.

22. See for example Chajes, *Between Worlds*, 5. The fact that possession was not a criminal offence explains why its documentation in judicial records is rare. See also Pearl, *The Crime of Crimes*, 42.

23. Owen Williams, 'Exorcising Madness in Late Elizabethan England: *The Seduction of Arthington* and the Criminal Culpability of Demoniacs', *Journal of British Studies* 47 (2008): 30–52.

24. The Italian abbess Benedetta justified the act of female sodomy for which she was accused before the Roman Inquisition by claiming that it was not she but either the angel Splenditello or Jesus Christ who made love with Sister Bartolomea. The fact that both possible possessing agents were male made the amorous relationship more plausible, while their angelic or divine status made it justifiable. The ecclesiastical officials at her second investigation did not accept this effort to blame either the angel or Jesus for her offence. Brown, *Immodest Acts*, ch. 5.

25. *Historical Notices of Scotish Affairs Selected from the Manuscripts of Sir John Lauder of Fountainhall*, ed. J. Laing (Edinburgh, 1848), vol. 1: 144.

26. Williams. 'Exorcising Madness', 30–52. Henry Arthington, *The Seduction of Arthington by Hackett especiallie, with some tokens of his unfained repentance and his Submission* (London, 1592).

27. Tausiet, 'From Illusion to Disenchantment', 52–3.

28. Ferber, 'Possession and the Sexes', 224. In late antiquity most possessions were believed to be the result of one's own sins. Brown, *Cult of the Saints*, 110.

29. *The Hammer of Witches*, 344.

30. See Monter, *Witchcraft in France and Switzerland*, 72. The woman was executed for her earlier witchcraft despite her innocence as a demoniac. The equation of possession with witchcraft violated classical witchcraft theory, but in this case the witchcraft and the possession appear to have been sequential, not coincidental.

31. See above, Chapter 3. On early Christianity see Fernando Cervantes, *The Idea of the Devil and the Problem of the Indian: The Case of Mexico in the Sixteenth Century* (London, 1991), 11. In the ninth century, however, an exorcism was intended to drive the demon out of either the body or the soul. Kieckhefer, *Forbidden Rites*, 144–5.

32. On this point see also Rodewyk, *Possessed by Satan*, 21–2. In contrasting the moral position of the witch and the demoniac, Michel Foucault asserts that the demoniac resists the Devil's power 'at the very moment she becomes his receptacle'. Foucault, *Abnormal Lectures*, 207. Such resistance was more common in Protestant than in Catholic possessions, when the demoniac and the Devil spoke in two voices and the demoniac resisted demonic temptation. In Catholic possessions the resistance came mainly from the exorcists, who Foucault claims made the system of relationships in possession 'triangular' and much more complicated than the simple polarity between witch and Devil in witchcraft. In Catholic possessions the demoniac's resistance to demonic power became evident only when she helped the exorcist.

33. Midelfort, 'Sin, Melancholy, Obsession', 134–5.

34. Newman, 'Possessed by the Spirit', 733–70.

35. Clark, *Thinking with Demons*, 433.

36. Midelfort, 'Sin, Melancholy, Obsession', 139.

37. Midelfort, 'The Devil and the German People', 113–14. The demoniac, Veronica Steiner, spoke with her own tender, Christian voice but also with a coarse, manly, blasphemous voice. She renounced her Lutheran faith and accepted Roman Catholicism. Midelfort, 'Sin, Melancholy, Obsession', 135–6. The Surey demoniac, Richard Dugdale, was reported to have spoken with two voices at once and without opening his mouth. Snape, '"The Surey Impostor"', 102.

38. Cervantes, 'Devils of Querétaro', 62.

39. Maggi, *In the Company of Demons*. The belief had originated in the culture of classical antiquity. On the modern belief that possessing devils were the familiars and also companions of the possessed see Malachi Martin, *Hostage to the Devil: The Possession and Exorcism of Five Contemporary Americans* (New York, 1992), 260.

40. On the predominance of the belief that sin was the proximate cause of possession in the Middle Ages see Muriel Laharie, *La Folie au moyen âge*, 27–8.

41. See Caciola, *Discerning Spirits*, 315–19.

42. Joseph Hansen, ed., *Quellen und Untersuchungen zur Geschichte des Hexenwahns im Mittelalter* (Bonn, 1901), 90.

43. Richard Kieckhefer, 'The Holy and the Unholy: Sainthood, Witchcraft and Magic in Late Medieval Europe', *Journal of Medieval and Renaissance Studies* 24 (1994): 355–85; Newman, 'Possessed by the Spirit'; Ferber, *Demonic Possession and Exorcism*, ch. 8. All three types were believed to have possessed special powers, including clairvoyance. A number of female saints were suspected of witchcraft or demonic possession. See Bynum, *Holy Feast and Holy Fast*, chs 4 and 5 on Catherine of Siena, Lidwina of Shiedam, and Columba of Rieti. The witch, however, was the mirror image of the saint, while the morally ambivalent demoniac was located somewhere in between. On the similarity of early modern perceptions of the witch, the demoniac, and the hysteric see Joanna Levin, 'Lady Macbeth and the Daemonologie of Hysteria', *English Literary History* 69 (2002): 21–55.

44. David Darst, ed., 'Witchcraft in Spain: The Testimony of Martín de Castañega's Treatise on Superstitions and Witchcraft (1520)', *Proceedings of the American Philosophical Society* 123 (1979): 319–20. Such men, according to Castañega, were necromancers who 'prophesied and spoke and said marvels'.

45. Midelfort, 'The Devil and the German People', 116–17 on this popular confusion in Lutheranism.

46. Pócs, 'Possession Phenomena', 115–16. The belief that people could be possessed by ancestral spirits existed only in popular culture. Christian demonologists denied its possibility. See above, Chapter 2, p. 47.

47. *New York Times*, 21 May 2010.

48. Jacques Fontaine, *Discours des marques des sorciers et de la reelle possession que le diable prend sur le corps des hommes* (Paris, 1611); Ferber, *Demonic Possession and Exorcism*, 84.

49. Walker, *Unclean Spirits*, 38; Swan, *A True and Breife Report*.

50. *Procès verbal fait pour délivrer une fille possédée*, 40–8.

51. Martin Del Rio, *Disquisitionum magicarum* (Cologne, 1755), Bk. 6, ch. 2, section 3, question 3. See Maxwell-Stuart, *Occult in Early Modern Europe*, 52–7. The Jesuits placed Prutenus under their care, and witchcraft was never mentioned. Del Rio boasted that 'One found none such among the Lutherans—and much else which modesty prevents me from repeating.' Ibid., 55.

52. Friedrich Hoffman, *Medicina consultatoria* (Halle, 1724), cited in Diethelm, 'Medical Teaching', 12. For another case of a young male demoniac who made a pact with the Devil see Midelfort, 'The Devil and the German People', 117.

53. The only time demoniacs were actually accused of witchcraft was when a witch whom they had named made a counter-accusation against them. See Blackwell, 'German Narratives', 242.

54. Rodewyk, *Possessed by Satan*, 113.

55. Walker and Dickerman, 'The Haunted Girl', 209–13.

56. Decker, *Witchcraft and the Papacy*, 108–10.

57. Bibliothèque nationale de France, MS 23,851.

58. Ibid., MS. 23,852, p. 491. She was however treated with relative leniency, being confined to house arrest for her lifetime.

59. *The Confessions of Madeleine Bavent*, 132–3.

60. On the charges against Françoise de la Croix and the difficulty in prosecuting her see Ferber, *Demonic Possession and Exorcism*, 100–4.

61. Decker, *Witchcraft and the Papacy*, 172.
62. Ibid., ch. 13.
63. Renate S. Klinnert, 'Von Besessenen, Melancholikern und Betrügen: Johann Weyers *De Praestigiis Daemonum* und die Unterscheidung der Geister', in Waardt et al., *Dämonische Besessenheit*, 104–5.
64. See Midelfort, *History of Madness*, 134. This point of view was particularly evident in Paracelsus.
65. Soili-Maria Olli, 'The Devil's Pact', 111–12. The charge was blasphemy.
66. Éva Pócs, 'Possession Phenomena', 115, argues that folk systems of witchcraft were influenced by the fact that from the end of the fifteenth century the Church's charges of possession became part of the persecution of witches.
67. Mather, *Memorable Providences*, 43–8.
68. Arthur Williamson, *Scottish National Consciousness in the Age of James VI. The Apocalypse, the Union and the Shaping of Scotland's Public Culture* (Edinburgh, 1979), 53.
69. 'May we not rightly hold the wicked and reprobate for possessed, which give themselves over to the Devil and do the work of the same?' Viret, *World Possessed*, 2nd Dialogue. sig. D4ᵛ. Clark, *Thinking with Demons*, 393, argues that Viret used the possession of demoniacs as an allegory for the condition of human society as it moved into the Last Days. St Paul frequently used the language of possession to describe the sinfulness of all human beings. Religious writers often used the language of possession and madness to identify sin in the age of the Reformation. Midelfort, *History of Madness*, 134.
70. Holmes, *Plain Dealing*, 78–81.
71. Jehl, 'Melancholie und Besessenheit', 63–71.
72. For a Lutheran statement of this view see Celichius, *Notwendige Erinnerung*.
73. Twentieth-century Catholic theologians consider demoniacs responsible for their actions when *not* in a trance state. Baglio, *The Rite*, 50.
74. Roper, *Oedipus and the Devil*, 177.
75. See Harley, 'Explaining Salem'. Thomas Darling's possession might have begun as a divine possession, but it did not lead to a debate whether it was demonic or divine. The only other discernment of an English possession was that of Richard Mainey, a Catholic exorcized by the Jesuits. Walker, *Unclean Spirits*, 46, 78. Quakers, especially Quaker women, could have what might be described as good possessions, in that the spirit could speak through them, but such claims ran counter to orthodox Calvinism. Anglican opposition to demonic possession might have foreclosed the possibility of discernment. See ibid., 78.
76. W. J. Anderson, 'Narratives of the Scottish Reformation, III: Prefect Ballentine's Report, *circa* 1660: Part One', *Innes Review* 8 (1957): 51.
77. Ibid.
78. See for example Cotton Mather's account of the spiritual travail of the Tocutt boy. *Memorable Providences*, 44–9.
79. Cervantes, 'Devils of Querétaro', 2–3.
80. Mather, *Memorable Providences*, 19.
81. Karlsen, *Devil in the Shape of a Woman*, 243.
82. *A Briefe Narration*, sig. B1 and B2ᵛ.
83. Barbara Rosen, ed., *Witchcraft in England, 1558–1618* (Amherst, 1991), 227.
84. Levack, *Witch-hunting in Scotland*, 123.
85. Almond, *Demonic Possession and Exorcism*, 153. Towards the end of the narrative the Devil apparently answered in his own voice when Darling fell into a trance.
86. Midelfort, 'The Devil and the German People', 113–14. One of these possessions was of a Catholic demoniac.
87. Ferber, *Demonic Possession and Exorcism*, 116. The theory that possession was punishment for one's sins persisted in sixteenth-century Germany, but it was increasingly common for demoniacs to be pious young girls. Midelfort, 'The Devil and the German People', 111–12.

88. For the possession of Kingesfielde see Sands, *Demon Possession*, ch. 3.
89. Midelfort, 'Sin, Melancholy, Obsession', 138.
90. Demos, *Entertaining Satan*, 129.
91. Samuel Willard, *A Briefe Account of a strange and unusual Providence of God, befallen to Elizabeth Knap of Groton*, in *The Mather Papers* (Collections of the Massachusetts Historical Society 8, 4th series, 1868), 555–71.
92. For a psychological analysis of Elizabeth Knapp's possession see Demos, *Entertaining Satan*, 97–131. The use of the word covenant for the pact was distinctly Calvinist.
93. Norton, *In the Devil's Snare*, 34–5.
94. On the role of the Devil as tempter in Protestant theology see Johnstone, 'The Protestant Devil', 173–205.
95. *A True Narrative of the Sufferings and Relief of a Young Girle*, 93.
96. Ibid., 84–5.
97. Levack, *Witch-hunting in Scotland*, 115–16.
98. L.A. Yeoman, 'The Devil as Doctor: Witchcraft, Wodrow and the Wider World', *Scottish Archives* 1 (1995): 95. On the afflictions of other Calvinist youth see Norton, *In the Devil's Snare*, 31.
99. Robert Wodrow, *Analecta or Materials for a History of Remarkable Providence*, vol. 2, ed. Matthew Leishman (Edinburgh, 1843), 314.
100. S.W. MacDonald, A. Thom, and A. Thom, 'The Bargarran Witchcraft Trial: A Psychiatric Reassessment', *Scottish Medical Journal* 412 (1996): 152–8.
101. Kaplan, 'Possessed by the Devil?', 751–4.

Chapter 9. Possession in the Age of Reason

1. Robert Mandrou, *Magistrats et sorciers en France au XVIIᵉ siècle* (Paris, 1968), chs 4–6; Brian P. Levack, 'The Decline and End of Witchcraft Prosecutions', in *Witchcraft and Magic in Europe: The Eighteenth and Nineteenth Centuries*, ed. Bengt Ankarloo and Stuart Clark (London, 1999), 28–30, 52–3.
2. Lederer, *Madness, Religion and the State*, 231.
3. On the connection between scepticism regarding possession and the decline in the publication of witchcraft pamphlets in England see Marion Gibson, *Reading Witchcraft: Stories of Early English Witches* (London, 1999), 186–90.
4. On this connection in Bavaria see Lederer, *Madness, Religion and the State*, 200–1.
5. Davies, *Witchcraft, Magic and Culture*, 28, argues that clergymen and doctors were interested in demonic power in the world, not human agency. See in particular Simon de Vries, *De Satan in sijn weesen*.
6. The most reliable account of this episode is B. Robert Keiser, 'The Devils of Toulon: Demonic Possession and Religious Politics in Eighteenth-century Provence', in *Church, State, and Society under the Bourbon Kings of France*, ed. Richard Golden (Lawrence, Kan., 1982), 173–221.
7. *The Case of Mrs. Cadiere*, 9–10, presents Marie-Catherine as the innocent victim of the lustful priest. It also describes the transformation of her divine possession into a demonic one, in which she could not pray and heard a voice saying that to save her soul she had to submit to possession by the Devil for a year, taking place before the sexual relationship had developed. See p. 7.
8. For the edict of Louis XIV see Levack, *The Witchcraft Sourcebook*, 163–6. Witchcraft was not fully decriminalized in France until 1791.
9. On these possessions and the charges of witchcraft they engendered see 'Bericht von dem Ausgang des Annabergischen Hexen-Wesens', in Hauber, *Bibliotheca*, vol. 3: 41–66. For the report of the hospital pastor whose son was the first to be possessed, see Johann Gottlieb Adami, *Kurze Nachricht von denen seltsamen und kläglichen Begebenheiten an Kindern und erwachsenen Personen zu Annaberg* (Altenburg, 1714). An investigation into this episode lasted until 1720.

10. Wolgang Behringer, *Witchcraft Persecutions in Bavaria: Popular Magic, Religious Zealotry and Reason of State in Early Modern Europe* (Cambridge, 1997), 346; Midelfort, *Exorcism and Enlightenment*, 8–9.

11. Blackwell, 'Controlling the Demoniac', 425–42.

12. Blackwell, 'German Narratives', 244, attributes the decline in the printing of possession narratives in Lutheran Germany to anti-Pietist pressure from Lutheran ecclesiastical authorities.

13. See above, Chapter 2.

14. Midelfort, *Exorcism and Enlightenment*, 11.

15. Henry Durbin, *A Narrative of some extraordinary things that happened to Mr Richard Giles's children, at the Lamb, without Lawford's-Gate, Bristol: supposed to be the effect of witchcraft* (Bristol, 1800). On the extent of publicity in this incident see Jonathan Barry, 'Public Infidelity and Private Belief? The Discourse of Spirits in Enlightenment Bristol', in Davies and Blécourt, *Beyond the Witch Trials*, 117–43.

16. Durbin, *Narrative*, 24. See also 36, where a man tried to hold Molly but the force was so great he could not restrain her.

17. Ibid., 39–41. Relief came after the girls' urine was thrown into the fire, although the stiffness returned three hours later.

18. Ibid., 24.

19. Davies, *Witchcraft, Magic and Culture*, 19–22.

20. Durbin, *Narrative*, 46, 48.

21. See Roy Porter, 'Witchcraft and Magic in Enlightenment, Romantic and Liberal Thought', in *Witchcraft and Magic in Europe: The Eighteenth and Nineteenth Centuries*, 239 on Wesley's inference of witchcraft from convulsions in 1770.

22. Davies, *Witchcraft, Magic and Culture*, 20–2.

23. Joseph Easterbrook, *An Appeal to the Public Respecting George Lukins* (Bristol, 1788).

24. Samuel Norman, *Authentic Anecdotes of George Lukins, the Yatton Demoniac* (Bristol, 1788); idem, *The Great Apostle Unmasked* (Bristol, 1788).

25. Davies, *Witchcraft Magic and Culture*, 23–6. Peach used the exorcism to secure the conversion of the woman to Roman Catholicism, recalling the practice of earlier Catholic exorcists.

26. James Heaton, *The Extraordinary Affliction and Gracious Relief of a Little Boy: Supposed to be the Effects of Spiritual Agency*, 2nd edn (Plymouth, 1822); Davies, *Witchcraft, Magic and Culture*, 19–22.

27. Ellenberger, *Discovery of the Unconscious*, 17.

28. Levi, *Inheriting Power*, 4–28. 'The evil spell did not seem to be attributed to the active operation of physically identifiable single individuals.'

29. On the reluctance of the Inquisition in Venice to deal with charges of *maleficium*, which could often be explained as having natural causes and were also hard to prove, see Ruth Martin, *Witchcraft in Venice 1550–1650* (Oxford, 1989), 193–206.

30. Midelfort, *Exorcism and Enlightenment*, 102–5. On Pietism and demonology in Germany see Diethelm, 'Medical Teaching', 12.

31. For this possession and exorcism see Herbert Haag, *Teufelsglaube* (Tübingen, 1974), 403–4.

32. Tausiet, 'The Possessed of Tosos', 263–80. It is unclear how many symptoms the demoniacs displayed. The official report claimed that they made the 'faces and violent gestures which are often seen in those truly possessed by the Devil'.

33. Maire, *Les Possédées de Morzine*.

34. Worobec, *Possessed*, 130, citing Ivan Gavrilovich Pyrzhov.

35. Diethelm, 'Medical Teaching', 12–14; Porter, 'Witchcraft and Magic', 229–32; Kay S. Wilkins, 'Attitudes to Witchcraft and Demonic Possession in France during the Eighteenth Century', *Journal of European Studies* 3 (1973): 349–60.

36. 'Possession du démon' in *L'Enclycopédie*, vol. 13: 167, identified possession as a mental malady, curable by medicine.

37. Porter, 'Witchcraft and Magic', 229. See also Diethelm, 'Medical Teaching', 13–15.

38. Worobec, *Possessed*, p. 130.
39. Alphonse Costadeau, *Traité historique et critique des principeaux signes dont nous nous servons pour manifester nos pensées,* 8 vols (Lyon, 1717–20).
40. François de Saint-André, *Lettres au sujet de la magie, des maleﬁces et des sorciers* (1725); Daugis, *Traité sur la magie,* 157–221.
41. Calmet. *The Phantom World,* 104–26. Quote at p. 112.
42. Charles-Louis Richard, *Dissertation sur la possession du corps & sur l'infestation des maisons par les démons* (Amiens, 1746). Reprinted in Nicolas Lenglet Dufresnoy, *Dissertations* vol. 2, Pt. 1: 191–241. See especially the *Avertissement* on p. 193. The essay gained the approval of the bishop of Amiens.
43. Lenglet Dufresnoy, *Dissertations,* vol. 1, Preface, cliii.
44. Wilkins, 'Attitudes to Witchcraft and Demonic Possession', 355, 358.
45. Jean Pierquin, *Conjectures sur les effets de l'obsession naturelle* (Paris, 1744); Wilkins, 'Attitudes to Witchcraft and Demonic Possession', 354.
46. Anthony Collins, *A Discourse of Free-thinking, occasion'd by the rise and growth of a sect call'd Free-Thinkers* (London, 1713), 28.
47. He estimated the number of the genuinely possessed to be approximately twenty or thirty out of five hundred. Feijoo, 'Demoniacos', 76.
48. Canon 72 of the *Constitutions and Canons Ecclesiastical of the Church of England, 1604* prohibited Anglican ministers from conducting dispossession by prayer and fasting without a licence. Gerald Bray, ed., *The Anglican Canons, 1529–1947* (Woodbridge, Suffolk, 1988).
49. Midelfort, *Exorcism and Enlightenment,* 88.
50. This definition excludes the identification of some clergy as 'secular', i.e. being active in the administration of the church in the parishes rather than the regular or monastic clergy that remained outside the system of diocesan clerical organization.
51. Charles Taylor, *A Secular Age* (Cambridge, Mass., 2007). For the argument that the Protestant Reformation contributed to the birth of this modern, secular world, see Brad S. Gregory, *The Unintended Reformation: How a Religious Revolution Secularized Society* (Cambridge, Mass., 2012).
52. See for example C. John Sommerville, *The Secularization of Early Modern England From Religious Culture to Religious Faith* (New York, 1992). For a critique of the theory of secularization see J.C.D. Clark, 'Secularization and Modernization: The Failure of a "Grand Narrative"', *Historical Journal* 55 (2012): 161–94.
53. Patrick Vandermeersch, 'The Victory of Psychiatry over Demonology: The Origins of the Nineteenth-century Myth', *History of Psychiatry* 2 (1991): 351–63. For the use of medical and psychiatric theory to support the revival of demonology and exorcism among fundamentalists and Pentecostals in Edwardian Britain see Rhodri Hayward, 'Demonology, Neurology, and Medicine in Edwardian Britain', *Bulletin of the History of Medicine* 78 (2004): 37–58.
54. On the difficulties seeing Restoration England as a period of secularization see Blair Worden, 'The Question of Secularization', in *A Nation Transformed: England after the Restoration,* ed. Alan Houston and Steve Pincus (Cambridge, 2001), 20–140.
55. Oesterreich, *Possession,* ch. 6, claims that possessions continued in modern times only in 'primitive' and uncivilized societies. On this argument see Keller, *The Hammer and the Flute,* 26–8.
56. Ellenberger, *Discovery of the Unconscious,* 18.
57. See Darrin M. McMahon, *Enemies of the Enlightenment: The French Counter-Enlightenment and the Making of Modernity* (New York, 2001), esp. 32–42.
58. See Jonathan I. Israel, 'Enlightenment, Radical Enlightenment and the "Medical Revolution" of the Late Seventeenth and Eighteenth Centuries', in *Medicine and Religion in Enlightenment Europe,* ed. Ole Peter Grell and Andrew Cunningham (Aldershot, 2007), 5–28.

59. Peter Elmer, 'Medicine, Witchcraft and the Politics of Healing in Late Seventeenth-century England,' in Grell and Cunningham eds, *Medicine and Religion in Enlightenment Europe*, 223–41.
60. MacDonald, 'Religion, Social Change, and Psychological Healing', 102, 122.
61. Levi, *Inheriting Power*, 23. Houston, *Punishing the Dead?*, 314; K.L. Parker, 'Richard Greenham's Spiritual Physicke' in *Penitence in the Age of Reformations*, ed. Katharine Jackson Lualdi and Anne T. Thayer (Aldershot, 2000), 71–83.
62. Italics mine.
63. Worobec, *Possessed*, 28–30.
64. Levack, 'Decline and End of Witchcraft Prosecutions'; idem, *Witch-hunting in Scotland*, ch. 6.
65. See Paul Christopher Johnson, 'An Atlantic Genealogy of Spirit Possession', *Comparative Studies in Society and History* 53 (2011): 393–425. Johnson argues that as the belief in demonic possession came to be viewed as irrational and a threat to public order, scholars began to associate what was called spirit possession with primitive societies in Africa and elsewhere.
66. Lederer, *Madness, Religion and the State*, 203.

Chapter 10. Possession: Past and Present

1. Rodewyk, *Possessed by Satan*, 120–7.
2. Carl Vogl, *Begone Satan! A Soul-stirring Account of Diabolical Possession*, trans. Celestine Kapsner (St. Cloud, Minn., 1935).
3. Ibid., 6.
4. Riesinger predicted that the furious rage of the Devil would be directed against the 'church of God'. In another possession the Devil reportedly gave the years 1952–5 as the predicted time of the Antichrist's appearance. Ibid, 41–2.
5. An Australian woman in Victoria died after her husband and three other charismatic Christians accidentally choked her in 1993. In 1995 ministers in a small Pentecostal sect in San Francisco pummelled a woman to death while trying to exorcize her. Two years later a deacon and two missionaries in Glendale, California caused the death of a woman by stomping on her chest in order to expel the occupying demon. In 2005 a Romanian nun died after the exorcist had gagged her and lashed her to a crucifix. For a list of 1,089 persons harmed by someone practising an exorcism or trying to remove a curse see http://whatstheharm.net/exorcisms.html
6. The German film *Requiem* is also based on this episode. The two priests and the woman's parents received only suspended jail sentences, but the punishment explains the reluctance of the Catholic Church in Germany to authorize exorcisms today. Most Germans seeking the expulsion of the demons that haunt them go to Poland or Switzerland for treatment.
7. The old ritual as amended in 1952 appears in the appendix to Malachi Martin, *Hostage to the Devil*. The new ritual begins with prayers, a blessing and sprinkling with holy water, the laying of hands on the possessed, and the making of the sign of the cross.
8. Reuters, 13 Oct. 2005. Some of the students have been laymen.
9. Baglio, *The Rite*, 7.
10. The head of the Congregation, Cardinal Joseph Ratzinger, who became Pope Benedict XVI in 2005, oversaw this initiative at the request of Pope John Paul II.
11. The *New York Times*, 13 Nov. 2010 reported that sixty-six priests and fifty-six bishops attended.
12. Quoted in Tausiet, 'From Illusion to Disenchantment', 45.
13. Amorth, *An Exorcist Tells His Story*.
14. *Padre Forte—eksorsisten*, a Norwegian documentary by Frederik Horn Akselsen.
15. Felicitas Goodman, *How About Demons? Possession and Exorcism in the Modern World* (Bloomington, Ind., 1988), 52.

16. Michael W. Cuneo, *American Exorcism: Expelling Demons in the Land of Plenty* (New York, 2001), 82.
17. The first Pentecostals, those associated with their founder, the American preacher and evangelist Charles Fox Parham, embarked on a mission in the early twentieth century to convert the world before the Second Coming. Goodman, *How About Demons?*, 55.
18. On the revival of exorcism among Pentecostals in Britain in the wake of the Welsh Evangelical Revival of 1904, see Hayward, 'Demonology, Neurology, and Medicine', 51–7.
19. See Blackwell, 'Controlling the Demoniac', 427, on possessions in the eighteenth century among charismatics in splinter groups from the mainstream confessions such as Pietists in Germany. The belief in the possibility of revelation in trance possessions, which represented a threat to the clerical hierarchies of the mainstream churches in the eighteenth century, finds its modern counterpart among modern Pentecostals.
20. Goodman, *How About Demons?*, ch. 4.
21. Cuneo, *American Exorcism*, ch. 6.
22. Ibid., 86.
23. Cuneo, *American Exorcism*, chs 7 and 8. On the Catholic roots of Pentecostalism see Walter J. Hollenweger, *Pentecostalism: Origins and Developments Worldwide* (Peabody, Mass., 1997), section 2.
24. Sands, *Demonic Possession*, 205–6.
25. Andrew Delbanco, *The Death of Satan: How Americans Have Lost the Sense of Evil* (New York, 1996).
26. Baglio, *The Rite*, 6.
27. Ibid., 124–5.
28. A woman had vomited seven black two-inch-long nails, which dissolved into a black liquid. Baglio, *The Rite*, 125.
29. Karen MacCarthy Brown, *Mama Lola: A Vodou Priestess in Brooklyn* (Berkeley, 2001), 110–12.
30. Some such dangerous possessions occurred when some of the children among the Haitian refugees known as the boat people were imprisoned by the United States Immigration and Naturalization Service in an upstate New York detention centre. Isolated and afraid, some of these children experienced possessions when they turned to spirits in this time of crisis, just as the first slaves transported to Haiti might have done when they were shipped to the new French colony in the seventeenth and eighteenth centuries. Brown, *Mama Lola*, 253.
31. Ibid., 252–3.
32. Cuneo, *American Exorcism*, 58 ff.
33. Paul Eberle, *Abuse of Innocence: The McMartin Pre-School Trial* (New York, 1993).
34. Baglio, *The Rite*, 133.
35. Ibid., 159.

Chapter 11. Conclusion

1. Monter, *Witchcraft in France and Switzerland*, 60, refers to the seventeenth century in this way, but the golden age, if by that is meant the period when demoniacs attracted the most attention, should be extended to include the last decade of the sixteenth century, when the number of possessions apparently peaked.
2. Clark, *Thinking with Demons*, 404.
3. Peter Brown, 'Sorcery, Demons and the Rise of Christianity: From Late Antiquity into the Middle Ages', in Brown, ed., *Religion and Society in the Age of Saint Augustine* (New York, 1972), 136.
4. Justin Martyr, *Second Apology*, 5. The apology was directed to the Roman Senate.
5. Martin, *Hostage to the Devil*, 11.
6. Baglio, *The Rite*, 5 claims that most exorcisms are routine, comparable to going to the dentist. The exorcisms of Chiesa and Gassner would probably fall into this category.

7. Delbanco, *The Death of Satan*.
8. Thomas, *Religion and the Decline of Magic*, 483–4.
9. Oesterreich, *Possession*, 189.
10. Tausiet, 'From Illusion to Disenchantment', 45.
11. Henningsen, *The Witches' Advocate*, viii.
12. Midelfort, 'The Devil and the German People', 112–13.
13. Midelfort, 'Catholic and Lutheran Reactions to Demon Possession', 642–5.
14. Midelfort, 'Sin, Melancholy, Obsession', 136–7; Bodo Nischan, 'The Exorcism Controversy' 31–51. Waite, *Eradicating the Devil's Minions*, 46–7.
15. Johann Ludwig Hartmann, *Pastorale Evangelicum* (Nuremberg, 1678), 1160–1.
16. *The Telegraph*, 7 July 2009; Sarah Ferber and Adrian Howe, 'The Man who Mistook his Wife for a Devil: Exorcism, Expertise and Secularisation in a Late Twentieth-Century Australian Criminal Court', in Waardt et al., *Dämonische Besessenheit*, 283.
17. Tuetey, *La Sorcellerie dans le pays de Montbéliard*, 34.
18. Ladame, *Les Possédés et les démoniaques à Genève*, 30–3 and *passim;* Monter, *Witchcraft in France and Switzerland*, 59–60.
19. Bossy, *English Catholic Community*, 266.
20. Mather, *More Wonders of the Invisible World;* Paul Boyer and Stephen Nissenbaum, *Salem Possessed* (New York, 1974); Karlsen, *Devil in the Shape of a Woman;* Norton, *In the Devil's Snare*.
21. Walker, *Unclean Spirits*, 40–1.
22. Ladame, *Les Possédés et les démoniaques à Genève*, 30–2.
23. Levack, *Witch-hunting in Scotland*, 125–6.
24. Kaplan, 'Possessed by the Devil?', 751–9.
25. *New York Times*, 13 Nov. 2010, p. A12.
26. Kaplan, 'Possessed by the Devil?', 745–8.
27. Michael Heyd, 'The Reaction to Enthusiasm in the Seventeenth Century: Toward an Integrative Approach', *Journal of Modern History* 53 (1981): 258–80.

Bibliography

Manuscripts

Bibliothèque nationale de France, manuscrits français nos. 23,851 and 23,852. Criminal proceedings against Louis Gaufridy 1611 and Magdelaine Demandols 1653.
British Library, MS. Harley 590, fols. 6–63. Account of the temptation and possession of Mr Brigges.
Huntington Library, San Marino, California. EL MS 5955/2. Examination in the prosecution of Anne Gunter, 1607.
National Archives of Scotland, Edinburgh. JC 10/4. Circuit Court Minute Books, 1677–99.
National Archives, London. STAC 8/4/10. Prosecution of Anne Gunter and Brian Gunter in the Star Chamber, 1607.
University of Nottingham. MS MiF 10/4. 'A note of the syght in Nottingham by one possessed the 5th of November 1597'.

Printed Primary Sources

Adami, Johann Gottlieb. *Kurze Nachricht von denen seltsamen und kläglichen Begebenheiten an Kindern und erwachsenen Personen zu Annaberg* Altenburg, 1714.
Ady, Thomas. *A Candle in the Dark: or, A Treatise Concerning the Nature of Witches and Witchcraft.* London, 1655.
——. *The Doctrine of Devils: proved to be the grand apostacy of these later times, an essay tending to rectifie those undue notions and apprehensions men have about dæmons and evil spirits.* London, 1676.
An account of the strange and wonderful manner in which John Fox, who some time ago lived near Nottingham, was sorely afflicted with an Evil Spirit. Glasgow, [n.d.].
Anderson, W.J., ed. 'Narratives of the Scottish Reformation, III: Prefect Ballentine's Report, *circa* 1660: Part One', *Innes Review* 8 (1957): 39–66.
The Anglican Canons, 1529–1947, ed. Gerald Bray. Woodbridge, Suffolk, 1988.
An Answer of a Letter from a Gentleman in Fife to a Nobleman. [Edinburgh], 1705.
Aquinas, Thomas. *Summa theologica*, ed. Fathers of the English Dominican Province. New York, 1947–8.
Arrest de la Cour de Parlement de Provence, portant condamnation contre Messire Louis Gaufridi. Aix-en-Provence. Aix-en-Provence, 1611.
Arthington, Henry. *The Seduction of Arthington by Hackett especiallie, with some tokens of his unfained repentance and his Submission.* London, 1592.

Aubin, Nicolas. *The Cheats and Illusions of Romish Priests and Exorcists, Discovered in the History of the Devils of Loudun.* London, 1703.
——. *Histoire des diables de Loudun.* Amsterdam, 1693.
[Baddeley, Richard]. *The Boy of Bilson: or, a true discovery of the late notorious impostures of certain Roman priests in their pretended exorcisme.* London, 1622.
Barrow, John. *The Lord's Arm Stretched Out in an Answer to Prayer.* London, 1664.
Baxter, Richard, *The Certainty of the Worlds of Spirits and, consequently, of the immortality of souls of the malice and misery of the devils and the damned.* London, 1691.
[Bee, Jesse et al.]. *The Most Wonderful and True Storie of a certaine Witch named Alse Gooderige . . . As also a true report of the strange torments of Thomas Darling, a boy of thirteen years of age, that was possessed by the Devill, with his terrible Fittes and terrible Apparitions by him uttered at Burton upon Trent in the County of Stafford and of his marvellous deliverance.* London, 1597.
Bekker, Balthasar, *De betoverde weereld*, 2 vols. Amsterdam, 1693.
——. *Die bezauberte Welt*, 4 vols in one. Amsterdam, 1693.
Benedicti, Jean. *La Triomphanti victoire de la vierge Marie, sur sept malins esprits, finalement chassés du corps d'une femme, dans l'Eglise des Cordeliers de Lyon.* Lyon, 1611.
Benivieni, Antonio, *De abditis nonnullis ac mirandis morborum et sanationum causis* (Florence, 1507). Trans. Charles Springer, *The Hidden Causes of Disease.* Springfield, Ill., 1954.
'Bericht von dem Ausgang des Annabergischen Hexen-Wesens'. In Hauber, *Bibliotheca sive acta et scripta magica.* Vol. 3: 41–66.
Bernard, Richard. *A Guide to Grand Jury-Men.* London, 1630.
Bérulle, Pierre de. *Traité de energumenes*, in *Les Oeuvres*, ed. F. Bouroing. Paris, 1644.
'Die Besessene Magd von Lebuss, zu Frankfurt an der Oder'. In Hauber, *Bibliotheca sive acta et scripta magica.* Vol. 3: 493–500.
Birette, Sanson. *Refutation de l'erreur du Vulgaire touchant les responses des diables exorcizez.* Rouen, 1618.
Blagrave, Joseph. *Astrological practice of physick . . . directing how to cast forth the said evil spirits out of any one who is possessed.* London, 1671.
Blendecq, Charles. *Cinq Histoires admirables, esquelles est monstré comme miraculeusement pas la vertu et puissance du sainct sacrement de l'Autel a esté chasse Beelzebub prince des diables.* Paris, 1582.
Boaistuau, Pierre. *Histoires prodigieuses et memorables, extraictes de plusieurs fameux autheurs, Grecs & Latins, sacrez & prophanes.* Paris, 1566. English translation: *Certaine Secrete Wonders of Nature* [by Edward Fenton], London, 1569.
Bodin, Jean. *De la démonomanie des sorciers.* 2nd edn Paris, 1587.
Boguet, Henri. *Discours execrable des sorciers*, ed. Nicole Jacques-Chaquin. Paris, 1980.
——. *An Examen of Witches*, trans. E. Allen Ashwin, London: John Rodker, 1929.
Boorde Andrew. *The Breviary of Helthe.* London, 1547.
Boulaese, Jean., *L'Abregee histoire du grand miracle par nostre Sauveur & Seigneur Jesus Christ en la saincte Hostie du Sacrament de l'Autel, faict à Laon.* Paris, 1573.
——. *Le Miracle de Laon en Lannoys*, ed. A.H. Chambard. Lyon, 1995.
——. *La Thrésor et entière histoire de la triomphante victoire du corps de Dieu sur l'esprit malign Beelzebub.* Paris, 1578.
Bourneville, Désiré-Magliore, ed. *La Possession de Jeanne Féry, religieuse professe du couvent des soeurs noires de la ville de Mons (1584).* Paris, 1886.
A Breife Narration of the Possession, Dispossession, and Repossession of William Sommers; and of some proceedings against Mr John Dorrell preacher, with answers to such objections as are made to probe the pretended counterfeiting of the said Sommers. Amsterdam, 1598.
Breton, J. le. *La Deffense de la vérité touchant la possession des Religieuses de Louviers.* Evreux, 1643.
Brinley, Richard. *A Discovery of the Impostures of Witches and Astrologers.* London, 1680.
Browne, Thomas. *Religio medici.* London, 1642.
Buisseret, François. *Histoire admirable et veritable des choses advenues a l'endroict d'une religieuse professe du couvent des Soeurs noires . . . possédée du malign espirit, &*

depuis delivrée. Paris, 1586. Reprinted and edited by Désiré Magloire Bourneville. Paris, 1886.

Burton, Robert. *The Anatomy of Melancholy*, ed. Thomas C. Faulkner, Nicolas K. Kiessling and Ronda L. Blair, 3 vols. Oxford, 1989–94.

Calef, Robert, *More Wonders of the Invisible World: Or, The Wonders of the Invisible World, Display'd in Five Parts*. London, 1700. Reprinted in *Narratives of the Witchcraft Cases, 1648–1706*, ed. George Lincoln Burr, 289–393. New York, 1914.

Calmet, Augustin. *An Historical, Critical, Geographical and Etymological Dictionary of the Holy Bible*, 2 vols. London, 1732.

——. *The Phantom World: or the philosophy of spirits, apparitions etc., etc.*, trans. Henry Christmas. Philadelphia, 1850.

Cardano, Girolamo. *De varietate rerum*. Basel, 1557.

Caron, Claude. *L'Antéchrist démasqué*. Tournon, 1589.

Carrington, John. *The Lancashire Levite rebuk'd, or, A farther vindication of the Dissenters from popery, superstition, ignorance and knavery unjustly charged on them by Mr Zachary Taylor in his two books about the Surey demoniak: in a letter to himself*. London, 1698.

——. *A Treatise Concerning Enthusiasme as it is an Effect of Nature: but is mistaken by many for either Divine Inspiration or Diabolical Possession*. London, 1655.

Casaubon Meric. *Of Credulity and Incredulity in Things Natural, Civil, and Divine*. London, 1668.

The Case of Mrs. Mary Catharine Cadiere against the Jesuit Father John Baptist Girard in a Memorial Presented to the Parliament of Aix. 2nd edn. London, 1732.

Celichius, Andreas. *Notwendige Erinnerung: Vonn des Sathans letzten Zornsturm und was es auff sich habe und bedeute, das nun zu dieser zeit so viel Menschen an Leib und Seel vom Teuffel besessen werden*. Wittenberg, 1594.

Charcot, Jean-Martin. *Clinical Letters on Diseases of the Nervous System*, ed. Ruth Harris. London, 1991.

Ciruelo, Pedro. *Pedro Ciruelo's A Treatise Reproving All Superstitions and Forms of Witchcraft*, trans. Eugene A. Maio and D' Orsay W. Pearson. Cranbury, NJ and London, 1977.

Collins, Anthony. *A Discourse of Free-thinking, occasion'd by the rise and growth of a sect call'd Free-Thinkers*. London, 1713.

The Confessions of Madeleine Bavent, trans. and ed. Montague Summers. London [1933].

Congnard, D.M. *Histoire de Marthe Brossier prétendu possedé*. Rouen, 1652.

Constitutions and Canons Ecclesiastical of the Church of England, 1604. Digital edition, 2005.

Cotta, John. *The Triall of Witchcraft*. London 1616.

[Crouch, Nathaniel]. *The Kingdom of Darkness: Or the History of Daemons, Specters, Witches, Apparitions*. London, 1688.

Daneau, Lambert. *A Dialogue of Witches*, trans. R.W. London, 1575.

Darrell, John. *An Apologie, or Defence of the Possession of William Sommers, a yong man of the Towne of Nottingham*. [1599].

——. *A Briefe Apologie Proving the Possession of William Sommers*. 1599.

——. *A True Narration of the Strange and Grevous Vexation by the Devil of 7 Persons in Lancashire and William Sommers of Nottingham*. 1600.

——. *A True Relation of the Grievous Handling of the William Somers of Nottingham*. London, 1641.

Darst, David (ed.), 'Witchcraft in Spain: The Testimony of Martín de Castañega's Treatise on Superstitions and Witchcraft (1520)', *Proceedings of the American Philosophical Society* 123 (1979): 298–322.

Daugis, Antoine Louis. *Traité sur la magie, le sortilege, les possessions, obsessions et malefices*. Paris, 1732.

Deacon, John and John Walker. *Dialogicall Discourses of Spirits and Devils, Declaring their Proper Essence*. London, 1601.

Dee, John. *The Private Diary of John Dee*, ed. James Orchard Halliwell. London, 1842.

Del Rio, Martín. *Disquisitionum magicarum*. Cologne, 1755.

——. *Investigations into Magic*, ed. and trans. P.G. Maxwell-Stuart. Manchester, 2004.

[Des Niau], *The History of the Devils of Loudun: The Alleged Possession of the Ursuline Nuns and the Trial and Execution of Urbain Grandier*, ed. and trans. Edmund Goldsmid. *Collectanea Adamantea.* Vol. 21. Edinburgh, 1887.

The Disclosing of a late counterfeyted possession by the devyl of two maydens within the Citie of London (1574). In Barbara Rosen, *Witchcraft in England, 1558–1618*, 231–9. Amherst, 1991.

Dorsch, Johann Georg. *Dissertatio de horrenda et miserabili Satana, eiusdem ex obsessis expulsion et obsessione.* Wittenberg, 1672.

Dove Speculum Anni, or, an almanac for the year of our Lord God 1678. London, 1678.

Duncan, Marc. *Discours sur la possession des Religieuses ursulines de Loudun.* Saumur, 1634.

Dunte, Ludwig. *Decisiones mille et sex casuum conscientiae.* Lübeck, 1664.

Durbin, Henry. *A narrative of some extraordinary things that happened to Mr Richard Giles's children, at the Lamb, without Lawford's-Gate, Bristol: supposed to be the effect of witchcraft.* Bristol, 1800.

Easterbrook, Joseph, *An Appeal to the Public Respecting George Lukins.* Bristol, 1788.

Eisengrein, Martin, *Unser liebe Frau zu Alten Oetting.* Ingolstadt, 1571.

'Endeckte Betrügerey bey einer Besessenen'. In Hauber, *Bibliotheca sive acta et scripta magica.* Vol. 3: 171–4.

Erasmus, Desiderius. *The Colloquies of Erasmus*, trans. Craig R. Thompson. Chicago, 1965.

Erschroeckliche gantz warhafftige Geschicht welche sich mit Apollonia Hannsen Geisslbrechts Burgers zu Spalt inn dem Eystaetter Bistumb Haussfrawn so den 20 Octobbris Anno 82. Von dem boesen Feind gar hart besessen . . . Ingolstadt, 1584.

'Erzählung von einer für zauberisch gehaltenen Krankheit'. In Hauber, *Bibliotheca sive acta et scripta magica.* Vol. 3: 252–63.

The Extraordinary Affliction and Gracious relief of a Little Boy: supposed to be the effects of Spiritual Agency. 2nd edn. Plymouth, 1822.

Fairfax, Edmund. *Daemonologia: a discourse on witchcraft as it was acted in the family of Mr Edward Fairfax, of Fuyston, in the county of York, in the year 1621*, ed. William Grainge. Harrogate, 1882.

Farmer, Hugh. *An Essay on the Demoniacs of the New Testament.* London, 1775.

Feijoo, Benito Jerónimo. 'Demoniacos'. In *Theatro Critico Universal.* Vol. 8: 76–151. Madrid, 1779.

Fernel, Jean. *De Abditis rerum causis libri duo.* Paris, 1548.

The Firebrand Taken out of the Fire, or the Wonderful History, Case and Cure of Mrs. Drake. London, 1654.

Fontaine, Jacques. *Discours des marques des sorciers et della reelle possession que le diable prend sur le corps des hommes.* Paris, 1611.

Gifford, George. *A dialogue concerning witches and witchcrafts.* London, 1593.

Glanvill Joseph. *A Blow at Modern Sadducism.* London, 1668.

——. *Sadducismus Triumphatus.* London, 1681.

Goulart, Simon. *Admirable Histories, Containing the Wonders of Our Time*, trans. Edward Grimelston. London, 1607.

Greene, John. *A Refutation of the Apologie for Actors.* London, 1615.

Gründlicher Bericht und Anzaig einer Warhafften Histori welcher massen zu Schmidweyler . . . ein Meydlein siben Jar lang weder gessen noch getruncken . . . Augsburg, 1585.

Guazzo, Francesco Maria. *Compendium maleficarum*, ed. Montague Summers. London, 1929.

Hansen, Joseph, ed. *Quellen und Untersuchungen zur Geschichte des Hexenwahns im Mittelalter.* Bonn, 1901.

[Harsnett, Samuel]. *A Declaration of Egregious Popish Impostures.* London, 1603. Reprinted in F.W. Brownlow, *Shakespeare, Harsnett and the Devils of Denham*, 191–413. Newark, Del., 1993.

——. *A Discovery of the Fraudulent Practises of John Darrel.* London, 1599.

Hartmann, Johann Ludwig. *Pastorale Evangelicum.* Nuremberg, 1678.

Hauber, Eberhard David, ed. *Bibliotheca sive acta et scripta magica. grundliche Nachricht und Urteile von solchen Buchern und Handlungen, welche di Macht des Teufels in leiblichen Dingen betreffen*, 3 vols. 2nd edn. Lemgo, 1739–45.

Heaton, James. *The Extraordinary Affliction and Gracious Relief of a Little Boy: supposed to be the Effects of Spiritual Agency*. 2nd edn. Plymouth, 1822.

Hédelin, François, abbé d'Aubignac. 'Relation de M. Hédelin, abbé d'Aubignac, touchant les possédées de Loudun au mois de Septembre 1637'. In Robert Mandrou, ed., *Possession et sorcellerei au XVIIe siècle*, 134–94. Paris, 1979.

Henckel, Elias Heinrich de. *Ordo et methodus cognoscendi et curandi energumenos seu a stygio cacodaemone obsessis expulsione*. Frankfurt and Leipzig, 1689.

Herolt, Johannes. *Sermones venerabilis ac devoti religiosi*. Lyons, 1514.

Hippocrates, *On the Sacred Disease*. In *The Genuine Works of Hippocrates*, trans. Charles Darwin Adams. 2 vols. New York, 1886.

The History of the Witches of Renfrewshire. Paisley: Alex Gardner, 1877.

Hobbes, Thomas. *Leviathan*. London, 1651.

Holland, Henry. *A Treatise against Witchcraft*. Cambridge, 1590.

Holmes, Nathaniel. *Plain Dealing*. London, 1652.

Horst, Jacob. *De aureo dente maxillari pueri Silesii*. Lipsy, 1595.

Humier, François. *Discours théologique sur l'histoire de Magdelaine Bavent*. Nyort, 1649.

Jolly Thomas. *The Surey Demoniack: or, An Account of Satan's Strange and Dreadful Actings in and about the Body of Richard Dugdale of Surey, near Whalley in Lancashire*. London, 1697.

Jonson, Ben. *The Devil is an Ass*. London, 1631. First performed 1616.

Jorden, Edward. *A Briefe Discourse of a Disease Called the Suffocation of the Mother*. London, 1603.

A Just Reproof to the False Reports and Unjust Calumnies Dropt in Two Late Pamphlets. Edinburgh, 1705.

Kramer, Heinrich. *The Hammer of Witches: A Complete Translation of the* Malleus Maleficarum, trans. Christopher S. Mackay. Cambridge, 2009.

Kurella, Ernst Gottfried. *Gedanken von Besessenen und Bezauberten*. Halle, 1749.

La Ménardière, Hippolyte-Jules Pilet de. *Traitté de la melancholie, sçavoir si elle est la cause des effets que l'on remarque dans les possédées de Loudon*. La Fleche, 1635.

Lancre, Pierre de. *On the Inconstancy of Witches: Pierre de Lancre's* Tableau de l'inconstance des mauvais anges et démons (1612), ed. Gerhild Scholz Williams. Tempe, Ariz, 2006.

Lange Johann. *Medicinalium epistolarum miscellanea*. Basel, 1554.

Lapide, Cornelius à. *The Great Commentary of Cornelius à Lapide*, trans. Thomas W. Mossman. London, 1890.

Laurens, André Du. *A Discourse of the Preservation of the Sight: of Melancholike Diseases, of Rheumes, and of Old Age*. London, 1599. Reprinted Oxford, 1938.

Lawson, Deodat, *A Brief and True Narrative of Some Remarkable Passages relating to Sundry Persons Afflicted by Witchcraft*. Boston, 1693.

Lemnius, Levinus. *De miraculis occultis naturae*. Frankfurt, 1593. Trans. *The Secret Miracles of Nature*. London, 1658.

Lenglet Dufresnoy, Nicolas, ed. *Dissertations anciennes et nouvelles sur les apparitions, les visions & les songes*. 2 vols. Paris, 1751–2.

Le Normant, Jean. *Histoire veritable et memorable de ce qui c'est passé sous l'exorcisme de trois filles possedées és pais de Flandre*, Paris, 1623.

The Life and Death of Lewis Gaufridi, a Priest in the Church of the Accoules in Marseilles in France. London, 1612.

Mackenzie, Sir George. *The Laws and Customes of Scotland in Matters Criminal*. Edinburgh, 1678.

Maldonado, Juan de. *Traicté des anges et demons*, trans. François de La Borie. Paris, 1605.

Mandrou, Robert, ed. *Possession et sorcellerie au XVIIe siècle: Textes inédits*. Paris, 1979.

Marescot, Michel. *A True Discourse upon the Matter of Martha Brossier of Romorantin, Pretended to be Possessed by a Devil*, trans. Abraham Hartwell. London, 1599.

Mather, Cotton. 'Another Brand Pluckt Out of the Burning, or More Wonders of the Invisible World'. In *Narratives of the Witchcraft Cases, 1648–1706*, ed. George Lincoln Burr, 308–23. New York, 1914.

——. 'A Brand Pluck'd out of the Burning' (1693). In *Narratives of the Witchcraft Cases, 1648–1706*, ed. George Lincoln Burr., 253–87. New York, 1914.

——. 'A Discourse on the Power and the Malice of the Devils'. In *Memorable Providences regarding Witchcrafts and Possessions*. 52–66. Boston, 1689, 1697.

—— *Memorable Providences regarding Witchcrafts and Possessions*. Boston, 1689.

Meade, Richard. *Medica sacra; or, a Commentary on the Most Remarkable Diseases, Mentioned in the Holy Scriptures*. London, 1755.

Mede, Joseph. *The Apostasy of the Latter Times . . . or the Gentiles Theology of Daemons*. London, 1644.

Menghi, Girolamo. *Compendio dell'arte essorcistica et possibilità delle mirabilis: e stupende operationi delli demoni e de' malefici*. Bologna, 1579; Venice, 1601.

——. *Flagellum daemonum seu exorcismi terribiles potentissimi et efficaces in malignos spiritus expellendos*. Venice, 1593.

——. *Fustis daemonum advirationes formidabiles et potentissimos ad malignos spiritus effigandos de oppressis corporibus humanis complectens*. Venice, 1602.

Michaelis, Sébastien. *The Admirable Historie of the Possession and Conversion of a Penitent Woman*, trans. William Aspley. London, 1613.

——. *Histoire admirable de la possession et conversion d'une pénitente*. Paris, 1613.

[Moore, Mary]. *Wonderfull News from the North, or, a True Relation of the Sad and Grievous Torments Inflicted upon the Bodies of Three Children of Mr George Muschamp*. London, 1650.

More, George. *A True Discourse concerning the Certain Possession and Dispossession of 7 Persons in One Familie in Lancashire*. [Middelburg], 1600.

The Most Strange and Admirable Discoverie of the three witches of Warboys, arraigned, convicted and executed at the last assises at Huntington, for the bewitching of the five daughters of Robert Throckmorton, esquire, and divers other persons, with sundry Divellish and grievous torments. London, 1593.

'Nachricht von dem ehemahlgen vermeynten Zauber-Wesen in der Chur-Sächsischen Berg-Stadt St Annaberg'. In Hauber, *Bibliotheca sive acta et scripta magica*. Vol. 3: 27–31.

'Nachricht von dem Hexenprocess in dem Stift Paderborn'. In Hauber, *Bibliotheca sive acta et scripta magica*. Vol. 2: 711–17.

Niau, des. *The History of the Devils of Loudun: The Alleged Possession of the Ursuline nuns, and the trial and execution of Urbain Grandier, told by an eye witness*, ed. Edmund Goldsmid. Collectanea Adamantea, 21. Edinburgh, 1887–8.

Norman, Samuel, *Authentic Anecdotes of George Lukins, the Yatton Demoniac*. Bristol, 1788.

——. *The Great Apostle Unmasked*. Bristol, 1788.

Nyndge, Edward. *A Booke Declaringe the Fearfull Vexasion of One Alexander Nyndge*. London, 1573.

—— *A True and Fearefull Vexation of one Alexander Nyndge, being Most Horribly Tormented with the Devill*. London, 1615.

Paracelsus. *Sämtliche Werke*, Pt. 1, ed. Karl Suhoff. Munich and Berlin, 1922–33; Pt. 2, ed. Wilhelm Matthiessen and Kurt Goldammer. Munich and Stuttgart, 1923.

Pardoux, Barthélemy. *De morbis animi liber*. Lyon, 1639.

Pegge, Samuel. *An Examination of the Enquiry into the Meaning of Demoniacs in the New Testament*. London, 1739.

Perkins, William. *A Discourse on the Damned Art of Witchcraft*. Cambridge, 1608.

Perraud, François. *Demonologie ou traitte des demons et sorciers: De leur puissance et impuissance*. Geneva, 1613.

Philo of Alexandria. 'On Giants', in *Philo*. Vol. 2, trans. F.H. Colson and G.H. Whitaker, 441–79. London, 1929.

Pichard, Rémy. *Admirable vertu des saincts exorcism sur les princes d'enfer possédants réellement vertueuse demoiselle Elisabeth de Ranfaing*. Nancy, 1622.

Pierquin, Jean. *Conjectures sur les effets de l'obsession naturelle,* in *Oeuvres physiques et géographiques.* Paris, 1744.

Pithoys, Claude. *La Descouverture des faux possedez.* Châlons, 1621.

——. *A Seventeenth-century Exposure of Superstition: Select Texts of Claude Pithoys (1587–1676),* ed. P.J.S. Whitmore. The Hague, 1972.

Pomponazzi, Pietro. *De naturalium effectuum causis, sive de incantationibus.* In *Opera,* 6–327. Basel, 1567.

—— *Les Causes des merveilles de la nature, ou les enchantements,* ed. H. Bussom. Paris, 1930.

La Possession de Jeanne Féry religieuse de couvent des Soeurs Noires de la ville de Mons (1584). Reprinted in D.-M. Bourneville, ed., *Histoire Admirable.* Paris, 1886.

Pratensis, Jason. *De cerebri morbis.* Basel, 1549.

'Le Procès du carroi de Marlou'. In *Les Sorciers du carroi de Marlou. Un procès de sorcellerie en Berry (1582–1583),* ed. Nicole Jacques-Chaquin, and Maxime Préaud. Grenoble, 1996.

Procès verbal fait pour délivrer une fille possédée par le malin esprit à Louviers (1591), ed. Armand Bénet. Introduction by B. de Moray. Paris, 1883.

A Relation of the Diabolical Practices of above Twenty Wizards and Witches of the Sheriffdom of Renfrewshire. London, 1697.

Remy, Nicolas. *Demonolatry,* trans. E. Allen Ashwin; ed. Montague Summers. London, 1930.

Richard, Charles-Louis. *Dissertation sur la possession des corps & sur l'infestation des maisons par les démons.* Amiens, 1746. Reprinted in Nicolas Lenglet Dufresnoy, *Dissertations anciennes et nouvelles.* Vol. 2, Pt. 1, 191–241.

Richeome, Louis. *Trois discours pour la religion catholique et miracles et images.* Bordeaux, 1598.

Riolanus, Johannes. *Ad libros Fernelii de abditis rerum causis commentarius.* In Riolanus *Opera omnia.* Paris, 1610.

Rituale Romanum Pauli V. Pont. Max. iussu editum. Antwerp, 1635.

Rogers, John. *Ohel or Beth-shemess: A Tabernacle for the Sun.* London, 1653.

Saducismus Debellatus. London, 1698.

Saint-André, François de. *Lettres au sujet de la magie, des malefices et des sorciers.* Paris, 1725.

Sanchez, Thomas. *In Praecepta Decalogi.* Lugduni, 1661.

Schaller, Daniel. *Herolt.* Magdeburg, 1595.

Schedel, Hartmann, *Liber chronicarum.* Nuremberg, 1493.

Scherer, Georg. *Christliche Erinnerung bey der Historien von jüngst beschehener Erledigung einer Junckfrawen.* Ingolstadt, 1584.

Scot, Reginald. *The Discoverie of Witchcraft,* ed. M. Summers. London, 1930.

——. *The Discoverie of Witchcraft . . . Whereunto is Added an Excellent Discourse of the Nature and Substance of Devils and Spirits.* London, 1665.

Scottish Diaries and Memoirs. Vol. 2: *1746–1843,* ed. J. D. Fyfe. Stirling, 1927.

The Second Part of the Boy of Bilson, or a True and Particular Relation of the Impostor Susanna Fowles. London, 1698.

Seiler, Tobias. *Daemonomania: Uberaus schreckliche historia von einem besessenen zwelfjährigen jungfräwlein zu Lewenberg in Schlesien in diesem 1605 jahr.* Wittenberg, 1605.

Semler, Johann Salomo. *Abfertigung der neuen Geister und alten Irrtümer in der Lohmannischen Begeisterung zu Kemberg.* Halle, 1760.

——. *Dissertatio theologico-hermeneutica de daemoniacis quorum in Evangeliis fit mentio.* Halle, 1760.

A Short Discourse Shewing the Most Certen and Principal and Good Meanes Ordeined of God to Discover, Expel and to Confound all the Sathanicall Inventions of Witchcraft and Sorcery. London, 1590.

Sinclair, George. *Satan's Invisible World Discovered.* Edinburgh, 1685.

——. *Satan's Invisible World Discovered . . . To which is added . . . the witches of Bargarran . . .* Edinburgh, 1780.

Spinoza, Baruch. *The Collected Works of Spinoza*, ed. Edwin Curley. Princeton, 1985.

——. *Spinoza. The Letters*, trans. Samuel Shirley. Indianapolis, 1995.

A Strange and True Relation of a Young Woman Possessed with the Devil. London, 1647.

Swan, John. *A True and Breife Report of Mary Glovers vexation and of her deliverance by the meanes of fastinge and prayer*. London, 1603.

Sydenham Thomas. *Dr Sydenham's method of curing almost all diseases*. 3rd edn. London, 1697.

Sykes, Arthur Ashley, *Enquiry into the Meaning of Demoniacks in the New Testament*. London, 1737.

Taxil, Jean. *Traicté de l'épilepsie, maladie vulgairement appellée au pays de Provence, la gouttete aux petits enfans.* Tournon, 1602.

Taylor, Zachary. *The Devil Turn'd Casuist, or the Cheats of Rome, Laid Open in the Exorcism of a Despairing Devil*. London, 1696.

——. *Popery, superstition, ignorance, and knavery, confess'd, and fully proved on the Surey Dissenters from the second letter of an apostate friend to Zach. Taylor*. London, 1699.

——. *The Surey Impostor*. London, 1697.

Thyraeus, Petrus. *Daemoniaci, hoc est: de obsessis a spiritibus daemoniorum hominibus liber unus.* Cologne, 1603.

Tillotson, John. *The Works*, ed. Thomas Birch, 3 vols. London, 1752.

Tooker, William, *Charisma or the Gift of Healing*. London, 1597.

A True and Full Relation of the Witches at Pittenweem. Edinburgh, 1704.

A True and Impartial Relation of the Informations against Three Witches. London, 1682.

A True and Most Dreadfull Discourse of a Woman Possessed with the Devill, who in the Likenesse of a Headlesse Beare Fetched her out of her Bedd . . . at Dichet in Somersetshire. London, 1584.

A True Narrative of the Sufferings and Relief of a Young Girle. Edinburgh, 1698. Reprinted in *A History of the Witches of Renfrewshire*. Paisley, 1877.

Vineti, Jean. *Tractatus contra demonum invocatores*. Cologne, 1487.

Viret, Pierre, *Le monde à l'empire et le monde demoniacle*. Geneva, 1561.

——. *The World Possessed with Devils, conteinying three dialogues*. London, 1583.

Visconti, Zacharia. *Complementum artis exorcisticae*. Venice, 1600.

Vries, Simon de. *De Satan in sijn weesen, aert, bedryf, en guychel-spel.* Utrecht, 1692.

Webster, John. *The Displaying of Supposed Witchcraft*. London, 1677.

Weston, William. *The Autobiography of an Elizabethan*, trans. Philip Caraman. London, 1955.

Weyer, Johann. *Witches, Devils and Doctors in the Renaissance: Johann Weyer*, De Praestigiis daemonum, ed. George Mora. Medieval and Renaissance Texts and Studies, 73. Binghamton, NY, 1991.

Whiston, William. *An Account of the Daemoniacks and of the Power of Casting out Demons*. London, 1737.

Willard, Samuel. *A Briefe Account of a strange and unusual Providence of God, befallen to Elizabeth Knap of Groton* in *The Mather Papers* [Collections of the Massachusetts Historical Society 8, 4th series, 1868].

Wodrow, Robert. *Analecta or Materials for a History of Remarkable Providence*. Vol. 2, ed. Matthew Leishman. Edinburgh, 1843.

Woolston, Thomas. *A Discourse on the Miracles of our Saviour: in view of the present controversy between infidels and apostates*. London, 1727.

[Zeideler, Georg Andreas]. *Historisches Send-Schreiben, von denen so genannten Wunderlichen Begebenheiten, welche sich an etlichen Knaben zu St Annaberg*. Chemnitz, 1713.

The Zurich Letters, ed. Hastings Robinson. Vol. 1. Cambridge, 1842.

'Zusatz zu der Historie und den Schrifften von den Annabergischen vermeinten Zauberischen Krankheiten'. In Hauber, *Bibliotheca sive acta et scripta magica*. Vol. 3: 577–86.

Secondary Sources

Almond, Philip C. *Demonic Possession and Exorcism in Early Modern England: Contemporary Texts and their Cultural Contexts*. Cambridge, 2004.

Amorth, Gabriele. *An Exorcist Tells His Story*, trans. Nicoletta V. Mackenzie. San Francisco, 1999.

Anglo, Sydney. 'Melancholia and Witchcraft: the Debate between Wier, Scot and Bodin'. In *Folie et déraison à la Renaissance*, ed. Jean Céard. Brussels, 1976.

——. 'Reginald Scot's *Discoverie of Witchcraft*: Scepticism and Sadduceeism'. In *The Damned Art: Essays in the Literature of Witchcraft*, ed. Sydney Anglo, 106–39. London, 1977.

Azouvi, François. 'Possession, révélation, et rationalité médicale au début du XVIIᵉ siècle'. *Revue des Sciences Philosophiques et Théologiques* 64 (1980): 355–62.

Babb, Lawrence. *The Elizabethan Malady: A Study of Melancholia in English Literature from 1580 to 1642*. East Lansing, Mich., 1951.

Backus, Irena, *Le Miracle de Laon: le déraisonnable, le raisonnable, l'apocalyptique et le politique dans les récits du miracle de Laon (1566–1578)*. Paris, 1994.

Baglio, Matt. *The Rite: The Making of a Modern Exorcist*. New York, 2010.

Barnes, Robin B. *Prophecy and Gnosis: Apocalypticism in the Wake of the Lutheran Reformation*. Stanford, 1988.

Barnstone, Willis. *The Restored New Testament: A New Translation with Commentary, including the Gnostic Gospels Thomas, Mary, and Judas*. New York, 2009.

Barry, Jonathan. 'Public Infidelity and Private Belief? The Discourse of Spirits in Enlightenment Bristol'. In *Beyond the Witch Trials*, ed. Owen Davies and Willem de Blécourt, 117–43. Manchester, 2004.

Bárth, Dániel. *Benedikció és exorcizmus a kora újkori Magyarországon* (Benediction and Exorcism in Early Modern Hungary), Budapest, 2010. Summary in English, pp. 439–50.

Bartra, Roger. *Melancholy and Culture. Essays on the Diseases of the Soul in Golden Age Spain*. Cardiff, 2008.

Bax, Mart. 'Women's Madness in Medjugorje: Between Devils and Pilgrims in a Yugoslav Devotional Centre'. *Journal of Mediterranean Studies* 1 (1992): 42–54.

Beattie, John and John Middleton, eds. *Spirit Mediumship and Society in Africa*. New York, 1969.

Bechtel, Guy. *Sorcellerie et possession: L'affaire Gaufridy*. Paris, 1972.

Behrend, Heike and Ute Luig. *Spirit Possession, Modernity and Power in Africa*. Oxford, 1999.

Behringer, Wolfgang. *Witchcraft Persecutions in Bavaria: Popular Magic, Religious Zealotry and Reason of State in Early Modern Europe*. Cambridge, 1997.

Bell, Rudolph M. *Holy Anorexia*. Chicago, 1985.

Benz, Ernst. 'Ergriffenheit und Besessenheit als Grundformen religiöser Erfahrung'. In *Ergriffenheit und Besessenheit. ein interdisziplinäres Gespräch über transkulturell-anthropologishe und psychiatrische Fragen*, ed. Jurg Zutt. Bern and Munich, 1972.

Bever, Edward. *The Realities of Witchcraft and Popular Magic in Early Modern Europe: Culture, Cognition and Everyday Life*. Basingstoke, 2008.

Biddle, Bruce J. and Edwin J. Thomas, eds. *Role Theory: Concepts and Research*. New York, 1966.

Bilinkoff, Jodi. 'A Spanish Prophetess and her Patrons: The Case of Maria de Santo Domingo'. *Sixteenth Century Journal* 23 (1992): 21–34.

Bilu, Yoram. 'Dybbuk, Aslai, Zar: The Cultural Distinctiveness and Historical Situatedness of Possession Illnesses in Three Jewish Milieus'. In *Spirit Possession in Judaism*, ed. Matt Goldish, 346–65. Detroit, 2003.

Bilu, Yoram. 'The Taming of the Deviants and Beyond: An Analysis of Dybbuk Possession and Exorcism in Judaism'. In *The Psychoanalytical Study of Society*, ed. L. Bryce Boyer and Simon L. Grolnick, 1–32. Hillsdale, NJ, 1985. Also in *Spirit Possession in Judaism*, ed. Matt Goldish, 41–72.

Blackwell, Jeannine, 'Controlling the Demoniac: Johann Salomo Semler and the Possession of Anna Elisabeth Lohmann (1759)'. In *Impure Reason: Dialectic of Enlightenment in Germany*, ed. W. Daniel Wilson and Robert C. Holub. 425–42. Detroit, 1993.

——. 'German Narratives of Women's Divine and Demonic Possession and Supernatural Vision, 1555–1800: A Bibliography'. In *Women in German Yearbook: Feminist Studies in German Literature and Culture* 16 (2000): 241–57.

Böcher, Otto. *Christus Exorcista: Dämonismus und Taufe im Neuen Testament*. Stuttgart, [1972].

Boddy, Janice. 'Spirit Possession Revisited: Beyond Instrumentality'. *Annual Review of Anthropology* 23 (1994): 407–34.

——. *Wombs and Alien Spirits: Women, Men and the Zar Cult in Northern Sudan*. Madison, Wisc., 1989.

Bossy, John. *The English Catholic Community, 1570–1850*. London, 1975.

Bouchet, Henri. *Relation sur l'épidémie de Morzine*. Lyon, 1899.

Bourguignon, Erika. *Possession*. San Francisco, 1976.

Bouwsma, William J. 'Anxiety and the Formation of Early Modern Culture'. In *After the Reformation: Essays in Honor of J.H. Hexter*, ed. Barbara Malament, 215–46. Philadelphia, 1980.

Briggs, Robin. *The Witches of Lorraine*. Oxford, 2007.

Broedel, Hans Peter. *The Malleus Maleficarum and the Construction of Witchcraft. Theology and Popular Belief*. Manchester, 2003.

Brown, Judith C. *Immodest Acts: The Life of a Lesbian Nun in Renaissance Italy*. New York, 1986.

Brown, Karen McCarthy. *Mama Lola: A Vodou Priestess in Brooklyn*. Updated edn. Berkeley, 2001.

Brown, Peter. *The Cult of the Saints: Its Rise and Function in Latin Christianity*. Chicago, 1981.

——. *Relics and Social Status in the Age of Gregory of Tours*. Reading, 1977.

——. *Society and the Holy in Late Antiquity*. Berkeley, 1982.

——. 'Sorcery, Demons and the Rise of Christianity: From Late Antiquity into the Middle Ages'. In *Religion and Society in the Age of Saint Augustine*, ed. Peter Brown, 118–46. New York, 1972.

Brownlow, F.W. *Shakespeare, Harsnett and the Devils of Denham*. Newark, Del., 1993.

Bunge, Wiep van. 'Eric Walton (1663–1697): An Early Enlightenment Radical in the Dutch Republic'. In *Disguised and Overt Spinozism around 1700*, ed. Wiep van Bunge and Wim Klever, 41–54. Leiden, 1996.

Burkhardt, Albrecht. 'Besessenheit, Melancholie, und *mal de mère* in Wunderberichten fränzosischer Heiligsprechungsprozesse des frühen 17. Jahrhunderts'. In *Dämonische Besessenheit*, ed. Hans de Waardt et al., 107–25. Bielefeld, 2005.

——. 'A False Living Saint in Cologne in the 1620s: The Case of Sophia Agnes von Langenberg'. In *Illness and Healing Alternatives in Western Europe*, ed. Marijke Gijswijt-Hofstra, Hilary Marland and Hans de Waardt, 80–97. London 1997.

Burns, Robert M. *The Great Debate on Miracles: From Joseph Glanvill to David Hume*. Lewisburg, 1981.

Burns, William E. *An Age of Wonders: Prodigies, Politics and Providence in England, 1657–1727*. Manchester, 2002.

Bynum, Caroline Walker. *Holy Feast and Holy Fast: The Religious Significance of Food to Medieval Women*. Berkeley, 1987.

Caciola, Nancy. *Discerning Spirits: Divine and Demonic Possession in the Middle Ages*. Ithaca, NY, 2003.

Calmeil, Louis-Florentin. *De la Folie, considérée sous le point de vue pathologique, philosophique, historique et judiciaire*, 2 vols. Paris, 1845.

Cambers, Andrew. 'Demonic Possession, Literacy and "Superstition" in Early Modern England'. *Past and Present* 202 (Feb. 2009): 3–35.

Cameron, Euan. *Enchanted Europe: Superstition, Reason and Religion, 1250–1750*. Oxford, 2010.

Cañizares-Esguerra, Jorge. *Puritan Conquistadors: Iberianizing the Atlantic, 1550–1700*. Stanford, 2006.

Caro Baroja, Julio. *The World of the Witches*, trans. O.N.V. Glendinning. Chicago, 1965.

Carroy-Thirard, Jacqueline. *Le Mal de Morzine: de la possession à l'hystérie (1857–1877)*. Paris, 1981.

Certeau, Michel de. *The Possession at Loudun*, trans. Michael B. Smith. Chicago, 1996.

——. *The Writing of History*, trans. Tom Conley. New York, 1988.

Cervantes, Fernando. 'The Devils of Querétaro: Scepticism and Credulity in Late Seventeenth-century Mexico'. *Past and Present* 130 (1991): 51–69.

——. *The Devil in the New World. The Impact of Diabolism in New Spain*. New Haven and London, 1994.

——. *The Idea of the Devil and the Problem of the Indian: The Case of Mexico in the Sixteenth Century*. London, 1991.

Chajes, J. H. *Between Worlds: Dybbuks, Exorcists, and Early Modern Judaism*. Philadelphia, 2003.

——. 'Judgments Sweetened: Possession and Exorcism in Early Modern Jewish Culture'. *Journal of Early Modern History* 1 (1997): 124–69.

Charcot, Jean-Martin. *Die Besessenheit in der Kunst*. Göttingen, 1988.

Clark, Stuart. 'Demons and Disease: The Disenchantment of the Sick (1500–1700)'. In *Illness and Healing Alternatives in Western Europe*, ed. Marijke Gijswijt-Hofstra, Hilary Marland and Hans de Waardt, 38–58. London 1997.

——. 'The Scientific Status of Demonology'. In *Occult and Scientific Mentalities in the Renaissance*, ed. Brian Vickers, 351–74. Cambridge, 1984.

——. *Thinking with Demons: The Idea of Witchcraft in Early Modern Europe*. Oxford, 1997.

Closson, Marianne. *L'Imaginaire démoniaque en France (1550–1650): genèse de la littérature fantastique*. Geneva, 2000.

Cohn, Norman. *Europe's Inner Demons: The Demonization of Christians in Medieval Christendom*. Chicago, 1993.

Cole, Michael. 'The Demonic Arts and the Origins of the Medium'. *The Art Bulletin* 84 (2002): 621–40.

Coons, Philip M. 'The Differential Diagnosis of Possession States'. *Dissociation*, 6 (1993): 213–21.

Cox, John D. *The Devil and the Sacred in English Drama, 1350–1642*. Cambridge, 2000.

Crabtree, Adam. *From Mesmer to Freud: Magnetic Sleep and the Roots of Psychological Healing*. New Haven and London, 1993.

——. *Multiple Man: Explorations in Possession and Multiple Personality*. New York, 1985.

Crapanzano, Vincent and Vivian Garrison. *Case Studies in Spirit Possession*. New York, 1977.

Crouzet, Denis, 'A Woman and the Devil: Possession and Exorcism in sixteenth-century France'. In *Changing Identities in Early Modern France*, ed. Michael Wolfe, 191–215. Durham, NC, 1997.

Cuneo, Michael W. *American Exorcism: Expelling Demons in the Land of Plenty*. New York, 2001.

Dall'Olio, Guido. 'Alle origini della nuova esorcistica. I maestri bolognesi di Girolamo Menghi'. In *Inquisizioni: Percorsi di ricerca*, ed. Giovanna Paolin, 81–219. Trieste, 2001.

Darr, Orna Alyagon. *Marks of an Absolute Witch: Evidentiary Dilemmas in Early Modern England*. Farnham, Surrey, 2011.

Daston, Lorraine and Katharine Parks. *Wonders and the Order of Nature, 1150–1750*. Cambridge, Mass., 1998.

Davies, Natalie Zemon. 'Boundaries and the Sense of Self in Sixteenth-century France'. In *Reconstructing Individualism: Autonomy, Individuality, and the Self in Western Thought*, ed. Thomas C. Heller, Morton Sosna, David E. Wellbery et al., 53–63. Stanford, 1986.

Davies, Owen. *Witchcraft, Magic and Culture, 1736–1951*. Manchester, 1999.

Decker, Rainer. 'Die Haltung der römisches Inquisition gegenüber Hexenglauben und Exorcismus am Beispiel der Teufelanstreibungen in Paderborn 1657'. In *Das Ende der Hexenverfolgung*, ed. S. Lorenz and Dieter Bauer. Stuttgart, 1995.

——. *Witchcraft and the Papacy: An Account Drawing on the Formerly Secret Records of the Roman Inquisition*, trans. H.C. Erik Midelfort. Charlottesville, 2008.

Delbanco, Andrew. *The Death of Satan: How Americans Have Lost the Sense of Evil*. New York, 1996.

Delcambre, Etienne and Jean Lhermitte. *Un Case énigmatique de possession diabolique en Lorraine au XVIIᵉ siècle: Elisabeth de Ranfaing, l'énergumène de Nancy*. Nancy, 1956.

Delumeau, Jean. *Sin and Fear: The Emergence of a Western Guilt Culture, 13th–18th Centuries*, trans. Eric Nicholson. New York, 1989.

Demos, John Putnam. *Entertaining Satan: Witchcraft and the Culture of Early New England*. New York, 1982.

Devlin, Judith. *The Superstitious Mind. French Peasants and the Supernatural in the Nineteenth Century*. New Haven and London, 1987.

Didi-Huberman, Georges. *Invention of Hysteria: Charcot and the Photographic Iconography of the Salpêtrière*, trans. Alisa Hartz. Cambridge, Mass., 2003.

Diethelm, Oskar, 'The Medical Teaching of Demonology in the Seventeenth and Eighteenth Centuries'. *Journal of the History of the Behavioral Sciences* 6 (1970): 3–15.

Dillinger, Johannes 'Beelzebulstreitigkeiten: Besessenheit in der Bibel'. In *Dämonische Besessenheit: zur Interpretation eines kulturhistorischen Phänomens*, ed. Hans de Waardt et al., 37–62. Bielefeld, 2005.

Djkhutzen Jan Frans van. 'Theatricality, Inwardness and the Demonic in Ben Jonson'. In *Dämonische. Besessenheit*, ed. Hans de Waardt et al., 145–62. Bielefeld, 2005.

Duden, Barbara. *The Woman beneath the Skin: A Doctor's Patients in Eighteenth-century Germany*, trans. Thomas Dunlap. Cambridge, Mass., 1991.

Duni, Matteo. *Under the Devil's Spell: Witches, Sorcerers, and the Inquisition in Renaissance Italy*. Florence, 2007.

Edwards, Mark U., Jr. *Luther's Last Battles: Politics and Polemics 1531–46*. Ithaca, NY and London, 1983.

Ellenberger, Henri F. *The Discovery of the Unconscious: The History and Evolution of Dynamic Psychiatry*. New York, 1970.

Elmer, Peter. 'Medicine, Witchcraft and the Politics of Healing in Late Seventeenth-century England'. In *Medicine and Religion in Enlightenment Europe*, ed. Ole Peter Grell and Andrew Cunningham, 223–41. Aldershot, 2007.

Erikson, Erik H. *Young Man Luther: A Study in Psychoanalysis and History*. New York, 1962.

Ernst, Cécile. *Teufelaustreibungen: Die Praxis der Katholischen Kirche im 16 und 17. Jahrhundert*. Bern, 1972.

Ferber, Sarah. 'The Abuse of History? Identity Politics, Disordered Identity and the "Really Real" in French Cases of Possession'. In *Women, Identities and Communities in Early Modern Europe*, ed. Stephanie Tarbin and Susan Broomhall, 29–41. Aldershot, 2008.

——. 'Charcot's Demons: Retrospective Medicine and Historical Diagnosis in the Writings of the Salpêtrière School'. In *Illness and Healing Alternatives in Western Europe*, ed. Marijke Gijswijt-Hofstra, Hilary Marland and Hans de Waardt, 120–40. London, 1997.

——. 'Cultivating Charisma: Elisabeth de Ranfaing and the Médailliste Cult in Seventeenth-century Lorraine'. In *Rituals, Images, and Words: Varieties of Cultural Expression in Late Medieval and Early Modern Europe*, ed. F.W. Kent and Charles Zika, 55–84. Turnhout, 2005.

——. 'The Demonic Possession of Marthe Brossier, France 1598–1600'. In *No Gods Except Me: Orthodoxy and Religious Practice in Europe 1200–1600*, ed. Charles Zika, 59–83. Melbourne, 1991.

——. *Demonic Possession and Exorcism in Early Modern France*. London, 2004.

——. 'Possession and the Sexes'. In *Witchcraft and Masculinities in Early Modern Europe*, ed. Alison Rowlands, 214–38. Basingstoke, 2009.

——. 'Reformed or Recycled? Possession and Exorcism in the Sacramental Life of Early Modern France'. In *Witches, Werewolves and Wandering Spirits*, ed. Kathryn Edwards, 58–9. Kirksville, Miss., 2002.

Ferber, Sarah and Adrian Howe. 'The Man Who Mistook his Wife for a Devil: Exorcism, Expertise and Secularisation in a Late Twentieth-century Australian Criminal Court'. In *Dämonische Besessenheit*, ed. Hans de Waardt et al., 281–92. Bielefeld, 2005.

Ferguson, Everett. *Demonology of the Early Christian World*. New York and Toronto, 1984.

Fishwick, Henry. *A History of Lancashire*. London, 1894.

——. 'The Lancashire Demoniacs'. *Transactions of the Historic Society of Lancashire and Cheshire* 35 (1883): 129–46.

Fix, Andrew. *Fallen Angels: Balthasar Bekker, Spirit Belief, and Confessionalism in the Seventeenth-century Dutch Republic*. Dordrecht, 1999.

——. 'Bekker and Spinoza'. In *Disguised and Overt Spinozism around 1700*, ed. Wiep van Bunge and Wim Klever, 23–40. Leiden, 1996.

Flint, Valerie. *The Rise of Magic in Early Medieval Europe*. Princeton, 1991.

Foucault, Michel. *Abnormal Lectures at the Collège de France 1974–1975*, trans. Graham Burchell. New York, 1999.

Freeman, Thomas. 'Demons, Deviance and Defiance: John Darrell and the Politics of Exorcism in Late Elizabethan England'. In *Conformity and Orthodoxy in the English Church, c. 1560–1660*, ed. Peter Lake and Michael Questier, 34–63. Woodbridge, Suffolk, 2000.

Freud, Sigmund. 'A Seventeenth-century Demonological Neurosis'. In *The Standard Edition of the Complete Psychological Works*, ed. James Strachey. Vol. 19: 67–105. London, 1975.

Frijhoff, Willem. *Wegen van Evert Willemsz: een Hollands weeskind op zoek naar zichzelf, 1607–1647*. Nijmegen, 1995.

Garnier, Samuel. *Barbe Buvée, en religion Soeur Sainte-Colombe et la prétendue possession des Ursulines d'Auxonne (1658–1663)*. Paris, 1895.

Garnot, Benoît. *Le Diable au couvent: les possédées d'Auxonne (1658–1663)*. Paris, 1995.

Garrett, Clarke. *Spirit Possession and Popular Religion: From the Camisards to the Shakers*. Baltimore, 1987.

Geertz, Gifford. 'Religion as a Cultural System'. In *Anthropological Approaches to the Study of Religion*, ed. Michael Banton, 1–46. London, 1966.

Geis, Gilbert and Ivan Bunn. *A Trial of Witches: A Seventeenth-century Witchcraft Prosecution*. London, 1997.

Gibson, Marion. *Possession, Puritanism and Print: Darrell, Harsnett, Shakespeare and the Elizabethan Exorcism Controversy*. London, 2006.

——. *Reading Witchcraft: Stories of Early English Witches*. London, 1999.

Gilman, Sander L., ed. *Hysteria beyond Freud*. Berkeley, 1993.

Godbeer, Richard. *The Devil's Dominion: Magic and Religion in Early New England*. Cambridge, 1992.

Goddou, André. 'The Failure of Exorcism in the Middle Ages'. In *Miscellanea Mediaevalia* 12: *Soziale Ordnungen in Selbstverständnis des Mittelalters*, 540–7. Berlin, 1980.

Goldish, Matt, ed. *Spirit Possession in Judaism: Cases and Contexts from the Middle Ages to the Present*. Detroit, 2003.

Goldstein, Jan. *Console and Classify: The French Psychiatric Profession in the Nineteenth Century*. Cambridge, 1987.

Goodman, Felicitas. *American Exorcism: Expelling Demons in the Land of Plenty*. New York, 2001.

——. *Ecstasy, Ritual and Alternate Reality*. Bloomington, Ind., 1988.

Görres, Johann Joseph von. *Die Christliche Mystik*, 5 vols. Graz, 1960.

Gow, Andrew. 'Challenging the Protestant Paradigm: Bible Reading in Lay and Urban Contexts of the Later Middle Ages'. In *Scripture and Pluralism*, ed. Thomas J. Heffernan and Thomas E. Burman, 161–91. Leiden and Boston, 2005.

Gowland, Angus. 'The Problem of Early Modern Melancholy'. *Past and Present* 191 (2006): 77–120.

——. *The Worlds of Renaissance Melancholy: Robert Burton in Context.* Cambridge, 2006.

Greenblatt, Stephen. 'Loudun and London'. *Critical Inquiry* 12 (1986): 326–46.

——. *Shakespearean Negotiations: The Circulation of Social Energy in Renaissance England.* Berkeley, 1988.

Haag, Herbert. *Bibel-Lexikon.* Zurich and Cologne, 1956.

Hacking, Ian. *Rewriting the Soul: Multiple Personality and the Sciences of Memory.* Princeton, 1975.

——. *The Social Construction of What?* Cambridge, Mass., 1995.

Hallett, Nicky. *Witchcraft, Exorcism and the Politics of Possession in a Seventeenth-century Convent: 'How Sister Ursula Was Once Bewitched and Sister Margaret Twice'.* Aldershot, 2007.

Halliczer, Stephen. *Between Exorcism and Infamy: Female Mystics in the Golden Age of Spain.* Oxford, 2002.

Harley, David. 'Explaining Salem: Calvinist Psychology and the Diagnosis of Possession'. *American Historical Review* 101 (1996): 307–30.

Harrell, David Edwin Jr. *All Things are Possible: The Healing and Charismatic Revivals in Modern America.* Bloomington, Ind., 1975.

Harris, Grace. 'Possession "Hysteria" in a Kenya Tribe'. *American Anthropologist* 59 (1957): 1046–66.

Harris, Ruth. 'Possession on the Borders: The "Mal de Morzine" in Nineteenth-century France'. *Journal of Modern History* 69 (1997): 457–78.

Hayward, Rhodri. 'Demonology, Neurology, and Medicine in Edwardian Britain'. *Bulletin of the History of Medicine* 78 (2004): 37–58.

Hengel, Martin. *Judaism and Hellenism: Studies in their Encounter in Palestine during the Early Hellenistic Period*, 2 vols. Philadelphia, 1974.

Henningsen, Gustav. *The Witches' Advocate: Basque Witchcraft and the Spanish Inquisition (1609–1614).* Reno, Nev., 1980.

Herzig, Tamar. 'Witches, Saints and Heretics: Heinrich Kramer's Ties with Italian Women Mystics'. *Magic, Ritual, and Witchcraft* (2006): 24–55.

Heyd, Michael. *'Be Sober and Reasonable': The Critique of Enthusiasm in the Seventeenth and Early Eighteenth Centuries.* Leiden, 1995.

——. 'The Reaction to Enthusiasm in the Seventeenth Century: Toward an Integrative Approach'. *Journal of Modern History* 53 (1981): 258–80.

Holmes, Clive. 'Witchcraft and Possession at the Accession of James I: The Publication of Samuel Harsnett's *Declaration of Egregious Popish Impostures'.* In *Witchcraft and the Act of 1604*, ed. John Newton and Jo Bath, 69–90. Leiden, 2008.

Houston, R.A. *Punishing the Dead? Suicide, Lordship, and Community in Britain, 1500–1830.* Oxford, 2010.

Hustvedt, Asti. *Medical Muses: Hysteria in Nineteenth-century Paris.* New York, 2011.

Huxley, Aldous. *The Devils of Loudun.* New York, 1952.

Isaacs, Ronald. *Ascending Jacob's Ladder: Jewish Views of Angels, Demons and Evil Spirits.* Northvale, NJ and Jerusalem, 1998.

Israel, Jonathan I. 'Enlightenment, Radical Enlightenment and the "Medical Revolution" of the Late Seventeenth and Eighteenth Centuries.' In *Medicine and Religion in Enlightenment Europe*, ed. Ole Peter Grell and Andrew Cunningham, 5–28. Aldershot, 2007.

——. *Radical Enlightenment: Philosophy and the Making of Modernity.* Oxford, 2001.

Jackson, Stanley W. *Melancholia and Depression: From Hippocratic Times to the Modern Times.* New Haven and London, 1986.

Jacques-Chaquin, Nicole and Maxime Préaud, eds. *Les Sorciers du carroi de Marlou: un procès de sorcellerie en Berry (1582–1583)* Grenoble, 1996.

Jehl, Rainer. 'Melancholie und Besessenheit im gelehrten Diskurs des Mittelalters.' In *Dämonische Besessenheit*, ed. Hans de Waardt et al., 63–71. Bielefeld, 2005,

Johnson, Paul Christopher. 'An Atlantic Genealogy of Spirit Possession'. *Comparative Studies in Society and History* 53 (2011): 393–425.

Johnson, Trevor. 'Besessenheit, Heiligkeit und Jesuitenspiritualitiät'. In *Dämonische Besessenheit*, ed. Hans de Waardt et al., 233–48. Bielefeld, 2005.

Johnstone, Nathan. 'The Protestant Devil: The Experience of Temptation in Early Modern England'. *Journal of British Studies* 43 (2004): 173–205.

Kallendorf, Hilaire. *Exorcism and its Texts: Subjectivity in Early Modern Literature of England and Spain.* Toronto, 2004.

Kallestrup, Louise Nyholm. '"Da kom den onde ånd ind i mit knae": i kulturhistorisk undersøgelse af djaevlebesaetttelser i Danmark efter Reformationem'. In *Religiøs tro og praksis i den dansk-norske helsat fra reformatasjonen til opplysningstid ca. 1500–181,* ed. Arne Bugge Amundsen and Henning Laugerud, 189–204. Oslo, 2010.

—— 'Knowing Satan from God: Demonic Possession, Witchcraft, and the Lutheran Orthodox Church in Early Modern Denmark'. *Magic, Ritual and Witchcraft* 6 (2011): 162–83.

—— 'Lay and Inquisitorial Witchcraft Prosecutions in Early Modern Italy and Denmark'. *Scandinavian Journal of History* 36 (2011): 265–78.

Kaplan, Benjamin J. 'Possessed by the Devil? A Very Public Dispute in Utrecht'. *Renaissance Quarterly* 49 (1996): 738–59.

Karlsen, Carol F. *The Devil in the Shape of a Woman: Witchcraft in Colonial New England.* New York, 1987.

Keck, David. *Angels and Angelology in the Middle Ages.* New York, 1998.

Keitt, Andrew W. *Inventing the Sacred: Imposture, Inquisition, and the Boundaries of the Supernatural in Golden Age Spain.* Leiden, 2005.

Keller, Mary. *The Hammer and the Flute: Women, Power, and Spirit Possession.* Baltimore and London, 2002.

Kendall, R. T. *Calvin and English Calvinism to 1649.* Oxford, 1979.

Kieckhefer, Richard. *Forbidden Rites: A Necromancer's Manual of the Fifteenth Century.* University Park, Pa., 1997.

——. 'The Holy and the Unholy: Sainthood, Witchcraft and Magic in Late Medieval Europe.' *Journal of Medieval and Renaissance Studies* 24 (1994): 355–85.

——. *Magic in the Middle Ages.* Cambridge, 1990.

Kiely, David M. and Christina McKenna. *The Dark Sacrament: True Stories of Modern-day Demon Possession and Exorcism.* New York, 2007.

Kihlstrom, John F. 'One Hundred Years of Hysteria'. In *Dissociation: Clinical and Theoretical Perspectives,* ed. Steven J. Lynn and Judith W. Rhue, 365–94. New York, 1994.

Killeen, Kevin. *Biblical Scholarship, Science and Politics in Early Modern England: Thomas Browne and the Thorny Place of Knowledge.* Aldershot, 2009.

Klass, Morton. *Mind over Mind: The Anthropology and Psychology of Spirit Possession.* Lanham, Md., 2003.

Klingner, Erich. *Luther und der deutsche Volksaberglaube.* Berlin, 1912.

Klinnert, Renate S. 'Von Besessenen, Melancholikern und Betrügen: Johann Weyers *De Praestigiis Daemonum* und die Unterscheidung der Geister.' In *Dämoniche Besessenheit,* ed. Hans de Waardt et al., 89–105. Bielefeld, 2005.

Krah, Ursula-Maria. '"Von boesen Feindt / dem Teuffel / eingenommen . . .": Das Motiv der Besessenheit in Flugschriften der Frühen Neuzeit'. In *Dämonische Besessenheit,* ed. Hans de Waardt et al., 163–76. Bielefeld, 2005.

Kreiser, B. Robert. 'The Devils of Toulon: Demonic Possession and Religious Politics in Eighteenth-century Provence'. In *Church, State and Society under the Bourbon Kings of France,* ed. Richard M. Golden, 173–221. Lawrence, Kan., 1982.

Ladame, Paul. *Les Possédés et les démoniaques à Genève au XVIIe siècle.* Geneva, 1892.

Laharie, Muriel. *La Folie au moyen âge XIe–XIIIe siècles.* Paris, 1991.

Lavenia, Vincenzo. 'I diavoli di Carpi e il Sant'Uffizio (1636–1639)'. In *Eretici, esuli e indemoniati nell'età moderna,* ed. Mario Rosa, 77–139. Florence, 1998.

Lea, H.C. *Materials toward a History of Witchcraft*, ed. A. C. Howland, 3 vols. Philadelphia, 1939.

Leblond, V. *Denise de la Caille, la possédée de Beauvais: ses crises de possession démoniaque: scènes d'exorcismes et de conjurations (1612–1613)*. Paris, 1908.

Lederer, David. '"Exorzieren ohne Lizenz ...": Befugnis, Skepsis, und Glauben in frühneuzeitlichen Bayern'. In *Dämonische Besessenheit*, ed. Hans de Waardt et al., 213–32. Bielefeld, 2005.

———. *Madness, Religion and the State in Early Modern Europe: A Bavarian Beacon*, Cambridge, 2006.

Leiris, Michel. *La Possession et ses aspects théâtraux chez les Ethiopiens de Gondar*. Paris, 1958.

Levack, Brian P. 'The Decline and End of Witchcraft Prosecutions'. In *Witchcraft and Magic in Europe: The Eighteenth and Nineteenth Centuries*, ed. Bengt Ankarloo and Stuart Clark, 1–93. London, 1999.

——— 'Demonic Possession in Early Modern Scotland'. In *Witchcraft and Belief in Scotland*, ed. Julian Goodare, Joyce Miller and Lauren Martin, 166–84. Basingstoke, 2008.

———. 'Possession, Witchcraft and the Law in Jacobean England'. *Washington and Lee Law Review* 52 (1996): 1613–40.

———. 'The Prosecution of Sexual Crimes in Early Eighteenth-century Scotland'. *Scottish Historical Review* 89 (2010): 172–93.

———. *The Witch-hunt in Early Modern Europe*. 3rd edn. Harlow, 2006.

———. *Witch-hunting in Scotland: Law Politics and Religion*. London, 2008.

Levi, Giovanni. *Inheriting Power: The Study of an Exorcist*, trans. L.G. Cochrane. Chicago, 1985.

Levin, Joanna. 'Lady Macbeth and the Daemonologie of Hysteria'. *English Literary History* 69 (2002): 21–55.

Lewis, I.M. 'Spirit Possession and Deprivation Cults'. *Man*, n.s. 1 (1966): 307–29.

———. *Ectastic Religion: An Anthropological Study of Spirit Possession and Shamanism*. Baltimore, 1971.

———. 'A Structural Approach to Witchcraft and Spirit-possession'. In *Witchcraft Confessions and Accusations*, ed. Mary Douglas, 293–309. London, 1970.

Limbeck, Meinrad. 'Satan und das Böse im Neuen Testament'. In Herbert Haag, *Teufelsglaube*, 271–388. Tübingen, 1974.

Lombardi, Paolo. *Il secolo del diavolo: Esorcismi, magia e lotta sociale in Francia*. Rome, 2005.

Lottin, Alain. *Lille: citadelle de la contre-réforme? (1598–1668)*. Dunkirk, 1984.

———. 'Sorcellerie, possessions diaboliques et crise conventuelle'. In *Histoire des faits de la sorcellerie*, 111–32. Angers, 1985.

Macalpine, Ida and Richard M. Hunter. *Schizophrenia 1677: A Psychiatric Study of an Illustrated Autobiographical Record of Demoniacal Possession*. London, 1956.

MacDonald, Michael. *Mystical Bedlam: Madness, Anxiety and Healing in Seventeenth-century England*. Cambridge, 1981.

———. 'Religion, Social Change, and Psychological Healing in England, 1600–1800', in *The Church and Healing*, ed. W.J. Sheils, 101–25. Oxford, 1982.

———. *Witchcraft and Hysteria in Elizabethan London: Edward Jorden and the Mary Glover Case*. London, 1990.

MacDonald, S.W., A. Thom and A. Thom. 'The Bargarran Witchcraft Trial – A Psychiatric Reassessment'. *Scottish Medical Journal* 412 (1996): 152–8.

McLachlan, Hugh and Kim Swales. 'The Bewitchment of Christian Shaw: A Reassessment of the Famous Paisley Witchcraft Case of 1697'. In *Twisted Sisters: Women, Crime and Deviance in Scotland since 1400*, ed. Yvonne Galloway Brown and Rona Ferguson, 54–83. East Linton, 2002.

Maggi, Armando. *In the Company of Demons: Unnatural Beings, Love and Identity in the Italian Renaissance*. Chicago, 2006.

———. *Satan's Rhetoric: A Study of Renaissance Demonology*. Chicago, 2001.

Maire, Catherine-Laurence. *Les Possédées de Morzine (1857–1873)*. Lyon, 1981.

Mandrou, Robert. *Magistrats et sorciers en France au XVIIᵉ siècle*. Paris, 1968.

——, ed. *Possession et sorcellerie au XVIIe siècle: Textes inédits.* Paris, 1979.
Martin, John Jeffries. *Myths of Renaissance Individualism.* Basingstoke, 2004.
Martin, Malachi. *Hostage to the Devil: The Possession and Exorcism of Five Contemporary Americans.* San Francisco, 1992.
Martin, Ruth. *Witchcraft in Venice 1550–1650.* Oxford, 1989.
Martinich, Aloysius. *The Two Gods of Leviathan: Thomas Hobbes on Religion and Politics.* Cambridge, 2002.
Maxwell-Stuart, P.G. *The Occult in Early Modern Europe: A Documentary History.* New York, 1999.
Métraux, Alfred. *Voodoo in Haiti,* trans. Hugo Charteris. Oxford, 1959.
Micale, Mark S. *Approaching Hysteria: A Disease and its Interpretations.* Princeton, 1995.
——. *Hysterical Men: The Hidden History of Male Nervous Illness.* Cambridge, Mass. 2008.
Michelet, Jules. *La Sorcière: The Witch of the Middle Ages,* trans. L.J. Trotter. London, 1863.
Midelfort, H. C. Erik. 'Catholic and Lutheran Reactions to Demon Possession in the Late Seventeenth Century'. *Daphnis: Zeitschrift für mittlere Deutsche Literatur* 15 (1986): 623–48.
——. 'The Devil and the German People: Reflections on the Popularity of Demon Possession in Sixteenth-century Germany'. In *Religion and Culture in the Renaissance and Reformation,* ed. S. Ozment. Sixteenth Century Essays and Studies 11 (1989): 99–119.
——. *Exorcism and Enlightenment: Johann Joseph Gassner and the Demons of Eighteenth-century Germany.* New Haven and London, 2005.
——. *A History of Madness in Sixteenth-century Germany.* Stanford, 1999.
——. 'Madness and the Problems of Psychological History in the Sixteenth Century'. *Sixteenth Century Journal* 12 (1981): 5–12.
——. 'Natur und Besessenheit: natürliche Erklärungen für Besessenheit von der Melancholie bis zum Magnetismus'. In *Dämonisches Besessenheit,* ed. Hans de Waardt et al., 73–87. Bielefeld, 2005.
——. 'Sin, Melancholy, Obsession: Insanity and Culture in Sixteenth-century Germany'. In *Understanding Popular Culture: Europe from the Middle Ages to the Nineteenth Century,* ed. Steven L. Kaplan, 113–45. Berlin, New York and Amsterdam, 1984.
Monson, Craig A. *Nuns Behaving Badly: Tales of Music, Magic, Art and Arson in the Convents of Italy.* Chicago, 2010.
Monter, E. William. *A Bewitched Duchy: Lorraine and its Dukes, 1477–1736.* Geneva, 2007.
——. *Witchcraft in France and Switzerland: The Borderlands during the Reformation.* Ithaca, NY and London, 1976.
Montgomery, John W., ed. *Demon Possession: A Medical, Historical, Anthropological and Theological Symposium.* Minneapolis, 1976.
Mullan, David George. *Narratives of the Religious Self in Early Modern Scotland.* Aldershot, 2010.
Nakanishi, Fumiaki. 'Possession: A Form of Shamanism?' *Magic, Ritual and Witchcraft* 1 (2006): 234–41.
Newman, Barbara. 'Possessed by the Spirit: Devout Women, Demoniacs and the Apostolic Life in the Thirteenth Century'. *Speculum* 73 (1998): 733–70.
Nischan, Bodo. 'The Exorcism Controversy and Baptism in the Late Reformation'. *Sixteenth Century Journal* 18 (1987): 31–51.
Norman, A.J. 'Witchcraft, Demoniacal Possession and Insanity'. *Journal of Mental Science* 57 (1911): 475–86.
Norton, Mary Beth. *In the Devil's Snare: The Salem Witchcraft Crisis of 1692.* New York, 2002.
Oesterreich, Traugott K. *Possession, Demoniacal and Other: Among Primitive Races in Antiquity, the Middle Ages and Modern Times.* New York, 1966.
Olli, Soili-Maria. 'The Devil's Pact: A Male Strategy'. In *Beyond the Witch Trials: Witchcraft and Magic in Enlightenment Europe,* ed. Owen Davies and Willem de Blécourt, 100–16. Manchester, 2004.
Ostorero, Martine. *Le Diable au sabbat: Littérature démonologique et sorcellerie (1440–1460).* Florence, 2011.

Ouerd, Michèle. 'Dans la Forge à cauchemars mythologiques: sorcières, practiciennes et hystériques'. In *La Sorcellerie*, 103–58. La Cahiers de Fontenay, nos 11–12. Paris, 1992.

Owen, A.R.G. *Hysteria, Hypnosis and Healing: The Work of J.M. Charcot*. New York, 1975.

Pagels, Elaine. *Revelations: Visions, Prophecy, and Politics in the Book of Revelation*. New York, 2012.

Park, Katharine and Lorraine J. Daston. 'Unnatural Conceptions: The Study of Monsters in Sixteenth- and Seventeenth-century France and England'. *Past and Present* 92 (1981): 20–54.

Parry, Glyn. *The Arch-Conjuror of England: John Dee*. New Haven and London, 2011.

Pattison, E. Mansell. 'Psychosocial Interpretations of Exorcism,'. *Journal of Operational Psychology* 8 (1977): 5–19.

Pearl, Jonathan. 'Demons and Politics in France, 1560–1630.' *Historical Reflections* 12 (1985), 241–51.

———. *The Crime of Crimes: Demonology and Politics in France, 1560–1620*. Waterloo, Ontario, 1999.

———. '"A School for the Rebel Soul": Politics and Demonic Possession in France'. *Historical Reflections* 16 (1989): 286–306.

Pfeifer, Samuel. 'Belief in Demons and Exorcism in Psychiatric Patients in Switzerland,' *British Journal of Medical Psychology* 67 (1994): 247–58.

———. 'Psychopathologie und Kausalattribution: Besessenheit als Metapher für psychisches Leiden', in *Dämonische Besessenheit*, ed. Hans de Waardt et al., 293–305. Bielefeld, 2005.

Pfister, Christian. *L'Energumène de Nancy: Elisabeth de Ranfaing et le couvert du Refuge*. Nancy, 1901.

Pócs, Éva. 'Possession Phenomena, Possession-Systems: Some East-Central European Examples'. In *Communicating with the Spirits*, ed. Gábor Klaniczay and Éva Pócs, 84–151. Budapest, 2005.

Popkin, Richard. 'Cartesianism and Biblical Criticism'. In *Problems of Cartesianism*, ed. Thomas M. Lennon, John M. Nicolas and John W. Davis, 61–81. Kingston and Montreal, 1982.

Porter, Roy. 'Witchcraft and Magic in Enlightenment, Romantic and Liberal Thought'. In *Witchcraft and Magic in Europe: The Eighteenth and Nineteenth Centuries*, ed. Bengt Ankarloo and Stuart Clark, 191–282. London, 1999.

Purkiss, Diane. 'Invasions: Prophecy and Bewitchment in the Case of Margaret Muschamp'. *Tulsa Studies in Women's Literature* 17 (1998): 235–53.

Quantin, Jean-Louis. *The Church of England and Christian Antiquity: The Construction of a Confessional Identity in the 17th Century*. Oxford, 2009.

Raiswell, Richard. 'Faking It: A Case of Counterfeit Possession in the Reign of James I'. *Renaissance and Reformation* 23 (1999): 29–48.

Raiswell, Richard and Peter Dendle. 'Demon Possession in Anglo-Saxon and Early Modern England: Continuity and Evolution in Social Context'. *Journal of British Studies* 47 (2008): 736–67.

Rapley, Robert. *A Case of Witchcraft: The Trial of Urbain Grandier*. Montreal, 1998.

Ribet, J. *La mystique divine*, 3 vols. Paris, 1879–83.

Richer, Paul Marie Louis Pierre. *Études cliniques sur la grande hystérie ou hystéro-épilepsie*. 2nd edn. Paris, 1885.

Rodewyk. Adolf. *Possessed by Satan: The Church's Teaching on the Devil, Possession, and Exorcism*, trans. Martin Ebon. Garden City, NY, 1975.

Romeo, Giovanni, *Esorcisti, confessori e sessualità femminile nell'Italia della Controriforma*. Florence, 1988.

———. *Inquisitori, esorcisti e streghe nell'Italia della Controriforma*. Florence, 1990.

Roper, Lyndal. 'Magic and Theology of the Body: Exorcism in Sixteenth-century Augsburg'. In *No Gods Except Me: Orthodoxy and Religious Practice in Europe 1200–1600*, ed. Charles Zika, 84–113. Melbourne, 1991.

———. *Oedipus and the Devil: Witchcraft, Sexuality and Religion in Early Modern Europe*. London, 1984.

Rosen, George. 'Psychopathology in the Social Process: Dance Frenzies, Demonic Possession, Revival Movements and Similar So-called Psychic Epidemics: An Interpretation'. *Bulletin of the History of Medicine* 36 (1962): 13–44.

Rosenthal, Judy. *Possession, Ecstasy and Law in Ewe Voodoo*. Charlottesville, 1998.

Rousseau, G.S. '"A Strange Pathology": Hysteria in the Early Modern World, 1500–1800'. In *Hysteria beyond Freud*, ed. Sander L. Gilman, 91–223. Berkeley, 1993.

Rubin, Julius H. *Religious Melancholy and Protestant Experience in America*. New York, 1994.

Ruggiero, Guido. *Binding Passions: Tales of Magic, Marriage, and Power at the End of the Renaissance*. New York, 1993.

Russell, Jeffrey Burton. *Lucifer: The Devil in the Middle Ages*. Ithaca, NY and London, 1984.

Sahlin, Claire L. *Birgitta of Sweden and the Voice of Prophecy*. Woodbridge, Suffolk, 2001.

Sands, Kathleen R. *Demon Possession in Elizabethan England*. Westport, Conn., 2004.

——. *An Elizabethan Lawyer's Possession by the Devil: The Story of Robert Brigges*. New York, 2002.

Sauzet, Robert. 'Sorcellerie et possession en Touraine et Berry aux XVIᵉ–XVIIᵉ siècles'. *Annales de Bretagne et des pays de l'ouest* 101 (1994): 69–83.

Schmidt, Jeremy. *Melancholy and the Care of the Soul: Religion, Moral Philosophy and Madness in Early Modern Europe*. Aldershot, 2007.

Schutte, Anne. *Aspiring Saints: Pretense of Holiness, Inquisition, and Gender in the Republic of Venice, 1618–1750*. Baltimore and London, 2001.

Schwartz, Hillel. *The French Prophets: The History of a Millennial Group in Eighteenth-century England*. Berkeley, 1980.

Screech, M.A. *Montaigne and Melancholy: The Wisdom of the Essays*. London, 1983.

Sharp, Lesley A. *The Possessed and the Dispossessed: Spirits, Identity and Power in a Madagascar Migrant Town*. Berkeley, 1993.

—— 'The Power of Possession in Northwest Madagascar: Contesting Colonial and National Hegemonies'. In *Spirit Possession, Modernity and Power in Africa*, ed. Heike Behrend and Ute Luig, 3–19. Oxford, 1999.

Sharpe, James. *The Bewitching of Anne Gunter: A Horrible and True Story of Football, Witchcraft, Murder and the King of England*. London, 1999.

——. 'Disruption in the Well-ordered Household: Age, Authority and Possessed Young People'. In *The Experience of Authority in Early Modern England*, ed. Paul Griffiths, Adam Fox and Steve Hindle, 187–212. Basingstoke, 1996.

Shaw, Jane. *Miracles in Enlightenment England*. New Haven and London, 2006.

Sheils, William J., ed. *The Church and Healing*. Oxford, 1982.

Shorter Edward. *From Paralysis to Fatigue: A History of Psychosomatic Illness in the Modern Era*. New York, 1993.

Showalter, Elaine. *Hystories: Hysterical Epidemics and Modern Media*. New York, 1997

Simplicio, Oscar di. *Inquisizione stregoneria medicina: Siena e il stato (1580–1721)*. Siena, 2000.

Skull, Andrew. *Hysteria: The Biography*. Oxford, 2009.

Sluhovsky, Moshe. *Believe Not Every Spirit: Possession, Mysticism, and Discernment in Early Modern Catholicism*. Chicago, 2007.

——. 'The Devil in the Convent'. *American Historical Review* 107 (2002): 1379–411.

——. 'Discerning Spirits in Early Modern Europe'. In *Communicating with the Spirits*, ed. Gábor Klaniczay and Éva Pócs, 53–70. Budapest, 2005.

——. 'A Divine Apparition or Demonic Possession? Female Agency and Church Authority in Demonic Possession in Sixteenth-century France'. *Sixteenth Century Journal* 27 (1996): 1039–55.

Snape, M.F. '"The Surey Impostor": Demonic Possession and Religious Conflict in Seventeenth-century Lancashire'. *Transactions of the Lancashire and Cheshire Antiquarian Society* 90 (1994): 93–114.

Snell, Otto. *Hexenprozess und Geistesstörung*. Munich, 1901.

Soergel, Philip M. *Wondrous in His Saints: Counter-Reformation Propaganda in Bavaria*. Berkeley, 1993.

Sommerville, C. John. *The Secularization of Early Modern England: From Religious Culture to Religious Faith*. New York, 1992.

Sorensen, Eric. *Possession and Exorcism in the New Testament and Early Christianity* (Wissenschaftliche Untersuchungen zum Neuen Testament 2, 157). Tübingen, 2002.

Souza, Laura de Mello. *The Devil and the Land of the Holy Cross: Witchcraft, Slavery, and Popular Religion in Colonial Brazil*, trans. D. G. Whitty. Austin, Tex., 2003.

Spanos, Nicholas P. 'Witchcraft in Histories of Psychiatry: A Critical Analysis and an Alternative Conceptualization'. *Psychological Bulletin* 85 (1978): 417–39.

Spanos, Nicholas P. and Jack Gottlieb. 'Demonic Possession, Mesmerism, and Hysteria: A Social Psychological Perspective on their Historical Interactions'. *Journal of Abnormal Psychology* 88 (1979): 527–46.

——. 'Ergotism and the Salem Witchcraft Trials'. *Science* 194 (1976): 1390–4.

Stephens, Walter. *Demon Lovers: Witchcraft, Sex and the Crisis of Belief*. Chicago, 2001.

Stoller, Paul. *Embodying Colonial Memories: Spirit Possession, Power and the Hauka in West Africa*. London, 1995.

Stronks, G.J. 'The Significance of Balthasar Bekker's *The Enchanted World* '. In *Witchcraft in the Netherlands: From the Fourteenth to the Twentieth Century*, ed. Marijke Gijswijt-Hofstra and Willem Frijhoff, 149–55. Rotterdam, 1991.

Szacsvay, Éva. 'Az ördög"uzés református szabályozása 1636-ban (I.)' (The Calvinist Regulation of Exorcism in 1636). In *Test, lélek, természet. Tanulmányok a népi orvoslás emlékeiből. Köszönt'o kötet Grynaeus Tamás 70. Születésnapjára*, ed. Gábor Barna and Erzsébet Kótyuk, 79–92. Budapest and Szeged, 2002.

Tausiet, 'Maria, From Illusion to Disenchantment: Feijoo versus the "Falsely Possessed" in Eighteenth-century Spain'. In *Beyond the Witch Trials*, ed. Owen Davies and Willem de Blécourt, 45–60. Manchester, 2004.

——. *Los posesos de Tosos (1812–1814): Brujeria y justicia popular en tiempos de revolución*. Zaragoza, 2002.

——. 'The Possessed of Tosos (1812–1814): Witchcraft and Popular Justice during the Spanish Revolution'. In *Dämonische Besessenheit*, ed. Hans de Waardt et al., 263–80. Bielefeld, 2005.

Taylor, Charles. *A Secular Age*. Cambridge, Mass., 2007.

Tellenbach, Hubertus. *Melancholy: History of the Problem, Endogeneity, Typology, Pathogenesis. Clinical Considerations*. Pittsburgh, 1980.

Temkin, Owsei. *The Falling Sickness: A History of Epilepsy from the Greeks to the Beginnings of Modern Neurology*. 2nd edn. Baltimore, 1971.

Tentler, Thomas N. *Sin and Confession on the Eve of the Reformation*. Princeton, 1977.

Thomas, Keith. *Religion and the Decline of Magic*. London, 1971.

Thorndike, Lynn. *A History of Magic and Experimental Science*, 8 vols. New York and London, 1958.

Todd, Margo. *The Culture of Protestantism in Early Modern Scotland*. New Haven and London, 2002.

Tolosano, Carmelo Lisón. *Demonios y Exorcismos en los Siglos de Oro*. In *La España Mental*, Vol. 1. Madrid, 1990.

Tuetey, Alexandre. *La Sorcellerie dans le pays de Montbéliard au XVIIᵉ siècle*. Dôle, 1886.

Turner, Bryan. 'Theoretical Developments in the Sociology of the Body', *Australian Cultural History* 13 (1994): 13–30.

Turner, R. H. 'Role Taking, Role Standpoint, and Reference Group Behavior'. *American Journal of Sociology* 61 (1956): 316–28.

Turner, Victor. *From Ritual to Theatre: The Human Seriousness of Play*. New York, 1982.

Twelftree, Graham. *Christ Triumphant: Exorcism Then and Now*. London, 1985.

——. *Jesus the Exorcist: A Contribution to the Study of the Historical Jesus*. Tübingen, 1993.

Tyacke, Nicholas. *Anti-Calvinists: The Rise of English Arminianism, c. 1590–1640*. Oxford, 1987.

Valente, Michaela. '"*Habent sua fata libelie*" : Il *Mondo incantatato* di Balthasar Bekker'. In *La centralità del dubbio*, ed. Camilla Hermanin and Luisa Simonutti, 665–83. Florence, 2011.

Vandendriessche, Gaston. *The Parapraxis in the Haizmann Case of Sigmund Freud*. Louvain and Paris, 1965.

Vandermeersch, Patrick. 'The Victory of Psychiatry over Demonology: The Origins of the Nineteenth-century Myth'. *History of Psychiatry* 2 (1991): 351–63.

Van der Hart, Onno, Ruth Lierens and Jean Goodwin, 'Jeanne Féry: A Sixteenth-century Case of Dissociative Disorder'. *Journal of Psychohistory* 24 (1996), 1–12.

Veith, Ilza. *Hysteria: The History of a Disease*. Chicago, 1965.

Venard, Marc. 'Le Démon controversiste'. In *La Controverse religieuse (XVIᵉ–XIXᵉ siècles)*, ed. Michel Peronnet, 45–60. Montpellier, 1979.

Vogl, Carl. *Begone Satan! A Soul-stirring Account of Diabolical Possession*, trans. Celestine Kapsner. St Cloud, Minn., 1935.

Waardt, Hans de. 'Prosecution or Defense: Procedural Possibilities following a Witchcraft Accusation in the Province of Holland before 1800'. In *Witchcraft in the Netherlands: From the Fourteenth to the Twentieth Century*, ed. Marijke Gijswijt-Hofstra and Willem Frijhoff, 79–90. Rotterdam, 1991.

——. *Toverij en Samenleving, Holland, 1500–1800*. The Hague, 1991.

Waardt, Hans de, et al., eds. *Dämonische Besessenheit: zur Interpretation eines kulturhistorischen Phänomens*. Bielefeld, 2005.

Waite, Gary. *Eradicating the Devil's Minions: Anabaptists and Witches in Reformation Europe, 1525–1600*. Toronto, 2007.

——. *Heresy, Magic, and Witchcraft in Early Modern Europe*. Basingstoke, 2003.

Walker, Anita M. and Edmund H. Dickerman. 'The Haunted Girl: Possession, Witchcraft and Healing in Sixteenth-century Louviers'. *Proceedings of the Annual Meeting of the Western Society for French History* 23 (1996): 202–18.

——. 'Magdeleine des Aymards: Demonism or Child Abuse in Early Modern France'. *Psychohistory Review* 24 (1996): 329–64.

——, 'A Notorious Woman: Possession, Witchcraft and Sexuality in Seventeenth-century Provence'. *Historical Reflections* 27 (2001): 1–26.

—— '"A Woman under the Influence": A Case of Alleged Possession in Sixteenth-century France'. *Sixteenth Century Journal* 22 (1991): 535–54.

Walker, D. P. 'The Cessation of Miracles'. In *Hermeticism and the Renaissance: Intellectual History and the Occult in Early Modern Europe*, ed. Ingrid Merkel and Allen G. Debus, 111–24. Washington, DC, 1988.

——. 'Demonic Possession Used as Propaganda in the Later Sixteenth Century'. In: *Scienze credenze occulte livelli di cultura*, ed. Leo S. Olschki, 237–8. Florence, 1982.

——. *Unclean Spirits: Possession and Exorcism in France and England in the Late Sixteenth and Early Seventeenth Centuries*. London and Philadelphia, 1981.

Walker, Timothy. *Doctors, Folk Medicine and the Inquisition: The Repression of Magical Healing in Portugal during the Enlightenment*. Leiden, 2005.

Watt, Jeffrey R. *The Scourge of Demons: Possession, Lust and Witchcraft in a Seventeenth-century Italian Convent*. Rochester, NY, 2009.

Weber, Alison. 'Between Ecstasy and Exorcism: Religious Negotiation in Sixteenth-century Spain'. *Journal of Medieval and Renaissance Studies* 23 (1993): 221–34.

——. 'Demonizing Ecstasy: Alonso de la Fuente and the Alumbrados of Extremadura'. In *The Mystical Gesture*, ed. Robert Boenig, 147–65. Basingstoke, 2000.

——. 'The Inquisitor, the Flesh, and the Devil: Alumbradismo and Demonic Possession'. In *Dämonische Besessenheit*, ed. Hans de Waardt et al., 177–91. Bielefeld, 2005.

Weber, Henri. 'L'Exorcisme à la fin du XVIe siècle: instrument de la contre réforme et spectacle baroque'. *Nouvelle revue du seizième siècle* 1 (1983): 79–101.

Webster, Tom. '(Re)possession of Dispossession: John Darrell and Diabolical Discourse'. In *Witchcraft and the Act of 1604*, ed. John Newton and Jo Bath, 91–111. Leiden, 2008.

Westaway, Jonathan and Richard D. Harrison. '"The Surey Demoniack": Defining Protestantism in 1690s Lancashire'. In *Unity and Diversity in the Church*, ed. R.N. Swanson, 263–82. Studies in Church History, 32. Oxford, 1996.

White, L. Michael, *Scripting Jesus: The Gospels in Rewrite*. New York, 2010.

Wilkins, Kay S. 'Attitudes to Witchcraft and Demonic Possession in France during the Eighteenth Century'. *Journal of European Studies* 3 (1973): 349–60.

Williams, Owen. 'Exorcising Madness in Late Elizabethan England: *The Seduction of Arthington* and the Criminal Culpability of Demoniacs'. *Journal of British Studies* 47 (2008): 30–52.

Williamson, Arthur. *Scottish National Consciousness in the Age of James VI: The Apocalypse, the Union and the Shaping of Scotland's Public Culture*. Edinburgh, 1979.

Wingens, Marc. 'Political Change and Demon Possession in the South of the Dutch Republic: The Confrontation of a Protestant Bailiff and a Catholic Priest in 1650'. In *Dämonische Besessenheit*, ed. Hans de Waaardt et al., 249–62. Bielefeld, 2005.

Wislicz, Tomasz. 'Talking to the Devil in the Early Modern Popular Imagination'. In *Faith and Fantasy in the Renaissance: Texts. Images, and Religious Practices*, ed. Olga Zorzi Pugliese and Ethan Matt Kavaler, 135–46. Toronto, 2009.

Worden, Blair. 'The Question of Secularization.' In *A Nation Transformed: England after the Restoration*, ed. Alan Houston and Steve Pincus, 2–40. Cambridge, 2001.

Worobec, Christine D. *Possessed: Women, Witches and Demons in Imperial Russia*. DeKalb, Ill., 2001.

Wright, Lawrence. *Remembering Satan*. New York, 1994.

Wygant, Amy. *Medea, Magic, and Modernity in France: Stages and Histories, 1553–1797*. Aldershot, 2007.

Yeoman, L.A. 'The Devil as Doctor: Witchcraft, Wodrow and the Wider World'. *Scottish Archives* 1 (1995): 93–105.

Zhang, Qiong. 'About God, Demons, and Miracles: The Jesuit Discourse on the Supernatural in Late Ming China', *Early Science and Medicine* 4 (1999): 4–36.

Zika, Charles. *Exorcizing Our Demons: Magic, Witchcraft and Visual Culture in Early Modern Europe*. Leiden, 2003.

Zuff, Jürg, ed. *Ergriffenheit und Besessenheit: ein interdiziplinäres Gespräch über transkulturell-anthropologische und psychiatrische Fragen*. Bern, 1972.

Index

hypochondria 126
hysteria 19, 26, 123–9, 134, 135, 187
hysterics 152–3

Imablichus of Syria 278 n. 91
illness
definition of 289 n. 1
possession and 18, 22, 26–9, 30, 36, 38,
45, 48, 60, 73–5, 96, 111, 113–38,
153, 225–6, 238, 242
Illuminism 178–9
Immaculate Conception, doctrine of 199
Index of Prohibited Books 109, 234
Ingolstadt 88
International Association of Exorcists 244
Italy 12, 16, 97, 99, 108, 136, 147, 166,
194, 199, 202, 226, 227, 243, 248,
249, 255, 256, 259, 263

Jackson, Elizabeth 124
James VI and I, king of Scotland and
England 25, 71
Janet, Pierre 293 n. 74
Jansenists 219, 237
Jeanne des Anges 20, 23–4, 54, 99, 128,
176, 180, 218, 224
Jesuits 88, 96, 97, 155, 248
Johnstone, James 195–6
Jolly, Thomas 73
Jonson, Ben 144
Jorden, Edward 116, 124–6, 129, 236
Jubilees, biblical book 51
Judas Iscariot 241
Justin Martyr 254

Kallendorf, Hilaire 145
Kansas City, Missouri 246
Karlsen, Carol 187–9
Kawalerowicz, Jerzy 145
Kemberg 220–1
Kempten, prince abbotship of 221
Kieckhefer, Richard 100, 101, 200
Killigrew, Thomas 104
Kingesfielde, Edmund 209
Kingesfielde, Mistress 5, 178, 207,
209–10, 211
King James Version of the Bible 33,
53, 115
Klass, Morton 29
Knapp, Elizabeth 143, 154, 211–13
Koelman, Jacobus 45
Kramer, Heinrich 61, 71, 101, 108–9,
192, 198

Lactantius 58

Ladame, Paul 128
Laird, Margaret 9
Lancashire 9, 14, 144, 158, 261
Lange, Johann 122
languages of demoniacs 11–12
Laon 67, 86, 142
Miracle of 42, 87, 158
Last Days 19, 65–70, 75, 82, 195, 206, 245,
253, 254 see also eschatology
Laud, William, archbishop 161
Lauderdale, earl of 72
Lavater, Ludwig 119
Lawson, Deodat 73
Lea, Henry Charles 128–9
Lederer, David 239
Leiden 126
Leipzig 237
Lemnius, Levinus 120
Lenglet Dufresnay, Nicolas 231
Lepanto, Battle of 160
Levi, Giovanni 98, 111
Leviathan, demon 53, 104, 135
levitation 2, 8, 9, 14, 15, 23, 135, 218,
222, 241
Lewis, I.M. 172, 185
Lidwina of Schiedam 11
Lieder, Georg 68
Lieder, Magdalena 7
Lierre 173
Lille 67
Livingston, John 213
Lohmann, Anna Elisabeth 48, 175, 220–1,
232, 235
London 5, 125
Lorde, André de 153
Loudun 3, 4, 6, 7, 8, 17, 87, 137, 142, 145,
178, 193
Louis XIV, king of France 219
Louis XV, king of France 231
Louvain 9
Louviers, Normandy 8, 54, 67, 86, 118,
151, 166, 176, 193, 202, 204
Lucifer, demon 53, 65, 67–8, 79, 241,
278 n. 90
Luís de Nazaré, friar 98–9
Lukins, George 223–4, 235
Lumsden, Margaret 72, 209
Luther, Martin 19, 32, 40, 109, 110
Lutheranism 30, 69, 88, 220, 265,
306 n. 45
Lutherans 87–90, 156, 202, 205, 232

MacGilchrist, John 74
McMartin Pre-School 253
Madrid 67, 178